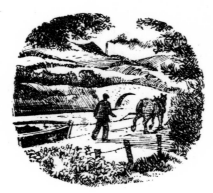

The Complete Book of Drawing and Painting

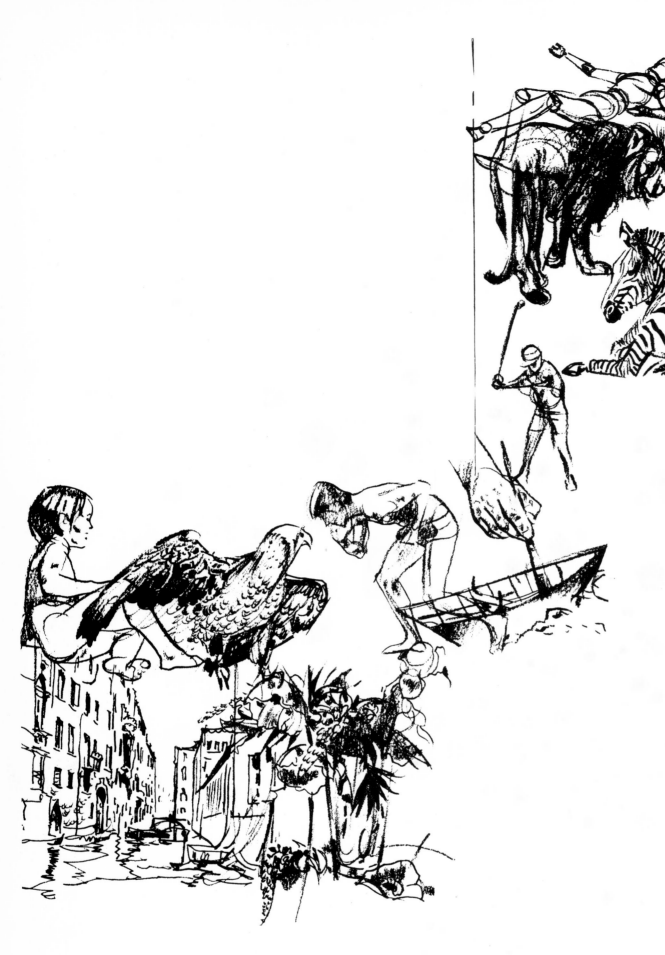

THE
COMPLETE
BOOK OF

AND

HUGH LAIDMAN

DRAWING
PAINTING

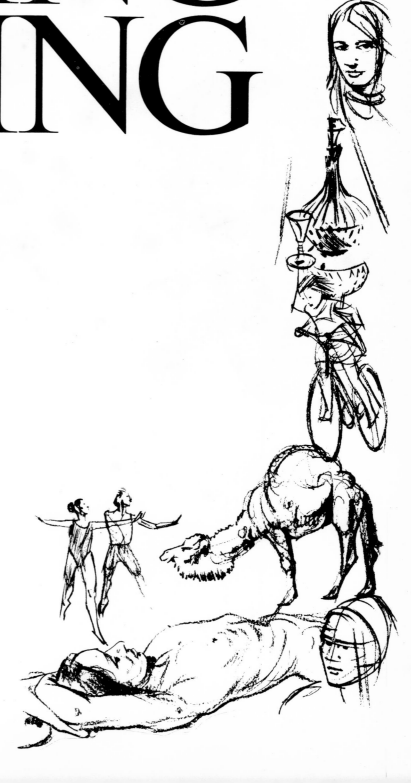

NELSON

Thomas Nelson and Sons Ltd
36 Park Street London W1Y 4DE
PO Box 18123 Nairobi Kenya
Thomas Nelson (Australia) Ltd
171-175 Bank Street South Melbourne
Victoria 3205 Australia
Thomas Nelson and Sons (Canada) Ltd
81 Curlew Drive Don Mills Ontario
Thomas Nelson (Nigeria) Ltd
PO Box 336 Apapa Lagos
© Hugh Laidman, 1973
First published in the UK by Thomas Nelson
and Sons Ltd in 1973
ISBN 0 17 141009 2
Printed in Japan

PREFACE

The base of creativity is knowledge. An outsider usually considers the art world a hotbed of creativity, although in reality it is frequently a deathbed of imitation. Knowledge of the basic tools and materials, plus at least an acquaintance with their potential, is a small step in the right direction. Knowledge of the tools and materials in relation one to the next is a giant step.

Most artists feel more at home in one medium. A watercolorist might say, "I am terrified of oil"; an oil painter, "I am terrified of watercolor." These may sound like extreme statements of an artist's sentiments, but in my experience they are two of the most common ones heard. The simple fact is that an ability to work in one medium serves to reinforce an artist's capabilities in the next one in which he chooses to experiment.

This book was written with the hope that lifting any mystery that surrounds a given process might remove the fear that is evidenced by so many specialists. The first step is to display the primary media available to today's artist, their potential and limitations, and the second step is to interrelate the potential and the limitations.

A fundamental in the entire creative process of the artist is a knowledge of drawing. He has to be able to rely on something more than the accidental in his approach to art. To distort effectively, the artist must first know how to draw correctly. To create anything of lasting artistic value, he must be capable of transmitting his feeling and emotions on a given subject.

CONTENTS

INTRODUCTION

This book is intended as a course in drawing and in painting in all media. Proved materials and proved methods are explored, and it will be seen how a knowledge of all can aid in the use of each. A subject difficult in one medium becomes simple in another. The transparent watercolor demonstration, on pages 66–67, for instance, explains the steps in painting a wet watercolor, while the acrylic demonstration (pages 130–131), identical to the watercolor in approach, shows a different end result. Acrylic gives the accident-prone artist a second chance in ways that the watercolor medium cannot. It is interesting also to see how, by using the same approach with an oil (pages 110–111), a painting can be made to have almost the freshness of a watercolor. By learning the similarities of the various media we become acquainted with the essential differences, which in turn can determine the proper medium for our particular talents and the job at hand. The hidden danger is that of becoming over-involved in technique, to the detriment of the main purpose of the artist, which is to express himself as freely as possible within whatever limitations the subject or media might impose.

Although most great artists have at one time or another been commissioned to communicate someone else's ideas, they have also invariably expressed their own. The closer they came to expressing their own feelings freely, the greater the final work, depending, to some extent at least, on the nature of these feelings. A specialist in realistic illustrative work might paint a soup can, slaving to the point of rendering accurately the minute letters that list the ingredients. Another artist, starting with the same can of soup, might create an infinitely more imaginative and interesting piece of work.

An artist, because of the intense individualism that must characterize his work, is often the worst of judges. He must decide, in the parlance of the art-show world, "what went wrong" and "what came off right," and why. In the case of the best entries in an art exhibit, no two artists are likely to concur, because a painting is a very personal expression and the viewer is automatically drawn toward the kind of work that comes closest to his own particular taste and aims.

The first recorded painters worked with a limited palette: black, ocher, and red-brown. Working in dank caves with limited light and a long work week devoted almost exclusively to getting enough to eat and to preserving the species, they did remarkably well. It is understandable why, to this day, artists seldom complain about poor working conditions, praying the while that the establishment with whom they work will not discover how much worse things in the art world once were.

After the cave painters came the Egyptians, then the Greeks, who in turn hired out to the Pompeians. At the time, encaustic painting was the thing. Encaustic painting employs beeswax. The available source of sugar was limited to honey, and the oversupply of wax was handed to the artists who struggled to improve their technique with the best materials at hand whatever there might be.

Through the ages, life has not been easy for the artist. Architects in medieval times created Gothic structures, a form that left little space for murals, so the artists, many of them, turned their talents to designing in stained glass. The Gothic art movement was best expressed in France; in Florence, for instance, the style found few takers. Giotto and his followers developed fresco, a method of painting on freshly spread, moist lime plaster. After Giotto came the school of Siena, and just as things seemed to be looking up for artists, Paolo Uccello began the early steps in perspective and set artists back or ahead, depending on the way you look at it.

Meanwhile, in Flanders, Van Eyck invented oil painting, which was the biggest revolution of all time in the development of the realistic portrait, landscape, or still life. Shortly afterward a series of painters—Da Vinci, Michelangelo, Raphael, and others—promoted what has since been referred to as the Renaissance.

Aside from the discovery of a few new colors and the loss of a number of trade secrets, nothing much happened in the world of painting materials until the recent rediscovery of casein paint and the invention of plastic paints. These last were originally intended not for artists, but for use as automobile finishes. The artists have taken them—and taken off with them—in many directions, and how successfully will be for future generations to judge.

ANALYZING THE OLD MASTERS

It is not obligatory for today's artist to study the work of the masters who preceded him, but it does help his own understanding of composition. A simple approach to analyzing the works of the old masters is first to select two or three shades of gray felt markers. Either from reproductions or from the original paintings in a museum or gallery, attempt to draw the pattern of the original, in simple tone in thumbnail size. The following examples are taken from paintings in the Louvre:

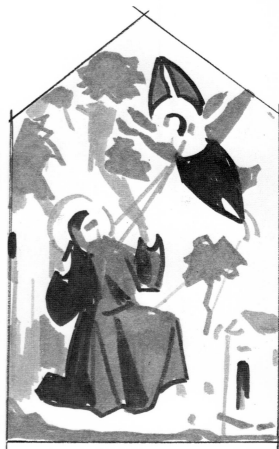
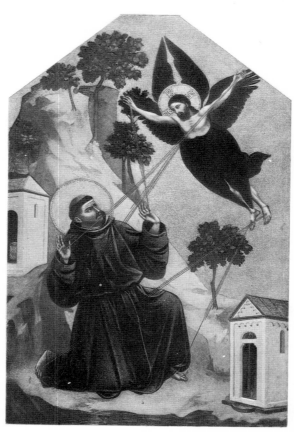

Giotto (above) is generally classified as an Italian primitive. Unhampered by linear and aerial perspective, he could proceed as best suited his aims and plans, with little regard to photographic correctness. This made the figure in *Saint Francis Receiving the Stigmata* stand out in simple relief from the background.

In analyzing the tonal design, a medium gray plus black was used. The term "primitive Italian" seems a misnomer when we realize how cleverly Giotto arranged his pattern. The term applies more to the time the drawing was completed than to a relative degree of sophistication.

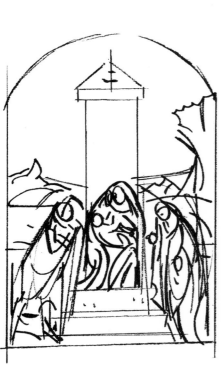
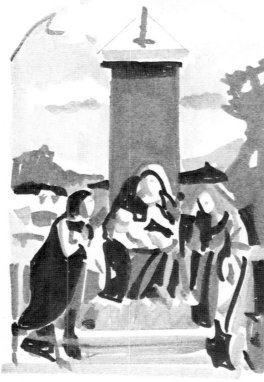
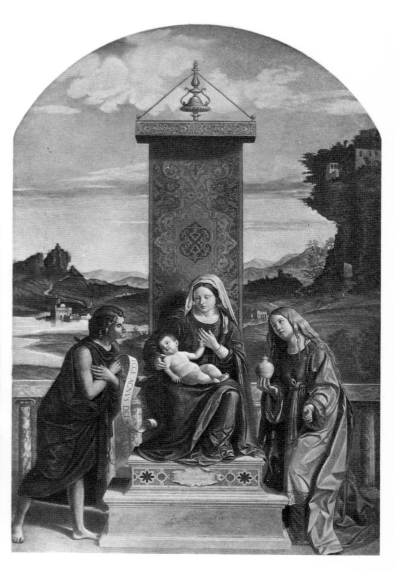

Cima da Conegliano, in his first thoughts on what was undoubtedly a commission to paint *The Virgin and the Child*, must have been a bit unhappy about the shape he had to fill. In his first plans he must have carefully worked out in linear form something like the sketches shown here. He might then have worked out a number of value patterns.

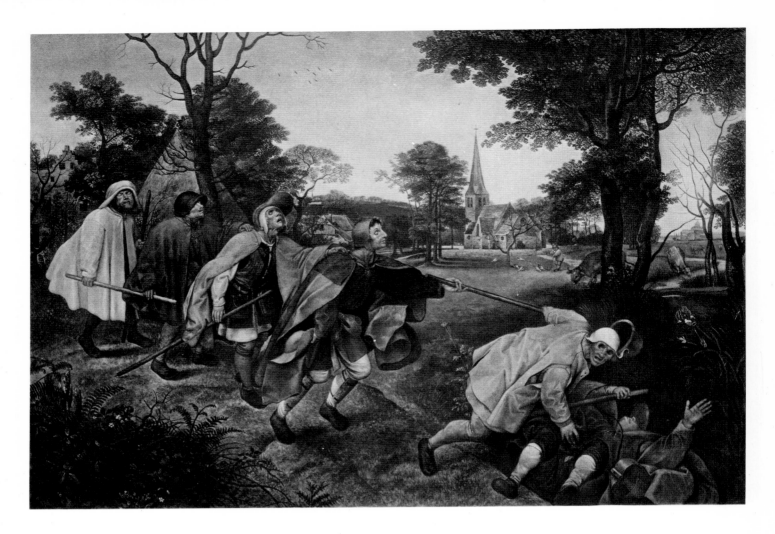

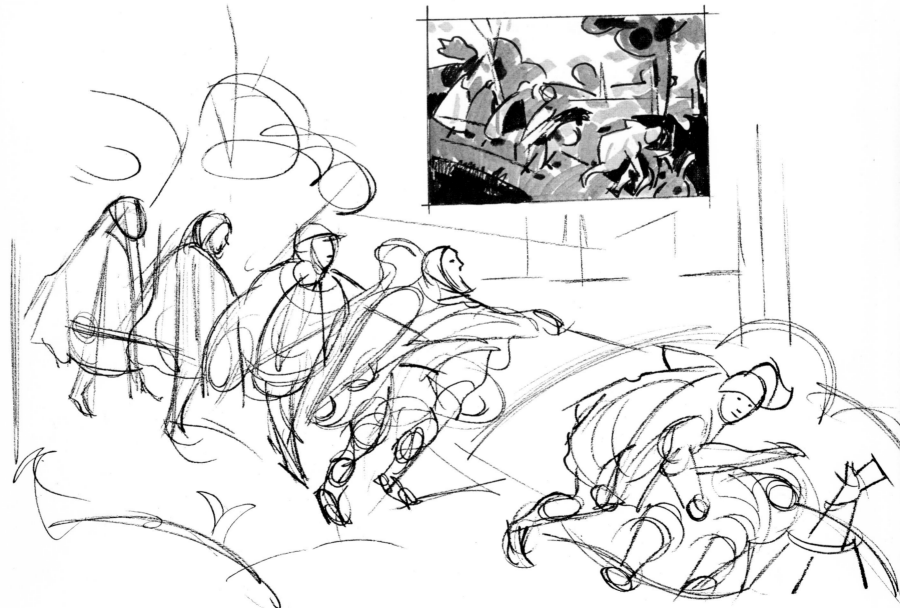

Pieter Brueghel had the priceless ingredient of a sense of humor, even if at times it approached the grotesque. The pattern of *The Parable of the Blind Men* gives an insight into his handling of a tremendously complicated subject in simple tone. The line drawing shows his mastery of subject. Faced with the active subject of blind men tumbling right out of the picture, he cleverly used devices to hold our attention on his subjects, even to the extent of a stop-sign hand in the right lower corner.

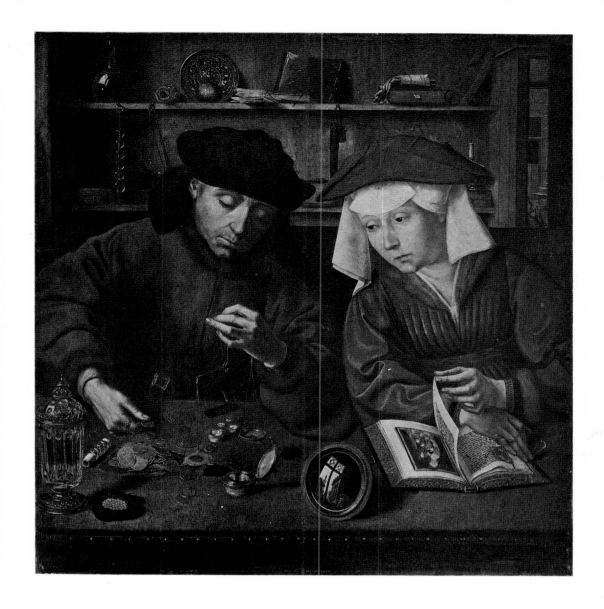

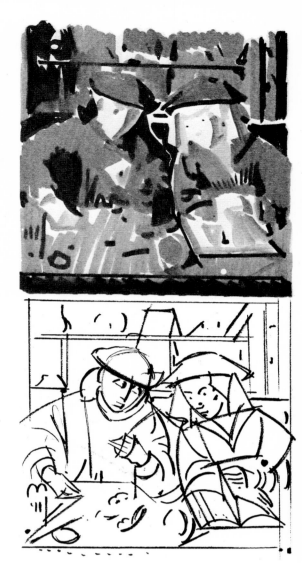

Quentin Massys began his career as a blacksmith. He fell in love with an artist's daughter, who convinced him to switch to painting. *Banker and His Wife* (above) was painted in the slow, built-up glazing technique, as against the *alla prima* technique of direct painting in oil. On the top, right, is re-created an interpretation in three tones of gray and black, and below it the lineal design. In studying the thinking behind the design of this painting, one is, as always, impressed by the basic simplicity of the painting. Within the simplicity of composition is a minuteness of detail and finish that would delight an en-graver of paper money. Strangely enough, there is little concern with light and shadow.

Comparing Holbein's *Erasmus* (below) to some current super-realist paintings, you might question whether, with all the technological advances, we have caught up with this work done some five hundred years ago.

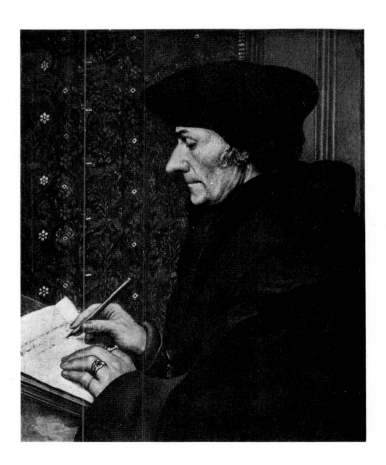

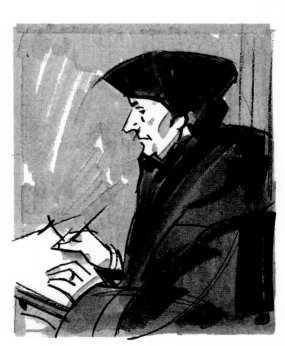

13

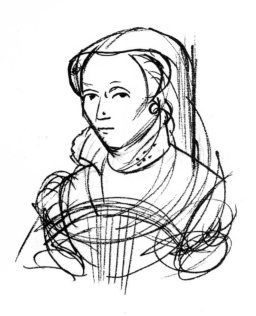
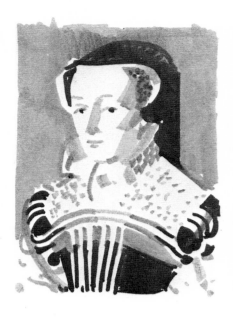
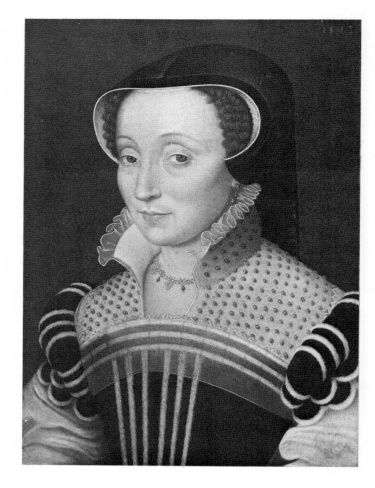

These portraits by two unknown French artists were painted in the sixteenth century, therefore designating them as "primitives." The possible thoughts of the artists are broken down in the tone and line sketches accompanying them. In both of the originals we note that the old masters have painted detail with superfluous care but still have not allowed the detail to overpower the over-all design and composition. (Above: *Portrait of Claudia.* Below: *A Kneeling Abbess.*)

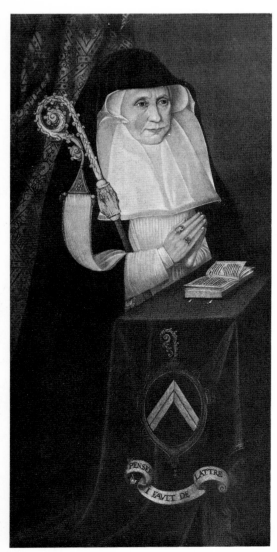
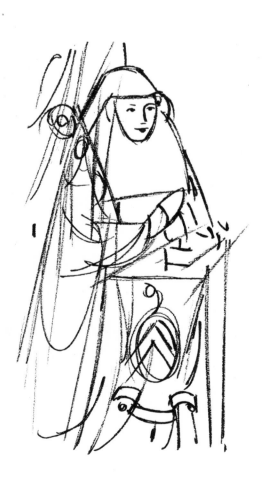
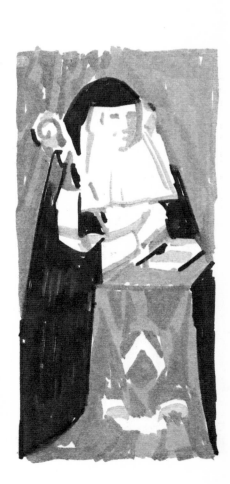

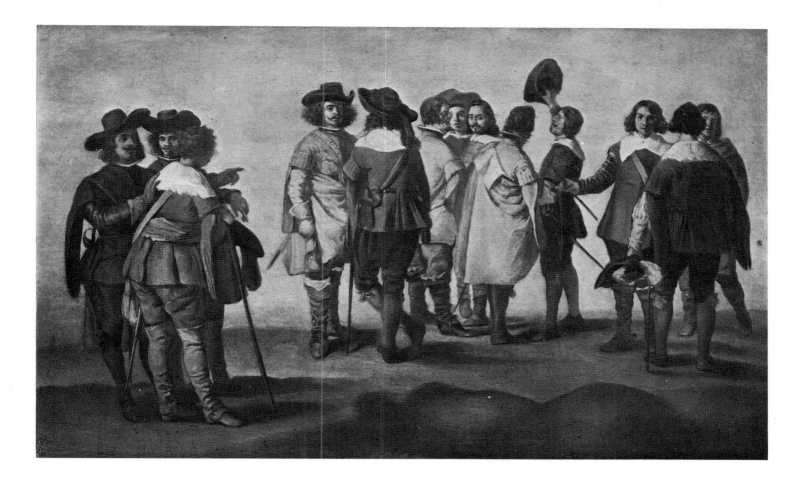

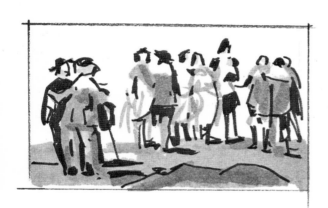
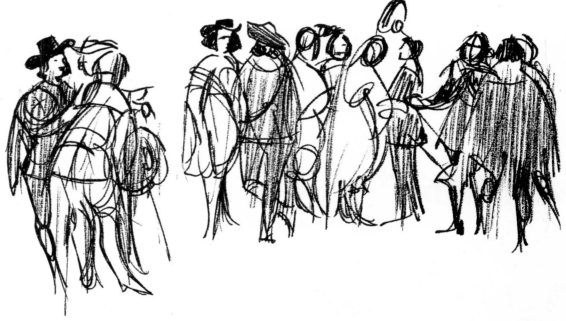

Reducing a rather complicated group of figures to two grays and black shows us the over-all pattern of a work. This is especially true in *A Meeting of Thirteen Personages* by Diego Rodríguez de Silva y Velázquez. The rough preliminary sketch is a simulation of what Velázquez might have done while working out a well-balanced composition to include all these personages. This method of study is not over-popular with schools today for it falls into the general category of copying. In reality, this is not copying in the bad sense of the word, but rather interpreting through one's own personality. Cézanne and others of similar stature did it. Copying this old master makes one realize the tremendous care he has taken in the placement of figures, and in their gestures, and how each person relates to his own group, and then how each group relates to the whole.

When student architects make sketches for proposed buildings, they usually are taught to group figures precisely as Velázquez has done here. The single figure can be uninteresting.

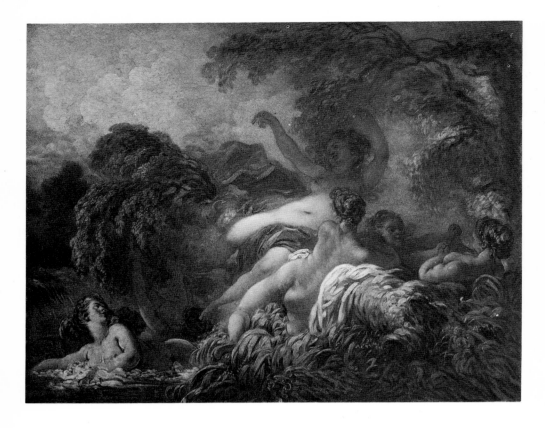

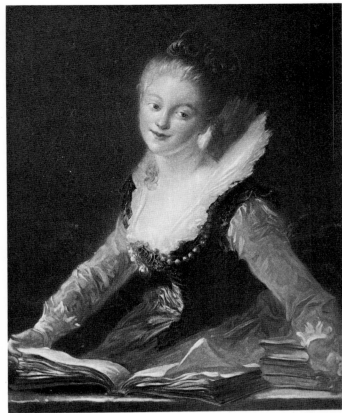

In *The Bathers* Fragonard not only shows his ability to paint ladies in complete abandon, but he also gives us a hint that he could easily be a master of landscape. In *A Study* (right), also by Fragonard, we see an example of his tremendous facility in brushwork. The piece, which many might labor over, was finished by him in a few hours. Both of these were done in his prime, near the age of fifty-seven. Shortly after, he was kicked upstairs, as administrator in the Conservatory of the Museum, to be in charge not only of his own but of other great works. This was the beginning of the end of a brilliant career.

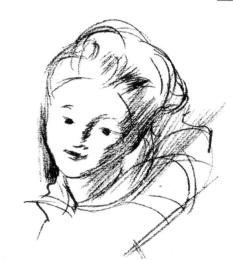

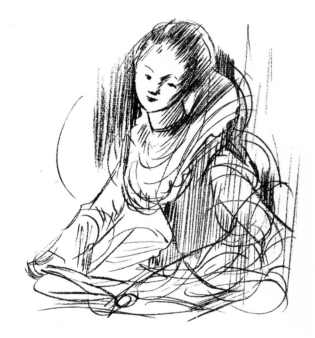

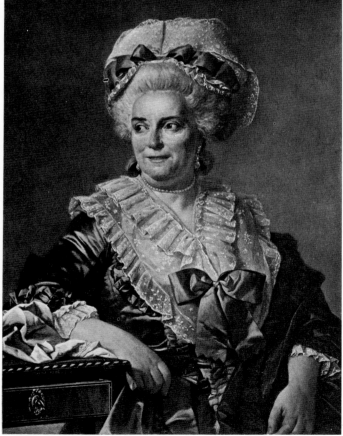

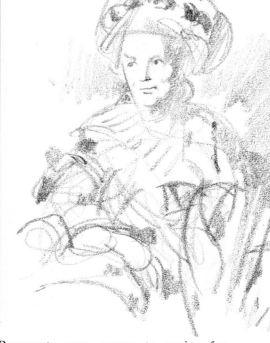

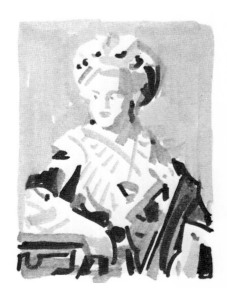

J. L. David, the artist of this *Portrait of Madame Pécoùl*, was a friend of Napoleon Bonaparte. Bonaparte offered him a refuge in his camp and later even offered him the use of the gallery of the old Academy of Architec-ture. Bonaparte was averse to posing for artists, but he did pose for David for three hours. David, in return, referred to him as "my hero." It was not an unusual turn of events for David to give up official portraiture when things went less than well for "his hero." He limited his portrait subjects to relatives and close friends. This portrait of his mother-in-law seems to qualify on both counts.

BLACK AND WHITE TECHNIQUES

The simplest beginning to most art forms is pencil and paper. This develops into a wide variety of techniques. The materials needed to become familiar with black-and-white media are inexpensive and readily available at art supply stores. Each is adaptable to multiple uses, but each has distinct advantages in obtaining unique effects. Most artists will find themselves more at home with one than the other, but the desired result will influence the selection. Here is a list of all materials used on pages 18 through 35.

Drawing pens: coarse, medium, and fine
Penholders
India ink
Erasers: artgum, kneaded, and sand
Single-edged razor
Cloth wiper
Pointed sable watercolor brushes: number 2 and number 6
Wolf pencils
Charcoal pencils and sticks

Graphite, Wolf, and Conte crayon: soft, medium, and hard
Conte and litho sticks: soft, medium, and hard
Set of warm gray hard pastels
Medium-size set of hard color pastels
Stumps
A variety of papers, from charcoal to smooth Bristol
Scratchboard, if you wish
A toothpick and a straightedge

The illustrations demonstrating the use of these materials are in realistic form because naturalistic interpretation offers a better opportunity to practice within an area that is simple to analyze. In his own work the artist will express himself in his own manner. The realistic approach, although good practice, is but one of many possibilities. It is only because we are accustomed through drawings and photographs to accept black-and-white interpretations that we recognize what's going on at all. A slavelike realism generally is worthless. It is only when the artist truly expresses something of himself, in whatever way he chooses, that the drawing becomes a work of art. The interesting fact is that an artist can express moods, feelings, and even some story, working in black and white only. Until he can do this, he can rarely work competently in color.

Broadly classified, pen and ink and brush and ink include both colored inks and scratchboard. Colored inks are generally difficult for the amateur to handle effectively. They lend themselves more to small-scale illustration. Reproduction is comparatively faithful to the original, which is usually drawn one-quarter larger, or "¼ up."

It is advisable to master the pen-and-ink and brush-and-ink techniques before attempting either colored inks or scratchboard.

Traditionally work to be reproduced is executed on a larger scale than it finally appears. Recently, however, artists working in a small scale have had the reproductions made on a somewhat larger scale. This, aside from making blunders more obvious, usually lends a freedom to the final reproduced work. This works both ways. A piece properly designed in large dimension should carry well in postage-stamp size. It is not the possibility of reproduction of any given work that concerns us, but rather what the reproduction process teaches us.

Most black-and-white work is relatively inexpensive to reproduce by letter press or lithography, those techniques employing only solid-line copy being less expensive than those using gray tones.

SCRATCHBOARD

Scratchboard drawing, in reproduction, is indistinguishable from a monotype, woodcut, or etching, depending on the artist's approach. The board used, in most cases, is a chalk-surfaced board that in turn can be covered with India ink or opaque, in black or a color. The white lines or areas are "scratched" out. This method is an adaptation of the ancient method of coating a surface with layers of varied color and then scratching into the surface to uncover the color required in the final design.

The method is generally used for extremely delicate work. In the illustrator's world, specialists in this technique were once in demand. Today, when much less restrained work is popular, the examples of scratchboard are less in evidence. The technique demands complete control and a reverse approach to the final working from black to white. Invariably the working drawing is made on another sheet of paper and then traced in light blue or white onto the surface to be scratched.

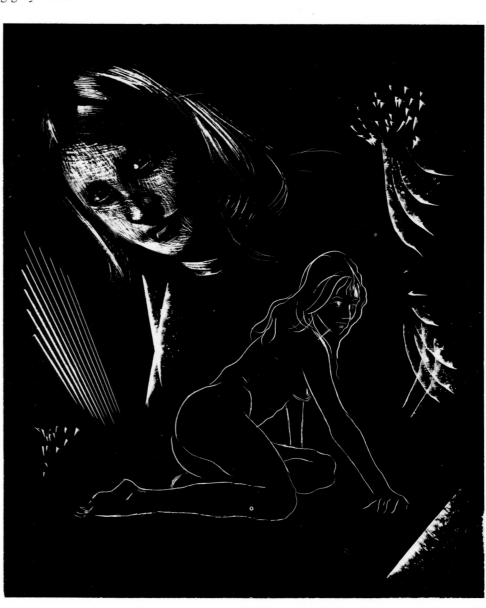

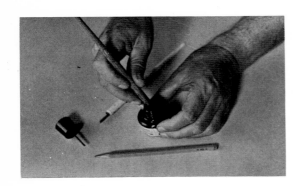

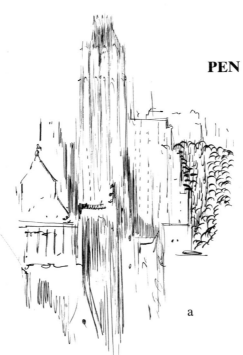

Most pen-and-ink drawings are first drawn in pencil, then traced onto a "plate finish" paper, since India ink, black and opaque, is difficult to erase and correct. When the final pen-and-ink drawing is completed over the pencil, the pencil is easily erased, leaving only the black ink lines.

The drawings on this page, however, were made directly in ink. Direct drawing has an advantage in the learning process. The artist is forced to concentrate on every line he puts onto the paper. Initially this may result in an over-tight, constrained line, but with practice the artist will gain the assurance needed to handle the medium more freely. It is possible that an artist, beginning his sketch in pencil with the knowledge that he may correct as he goes along, may feel freer to experiment. However, having less to think about, he may be lax about the job at hand.

Practice first to learn the possibilities of the various nibs. As restricted as the medium seems at first, you will soon develop a facility with the pen and discover tricks peculiar to your own needs.

Pen-and-ink sketches may and should be executed on a small scale. Later, with an opaque projector, it is interesting to enlarge the work to get an altogether new aspect.

(a) The tall buildings seem to call for vertical lines.

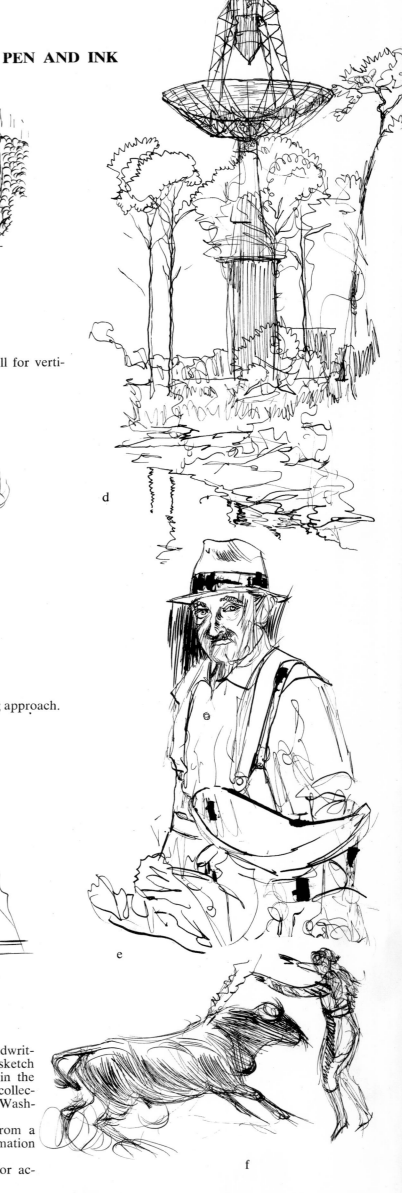

d

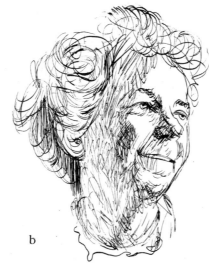

b

(b) A kind of scribbling or doodling approach.

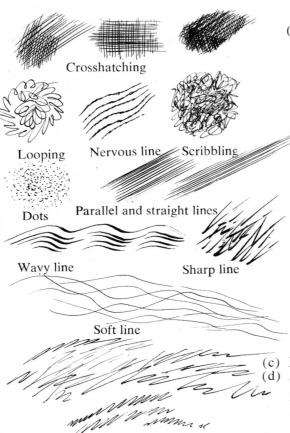

Crosshatching

Looping   Nervous line   Scribbling

Dots   Parallel and straight lines

Wavy line   Sharp line

Soft line

Jagged line

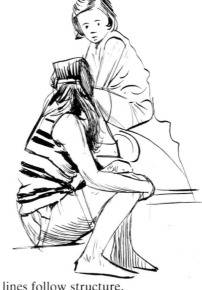

c

(c) Here lines follow structure.
(d) A linear approach, almost like handwriting. This was an informational sketch used later for a finished painting in the studio. The final painting is in the collection of the National Gallery in Washington.
(e) A straightforward sketch, lifted from a sketchbook, carrying enough information to carry on to a finished work.
(f) The action of the bullfight calls for action lines to express motion.

e

f

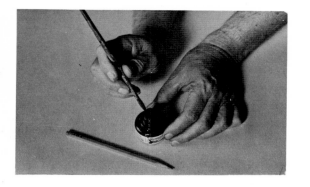

Hold the brush by the ferrule for rigid control (a).

Hold the brush handle for a looser line (b).

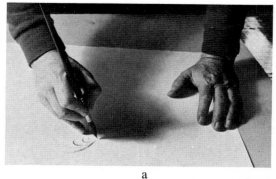

a

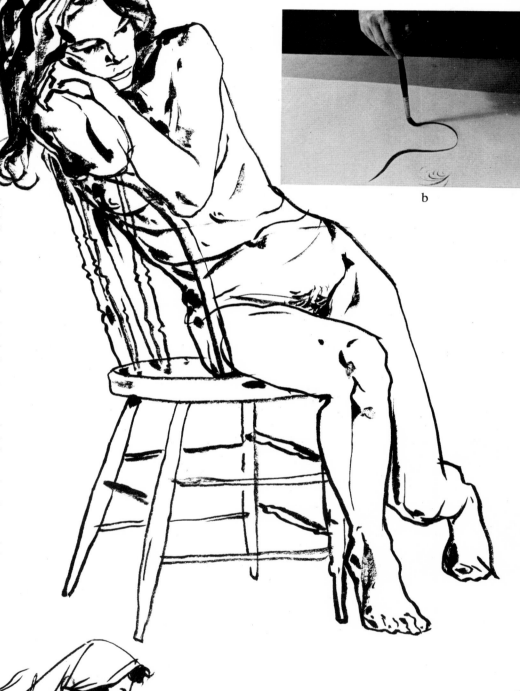

b

BRUSH AND INK

Line effects impossible with pen and ink can, and should be, attempted in brush and ink. The brushes used will range from sable hair watercolor brushes numbers two to six. They should be washed out well after use. India ink has a tendency to shorten the life of good brushes.

For rigid control of lines either straight or wavy, use a straightedge as shown on page 51.

There are limitless examples of what can be accomplished with a well-charged brush, or, for that matter, with what is called dry-brush technique. The drawings on this page were partially done in dry brush.

The advantage of the brush is its capacity to hold a large amount of ink plus its potential for the extremely fluid line.

Brush-and-ink techniques offer the opportunity to use papers impractical in pen techniques. Metal nibs will catch and make for accidents.

For the figure on the chair, a number six brush on a Japanese paper, Troya, was used.

For the lady in the marketplace and for the partridge, a number four brush was used on the same paper. The partridge was drawn from a stuffed museum bird. Live birds seldom remain still long enough for the observer to learn what they look like in detail.

Draw and trace and draw and trace again, attempting each time to simplify and improve on the last sketch.

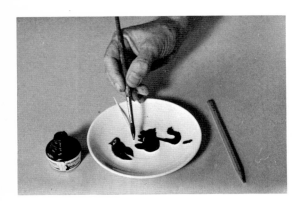

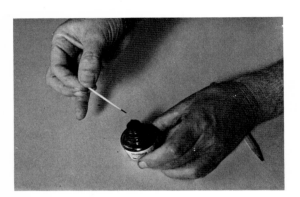

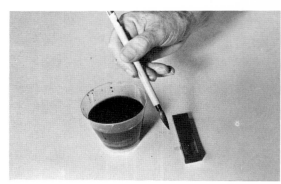

Using a Japanese ink block

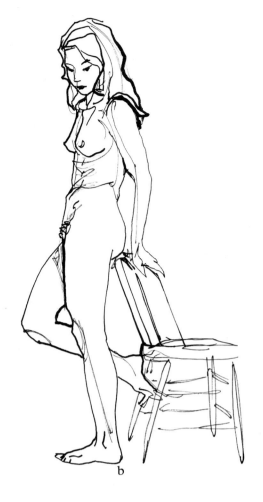

b

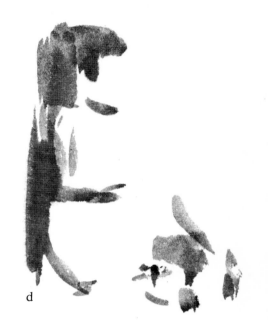

d

INK WASH

Methods of getting ink onto paper are not restricted to pens and brushes. The girl leaning on the chair (a) was drawn with pen and ink; the same girl, leaning on the same chair (b), with a toothpick dipped in ink. Sensitive drawings have been made with a matchstick dipped in ink.

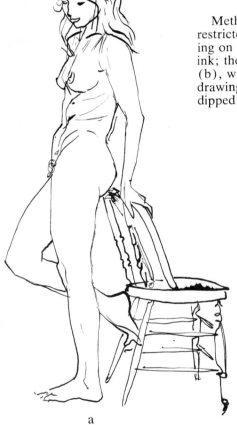

a

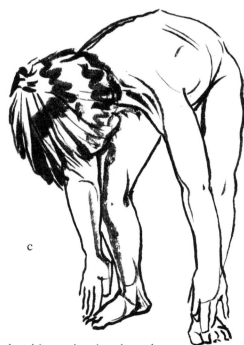

c

An approach to sketching using brush and ink on paper is shown in (c).

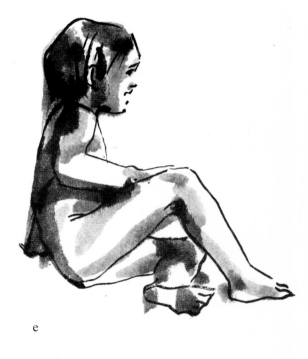

e

In (d) India ink was diluted with water to give a gray tone. By squinting at the subject at the start of the sketch, it is possible to see the simple light and dark pattern of the figure.

Once this is dry, define the drawing with solid ink lines. (e)

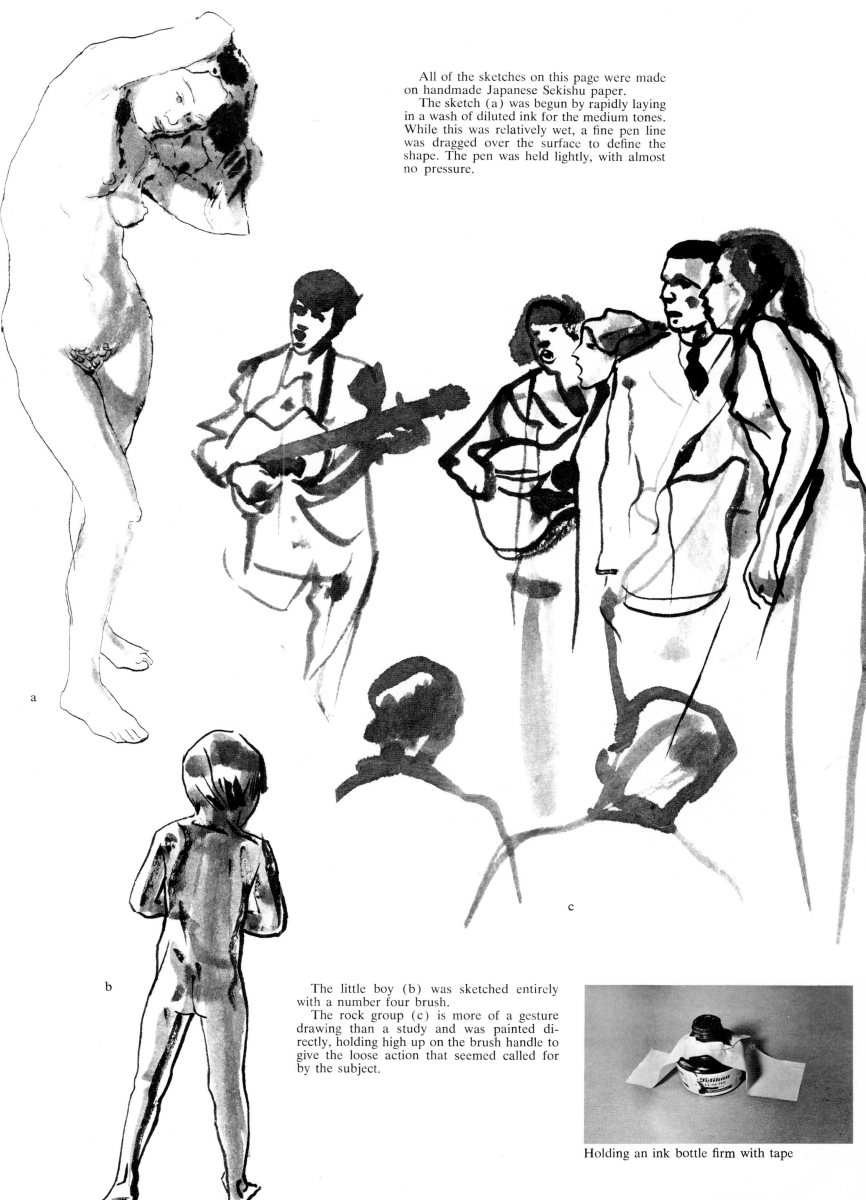

All of the sketches on this page were made on handmade Japanese Sekishu paper.

The sketch (a) was begun by rapidly laying in a wash of diluted ink for the medium tones. While this was relatively wet, a fine pen line was dragged over the surface to define the shape. The pen was held lightly, with almost no pressure.

a

b

c

The little boy (b) was sketched entirely with a number four brush.

The rock group (c) is more of a gesture drawing than a study and was painted directly, holding high up on the brush handle to give the loose action that seemed called for by the subject.

Holding an ink bottle firm with tape

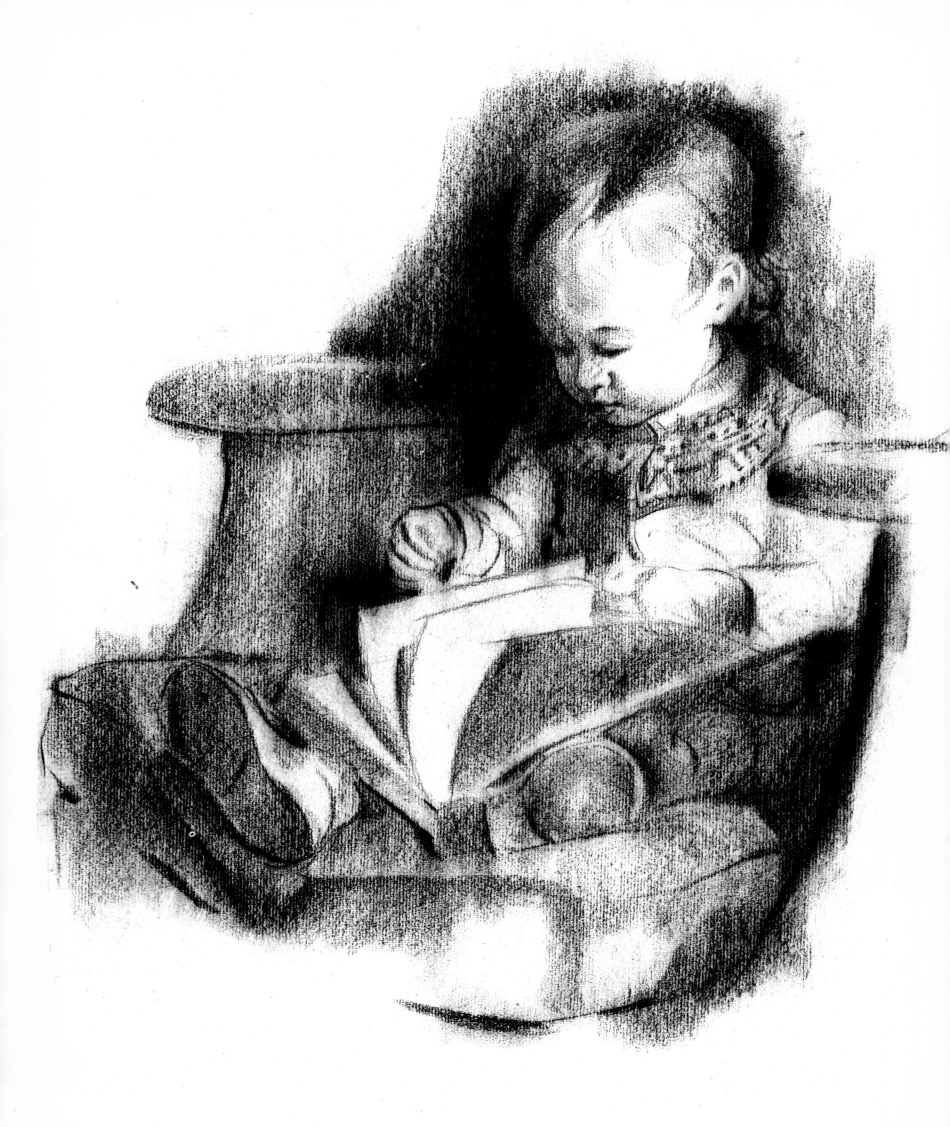

This is a preliminary drawing for an oil painting. It was executed rapidly, using, for the most part, a Conte stick held as shown on page 26, example (b). This method affords a chance to get large toned areas onto the surface quickly and effectively. No smudging technique was used. The limited linework was made with a medium-soft Conte pencil.

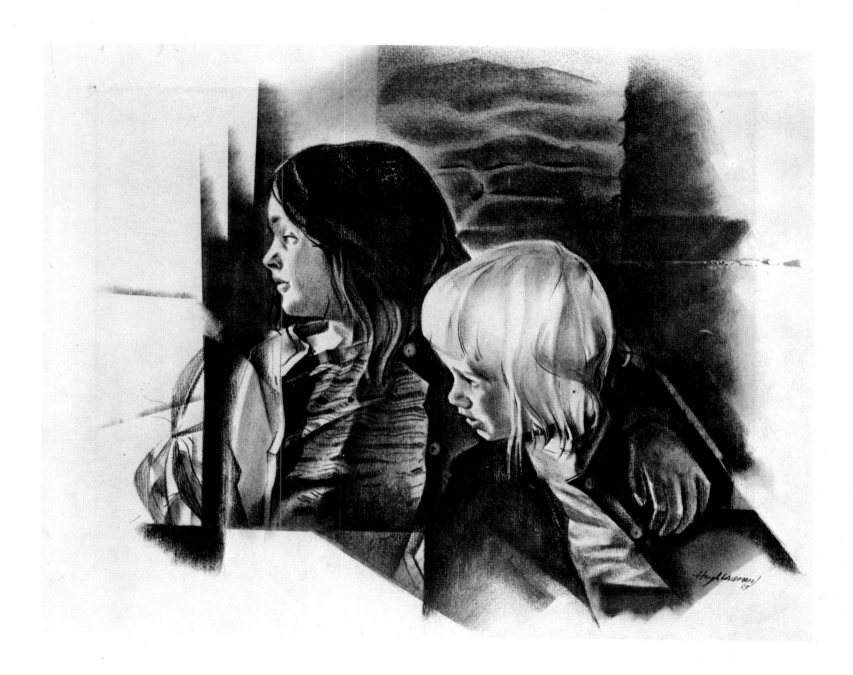

The picture *Jinx and Bon* used a combination of many black-and-white techniques. It was drawn first in charcoal, corrected and redrawn in Conte crayon and sticks, erased to produce soft effects, and reworked over the erasures.

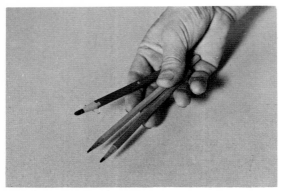

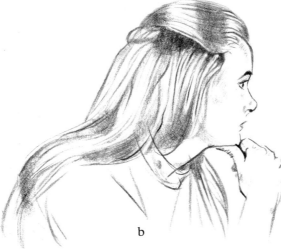

b

(b) Drawing made with a 2B graphite pencil. The softer B pencils allow for more immediate response and consequently a freer rendition of the subject. It is a good practice occasionally to draw with an extremely hard pencil. The hard pencil makes "faking" it with smudges more difficult and forces a more disciplined approach.

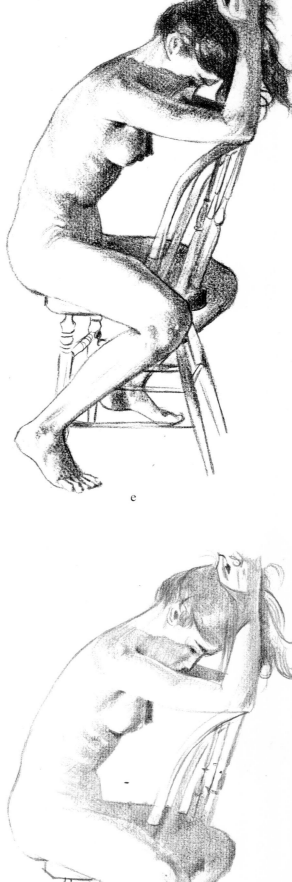

PENCILS AND CRAYONS

The selection of your pencil, both degree of hardness and type, will determine to a great extent the final appearance of the drawing. If you attempted to use charcoal, Conte, or Wolf pencil over a graphite underdrawing, you might find such a slippery graphite surface as to make further drawing impractical. There will be no difficulty using graphite pencil as a final technique.

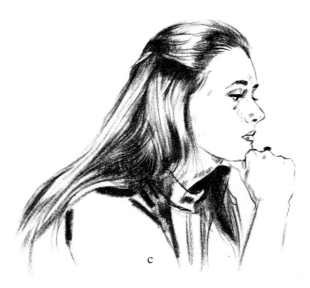

c

(c) A Wolf B pencil sketch.

(d) A charcoal pencil.

The nude on the chair was drawn on Fabriano text paper with a 2B Wolf pencil. The bottom identical drawing (f) was done with graphite pencil. The graphite rendition is generally more difficult to reproduce.

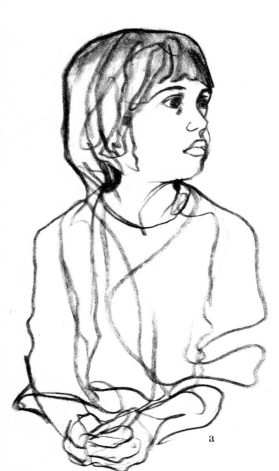

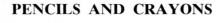
(a) A line drawing made in charcoal pencil.

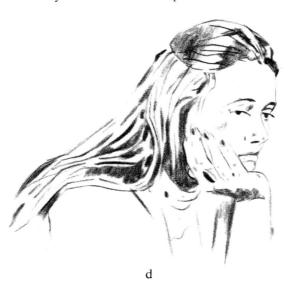

d

e

f

This last bit is true, but it is amusing to recall what one of our late great artists replied when he was told that the engravers were having difficulty reproducing his work. "Get better engravers." This verbal conflict took place in the late nineteenth century and is the last authenticated victory of any artist over an engraver.

SMUDGING

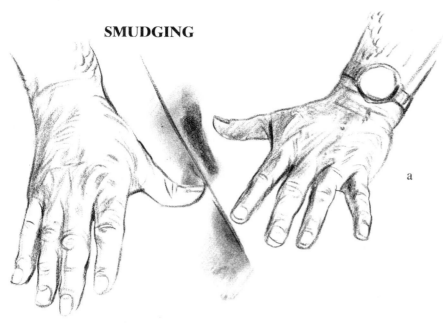

(a) Make a smudge gradation with the fingers or thumb. For more definitive edges, use a sheet of tracing paper as a mask.

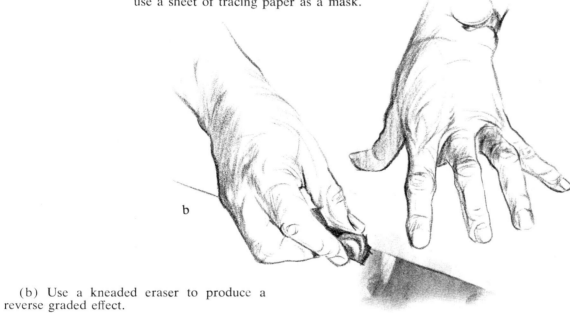

(b) Use a kneaded eraser to produce a reverse graded effect.

(c) Use a frisket to create predecided shapes. This controls undesired smudging and otherwise messy work.

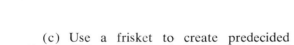

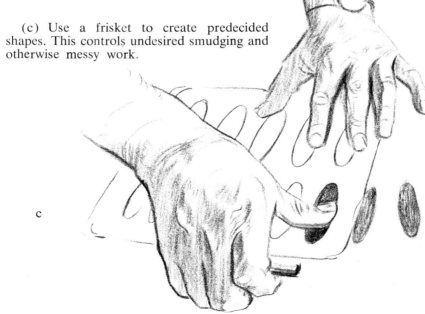

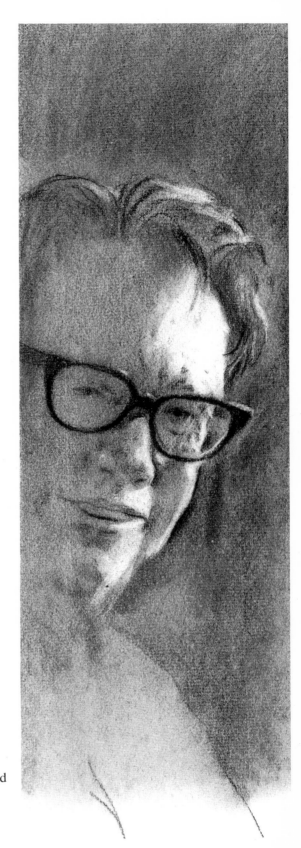

(d) This portrait was sketched lightly with charcoal to arrange its placement on the paper. An over-all tone was smudged onto the paper. The lighted areas were erased to the proper tone, highlighting from dark to light. The details and accents came last. Always wait until you have completed the head before "putting on" the glasses.

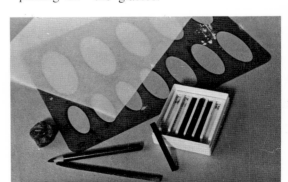

Materials used on this page

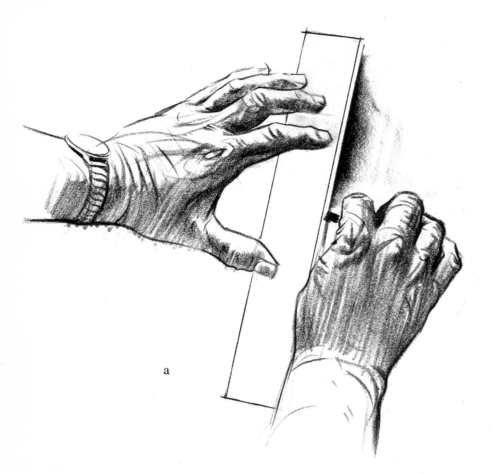

a

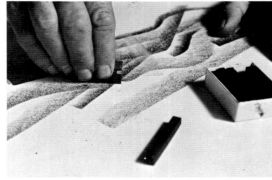

d

CONTE AND LITHO STICKS

Both Conte and litho sticks come in varying degrees of hardness to softness. Generally, the harder grades work for more detailed work, the softer grades for a larger, more abandoned approach. The three sketches on this page were made with a combination of Conte sticks and Conte pencils, medium grade.

(a) A medium Conte stick was used to make a straight toned line. The straightedge used is a ruler of ¼-inch-thick plastic, sanded to a smooth surface on the edges. There are usually such scraps of plexiglass for the asking around plexiglass supply houses or sign painters' shops. This makes a multiple-purpose ruler for the artist, most practical because he can see through it when putting down lines or tones.

(b) Experiment with the stick (a litho stick was used here) to create a variety of controlled tones and lines.

(c) Interesting effects can be achieved using the sharp or dulled edge of the square sticks.

If you are using thin paper, it will be a must to work on a pad or at least a backing of a number of sheets of paper. Even with relatively heavy paper, the sticks are so sensitive to the surface that any relief will show. It is possible to make use of this characteristic by deliberately working on thin paper over a textured surface. (See page 33.)

Litho sticks on plate-finish paper make possible interesting effects. A single-edged razor may be used to scrape off sections of dark tone (d).

(e) Delicate corrections may be made with an Exacto knife.

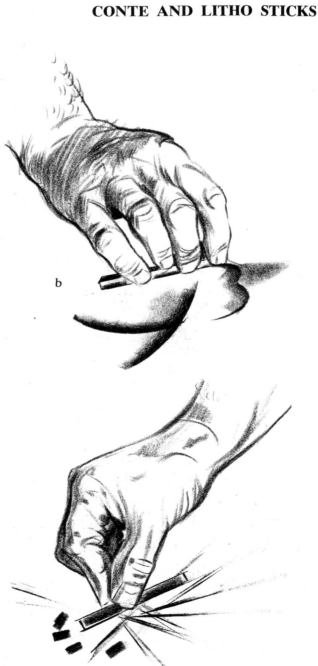

b

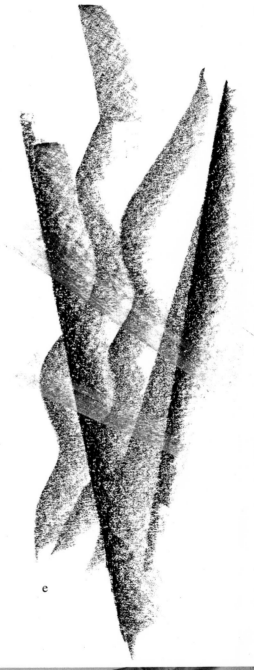

e

c

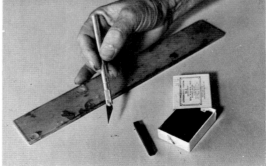

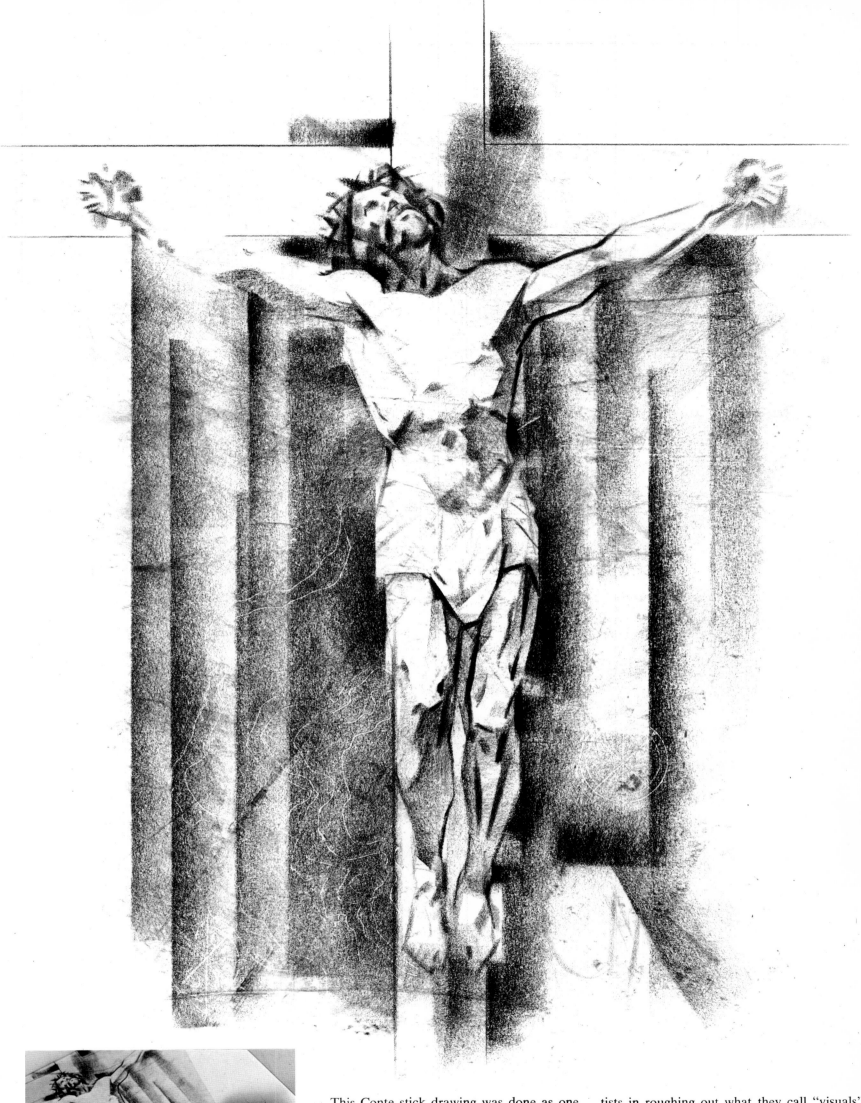

This Conte stick drawing was done as one of a number of preliminary drawings preceding a mural commission. It was drawn on a good grade of heavy tracing paper. Tracing paper of this quality is sold in rolls in architectural supply stores and in pads of varying sizes in art stores. A less transparent paper, called visual paper, with a responsive surface is sold in pads. Visual paper is so named because it is frequently used by advertising artists in roughing out what they call "visuals" or rough layout work, which gives an idea of a finished ad.

For this drawing, paper that had been used as a pad under another sketch was employed. The incised lines caused by tracing a past drawing resulted in the fine white lines in the final drawing. This becomes a technique of working on page 35. See the illustration of the vulture (2).

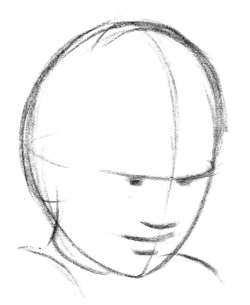

First, the blocking out and the placement on the page

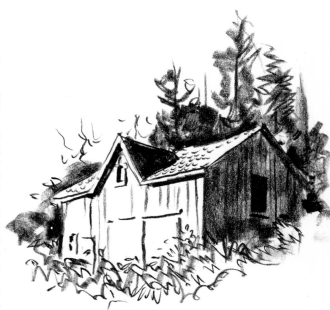

a

SKETCHING TECHNIQUES

In addition to the use of pencils and crayons already described, sketching is also done with sause and stumps. This may sound a bit gory, but stump is a word applied to sticks of tightly rolled paper, made with a point for shading and blending of pastel, charcoal, crayon, and pencil.

The term "lead pencil" is a misnomer. It is really a graphite pencil. Pencils for drawing also include charcoal, Wolf, and Conte pencils. All pencils come in a variety of degrees of hardness, and some in shapes peculiarly suited to special kinds of drawing.

The traditional barn is a subject favored by the beginner for the simple reason that it is an easy subject and the artist's audience seems never to tire of it. In (a) we have a graphite pencil sketch. In (b) the same subject in charcoal pencil.

In (c) we have a subject dear to Whistler's heart, but more likely he used London as subject matter because he was there. That's why this sketch is in pencil—it was what happened to be available.

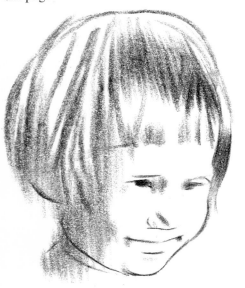

Next, the general tonal pattern

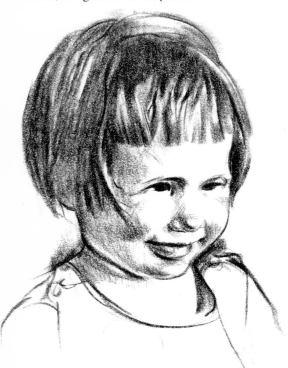

. . . and finally, the details

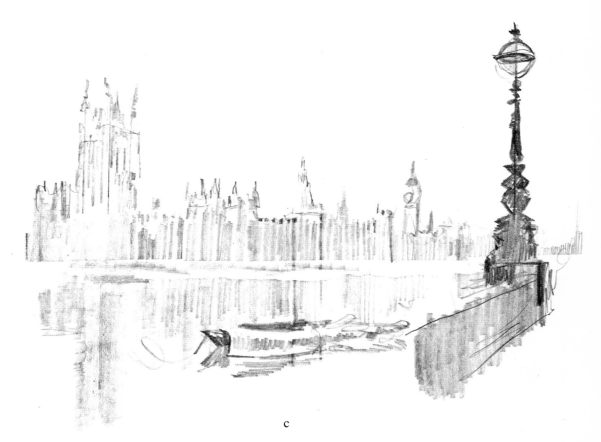

b

c

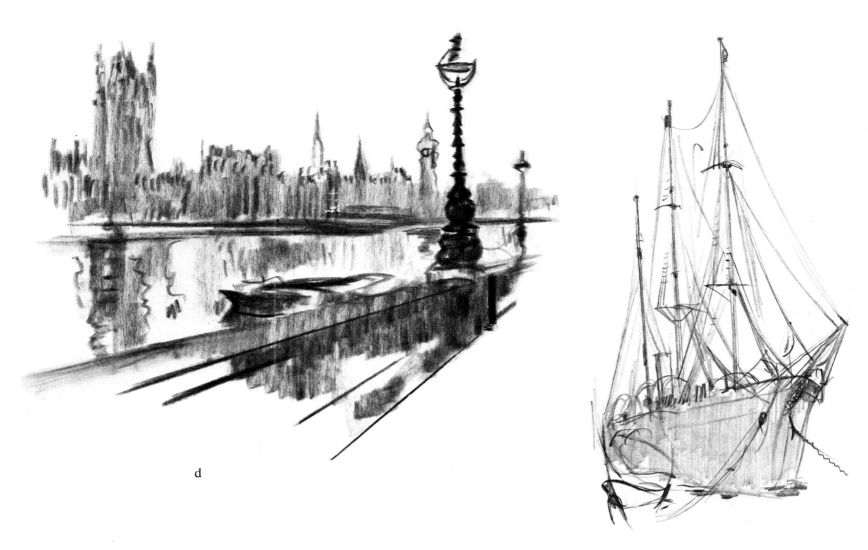

d

The charcoal sketch (d) is a repeat of the London scene to show the change in mood caused by the medium.

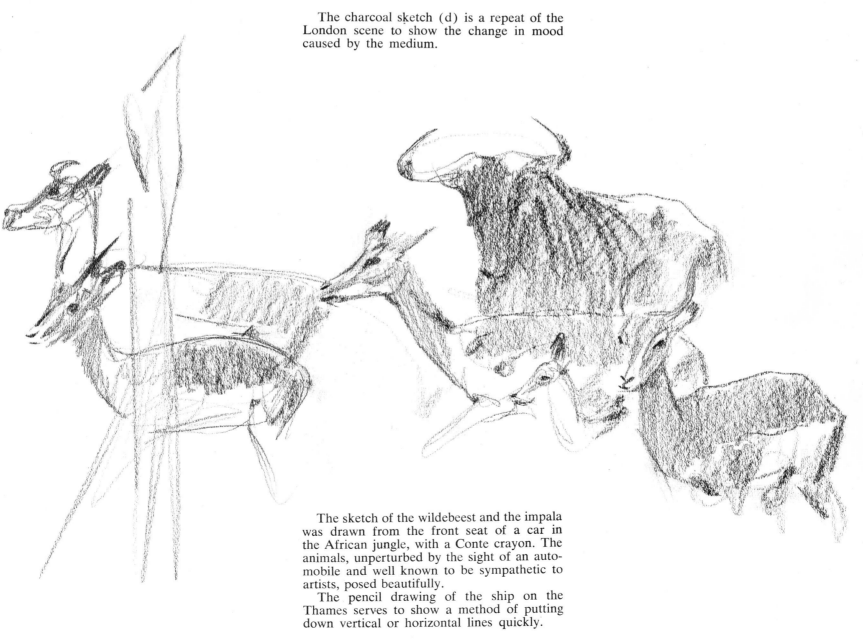

The sketch of the wildebeest and the impala was drawn from the front seat of a car in the African jungle, with a Conte crayon. The animals, unperturbed by the sight of an automobile and well known to be sympathetic to artists, posed beautifully.

The pencil drawing of the ship on the Thames serves to show a method of putting down vertical or horizontal lines quickly.

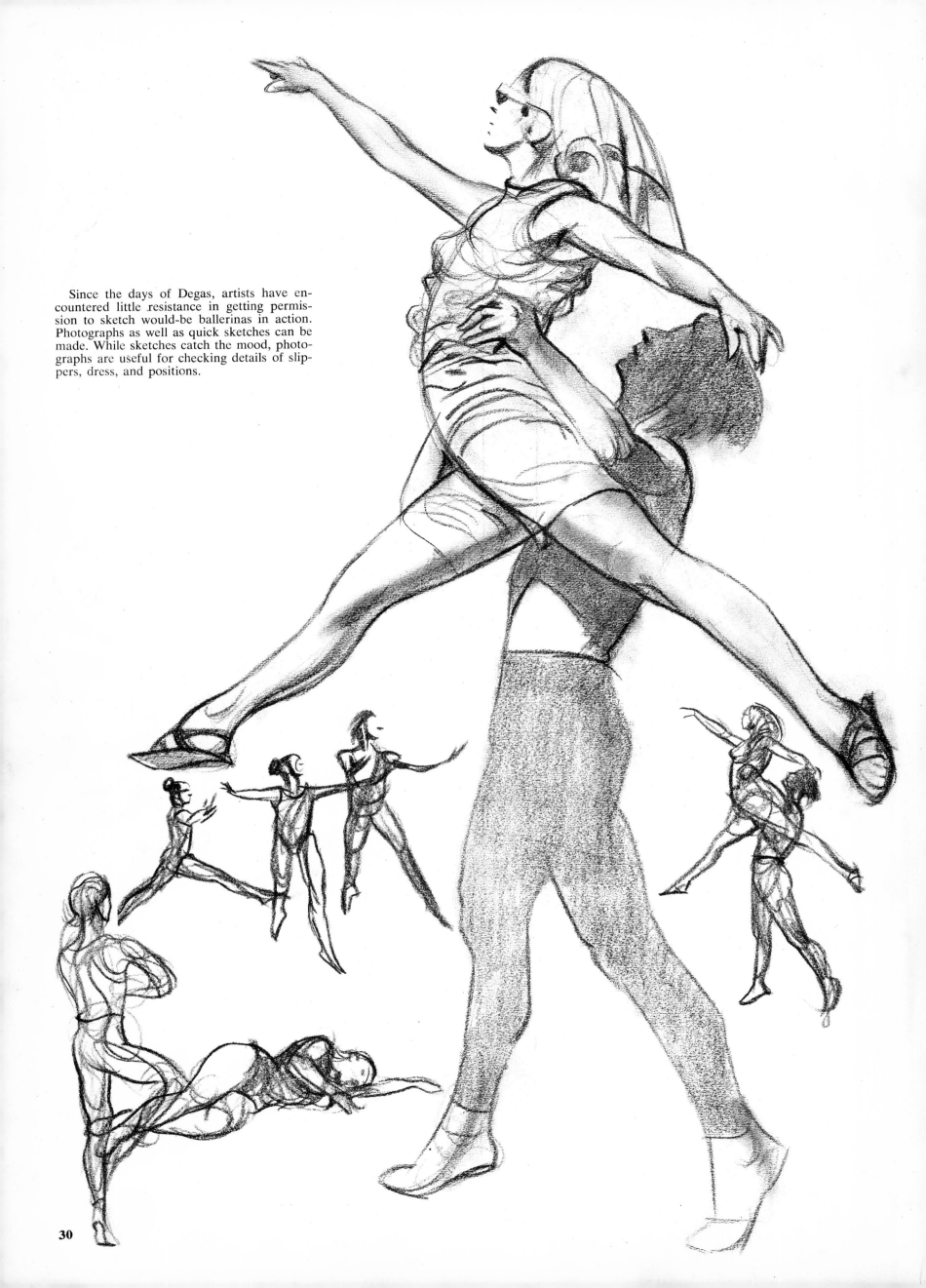

Since the days of Degas, artists have encountered little resistance in getting permission to sketch would-be ballerinas in action. Photographs as well as quick sketches can be made. While sketches catch the mood, photographs are useful for checking details of slippers, dress, and positions.

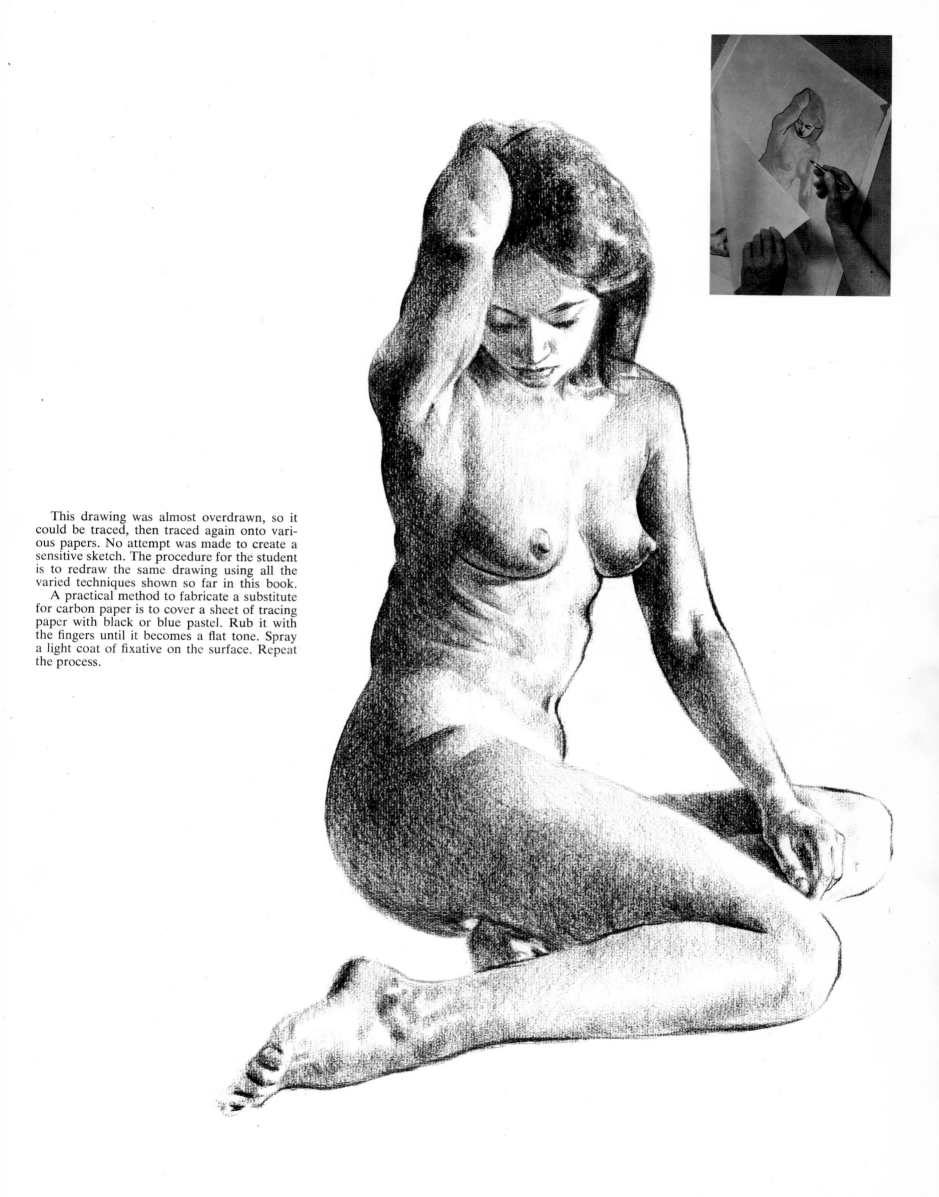

This drawing was almost overdrawn, so it could be traced, then traced again onto various papers. No attempt was made to create a sensitive sketch. The procedure for the student is to redraw the same drawing using all the varied techniques shown so far in this book.

A practical method to fabricate a substitute for carbon paper is to cover a sheet of tracing paper with black or blue pastel. Rub it with the fingers until it becomes a flat tone. Spray a light coat of fixative on the surface. Repeat the process.

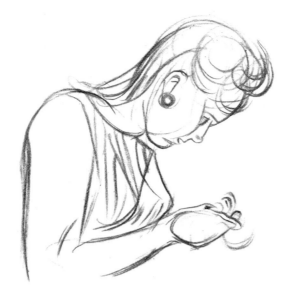

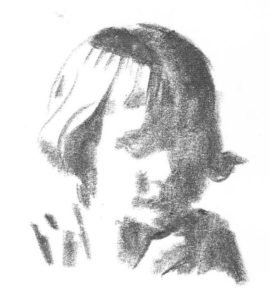

TECHNIQUES IN GRAYS

(a) The outline sketch of a girl painting her fingernails was done in charcoal. Charcoal leaves a surface not only easily changed and erasable but also compatible with the application of pastel or chalk sticks.

(d) A different approach. Instead of beginning a sketch with a careful line drawing, begin by making a tone pattern. This practice is excellent for analyzing the composition of any drawing.

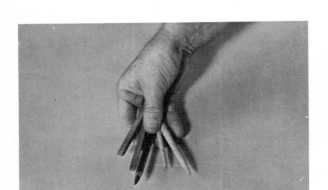

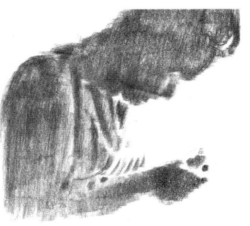

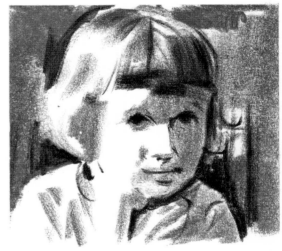

Gray pastels in a variety of rigidly controlled tones (originally manufactured to fill the needs of commercial artists in their constant quest for speed of execution) are an effective tool for the fine artist.

They are sticks of hard pastel, boxed in a series of graduated tones in either warm or cool tones. The surfaces most adaptable to their use are bond paper, tracing paper, and visual paper, used over a pad of other paper to provide a slightly resilient surface. As in the case of the Conte or litho sticks, they lend themselves not only to straightforward techniques but also to application as shown here. Aside from their use as a graduated medium, they can be applied in solid form, for no matter how hard and long the artist applies them to the paper, they will never mark the surface with a deeper tone than that for which the specific pastel was designed.

In practice, this quality makes possible the artist's returning to a given tone at any time with no concern as to matching. This tends to limit the artist to producing simpler compositions, and this is a good discipline.

(b) A medium-gray stick was used to create the general form of the drawing. It is wise not to obliterate completely the drawing underneath.

(e) The darker gray is applied. Think not only of the areas you are covering but also of the shapes and design of the areas left untouched.

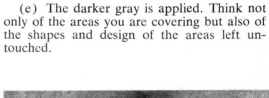

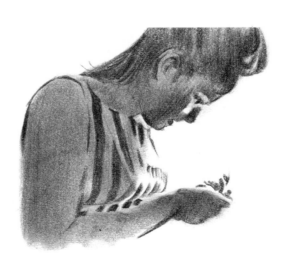

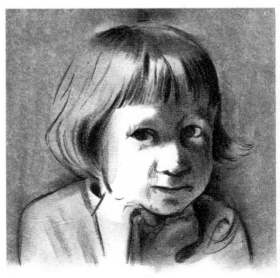

(c) A dark tone was used to finish the drawing. In following this procedure, you may find that a succeeding step may pick up the preceding tone, making it difficult to gain the effect you are attempting. Spraying with workable fixative after each step eliminates this problem.

(f) Carry the sketch a step further. Beyond a certain point, continuation of working will help little, if at all. One of the most difficult problems is to learn when to stop. One learns most through trial and error.

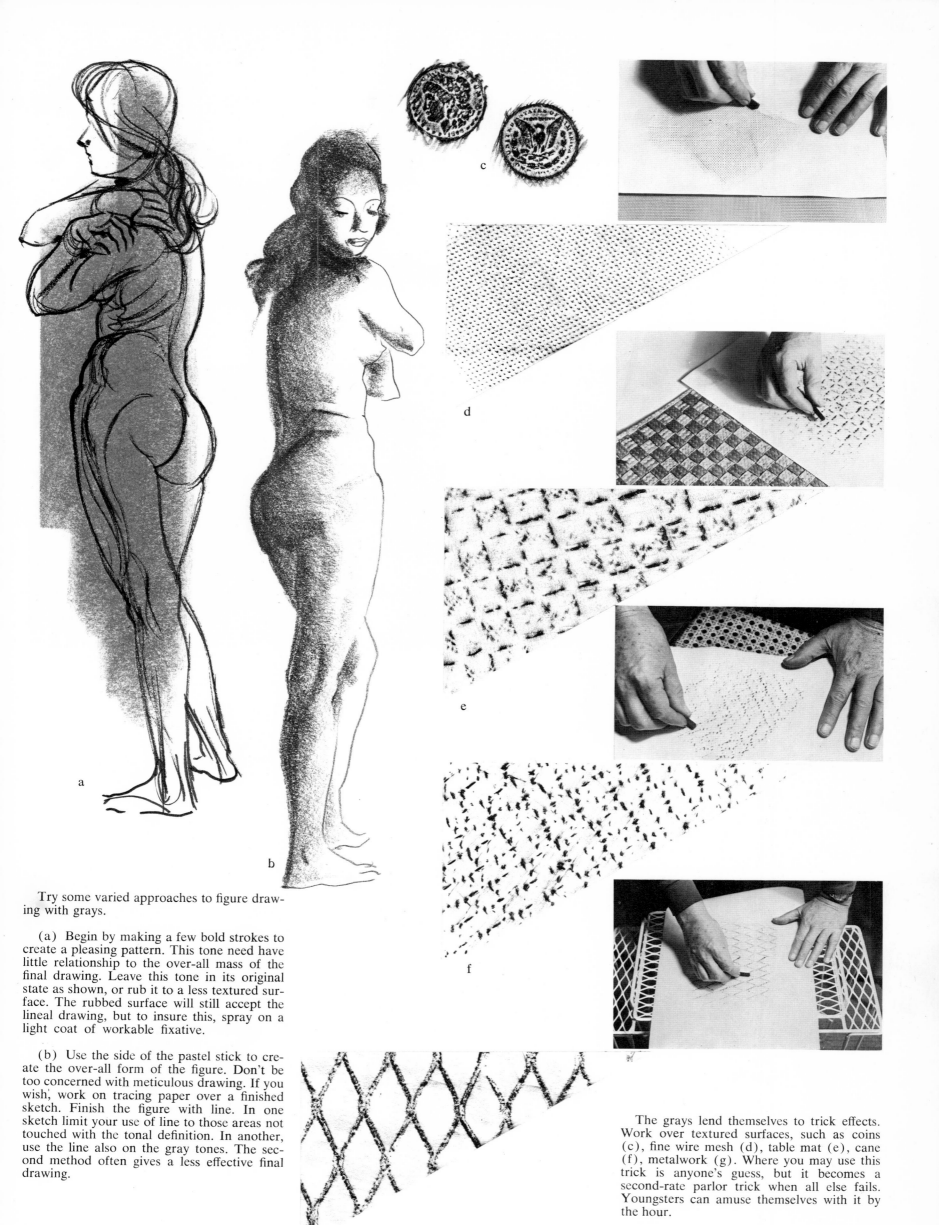

Try some varied approaches to figure drawing with grays.

(a) Begin by making a few bold strokes to create a pleasing pattern. This tone need have little relationship to the over-all mass of the final drawing. Leave this tone in its original state as shown, or rub it to a less textured surface. The rubbed surface will still accept the lineal drawing, but to insure this, spray on a light coat of workable fixative.

(b) Use the side of the pastel stick to create the over-all form of the figure. Don't be too concerned with meticulous drawing. If you wish, work on tracing paper over a finished sketch. Finish the figure with line. In one sketch limit your use of line to those areas not touched with the tonal definition. In another, use the line also on the gray tones. The second method often gives a less effective final drawing.

The grays lend themselves to trick effects. Work over textured surfaces, such as coins (c), fine wire mesh (d), table mat (e), cane (f), metalwork (g). Where you may use this trick is anyone's guess, but it becomes a second-rate parlor trick when all else fails. Youngsters can amuse themselves with it by the hour.

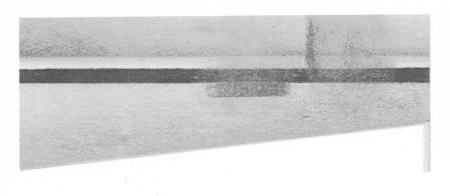

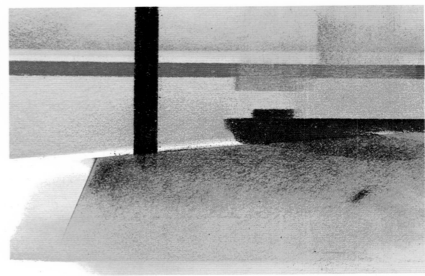

(1) This was done with two tones of nu-pastel, using a piece of paper as a frisket to make the hard edge.

(2) Add a complementary color, and then an analagous one to proceed with an abstract pattern.

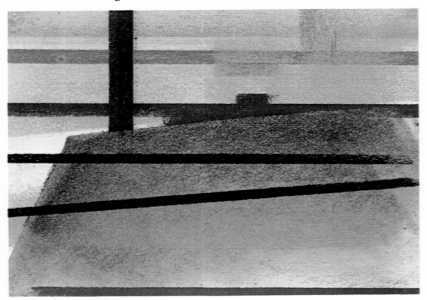

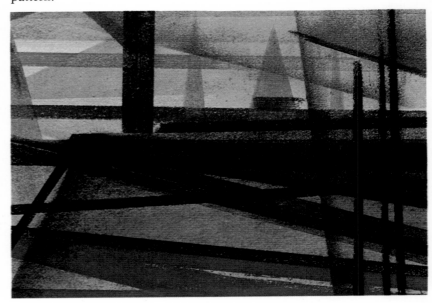

(3) Spray the already covered areas with workable fixative if you do not wish the ensuing tones to blend into the original ones.

(4) An abstract pattern approach to gaining familiarity with a medium will usually reveal a great deal about an artist. There could be an open field for analyzing abstract patterns. Here the designs are purposeful, not accidental.

Crested cranes have a brilliant pattern of colors.
(a) First the birds were drawn in colored pencil in a line pattern, coming fairly close to the colors of the bird.
(b) The next step was to fill in the colors with broad strokes.

HARD PASTEL

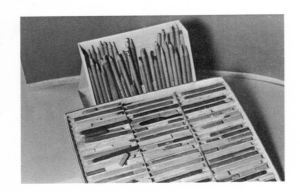

Hard pastels are sold under a number of trade names. Pastel pencils, matched to the color of the pastel sticks, are also available. Explore the effects and textures possible in this medium.

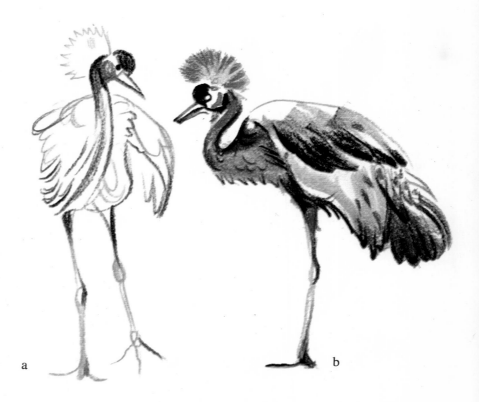

a   b

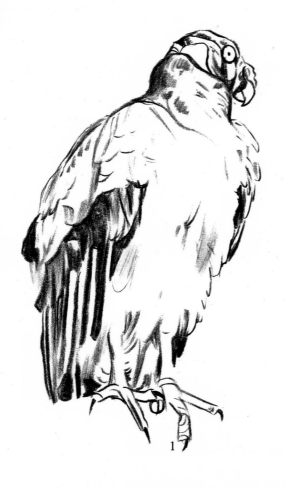

1

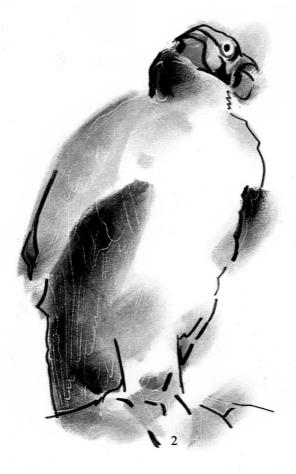

2

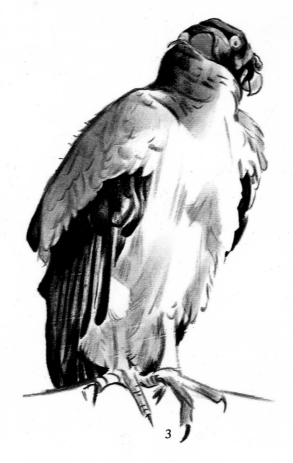

3

(1) Make a working drawing in pencil. Trace it onto the finish paper without benefit of carbon paper. This will incise the drawing into the final working surface. Use a soft surface, a pad, or a number of sheets of paper under the drawing paper for a cushion.

A ball-point pen is an ideal instrument with which to trace, although you can use the pointed end of the handle of a brush.

(2) The resulting incised line drawing will be almost invisible unless viewed in a strong sidelight. Use a selection of colors considerably more intense than those seen in the subject to block in the general pattern of the bird. The incised lines will not accept the color, and you will have a clear white line drawing of your bird.

(3) You may rub these areas to create a smooth-looking surface, but be careful not to overdo it and consequently lose the white lines. Spray with workable fixative. Let dry and continue to give form to the bird with pastel or Conte or both.

Try using tracing paper for your color application.

1a. Draw an extremely strong black-and-white sketch on any surface.

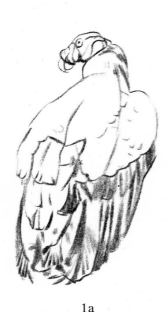

1a

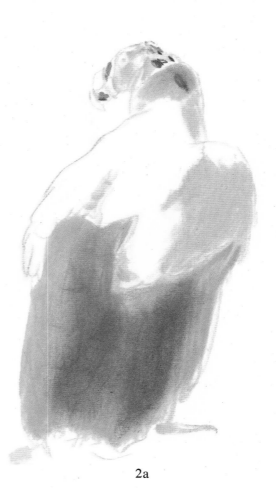

2a

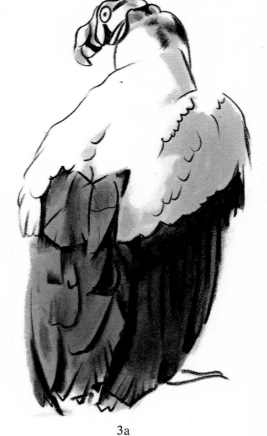

3a

2a. Tape the tracing paper over the drawing. Apply the color to the drawing, using the covered drawing as a guide. Rub the pastel with finger or stump so that the drawing underneath is visible.

3a. Finish the drawing with strong accents of darker tones and color. Fix and mount the traced drawing.

Try tracing the vulture in a variety of colors.

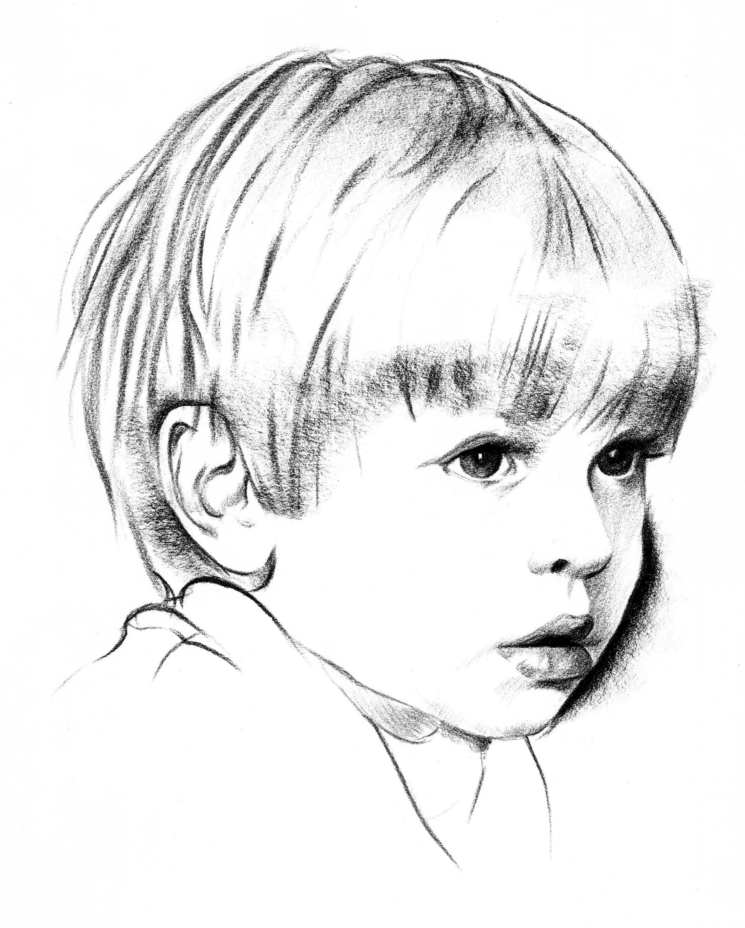

This moderately comprehensive drawing of a boy's head is the size of the original sketch shown on pages 38–39. Trace it and experiment with the techniques shown.

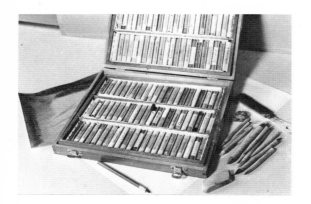

TRADITIONAL PASTEL

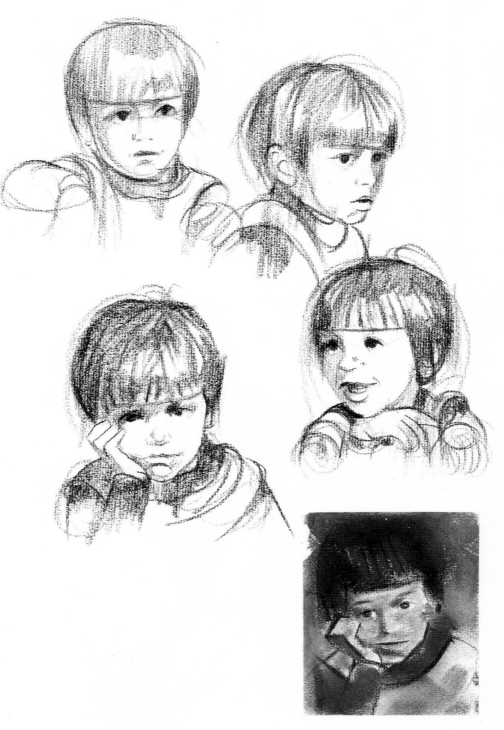

These pastels come in round sticks with an infinite variety of colors, shades, and tones. They are softer than the square sticks and considerably more adaptable to use by the fine artist. Artists frequently combine their use with the harder, more easily managed square sticks.

Pastel is, like watercolor, acrylic, and oil, a permanent medium. Pastel is ground pigment mixed with gum and formed into a stick. There is an inference, because of a secondary use of the word to designate a soft, pale shade, to think of pastels as something less than a strong, vigorous medium. This is an unfortunate misconception because pastel also lends itself to brilliant and strong design. The dangers in using pastel, apart from use by individuals allergic to dust particles, is in overworking into a muddy finish. Like working in watercolor, the best method is the direct "get it down and forget it" approach. Unlike watercolor, pastel, after a coat of fixative, gives the artist a second chance, never, however, with the same potential of the first try.

The surfaces for pastel painting are many, and each creates its own final characteristics. Traditional pastel papers are used mostly, but special velvet surfaces, as well as sandpaper sheets, produce interesting effects.

For delicate passages, a palette of sandpaper is used. Colors are picked up with a separate stump for each color and then applied to the drawing surface.

To appreciate the possibilities of pastel, experiment with varied colors, first strongly applied and then briskly rubbed, one color into the next.

It is wise to use a sheet of paper over the finished areas to avoid smudging the work in progress. During the process of painting a pastel, frequently tap or blow off the excess particles.

To approach a portrait in any medium, the artist must first determine the direction the final portrait is to take by way of many thumbnail sketches. In the case of the subject opposite, will the boy be pensive, devil-may-care, sad, or happy? It is the thinking that precedes the portrait, more than the technique, that counts; likeness of the spirit of the subject more than a proper definition of a set of features.

So far we have stressed the technique and use of the materials, but it is the artist's expression of his feelings about the subject that is most important. A technically clumsy execution, rich in emotion, will be a much more lasting piece than a slick exhibition of the tricks of the trade. Knowledge of the media's peculiarities will afford the artist more opportunities to express his feelings with assurance.

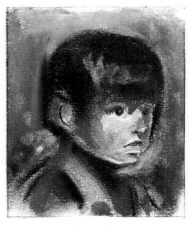

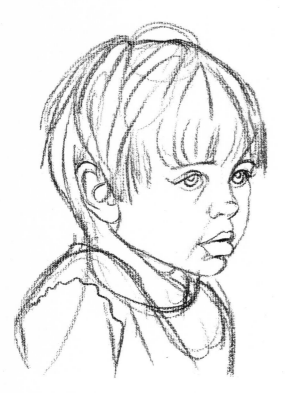

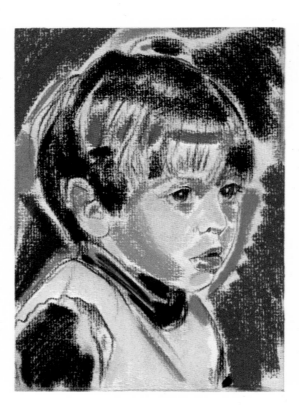

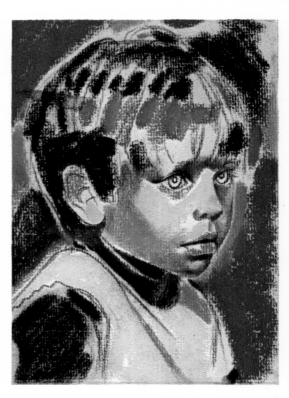

The Direct Approach

Most viewers of the preceding sketches would probably have selected the pastel sketch with chin in hand to carry to completion, but here the simplest was chosen to clarify the exercise step by step.

1. Sketch the chosen pose to size directly and lightly in charcoal. If you prefer, sketch it on a work sheet, then trace it onto your paper.

2. The second step is to cover the whole portrait area with pastel. Use colors either close to nature or from your impression of what you see. Maybe it's your blue period. Keep the colors isolated one from another.

3. Now, and not before, is the time to begin concentrating on the features. I have yet to see a beginner who does not start with the complete rendition of the eyes, but this approach invariably spells ruin to the final work. It is much more difficult to begin with specific features than it is with the over-all pattern.

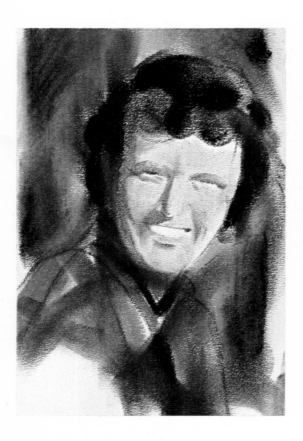

The Smudging Approach

1a. Begin the sketch with no outline drawing by smudging areas of fairly true color in an almost abstract arrangement. If you wish to check your ability to match color, take a small smudge on a separate slip of paper. Walk to the model or the background and hold the chip of color up to the area you want to match.

2a. Once you have come close to the over-all pattern in true color, begin the process of defining the structure. The ability to match colors at a distance takes years to master, but, whether you wish to stray from true color or stick to the facts, it follows that you must have more than an accidental approach.

A traditional pastel approach is to start with a toned paper. Both Ingres and Michelet papers come in a selection of light and dark shades. In drawing this type of portrait, the paper tone becomes the middle or over-all tone. In this case, white chalk is used for lighter areas and highlights. Dark shadows are in black.

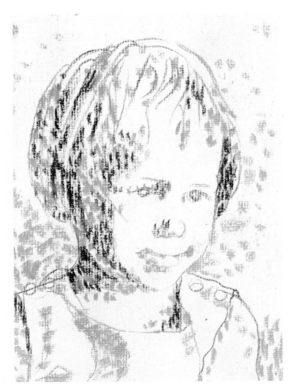
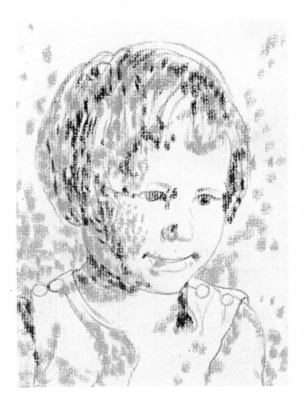
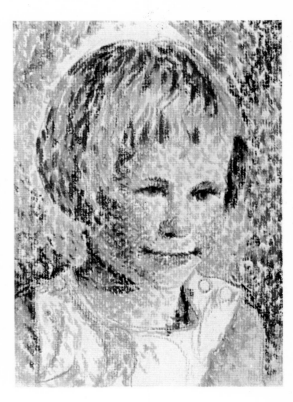

The Pointillist Approach.

1. Make a light charcoal outline drawing, then place dots of cool color over it, as here. In effect, this is a kind of underpainting. When these cool colors show through or appear next to the warmer complementary colors (added later), they mix in the viewer's eye, giving a far more vibrant color than that obtained by premixing colors.

2. This is not a rapid approach, but a cautious one, allowing the artist plenty of time to analyze his work as he proceeds. With occasional coatings of fixative, it is possible to change and change again to create just the desired effect. There is the constant danger that the artist may lose his original sketch, but, theoretically at least, the process allows for improving as the painting progresses.

3. The application of dots of warm and cool colors is continued until the sketch does what you want it to do. Pointillism works equally well with other subjects and is probably most effective in landscapes.

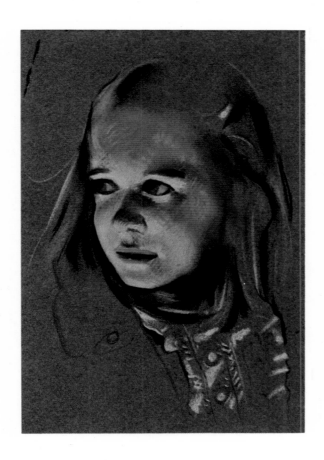

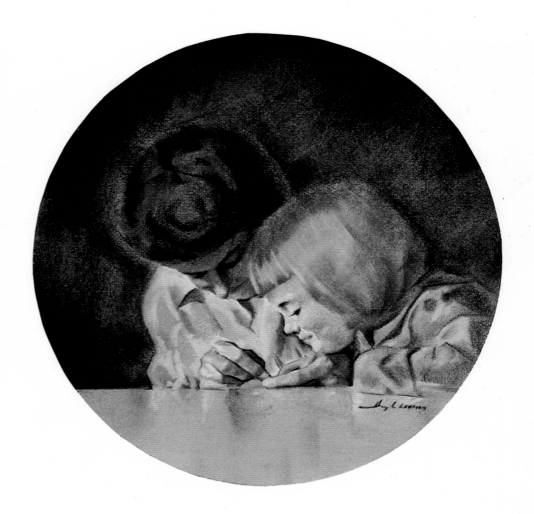

Colored paper was again used as the base for this pastel. Although more difficult to execute, it is an effective method, and probably the most popular.

The circular painting is an example of the use of a combination of all the approaches so far discussed.

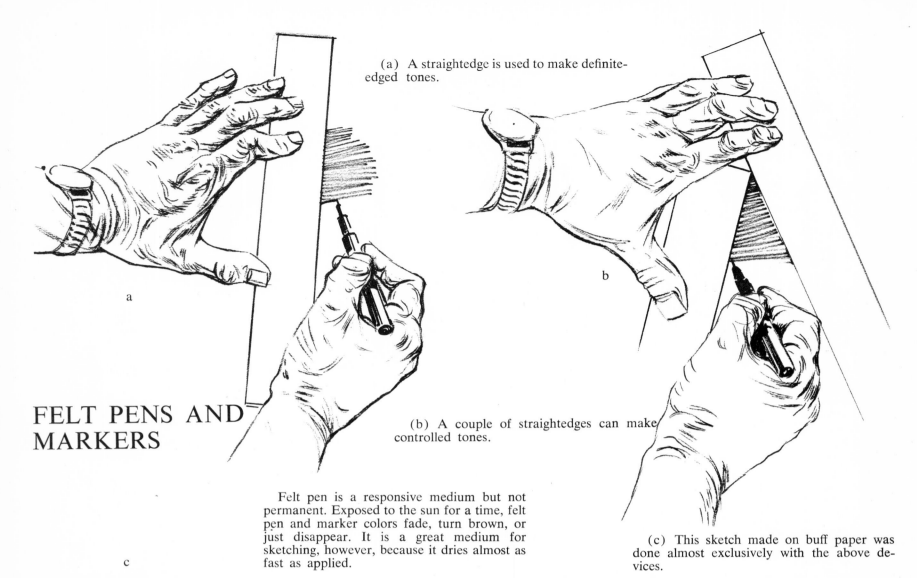

(a) A straightedge is used to make definite-edged tones.

(b) A couple of straightedges can make controlled tones.

(c) This sketch made on buff paper was done almost exclusively with the above devices.

FELT PENS AND MARKERS

Felt pen is a responsive medium but not permanent. Exposed to the sun for a time, felt pen and marker colors fade, turn brown, or just disappear. It is a great medium for sketching, however, because it dries almost as fast as applied.

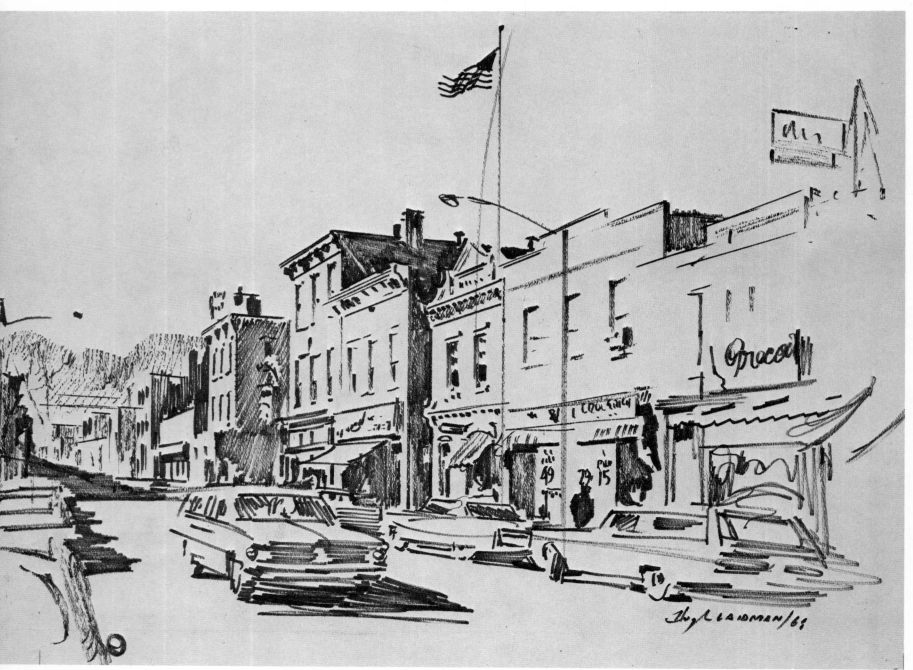

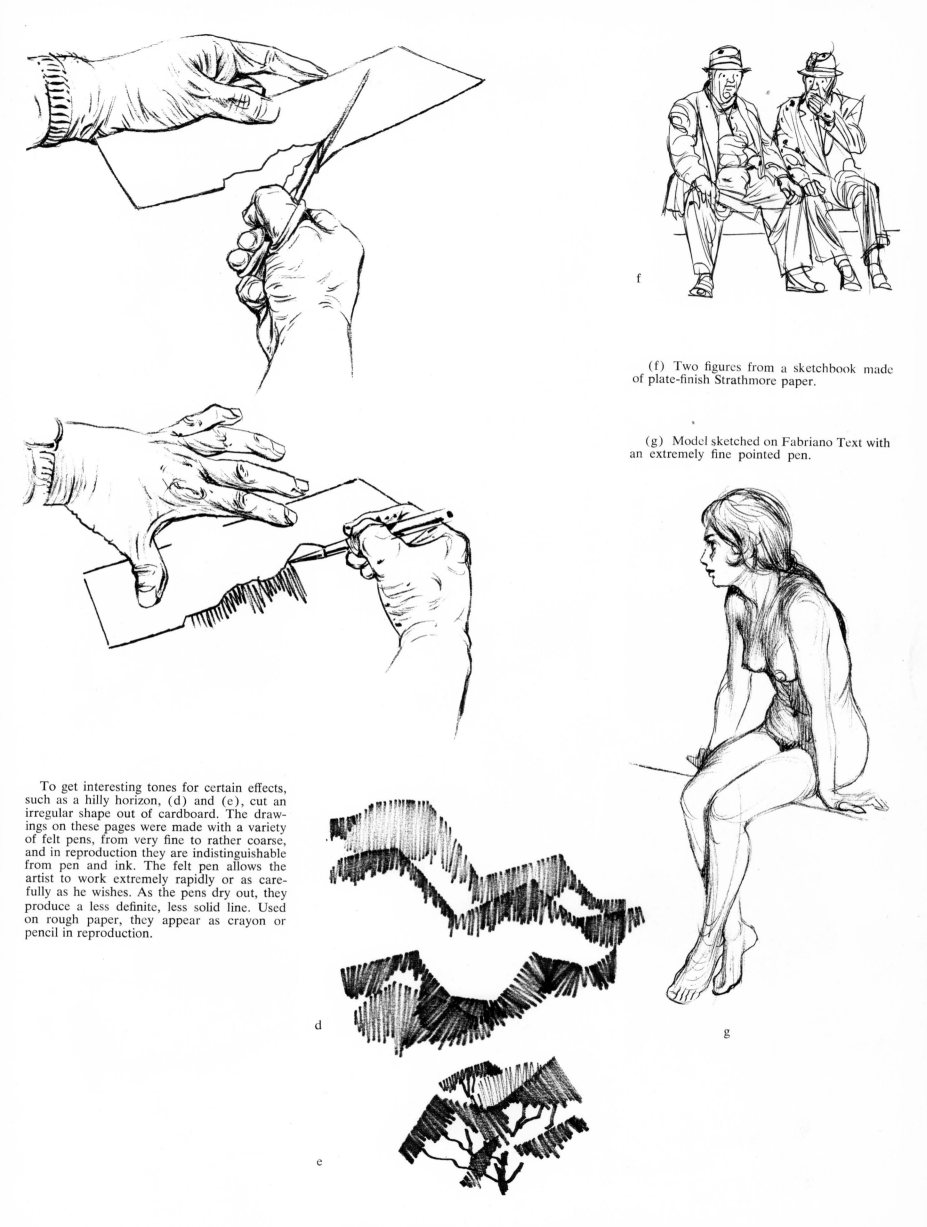

(f) Two figures from a sketchbook made of plate-finish Strathmore paper.

(g) Model sketched on Fabriano Text with an extremely fine pointed pen.

To get interesting tones for certain effects, such as a hilly horizon, (d) and (e), cut an irregular shape out of cardboard. The drawings on these pages were made with a variety of felt pens, from very fine to rather coarse, and in reproduction they are indistinguishable from pen and ink. The felt pen allows the artist to work extremely rapidly or as carefully as he wishes. As the pens dry out, they produce a less definite, less solid line. Used on rough paper, they appear as crayon or pencil in reproduction.

d

e

f

g

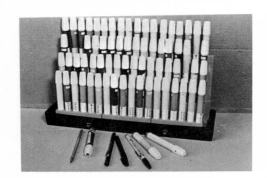

Color markers are felt pens with a broader tip. To use them with any degree of success, you need a complete set of colors with many shades and tones (above). The marker of any given color is incapable of making other than one specific tone, so markers are manufactured in degrees from light to dark in most shades. They are transparent, however, and when used one over the other, they will give multiple-color effects.

These colors are not permanent, but are so responsive and simple to use that they have become a sort of career for those in the commercial world where permanence in anything is the last consideration.

(a) Starting with a simple felt pen sketch, we interpret the head in intense color with little relation to the colors of nature. It is always interesting to experiment in this way.

(b) The style seems to express the character of the subject here and points to the possibility of utilizing brilliant colors separated by black, simulating stained glass. This style can also be copied using oil or acrylic.

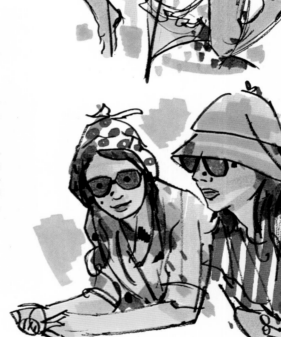

c

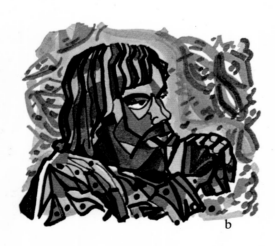

a

b

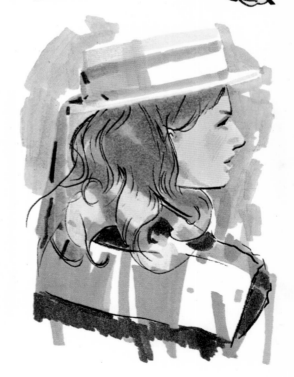

d

(c) A more serious approach is shown in the two sketches of *Birds of Kyalami*. These sketches were started in black felt pen (on location) and developed later with color.

(d) *The Girl in the Straw Hat* (at the races) was sketched directly in color and accented with black.

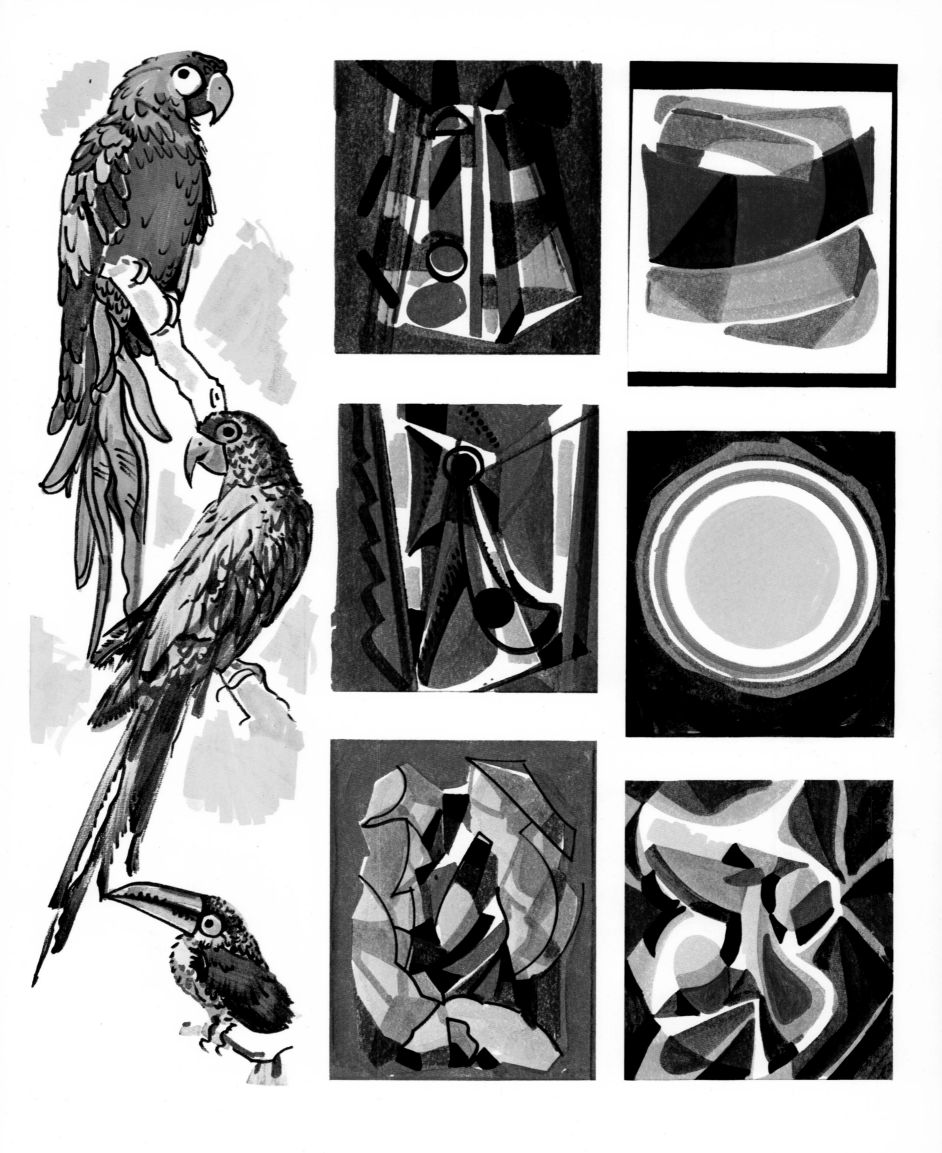

It is often impractical to take a complete selection of color markers for outdoor sketching, but six or so, which represent the color wheel fairly well, should be possible. A limited palette encourages far more intelligent work.

The parrot, the macaw, and the aracari show how fitting the medium is for the "camp" style. The small abstracts show another excellent use of color markers. They are quick notes that, when projected to gigantic size, serve as good preliminary studies for more serious works in other media.

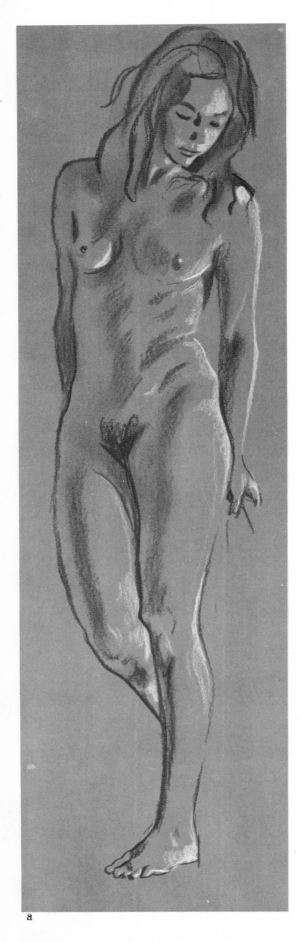

a

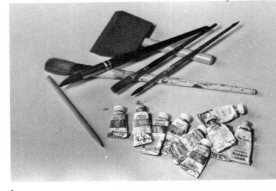

b

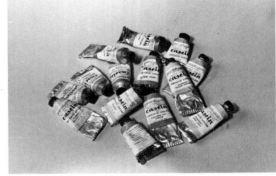

c

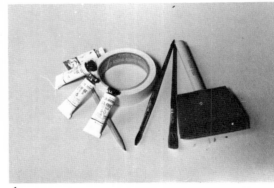

d

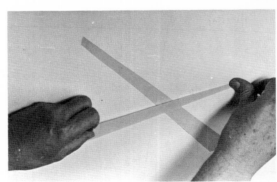

e

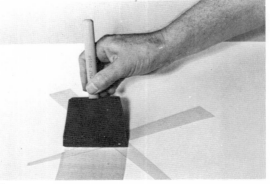

f

Strictly speaking, the term gouache—a method of painting with watercolors—covers all of them. For a long time casein was the most popular. This is an extremely versatile medium. It can be applied thinly as in transparent watercolor, or in heavy impasto. The latter method employs just enough water with the casein to make it workable, so that it resembles an oil, especially when varnished.

Casein may be used as the underpainting for an oil painting. The casein in this case should be applied sparingly, left to dry, then isolated from the subsequent oil glazes by a coat of casein varnish. Once you have painted on this in oil, you cannot retract and go back to casein. The casein requires a more absorbent surface, and the oil surface will cause the casein to flake off. It is also prone to ruin brushes. Perhaps because of these difficulties, although it is a good medium, casein has largely been replaced by acrylics.

Here are a few facts to bear in mind when using casein. For the palette, use a nonabsorbent metal or plastic one, or else ceramic, such as an old white plate. Water is the vehicle, but special drying retarders are available.

Casein may be applied to most surfaces. Gesso board is good, but quality paper or illustration board works equally well. There is a casein varnish, and even sprayable films, tailored for use with casein.

The most difficult aspect of painting in gouache is the spelling of the word. Gouache consists of opaque colors ground in water and mixed with a gum preparation. Gouache is extremely adaptable to painting flat areas of color. Since it is opaque, one color may be painted over the next. To a limited degree, it can be used in much the same way as transparent watercolor. Gouache is an excellent way to learn to paint with transparent watercolors; you can correct your mistakes almost immediately because it dries so quickly.

Used in conjunction with black or colored markers, gouache lends itself to minor works in camp style.

(a) A tone of retouch gray was painted on the paper surface. The drawing was then made on top of this in Conte crayon and white chalk. Any of the opaque paints, brushed on in a smooth, flat style, make a good base for working in crayon and stump techniques.

(b–c) A variety of brushes, rounds, and chisel edge, a flat urethane paint applicator, pencils, paper, and paints are the simple requirements for painting in gouache.

In photo (b) designers' colors are shown, but casein colors can be used interchangeably.

(d) Here four tones of retouch grays are shown. Using the grays is excellent practice to gain a sense of tonal values.

(e) Tape is cut to form interesting shapes and then pasted down on a sheet of paper.

(f) A paint applicator is dragged over the pasted tape. The tape is removed and repeatedly pasted down and painted over, to gain effects as shown on the right.

WORKING WITH OPAQUES: CASEIN, GOUACHE, POSTER AND DESIGNER COLORS

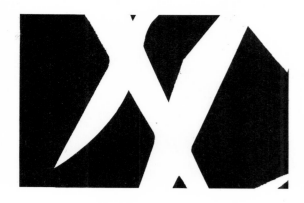

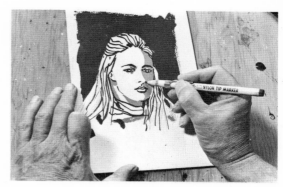

The five abstract patterns at left, done in retouch gray poster paints, were made, as shown at the bottom of page 44, by pasting down masking tape cut into strips, painting over them, and then removing the tape. Poor-quality paper without a fairly durable surface may peel when the tape is removed.

4

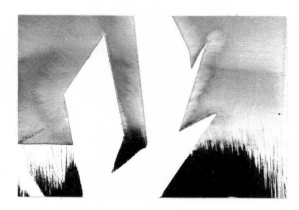

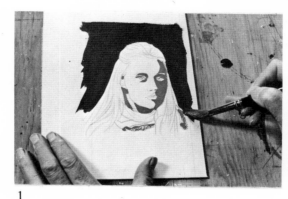

1

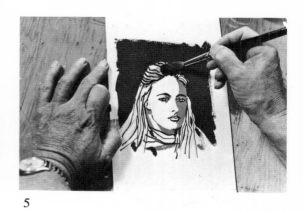

5

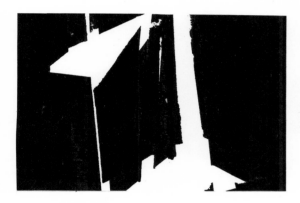

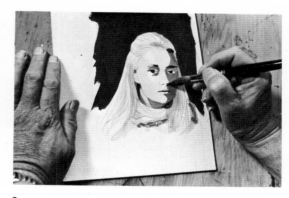

2

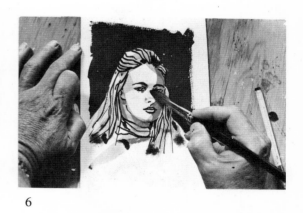

6

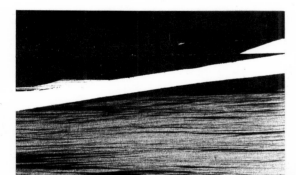

The seven progressive stages (from top to bottom) in drawing the girl in two different techniques show simple methods of completing a pencil sketch. A number of retouch grays were used for the opaque paint.

Illustrations 1, 2, and 3 show using opaques only, while 4, 5, 6, and 7 show the addition of line work using a permanent ink felt pen.

3

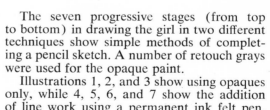

7

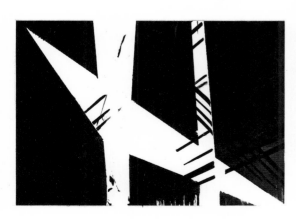

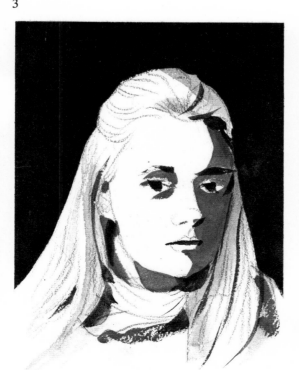

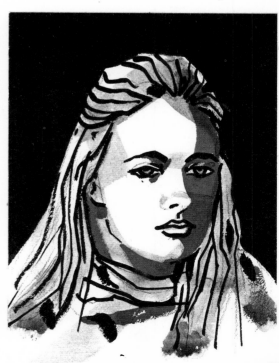

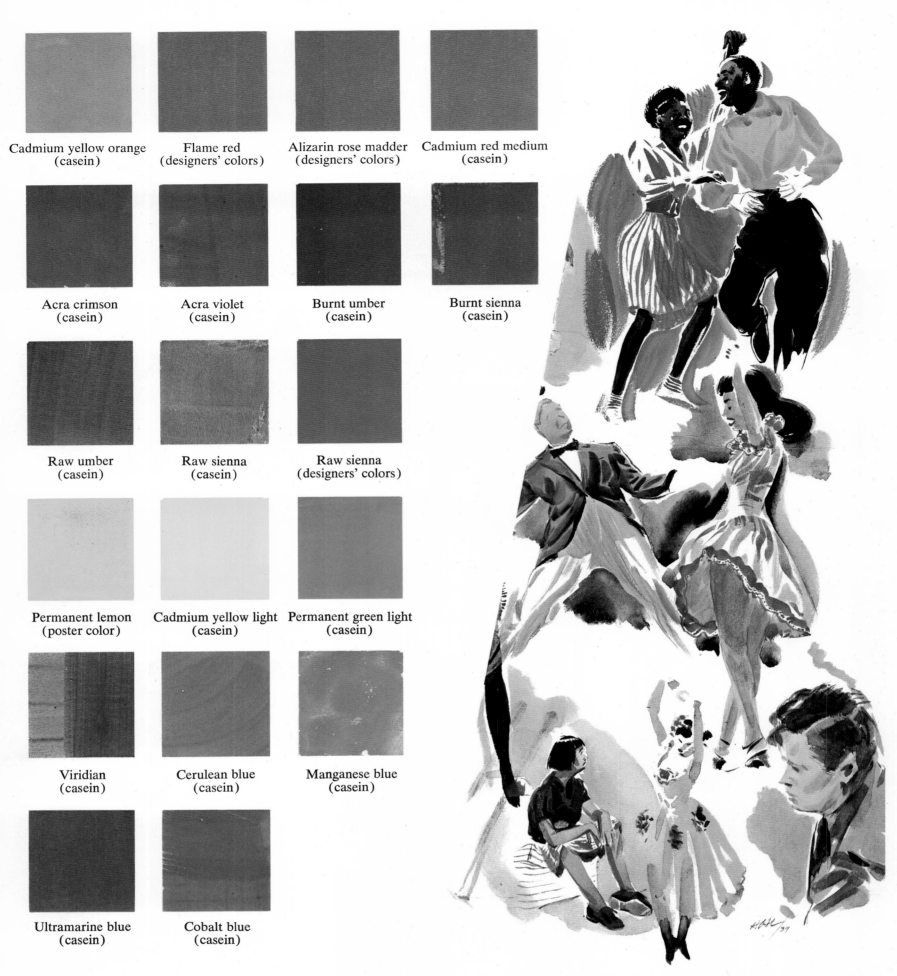

Cadmium yellow orange
(casein)

Flame red
(designers' colors)

Alizarin rose madder
(designers' colors)

Cadmium red medium
(casein)

Acra crimson
(casein)

Acra violet
(casein)

Burnt umber
(casein)

Burnt sienna
(casein)

Raw umber
(casein)

Raw sienna
(casein)

Raw sienna
(designers' colors)

Permanent lemon
(poster color)

Cadmium yellow light
(casein)

Permanent green light
(casein)

Viridian
(casein)

Cerulean blue
(casein)

Manganese blue
(casein)

Ultramarine blue
(casein)

Cobalt blue
(casein)

Color sketch in opaques, done for a magazine in the 1930s

Artists seldom agree on an exact list of colors necessary to the complete palette. Similar colors appear in the various media, though the names of the colors may differ. The more inexpensive the paint, the more likely it is to have some exotic name, often incomprehensible to the professional. Above are swatches of color directly from an assortment of opaque media.

A starting palette should comprise varieties of the primaries, red, blue, and yellow. The best approach to any given selection of colors is the simplest assortment. It is also true that various subjects call for different colors. The colors shown, or their equivalents, plus black and white, will answer most needs of the beginning artist. In opaque techniques like casein, ten times as much white will be used

as any other color. White rather than diluted paint is used to create light tones.

To become familiar with colors, purchase paints with a color chart that can be kept close at hand. No mechanical reproduction can be in absolutely true color, including this reproduction, so the final judgment will be made through the paints themselves and the eye of the artist.

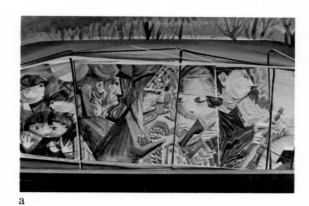

a

A preliminary drawing of Christ for a mural which was to be fabricated in square and triangular commercial tile. The commercial tile colors were limited. The opaque medium lent itself to accurate color matching.

This finished sketch was coated with clear plastic spray to protect it against much handling by committees.

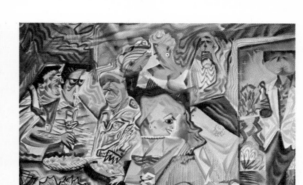

b

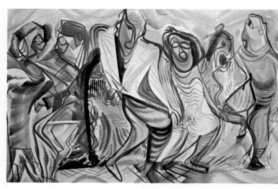

c

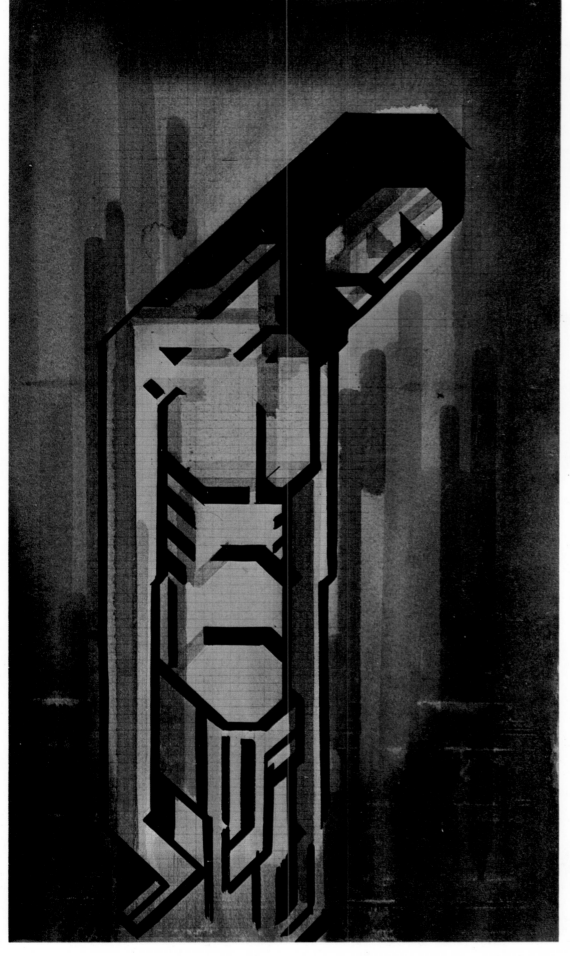

This triptych was painted at various times with a variety of opaque media. Some passages were painted over and over. The family in the car was a family in heavy traffic at one stage. From a concept standpoint, all three paintings are distorted in cartoon fashion.

The top painting (a), entitled *Ride in the Country*, is a satire on today's togetherness; no one is enjoying the scenery except one child, too young to know.

The painting *Cocktail Party* (b) shows typical characters at this kind of event.

Painting (c), like the preceding two, was painted in the early 1950s, prior to today's type of dancing, dress, and hairstyle. The pattern of (a) is mechanical and static. The pattern of (b) is deliberately jammed and confusing. The pattern of (c) is rhythmic-flowing, full of action. At the time, opaque was by far the easiest medium to capture all three situations.

47

WATERCOLOR

Watercolor is a most expressive and (when properly used) permanent medium. It was first employed by the Chinese, then the Japanese, Persians, and East Indians. In Eastern painting it retained its popularity even with the advent of oil painting. This was not surprising, since the delicate and exquisite handling of brush and medium was also used in manuscript work. Watercolor might well be listed as a basic form of pictorial art. The substitution of other carrying vehicles for water, such as eggs (tempera), oil, and plastic, were later innovations.

Watercolor dries quickly and is therefore ideal for works requiring speed in execution. The tools and materials are easily transportable, making it a capital medium for on-the-spot painting. These qualities alone made it the medium for an artist's more personal work even when oil painting became more popular. Not surprisingly, we find that some of the truest expressions of the great masters were made and overlooked, until the current deeper appreciation of the watercolor medium set in.

Watercolor, as we know it today, developed through an interminably long period of combinations of line and tinting, or worked-over disasters, of opaque and transparent applications of painstakingly arduous building of layer upon layer of glazes, to today's direct, bold approach.

In the beginning of the nineteenth century Peter de Wint, using a palette that was surprisingly brilliant for the time, soaked his paper and brushed his color into the wet surface. Turner followed a similar approach, with the result that his oils greatly benefited from it. Today's artists generally assume that the smashing wet-in-wet techniques are a recent discovery.

We can approach watercolor using the old masters' approach, but we now find far fewer obstacles in our way. For one thing, we can purchase colors in tubes instead of having to grind and prepare them ourselves.

It is difficult to believe that Winslow Homer was not aware that his best works were in the watercolor medium. The misconception very likely began because he and earlier American artists of note worked in a society that quite stupidly thought oils a more important medium. At that time, if an artist did get some training, it was usually in Paris, where watercolor was never an "in" medium. Sargent said that watercolor was his best medium and that he was more capable of great artistic expression through this medium than through oil. If any lesson is to be learned from all this, it is that the use of one medium has a distinct value in advancing the accomplishments in another.

In no other medium is the selection of the proper and best materials more important than in watercolor. Only a master should think of creating a work of art with anything but the very best materials. The beginner, usually working with inferior materials, may draw his own conclusions. It is true that the novice may create a work that in time may become a milestone in the history of painting, but the best paint and the best red sable brush and the finest rag paper make success that much more possible.

A large expensive brush will retain its shape and resilience long after a series of cheap ones have deteriorated. The finest tube paint will cover a given area with more brilliant or subtle color than the cheap grades, and the best paper will react to the paint and the brush much more closely to the effect that is desired. It is assumed, of course, that you are not approaching the project aimlessly. Even in the watercolor medium, which at times appears to rely on accidental passages, the only hope is through consistent control.

A practical start in watercolor is to use material and procedures both in the studio and outdoors. Therefore, a palette should be chosen that can be conveniently held in the field, as well as placed on a table indoors. The basic equipment needed—colors, brushes, palette, sponge, and water container—is shown below.

In all painting, with the possible exception of miniature, the brush should be held some distance from the ferrule, and be full of color. The action then becomes a combination of both hand and arm motion, with the brush held almost vertically, with a slight inclination in the direction of the stroke.

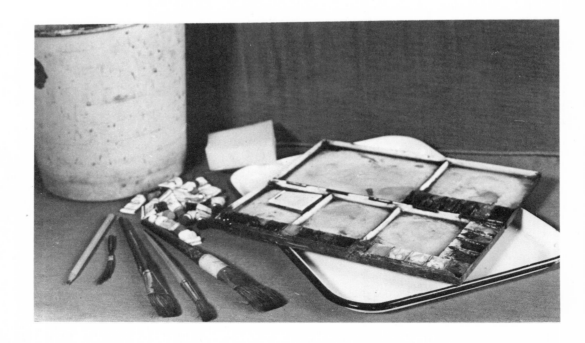

As good a way as any to get started in watercolor is through what might seem to the casual passerby aimless doodling (a–e). Frequent practice, without too long concentration on practice strokes, always helps one to become a better watercolorist.

(1) Place a couple of pieces of paper on the drawing board or work table—one a good watercolor paper, the other of lesser quality. Wet both on both sides. (2) Mop up the excess water and flatten both by smoothing them onto the board. (3) A small squeegee normally used for cleaning car windows can be useful. The chances of damaging the surface of the inferior paper are high. You can use a protective layer of another piece of paper if you run into this trouble. (4) As good a method as any to press the paper onto the surface is with your palm and the side of your hand. All air bubbles trapped under the wet paper must be pressed out. (5) It is often necessary to pick up a corner of the paper and press it down again as you hold it taut. Press from the center outward toward the edges. You may redampen, blot, or start all over again to get the paper to adhere flatter than any pancake.

Once the papers are down and flat, open a tube of color. For the sake of this reproduction, black was used, but more interesting patterns can be obtained with two colors, preferably complements.

If the tube is difficult to open, heat the cap with a match. Caps are bound to stick in time. A pair of pliers will help, or holding the top of the tube under a hot-water tap. Chances are you'll have no difficulty with brand-new tubes.

Practice the strokes as shown. Most of the time here, the heel of the brush was used. Aside from getting a few very different effects with this method, it is not too good for your brushes. Try out all your brushes, until you begin to get the feel of each brush and gain greater control.

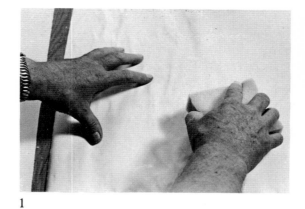

1

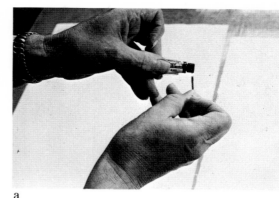

a

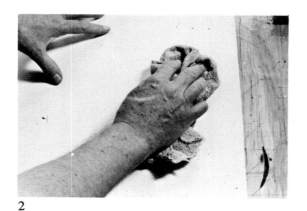

2

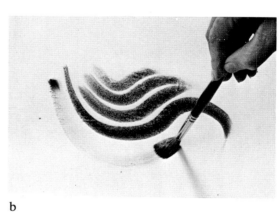

b

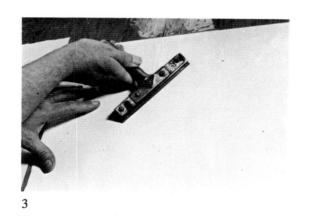

3

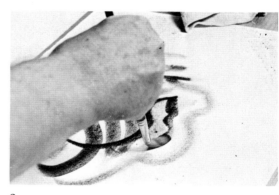

c

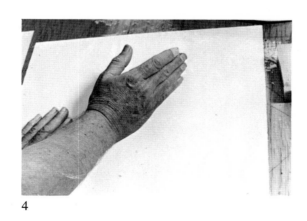

4

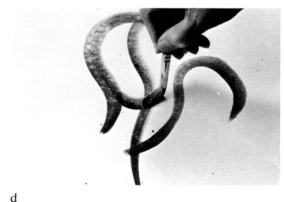

d

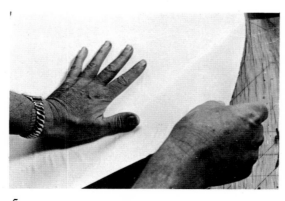

5

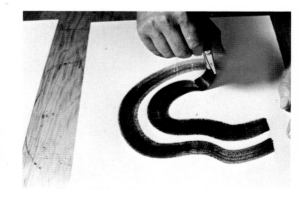

e

PRACTICE STROKES

After you have gained a certain control of the brush, the next attempt is to do more with it than make lines.

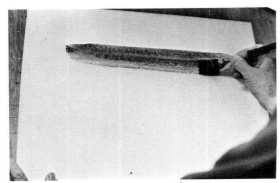

1. "Paste" a sheet of paper flat on a firm surface (a board or table) with water; then, with a brush well loaded with color, paint much as you would on any house-painting job, back and forth in broad strokes. The painting will start out being fairly uneven, but the slight moistness of the surface will tend to smooth out the rough spots.

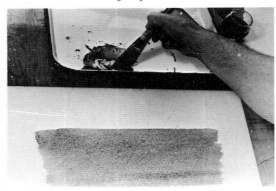

2. Go back to your palette (the butcher tray here is excellent for watercolor) and pick up more paint on the brush.

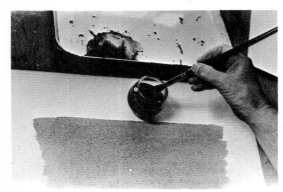

3. Add water to the brushload of paint.

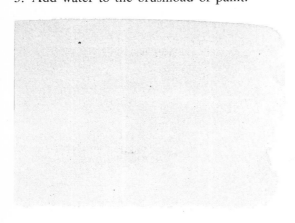

4. With the same back-and-forth strokes, try for an even tone.

5. Full of water, but with less color on the brush, try for a light, even tone.

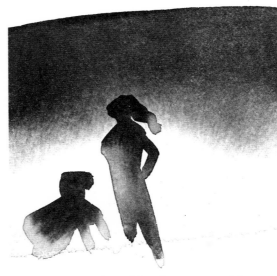

6. Now starting with a deep tone, add water to the brush to get a graded tone. Once this is *dry*, paint a few forms over the dried graded area.

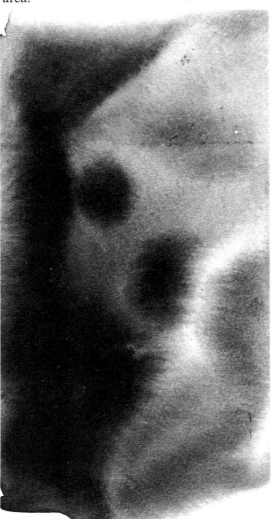

7. On a wet tone, graded or flat, introduce a few brushfuls of strong color. Experiment by pushing the pattern around with brush.

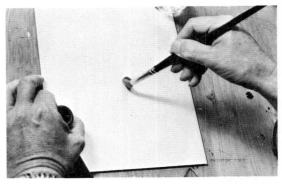

8. With a brush full of clear water, paint a small area on dry paper.

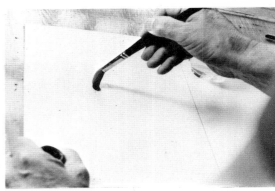

9. Fill the brush with paint and paint into the area.

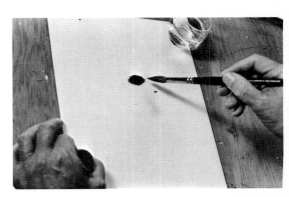

10. Drip a bit of color into a similar area.

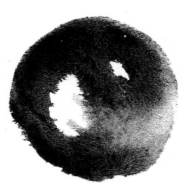

11. The paint will spread around the area you wet but will be contained within it.

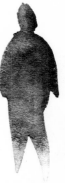

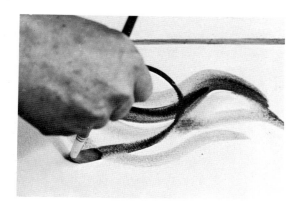

1. On page 49 we were content to dawdle a bit with simple lines. Here we run one line into the next.

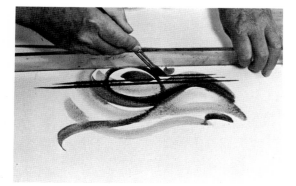

2. With a ruler to control the brush cross a few wet lines over each other, using a pointed brush.

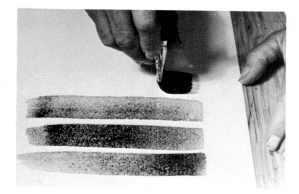

3. With a chisel brush make a series of multitoned lines.

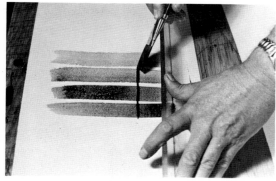

4. With the edge of the brush make some narrow lines. When these touch the wet surface they will begin to spread out, but on dry areas they will remain intact. This technique is used again and again in watercolor painting.

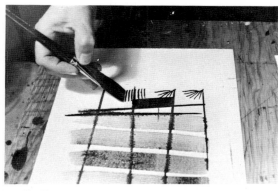

5. Experiment with the edge of the chisel brush.

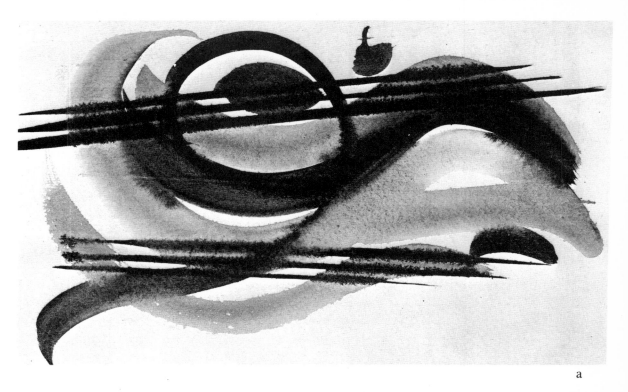

a

6. Use a chisel brush for scallop line and skipping technique. Experimenting in this manner shows what happens on various surfaces, smooth or rough, wet or dry. On a rough surface, with rapid strokes, you can get a skipping effect, which is ideal for getting glistening whites into a watercolor.

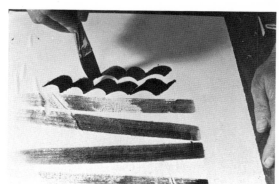

b

c

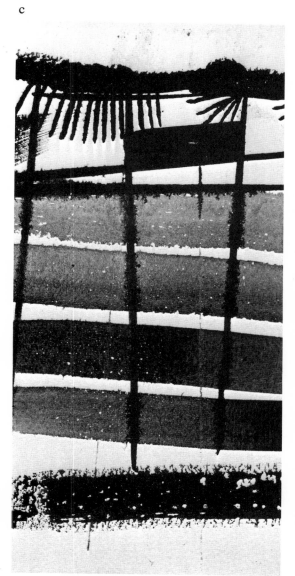

Practice strokes of all descriptions with the chisel brush. This versatile tool is happily less expensive than the large pointed sable brush. These two brushes, the chisel and the pointed, are the workhorses of the watercolorist.

Illustrations a, b, and c show more clearly the experimental designs made in these demonstrations.

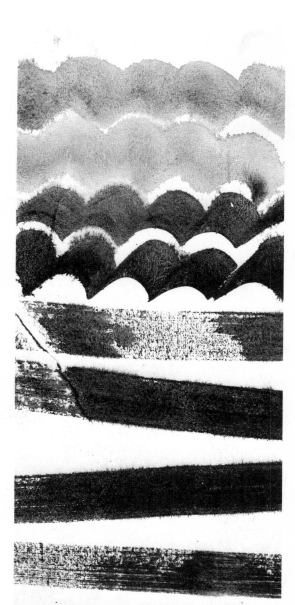

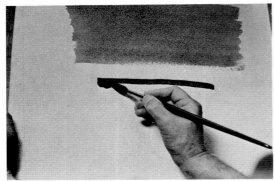

1. Here a brand-new pointed sable brush is used. By any standard, this is the single most expensive tool of the watercolorist.

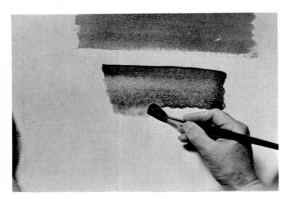

2. Practice laying down flat washes, then graded washes.

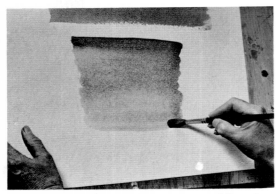

3. Run the graded wash out, adding just clear water. See also (a).

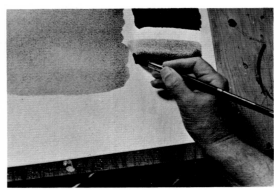

4. Paint a light-to-intense wash, adding color as you progress.

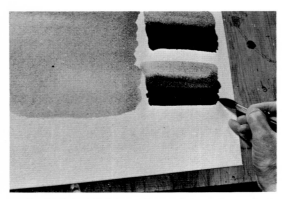

5. Paint a light wash, and introduce dark passages. See also (b) and (c).

a

b

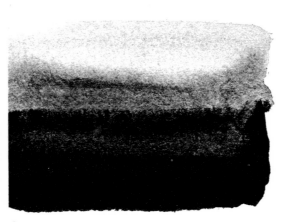

c

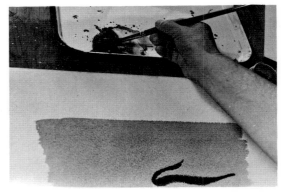

6

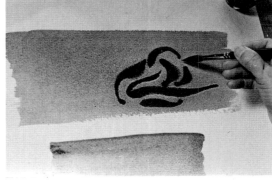

7

8

6, 7, 8. The most difficult strokes of all are controlled wet-in-wet strokes. Into a wet area, this time a simple tone, the brush was filled with plenty of wet color, so full that if care was not used, the paint might drip. The desired lines were painted into the wet (hence the term "wet-in-wet"). The same procedure can be used in both oil and acrylic, where it is less prone to accidental effects.

The next step is to practice all the strokes mentioned in the last four pages, incorporating them into a line drawing.

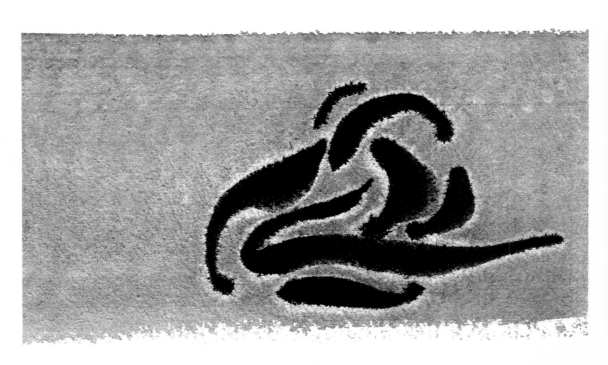

In this case, the drawing is too dark, but made so for purposes of clarity in the demonstration. The paper was wet on both sides, adhered to the board, and blotted until almost dry. Only tones from black through gray to near-white were used—no other color.

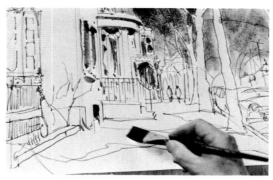

5. With a chisel brush the sidewalk area is rapidly wetted.

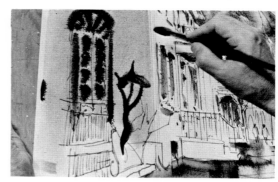

10. . . . adding a few light tones, with a brush wet with little paint.

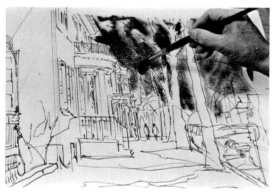

1. First the sky areas were wet, leaving those parts dry that were to be left white or were to be worked on later.

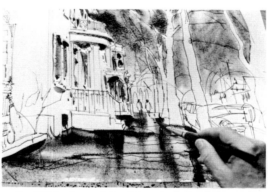

6. With the same brush, the general tone of the sky is introduced into this area.

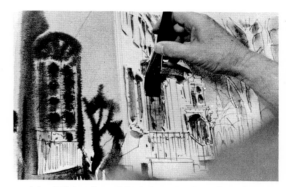

11. With the chisel brush, I painted into shadow areas that had dried and therefore did not pick up the paint.

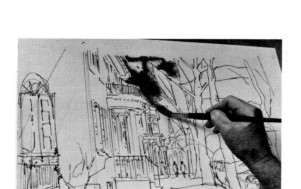

2. A further development of the above.

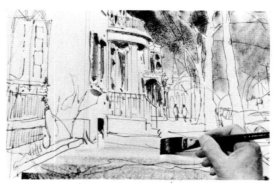

7. With the original brush full of the color that would be reflected onto the walk, the walk was finished in wavy vertical strokes.

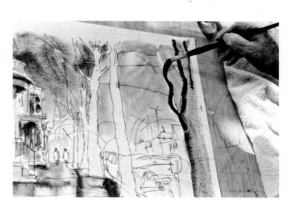

12. With the pointed sable I begin the large mass of the trunks of the trees,

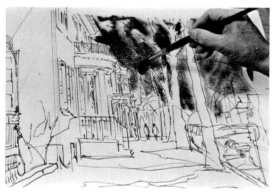

3. Filling in the dark windowpanes.

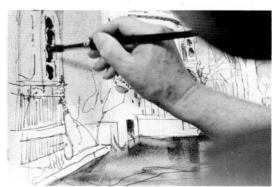

8. A wet-in-wet technique was begun on some foreground windows. Note how the sidewalk area is drying lighter than painted.

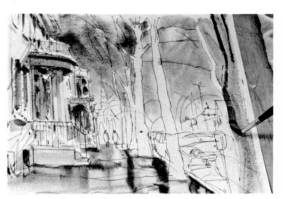

13. . . . and continue into the smaller branches.

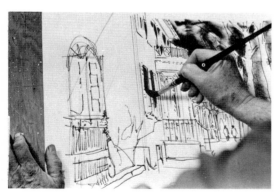

4. Washing and drying the brush between operations.

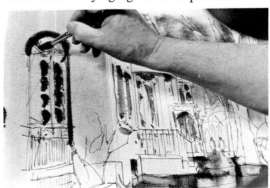

9. Painting darker than I wished the final windows to be, and allowing the paint to spread, I continued,

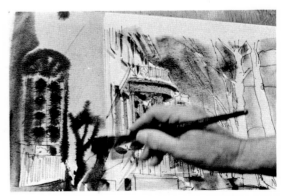

14. The background trees still had wet spots surrounding them, so I picked another spot to work.

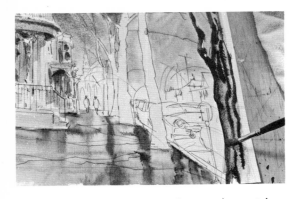 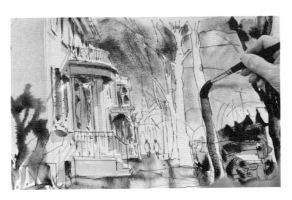 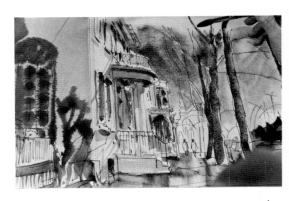

15. The attempt was made to paint wet-in-wet bark on the trees. As it turned out, the paper was not wet enough. To correct this, one should wait until it dries, then wet the trunk and begin again.

16. At this point, the old saying, "It takes two people to make a painting. (One to do the painting, and another to stop him when he is through,)" comes to mind.

17. Continue anyway, this being practice, and learn as much from what goes wrong as from what goes right. Sometimes small accidents turn out to be happy ones.

18. Detail of the finished watercolor.

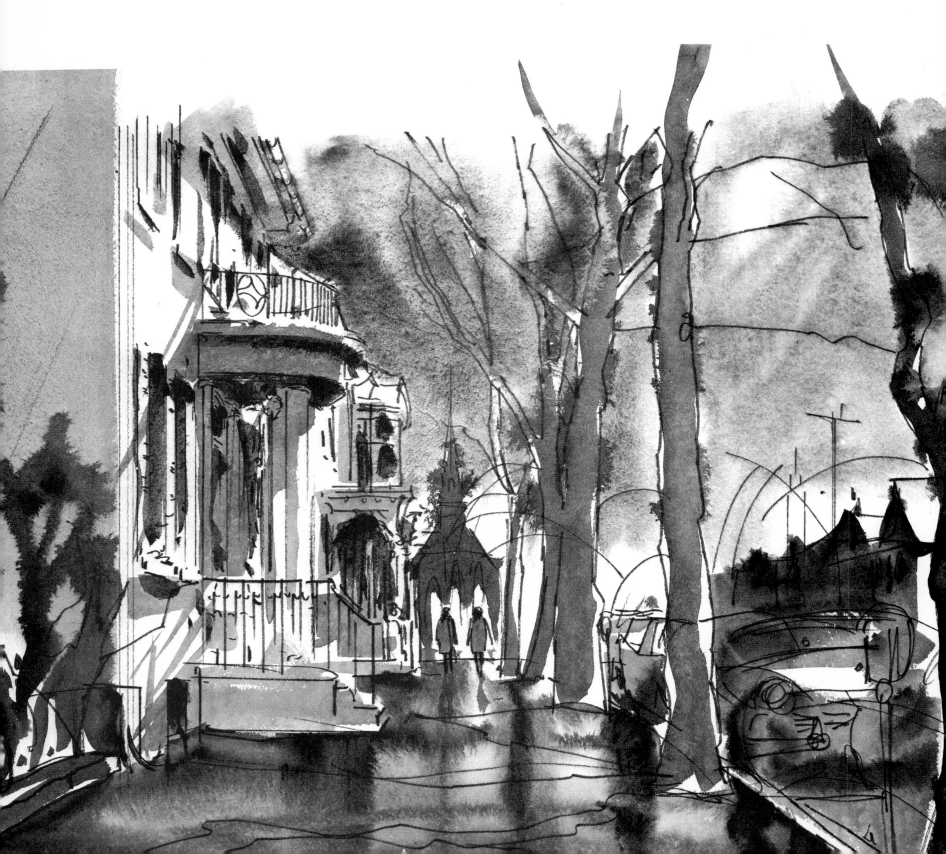

Strokes made in the Japanese style

After work on a watercolor, such as the one on the previous page, further practice in the brush is advisable to perfect strokes and discover new effects. With a clean brush charged in clear water, dip just the tip into either ink or watercolor and begin making the strokes as shown. There are complicated procedures in which each section of the brush is charged with a lessening degree of color, so that the heel is filled with plain water, the middle with half-intensity color, and the tip with full intensity. It would be most valuable to study and practice these essentially Japanese methods and strokes, but for the moment a general idea of how they apply to the work of a watercolorist is sufficient.

a. The brush held in a vertical position and pulled toward the painter.

b. The brush held in an oblique position and pulled toward the painter.

c. With the handle of the brush held toward the painter and pulled toward the painter.

d. The brush turned as the stroke proceeds.

e. Twirling strokes, with the brush held high on the ferrule.

f. A stroke that starts wide at the heel, progressing to the very tip of the brush.

g. A stroke that starts with just the tip, then is turned and pressed toward the heel and ends with just the tip touching.

h. A side stroke that will give a graded stroke if the ink is properly distributed in the brush from light in the heel to deep in the tip.

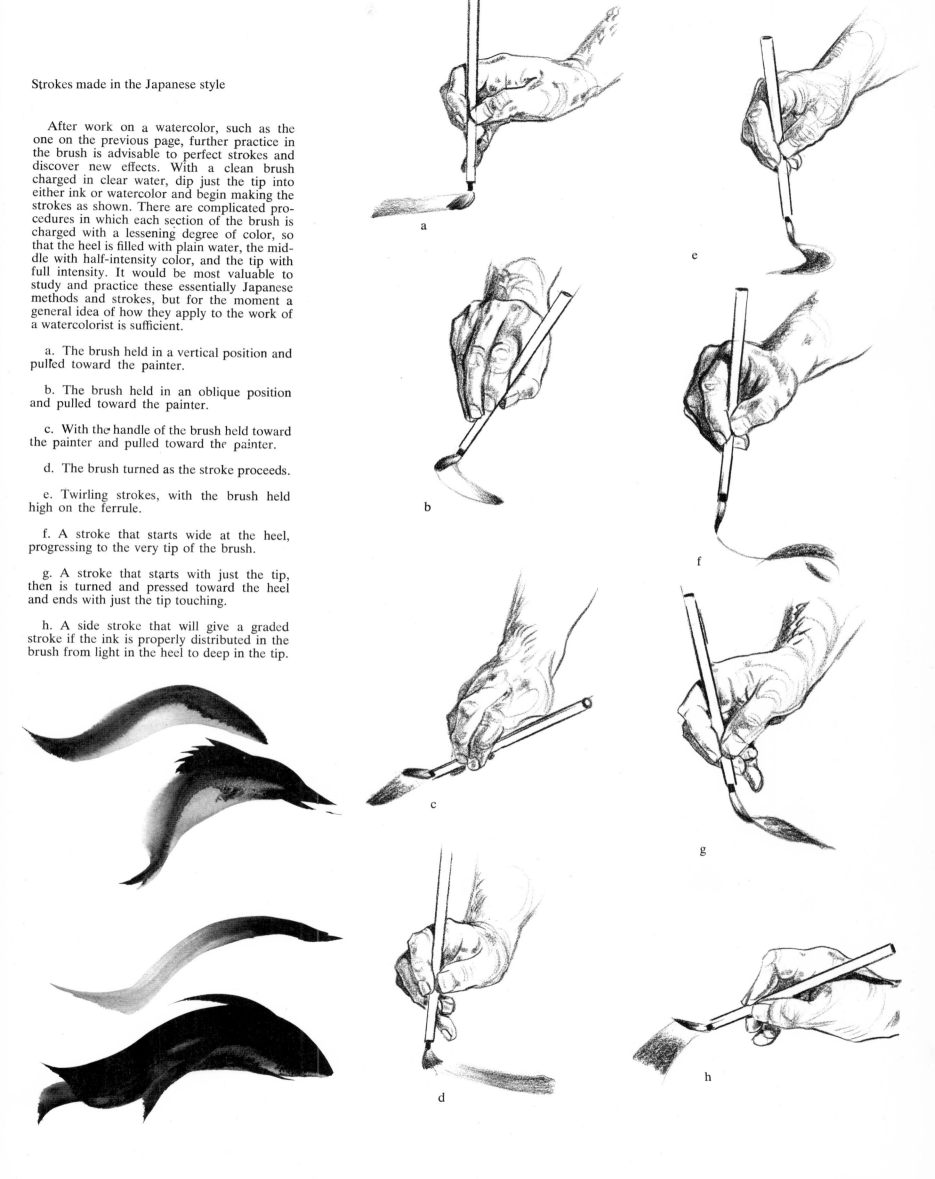

All painting is a tremendously individual pursuit. The artist must express his feeling about each specific subject and not employ a collection of tricks under the heading of "how to paint skies," "how to paint rocks," "how to paint trees," or "how to paint reflections." Once any artist is caught in the snare of a clever way to make cumulous clouds or a fast way to give the effect of a birch tree trunk, he might as well give up thinking he will be a great artist. There are gimmicks and there are things to give immediate effects, but they are not to be encouraged as a general practice. Each painting must be as individual as the artist feels his subject to be. Each painting or drawing should be a new experience for the artist as well as for the viewer.

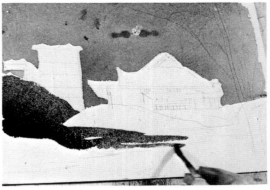

5. It would seem logical at this point to paint the structures. However, to avoid any chance of such a wash accidentally touching the not yet dry sky wash, the shadows on the snow were painted first.

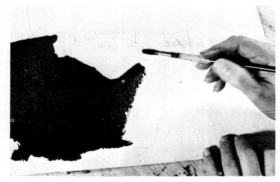

1. The sketch of the unused station, used for another practice in watercolor, presents an involved building outline. A sky wash, working from the top of the drawing to this outline, would have run the danger of leaving a hard edge of paint around the snow-covered buildings. The easy way out was to turn the sketch around and begin at this area. The wash flowed away from the outline of the buildings and, more important, was simpler to control while painting around the outline.

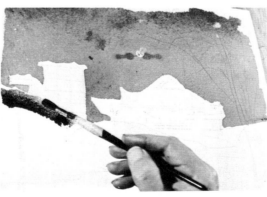

3. With the wash finished, the excess liquid was picked up with a squeezed-out brush. This kept it from spidering back into the sky.

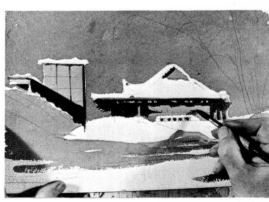

6. Painting a watercolor is a matter of timing. The large sky wash was still damp. The sides of the building were painted carefully to avoid any contact with the sky wash.

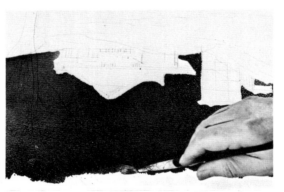

4. As the wash dried, not only did it lighten, but the paper buckled. Working on this uneven surface was difficult. One answer was a pushpin, used here pinned through the sky area, to flatten the paper. This was a display of the devil-may-care attitude a watercolorist must acquire before he can hope to master the medium. He must balance gay abandonment with rigid control—rather like riding to the hunt.

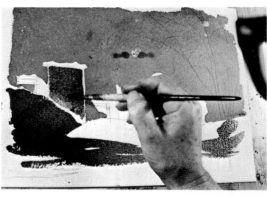

7. After the wash on the buildings was dry, the shadows on the sides were added.

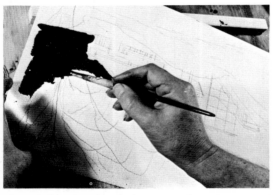

2. With the paper still at an angle, the traditional wash was laid in from side to side. Watercolor always dries to a lighter tone than it appears when wet. Even as we proceeded, it lightened.

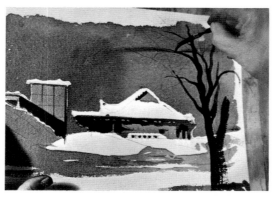

11. Near their extremities the branches were so small that a striper brush was used for the finishing strokes.

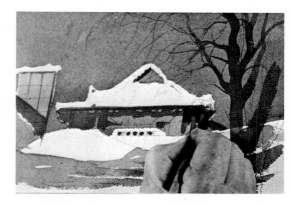

13. Details were now filled in and others were strengthened.

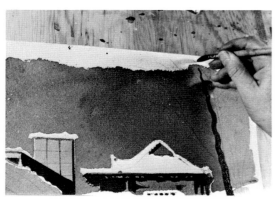

8. Everything was dry at this stage. Then the tree was superimposed, starting at the bottom with a fully charged brush.

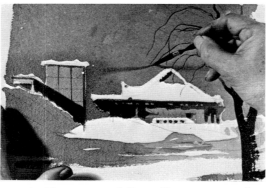

12. Even more delicate lines were used to indicate the twigs.

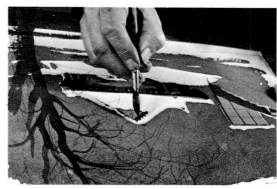

14. And the shadows were accented with the tip of the brush.

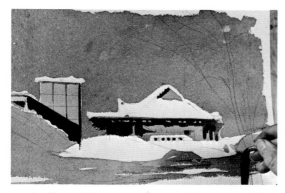

9. The line of the trunk became naturally thinner at the top.

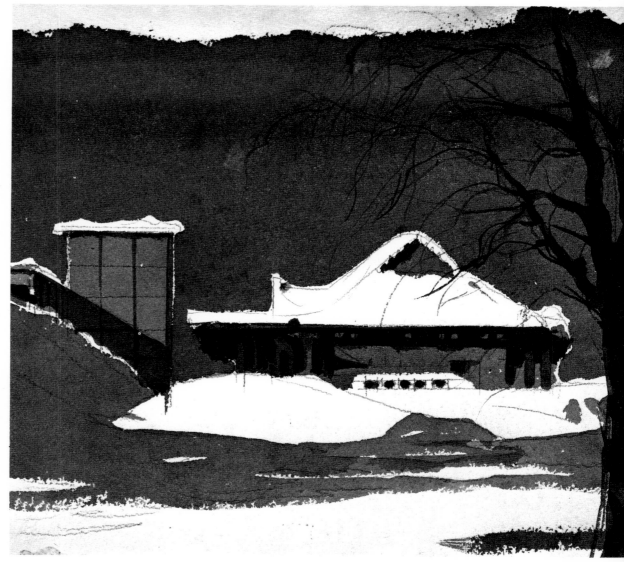

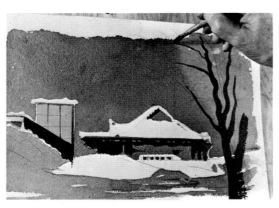

10. The branches got smaller as they divided and divided again away from the trunk.

15. The finished watercolor.

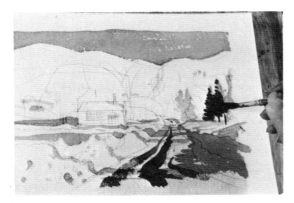

4. Then the mass of the evergreens.

A further demonstration, using much the same technique.

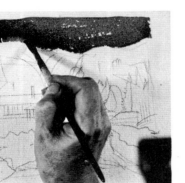

1. The sketch was slightly tilted to allow the wash to run from the top to the contour of the mountains. A pool of paint formed. At this point the brush should be dried on a rag or squeezed between the fingers to take up the excess pool of paint.

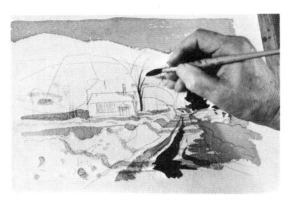

5. And the skeleton of the hardwoods.

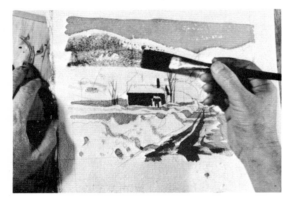

6. With the chisel brush pressed against the paper, the stroke left behind it sparkles of white on the distant mountains.

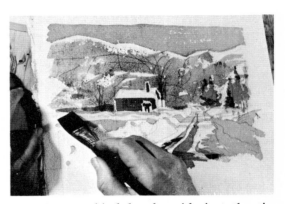

7. A wet chisel brush, with just the tip touching the paper, produced a solid tone.

8. Accents and detail were completed.

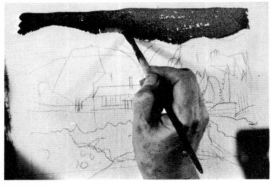

2. Strong shadows were added to the snow.

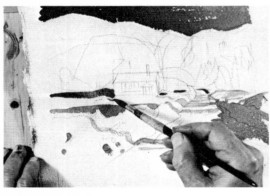

3. After the shadows dried, the ruts in the road were painted.

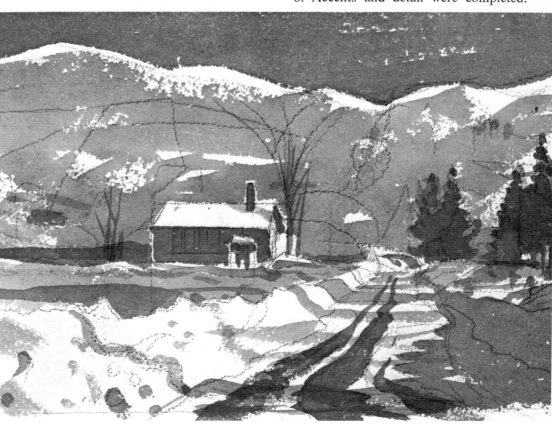

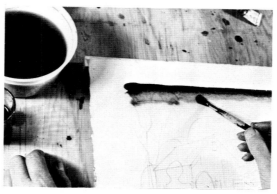

1. The sky was begun with a stroke from left to right in full-intensity color. Because the paper was slightly moist, as the brush proceeded down the page, the tone became lighter.

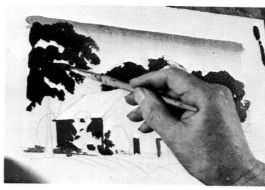

5. Next came the foreground trees. The procedure of painting an area only after waiting for the previous area to dry is possibly the simplest method in watercolor painting.

In painting watercolors, it is wise to have two supplies of water; otherwise in short order there will be no clear water. In the illustration is a partially filled bowl of water, used to clean the brush. Out of the picture a bowl of clear water was handy.

Traditionally, a dark-top-to-light-bottom wash is best obtained by starting at the top with the darkest tone, then brushing from left to right, and left to right again, adding water as you go.

In this case, the area to be shown in graded color was relatively small. The entire surface was dampened slightly with a sponge.

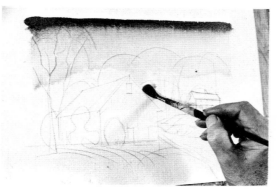

2. By the time the barn area was reached, the surface was almost dry.

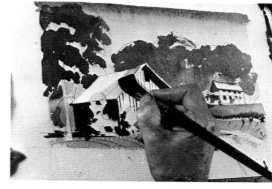

6. Again the paint had to dry before the simple tones and colors and the lines to show the barn siding were added.

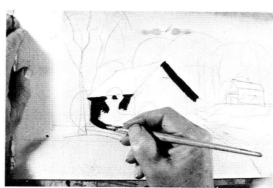

3. The dark shadow areas of the barn and the cast shadow on the eave side were painted, using a different brush.

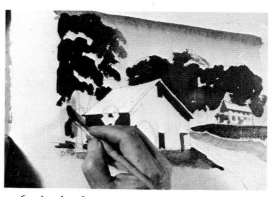

7–8. Bit by bit, the small watercolor began to take shape. As an exercise, this type of painting shows the safest and surest approach. The result may lack spontaneity, but the technique is successful where rigid control is important.

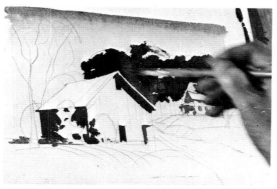

4. The background trees were painted in quick strokes.

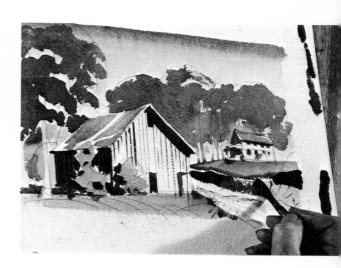

To show still a different approach, a line drawing was made of this street scene before starting the wet watercolor. Any pen used for this purpose must produce a line that is not soluble in water; otherwise, of course, the outlines will smear. The rest of the step-by-step procedure shown follows the same order described on the previous pages.

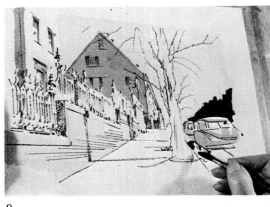

4

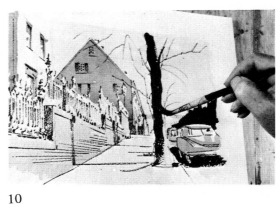

8

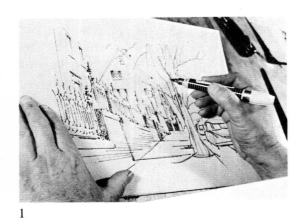

1

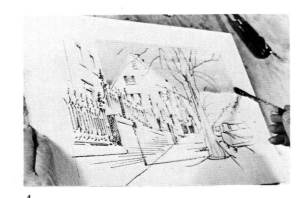

5

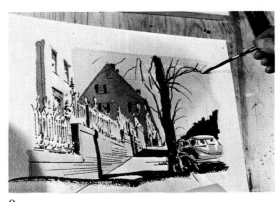

9

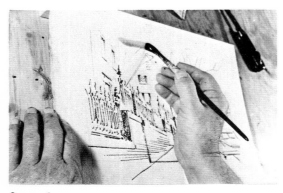

2

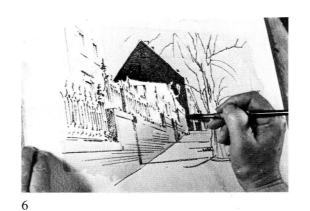

6

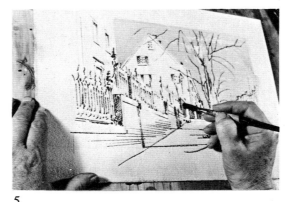

10

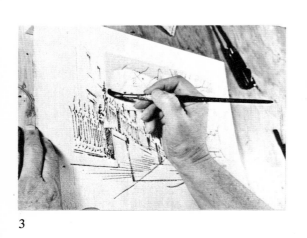

3

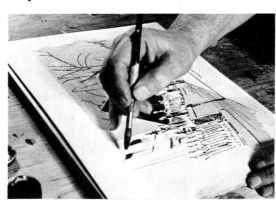

7

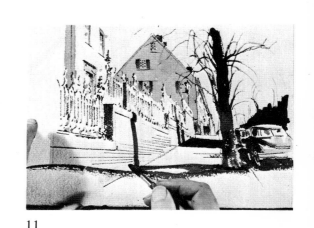

11

60

Practicing handling your paintbrush on one sketch after another is the only way to learn what happens when the paint hits the paper. The use of either black or a limited amount of color is the best way to acquaint yourself with the limitations and possibilities of the medium.

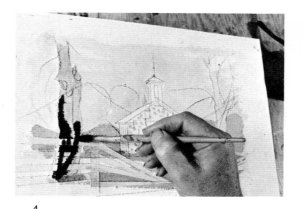
4

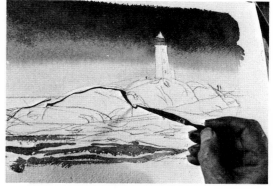
2. A dagger brush was used for the rock definitions.

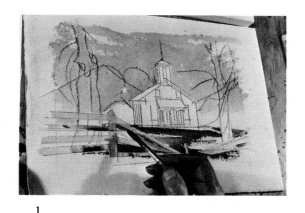
1

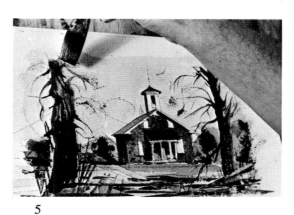
5

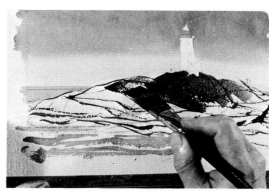
3. For the planes of the rocks a chisel brush was the best tool.

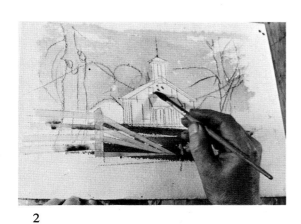
2

For *The Meeting House* (above and left), masking tape was stuck over the fence before the painting was begun. This was to protect it from the brush. (See also the liquid frisket method, page 63.) After the painting was dry, the tape was removed and the board fence was entirely white. This can be a useful device for many subjects. The other step-by-step illustrations follow the general procedure outlined in the earlier demonstrations (below and right).

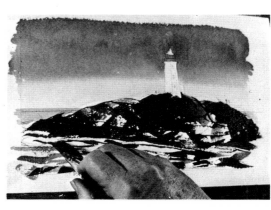
4. The same brush was used on edge for the linear treatment of the water.

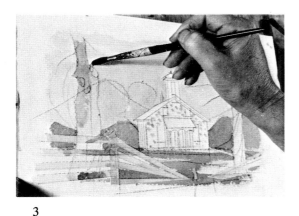
3

For *The Lighthouse* (below and right column) the sky area was wet with a slightly tinted wash.

1. Then the sketch was tilted upside down, and a heavy foreboding sky was brushed in.

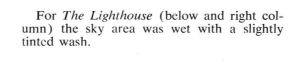

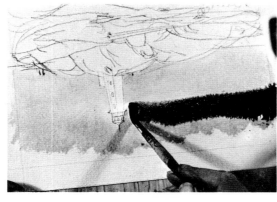

5. A straightedge obviously was best employed for making a straight edge.

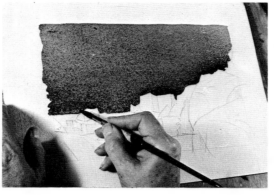

For this demonstration a small sheet of paper (300# d'Arches) was used. In this size there is little likelihood of its buckling, even without its being fastened down to a more rigid surface. There are further advantages. The paper can be held at any angle and the paint made to flow at will.

4. The semidry brush made a fine tool to pick up the excess paint. In addition to being an excellent "sopper-upper," the brush worked well for outlining the rocks.

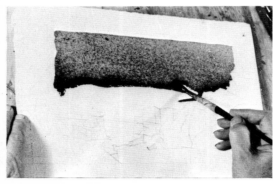

1. A pool of moderately deep color was made in a small glass; then, with occasional replenishing from the glass, a sky wash was started from the top.

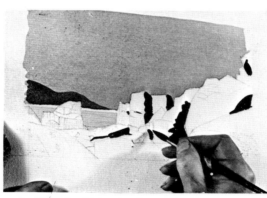

5. The sky wash dried considerably lighter —it always does, but more so in some colors than in others. This is a never-ending source of surprise to all watercolorists. The background mountains were now started.

Opposite page top: A demonstration using liquid frisket. This material, which is similar to rubber cement, was used to keep the driftwood white while washes for the sky were laid down. The shadows were added later.

A dried blob of rubber cement makes an excellent pickup. The painting must be completely dry or the paper comes up with the frisket.

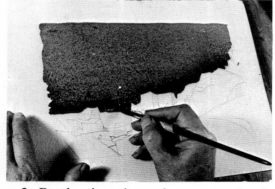

2. By the time the rocks were rendered, there was more paint than needed.

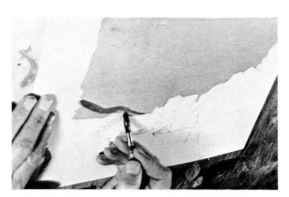

6. The shadows on the rocks were quickly painted with a brush, well charged with a dark tone, darker than anything so far used.

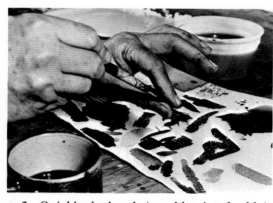

3. Quickly the brush (an old pointed sable) was squeezed dry. It could have been washed prior to squeezing it dry, but it was fairly obvious that the paint was about to run, or, worse yet, bleed into the simple, smooth wash.

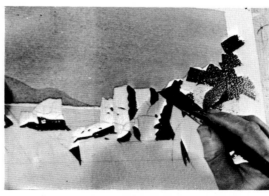

7. To get the feeling of ruggedness and sharp edges, for the foreground rocks a semidry chisel brush was used.

Opposite page bottom: The church in Nova Scotia shows a wet wash made into very wet sky (the paper having been well moistened beforehand). Let the paint blossom and run—and see what happens.

Here, liquid frisket was used, indicating clothes hanging on a line. After the painting was completely dry, this was picked up as in the highlights of the previous beach scene.

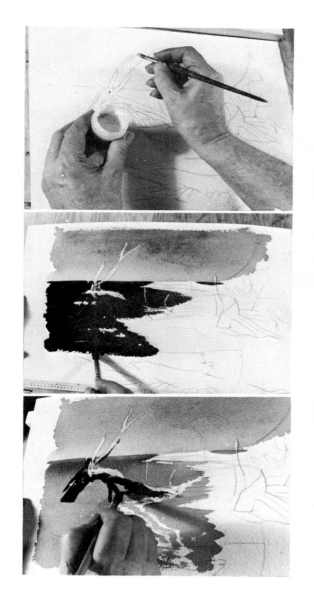

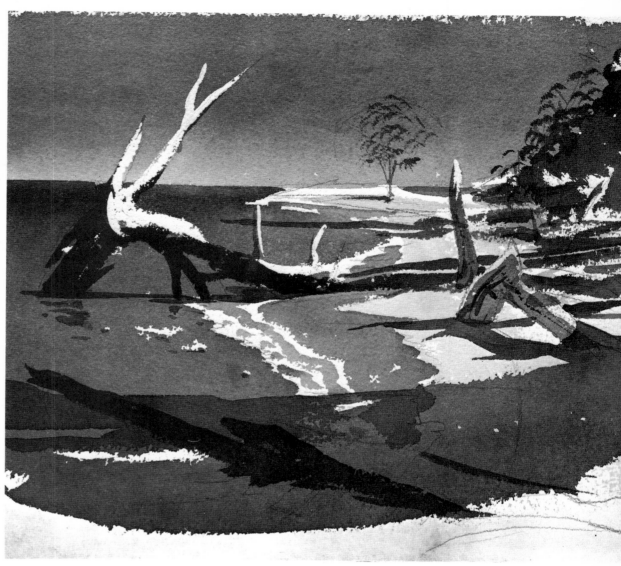

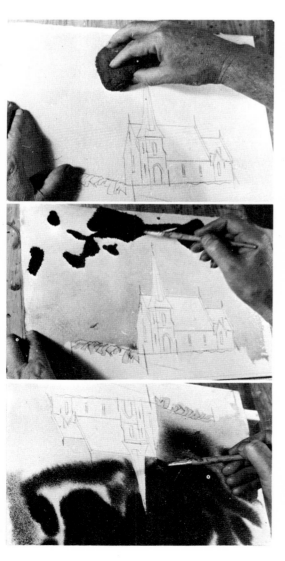

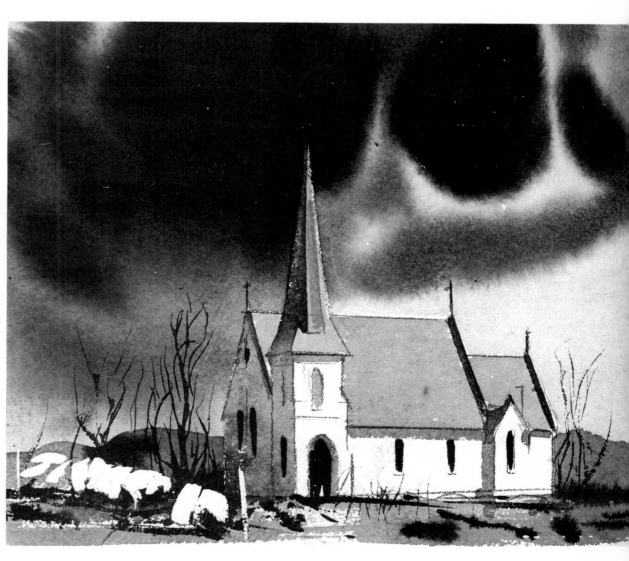

STRETCHING WATERCOLOR PAPER

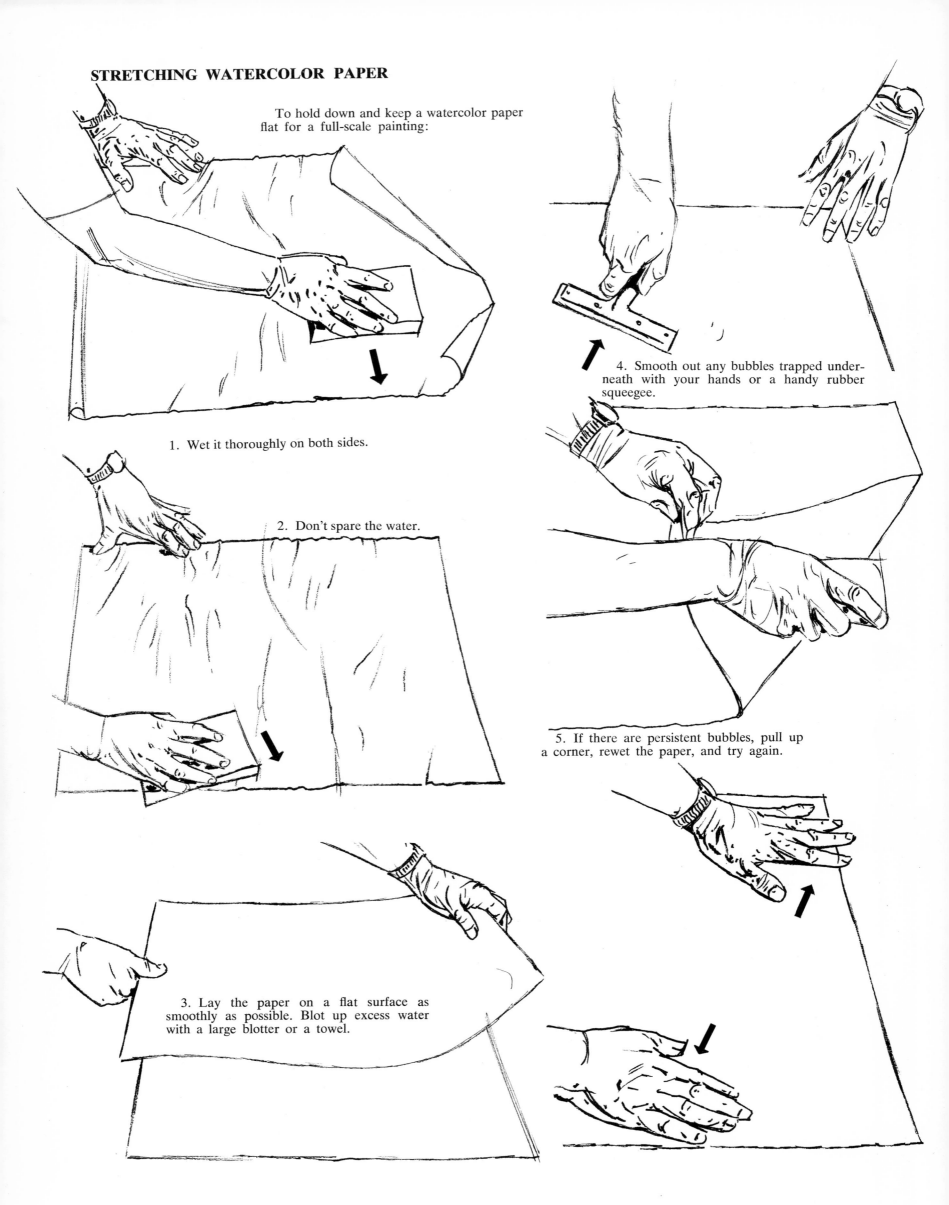

To hold down and keep a watercolor paper flat for a full-scale painting:

1. Wet it thoroughly on both sides.

2. Don't spare the water.

3. Lay the paper on a flat surface as smoothly as possible. Blot up excess water with a large blotter or a towel.

4. Smooth out any bubbles trapped underneath with your hands or a handy rubber squeegee.

5. If there are persistent bubbles, pull up a corner, rewet the paper, and try again.

6. If a rag paper has been wet thoroughly, it should stay tightly pasted to the flat surface for an entire painting session.

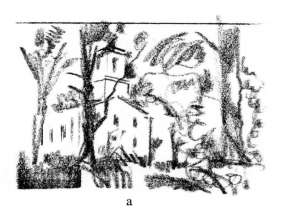

a

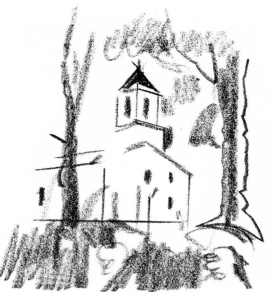

b

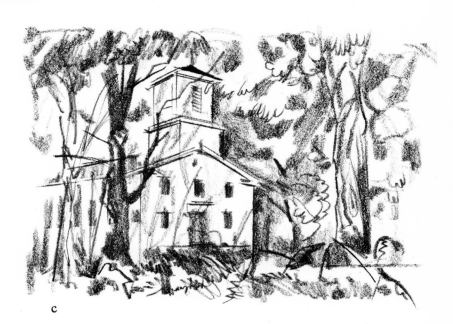

c

Odd as it may seem to anyone but an artist, the process of becoming or of being a painter is largely involved not with finger dexterity but with mental facility.

This little church had frequently intrigued me as a subject for a painting, until I stopped to examine it closely. There was a cemetery in the foreground. If the painting was ever to be sold and not just gather prizes, the cemetery would have to go. Another difficulty was a lineman's nightmare of poles, transformers, and wires cutting the scene into an unhappy composition. Added to this, a caretaker dropped in to park his car in the center of my painting. This all made sketch (d).

The subject had intrigued me. What was it I saw driving past at fifty miles an hour? Was it (a) a horizontal sketch of the church half hidden by maples? Was it (b) a vertical sketch? Was it (c) lively sunlight on the brilliant white clapboard? I transplanted a tree or two for better composition.

All this had to happen either on paper or in my mind before I began work on the watercolor shown on the following pages.

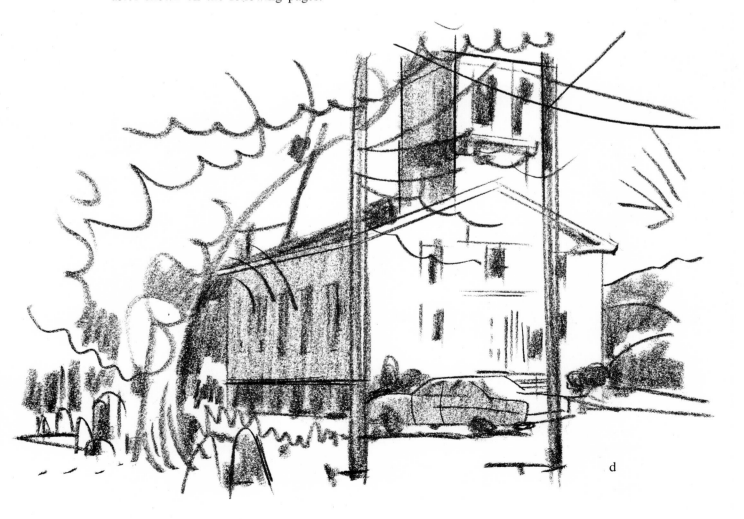

d

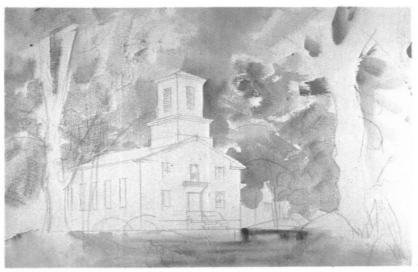

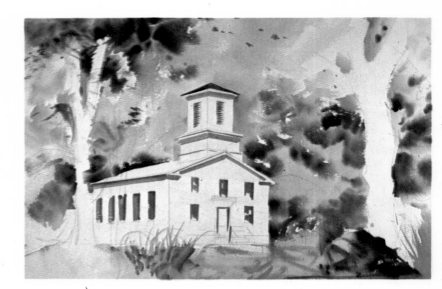

1. This painting was begun after the paper had been wet to a flat surface (as shown on page 64) and allowed to become relatively dry. Moistness can be checked by dabbing a touch of paint on the corner. If the paint runs, begin the blotting and smoothing process shown on page 64. A square-edge brush was used for outlining (in plain water) the areas around the church. The next step needed courage. With a brush well filled with blue and a touch of orange, the sky areas around the church steeple and roof were painted in. Then, with the same brush washed clean, the autumn colors were slapped in.

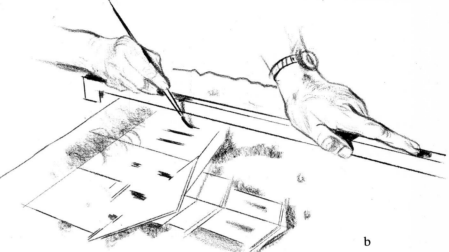

b

COLOR DEMONSTRATION: CHURCH

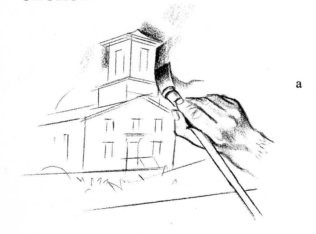

a

2. Whereas total abandonment in attacking a color area like this can be disastrous, the frightened painter is lost before he begins. The brush was filled with a combination of deep cool and warm colors; then, using the bridge as shown in the hand sketch, the geometry of the church, the windows, the doors, and the roof were done forcefully. With the same strong color, but a bit warmer in tone, the darker sections of the tree foliage and the foreground were developed.

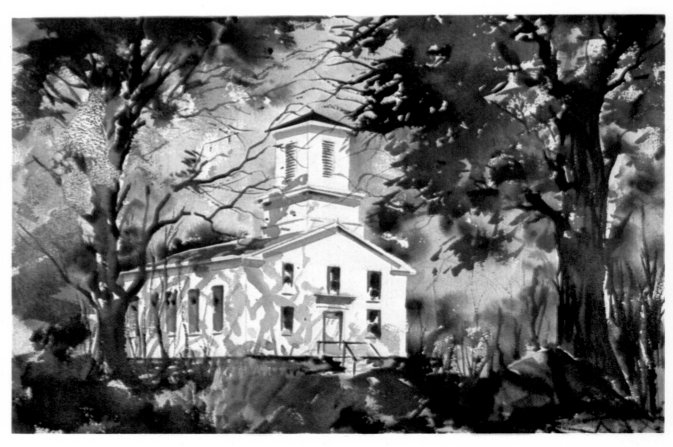

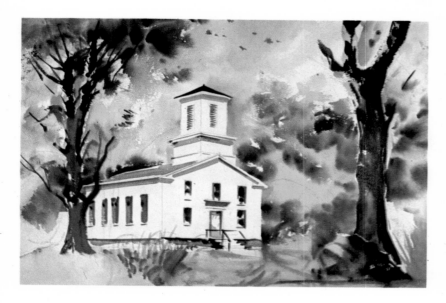

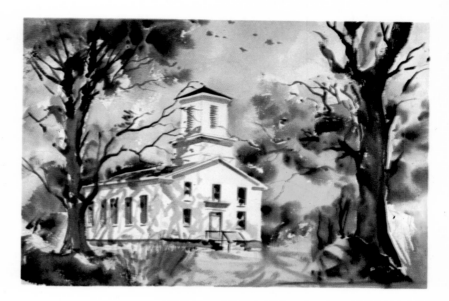

3. Unpainted areas were left to become the main structure of the maples. Once the areas painted as shown in step (2) were relatively dry, the trunks and main branches were added. With the brush heavy with liquid paint, work could proceed because heavy paint does not usually run into areas already painted. This shouldn't be trusted entirely, however. Check this by making a practice stroke near the edge.

4. The shadows that gave form to the building were painted from a pool of cool bluish gray directly over a dry surface and allowed to dry, so that they would dry not flat but rather transparent and graded in tone. You need not worry about how to do this. It is the nature of the paint to dry in this manner, more so if the painting is at a slight

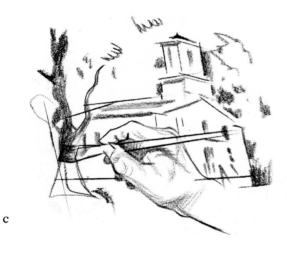

c

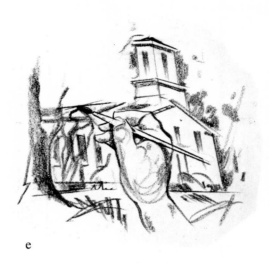

e

In the hand sketch (c) an entire trunk is painted with a square-edge brush, one edge of it dipped in dark color, the other in light. In sketch (d) a pointed sable brush is used in a kind of concentric series of motions to represent a rhythmic foreground area of underbrush.

angle. Again, beware of a timid, less than direct approach. For these shadows to do what is intended of them—to create not only a feeling of form but of sunlight—they must be painted in bold, slashing strokes (e).

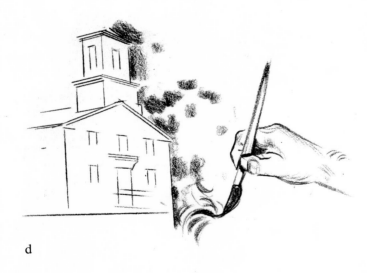

d

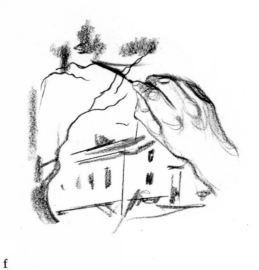

f

Opposite page:

5. The finishing strokes are probably the most direct of any in the painting. Over a now-dry surface, the pattern of the foreground elements in the trees and on the grass were painted in. All these things were done to bring the viewer's gaze toward the simple little church in the sunlight.

For your own practice, paint a similar scene in entirely different colors. Color it spring, then winter, then summer.

In sketch (f) a dagger brush is used to indicate the fine branches. It is possible, with this relatively inexpensive brush, to drag quite effective small branchlike lines onto the surface.

STRETCHING PAPER WITH TAPE

A simple yet highly satisfactory method of stretching watercolor paper to present a relatively smooth surface is to use wet tape to hold down the edges. The paper will buckle slightly during the painting process, but usually not enough to make painting impractical. One advantage of this method is that, once the painting is completed and left to dry, the surface will return to its taut, flat state. With a razor it is then possible to cut the painting from the board, leaving a reinforced edge of tape.

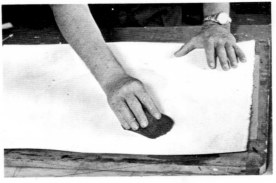

1. With a sponge moisten both sides of the paper. The proper painting surface will be the one that allows the watermark to be read when held up to the light.

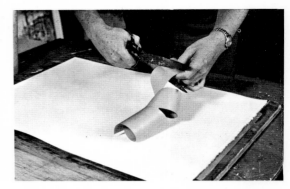

2. Cut four pieces of tape to lengths a bit longer than the dimensions of the paper.

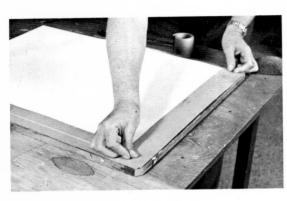

3. Press the moistened paper tape onto one edge. Masking tape and other adhesive tapes will not work because you are adhering to a moist surface.

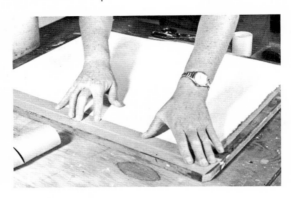

4. Continue taping down all sides. Keep the paper surface as flat as possible during the operation. As it dries, it will tighten and become flat.

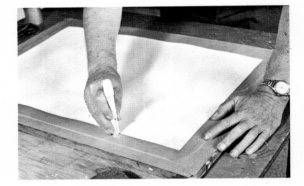

5. Unless you are uncommonly fortunate, the tape will not adhere perfectly to the surfaces. As it dries, continue to press it onto the board to insure a good bond.

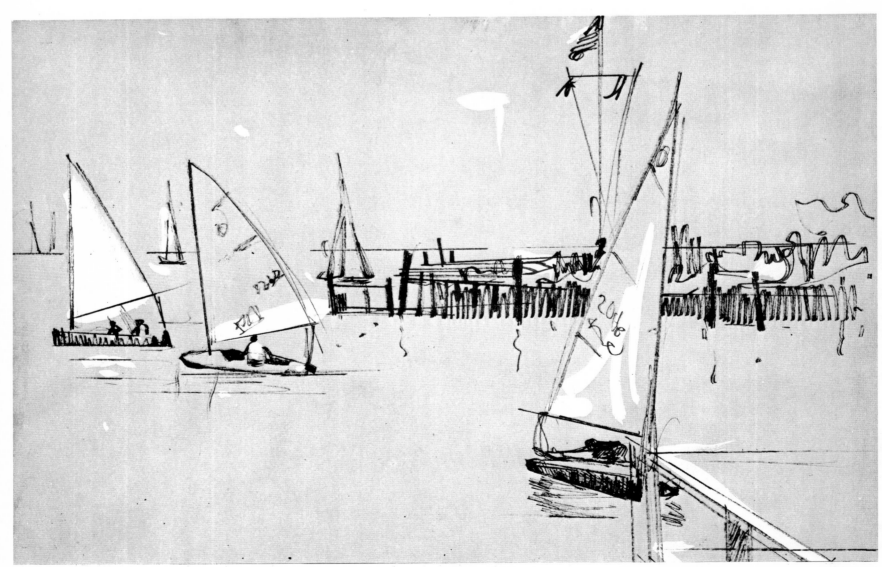

A simple practical subject. Sketch something like it, or trace this. Practice the following procedures: Paint an over-all tone, leaving the white paper to represent the sails. Paint a sky area with wet-in-wet clouds. Paint the water as flat as a millpond. Then put in shimmers and reflections. Once the areas are dry, paint quick, one-stroke hills and background docks. Keep experimenting until it is no longer so much a picture as it is an experimental ground for seeing what happens in many different circumstances. This is merely a method of gaining control of the medium prior to handling a more complicated subject such as on page 70.

ON-THE-SPOT SKETCH

A logical starting point for a studio water-color is the on-the-spot sketch. While sketching, if you have a camera, you may want to take a few local color shots. Some artists prefer to "write down" color notes. Quick sketches inexplicably catch the mood and atmosphere of a place. Select one or a combination of sketches to develop into a painting.

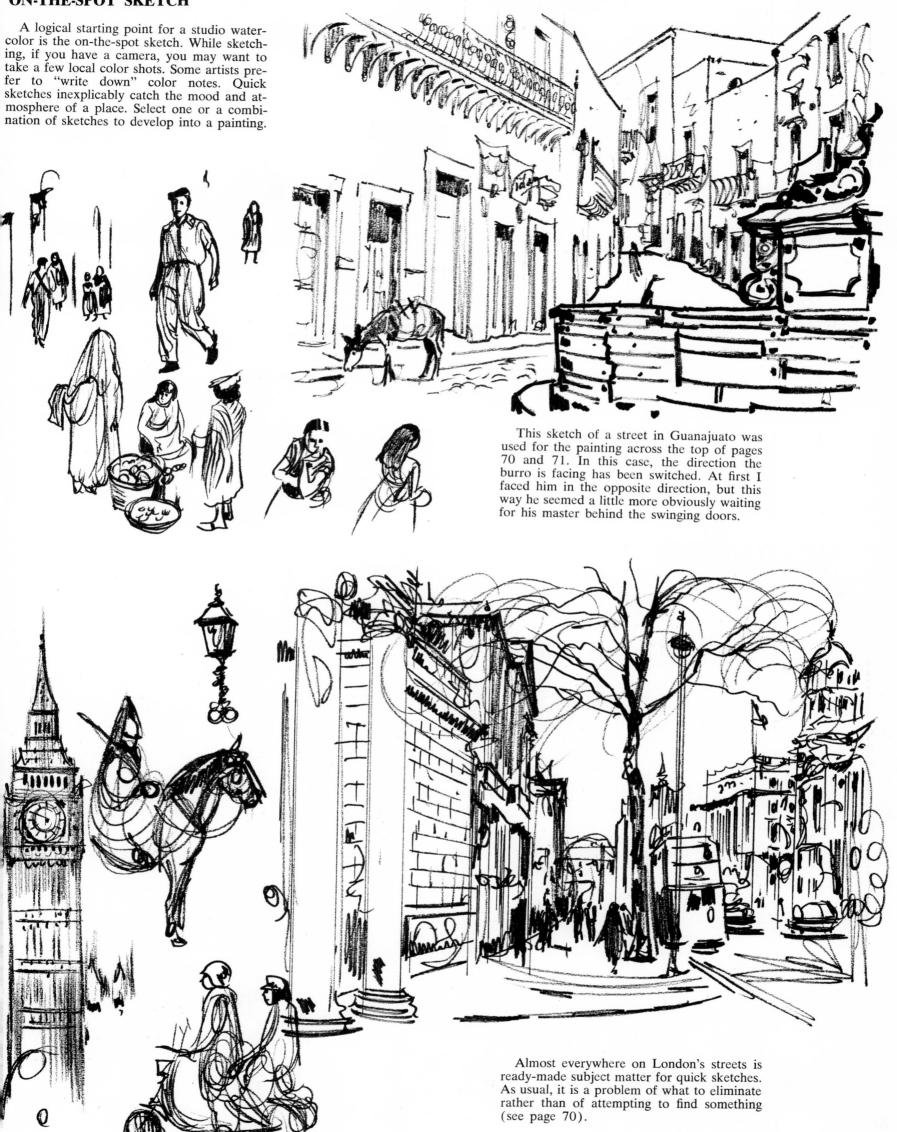

This sketch of a street in Guanajuato was used for the painting across the top of pages 70 and 71. In this case, the direction the burro is facing has been switched. At first I faced him in the opposite direction, but this way he seemed a little more obviously waiting for his master behind the swinging doors.

Almost everywhere on London's streets is ready-made subject matter for quick sketches. As usual, it is a problem of what to eliminate rather than of attempting to find something (see page 70).

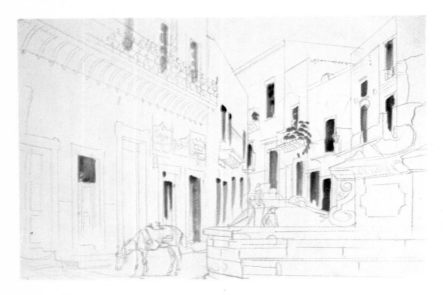

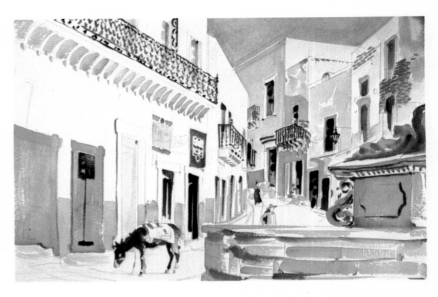

1. The street scenes of Mexico (top) and London (bottom) both were painted following similar procedures. Details of people and objects were brushed in over a carefully penciled drawing. The Mexico scene would be brilliant sunshine, the London scene wet. Both were painted in brilliant color in the early stages.

2. The sky was executed first. Skies are generaly darker than one thinks. Next came the strong color washes. Dabs for colored signs and filigree, considerably brighter than they seemed to appear in nature, were added.

PREPARATION FOR TWO WATERCOLORS: MEXICO AND LONDON

The painting of a London street (seen below) followed the same procedure as the painting of Mexico, except for the following. As a final step, the entire painting was dampened lightly with a sponge. Into this moist surface were brushed yellow ocher into the lower sky, and a gray, made of Hookers green No. 2 and burnt umber, into the high clouds. Work on the moist surface was finished with the same pool of color, on the pillars at left and the sidewalk at right, painting over everything, except the bus and a few bright spots indicating pedestrians. Once this was thoroughly dry, quick strokes of bright, opaque color pointed up the flags, back lights on cars, lights in the office windows, the Union Jack, and highlights. The paper used was 90-pound rough watercolor sheet, size 22 x 30.

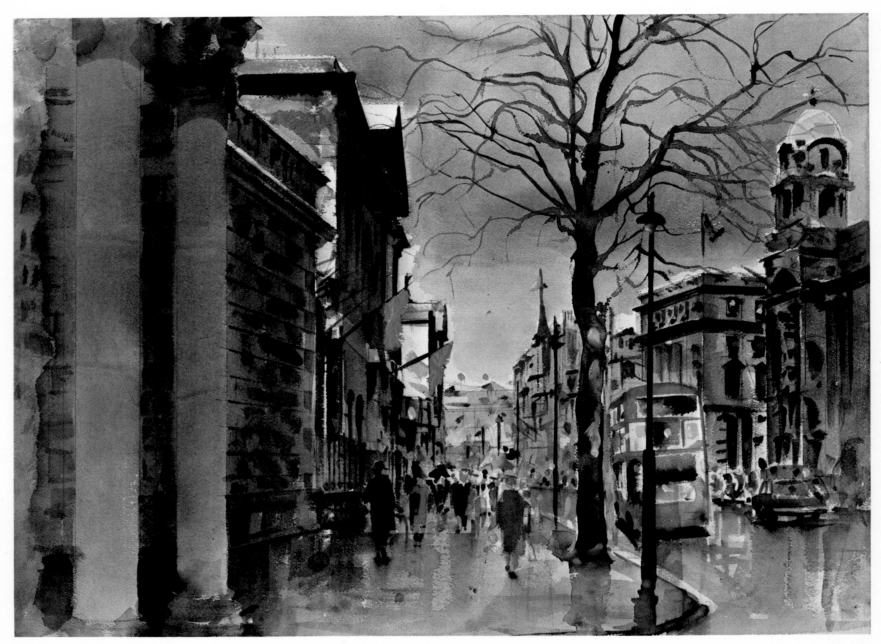

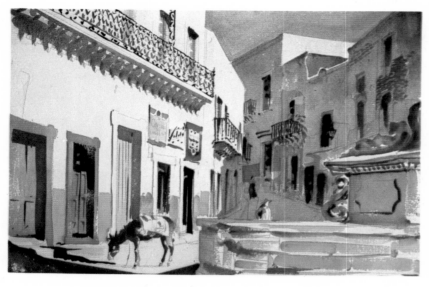

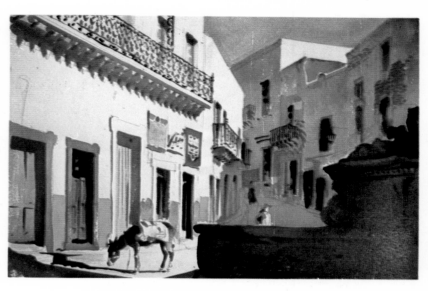

3. Here a combination of indigo and Indian red was mixed, and then this warm tone painted over the fountain area and street shadows. A 1½-inch square-edge brush was used, making quick strokes of the brush to miss spots on the paper and produce a sunlight effect.

4. Once the foreground was dry, a deep, transparent mass of ultramarine blue and burnt umber was painted over the fountain to put it in shadow.

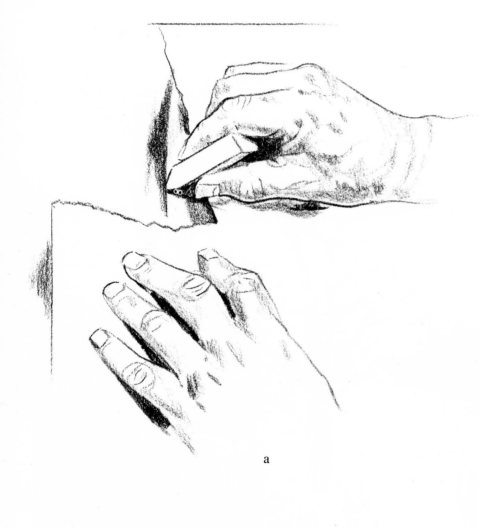

a

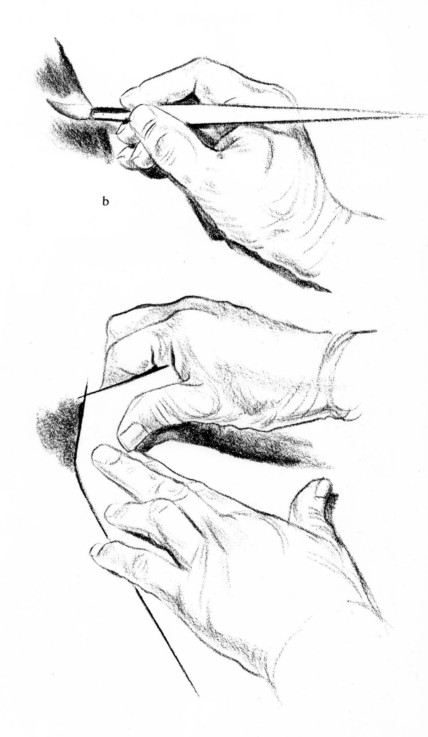

b

b–1

MAKING CORRECTIONS

It is part of painting in watercolor to have things not always go as planned. Watercolors can be changed or repaired, in certain instances, by erasing (a), or rewetting a small area with a brush and blotting up the color, as in (b) and (b–1). Bear in mind that these can never be major changes.

Pastel may be used with great restraint to change a small area. When the painting is framed and under glass, it is difficult to see where the change was made.

PREPARATION FOR DRAWING FLOWERS

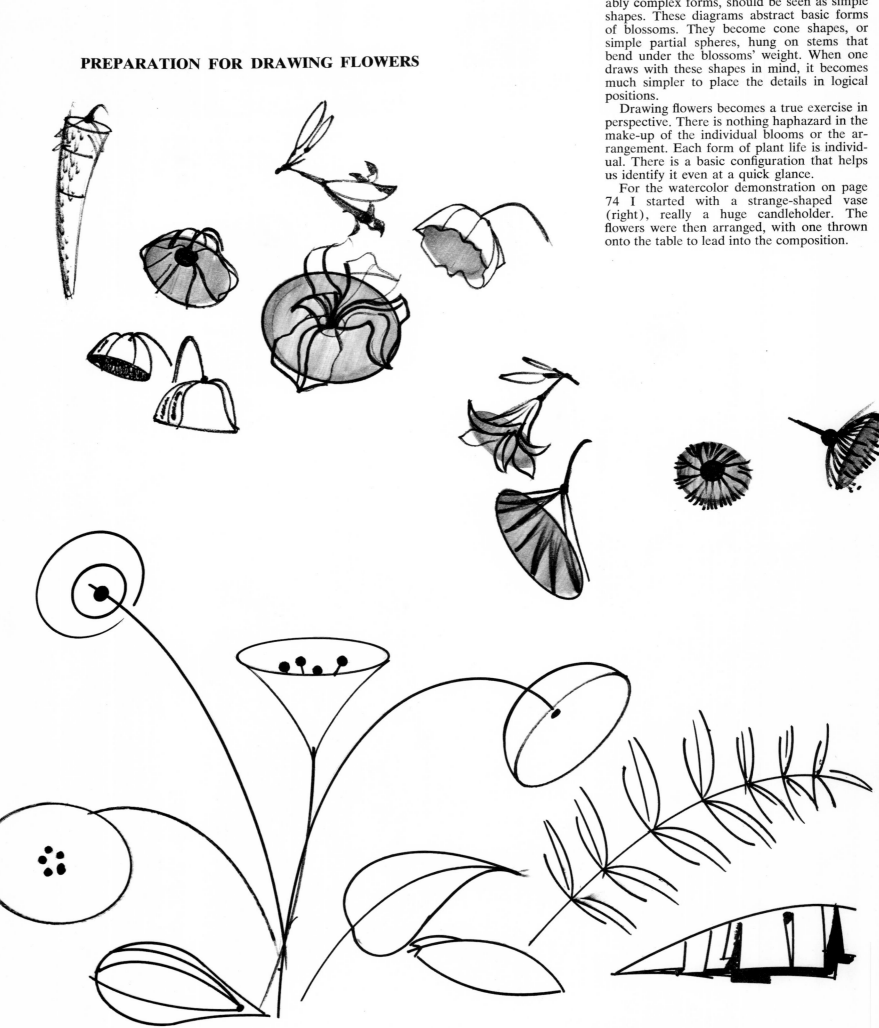

Flowers, which at first glance have remarkably complex forms, should be seen as simple shapes. These diagrams abstract basic forms of blossoms. They become cone shapes, or simple partial spheres, hung on stems that bend under the blossoms' weight. When one draws with these shapes in mind, it becomes much simpler to place the details in logical positions.

Drawing flowers becomes a true exercise in perspective. There is nothing haphazard in the make-up of the individual blooms or the arrangement. Each form of plant life is individual. There is a basic configuration that helps us identify it even at a quick glance.

For the watercolor demonstration on page 74 I started with a strange-shaped vase (right), really a huge candleholder. The flowers were then arranged, with one thrown onto the table to lead into the composition.

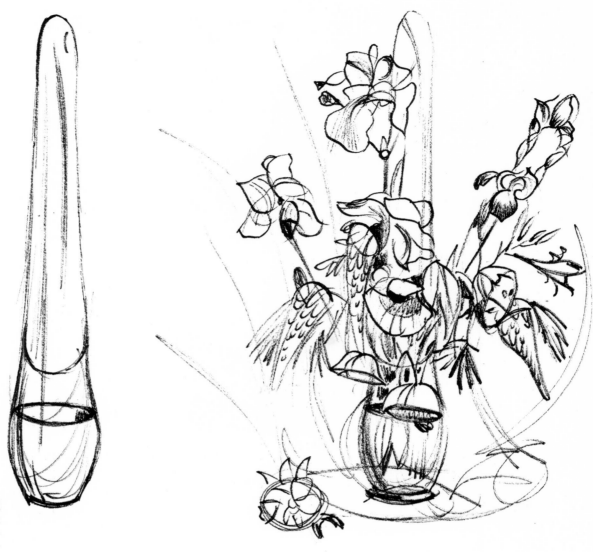

Children and the bowl of flowers (right and page 75) is a combination of two of the most difficult problems in watercolor. How it developed was simple. In painting flower paintings, I discovered that I was forced to wait for the color to dry on the variously colored blooms. To allow me to continue working, I recomposed this painting and painted the children along with the flowers. Of course, I first made a number of sketches of the flowers and the children separately, but I had only one transparency of the children. It would have been helpful to have had the children as models or at least have a number of photos of the children. It is interesting to note, however, that in this painting, in which I was more involved in its composition than in its multiple portraiture, the finished work showed a good likeness of the children.

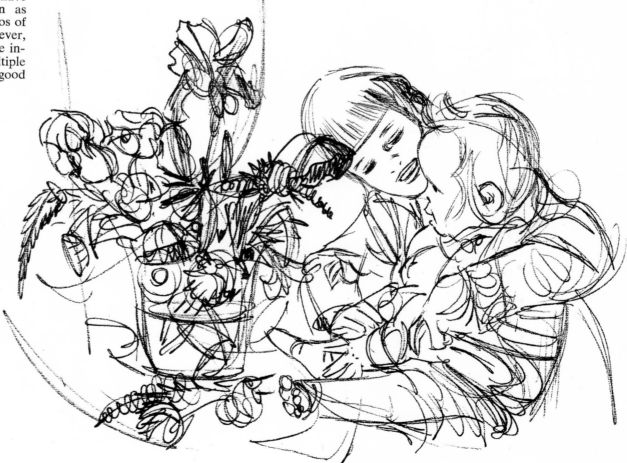

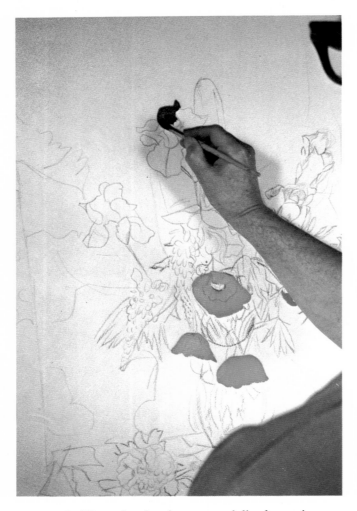

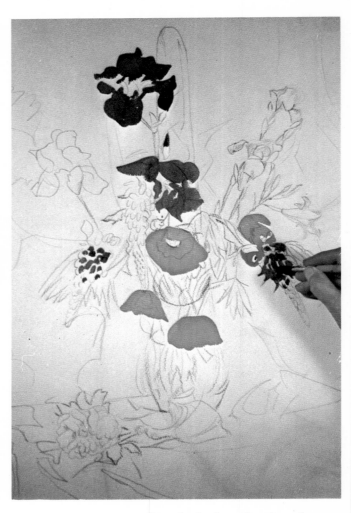

1. First, the sketch was carefully drawn in pencil on a piece of 90-pound watercolor paper. The paper was then dampened and stretched onto the table. Over this sketch, each flower was painted in its entirety in a single over-all tone of its predominant color.

2. From a small pool of color of each variety of flower, the flowers and leaves were painted. Those areas that would take a different color or highlight were left blank.

COLOR DEMONSTRATION: FLOWER PAINTING

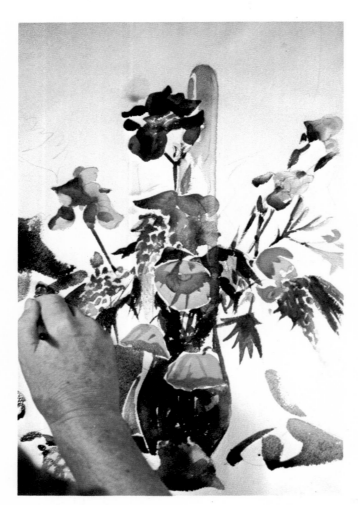

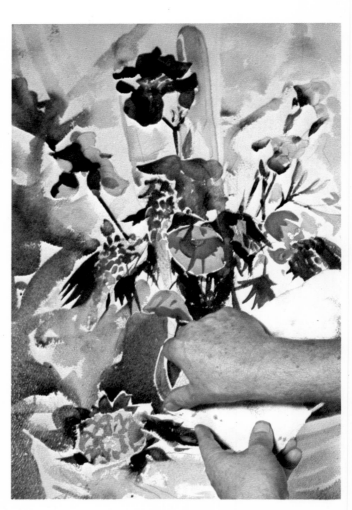

5. The background area was redampened, using care not to touch the recently painted areas. The larger areas are best dampened lightly with a sponge and the smaller ones with a brush. Into the dampened area, the shadows of the dropcloth were quickly brushed.

6. A few areas were puddling into what might have become an accident, so a blotter was used to remove excess water. At right is an example of the same approach, with the addition of the children and other elements as explained on page 73.

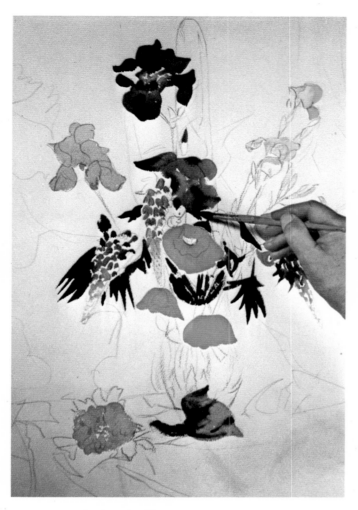

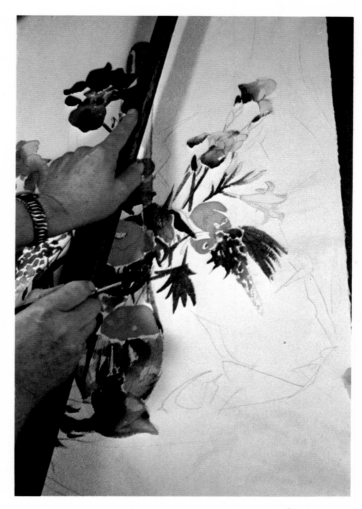

3. While the flowers were still moist, the darker tones were painted, wet into wet. Shadow tones were a combination of the original pool of color plus the complement of the color. The results are more vibrant than they would have been if black had been used.

4. For delicate sections of the painting, around the vase and areas where rigid control was necessary, the hand was steadied with a bridge—a rigid stick raised off the paper by means of two small blocks, one at either end.

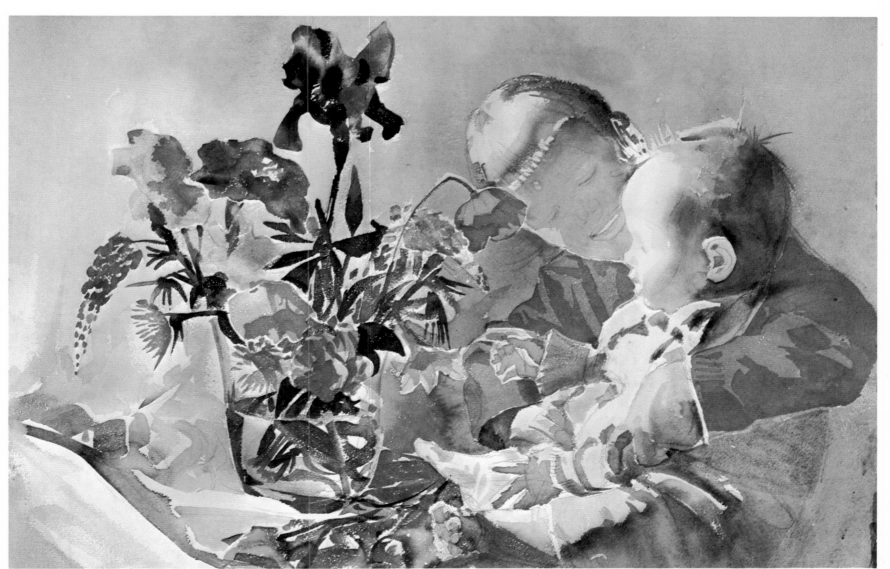

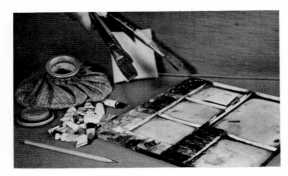

a

PAINTING OUT OF DOORS

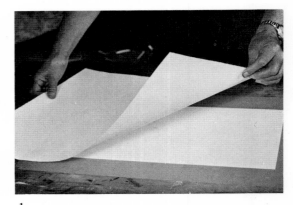

1

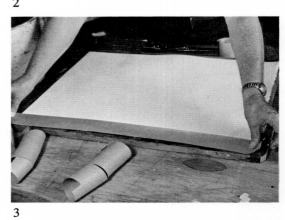

2

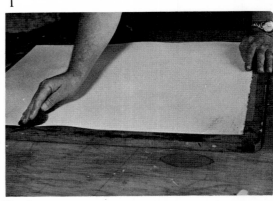

3

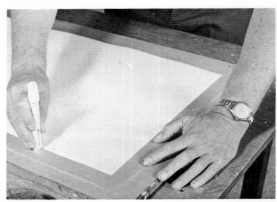

4

There is no substitute for painting out of doors. Watercolor lends itself extremely well to quick impressions as well as to more comprehensive paintings in a minimum of time. Although there are records of both Dürer (fifteenth century) and Rembrandt (seventeenth century) painting on-the-spot sketches, it was not until Constable and Turner (in the nineteenth century) began painting in color from actual observation that we began to see the true value of the practice.

The impressionists, in the mid- and late-nineteenth century, believed that only from painting their impressions directly from nature could they possibly begin to capture the feeling and essence of a scene. Whether or not one agrees with the impressionists, painting from the subject out of doors is a big part of the painting experience.

In painting out of doors with watercolor, as with any other medium, a prime consideration is the transportability of the materials. The lighter and less complicated these are the better. A simple enameled palette (a) is preferable to a watercolor box-palette combination. Tube colors are easily carried in one's pocket.

It is not always practical to pick a spot in the shade. When painting in brilliant sunlight, the paper will reflect the light, making it impossible to determine colors and to put them down in anything like their proper hue and intensity.

The answer is color-corrected sunglasses. This type of glass was developed for fighter pilots of World War II. Most optometrists can supply them, either by prescription or otherwise. The alternative, as used by Sargent, is a beach umbrella—dramatic but unwieldy.

It is quite simple to sit on the deck with paint and palette on the ground, and with pad or board and paper held between the knee. One can also use a campstool with painting on the ground, or stand at a collapsible easel.

Painting blocks are available in various sizes in paper weights of 70 and 140 pounds, in both very rough and rather smooth finishes. They are all inclined to buckle a bit during the painting process but are certainly a good answer for the painter who intends to do more than a single painting.

A method of taping down paper on board is shown , right (1–4). One sheet of paper is stretched over the next, a practical procedure for larger paintings.

When 300-pound paper is used, this is heavy enough merely to be clipped to a sheet of plywood.

The spiral-bound sketchbooks are useful, but only for smaller works.

Even out of doors, it is sometimes practical to use the method of stretching paper shown on page 64. This works well with most surfaces of paper, rough to smooth, and has the added advantage of allowing the use of a lighter and less expensive paper.

The artist painting out of doors will find that the needs of the hunter and other outdoor sportsmen have caused the suppliers of such clothes to answer most of his needs also. There are jackets with capacious pockets, high boots for marshland and the like. There are insect repellents, for insects are probably the greatest villains for frustrating artists. Depending on your taste, you must be well prepared in the food and drink line. Nothing quite takes the place of a cold martini or a glass of wine and a snack while waiting for a passage to dry.

On the opposite page a number of methods of using a variety of vehicles are shown. The common advantage of all of them is that the artist is above his subject. In most cases he is shielded from the onlooker by a mass of steel.

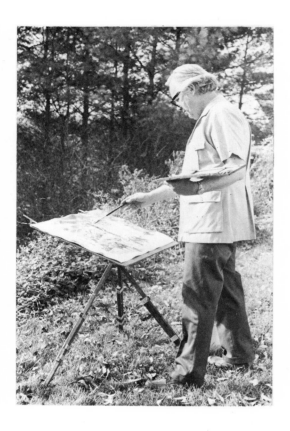

(1) Take along an enamel palette, a No. 12 watercolor brush, and a large pail of water; tube watercolors are carried to the spot in the pockets of a summer bush jacket. The easel is a traditional wooden affair that is easily collapsible . . . in fact, it collapsed while I was using it, directly after the photo was taken.

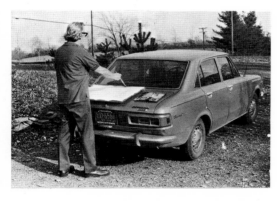

(2) The rear trunk of many sedans makes a fine painting surface.

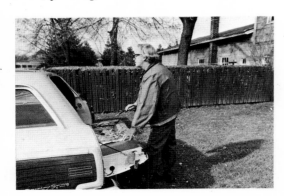

(3) An even better painting area is the rear tailgate of the traditional station wagon. Aside from its practical height for use while standing, it completely frustrates the onlookers in coming between the artist and his subject.

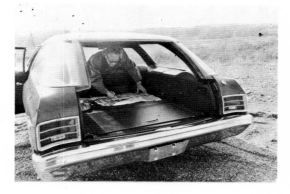

(4) A practical method of using the station wagon, even models with the hideaway tailgate, is that of kneeling on the second seat. The scene to be painted will be framed in the rear opening. The attitude of the body is a bit ludicrous, but this is a quite comfortable painting position. It is great for painting in inclement weather.

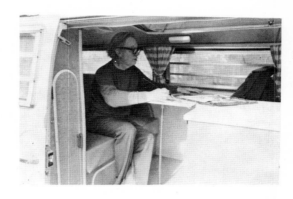

(5) Vans make excellent mobile studios. Some of them, notably those made for camping, come complete with a table.

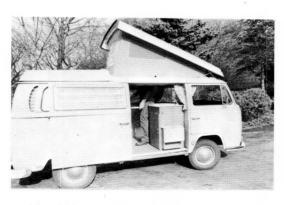

(6) Older models of the camper have a pop-up top that enables you to view in any direction. Either type makes painting in poor weather conditions possible.

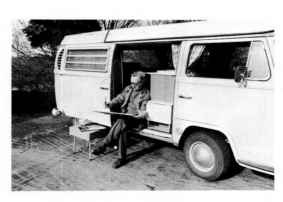

(7) Campers are the right height for a kind of relaxed sitting position. In this case, the camper carried its own water supply and a built-in side table for the palette.

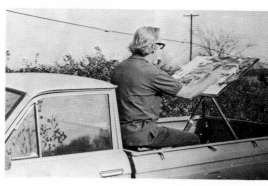

(8) The back of a pickup truck provides an ideal painting platform. The artist, even while sitting, is above the crowd and in a better position to see what's going on.

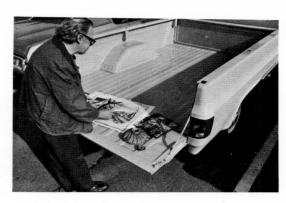

(9) A favorite position for outdoor sketching or painting is at the tailgate of a pickup truck. This gives the artist a chance to step back once in a while to see how the painting is coming along.

In some of these pictures an ice bag will be noted. This is used as a water carrier. Not only will an ice bag cling to most surfaces regardless of the angle, but it can be carried, filled, in one's pocket.

In general, the same tools and materials are used in outdoor sketching as in the studio, so there is little jump in procedure from the studio to the great outdoors.

Today's vehicles seem to have been made with the outdoor watercolorist in mind. However, unless the artist has little regard for the interior of his vehicle, he will find it wise to be prepared with a dropcloth of some type to protect the interior finish.

A note of warning: If you paint in the snow and cold with the heater going full blast, make sure that the exhaust fumes are not seeping into the car. This would be highly improbable in a new vehicle, but a lot of artists don't have new cars.

77

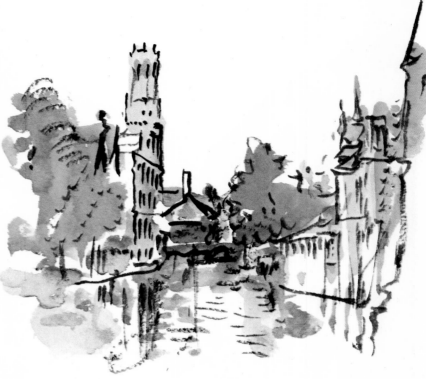

(1) In a quick, on-the-spot watercolor out of doors, it is a good idea to start with a mass of color with no regard for detail, but great attention to the over-all pattern. In this demonstration two sketches were made to show the two steps. In so doing mistakes were discovered in the first one.

(2) A waterproof felt pen was used for the outlines. After a wait for the color washes to dry, the steeples, windows, bridges, and other details were delineated. Another approach would have been to use watercolor or India ink for defining lines instead of the felt pen.

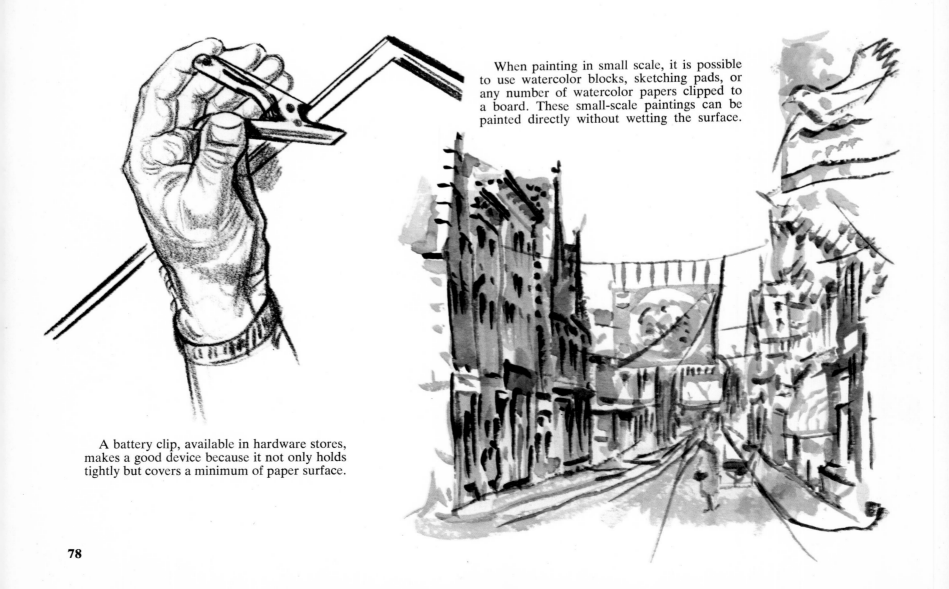

When painting in small scale, it is possible to use watercolor blocks, sketching pads, or any number of watercolor papers clipped to a board. These small-scale paintings can be painted directly without wetting the surface.

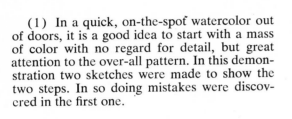

A battery clip, available in hardware stores, makes a good device because it not only holds tightly but covers a minimum of paper surface.

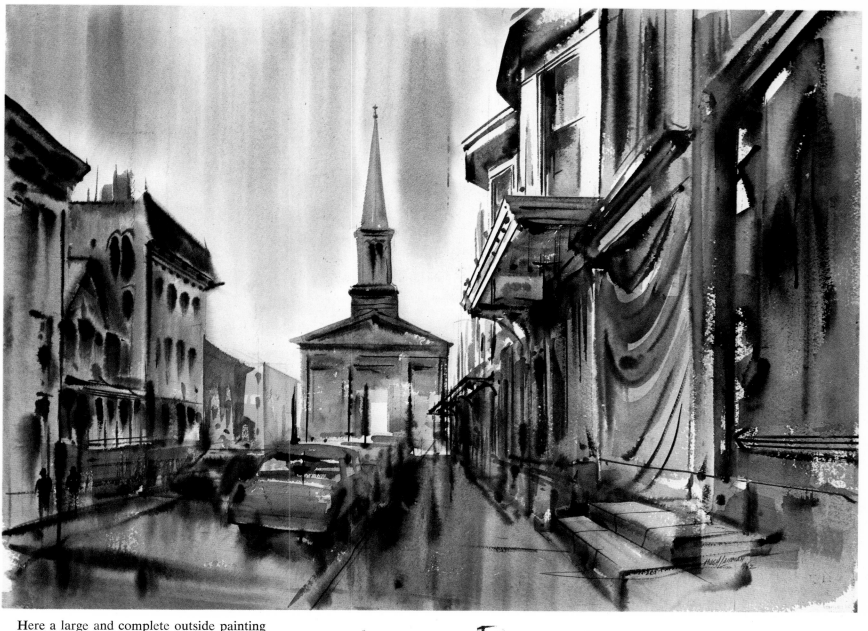

Here a large and complete outside painting was made using only one large, square-edged brush. It wasn't intended that way, but it so happened that the one brush was all that was available at the moment.

This is how to use the same brush in different ways:

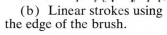

(a) Bold vertical strokes.

(b) Linear strokes using the edge of the brush.

(c) Thin to thick elliptical strokes using the brush held in one position.

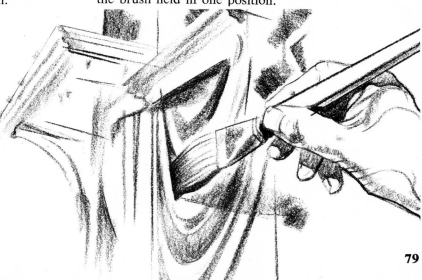

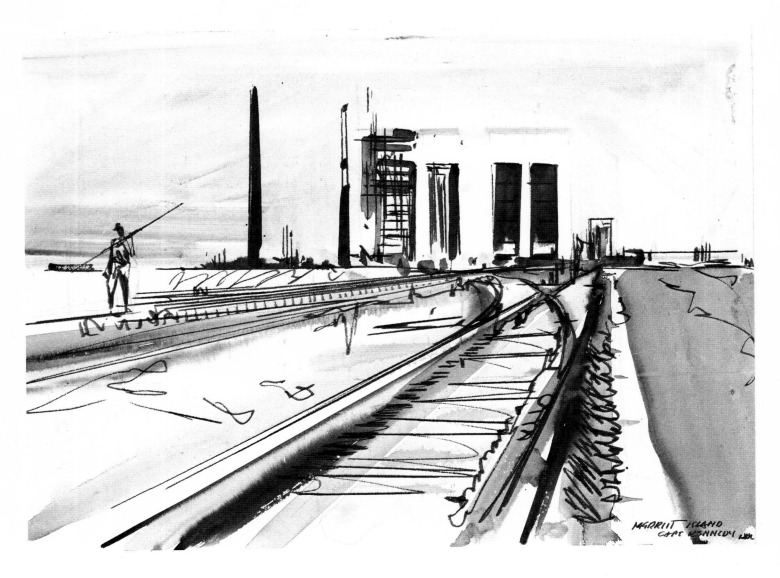

Two watercolor impressions of the U. S. space program made on the spot at Merritt Island·Launch Center

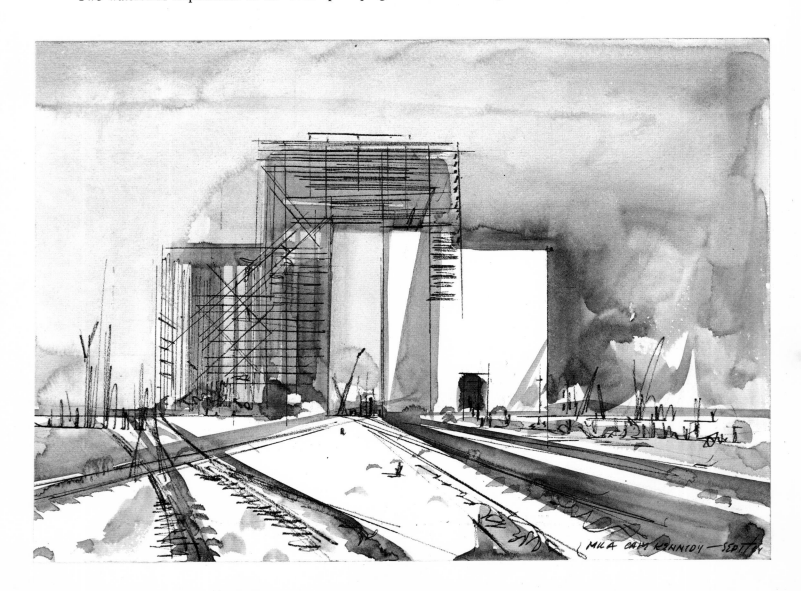

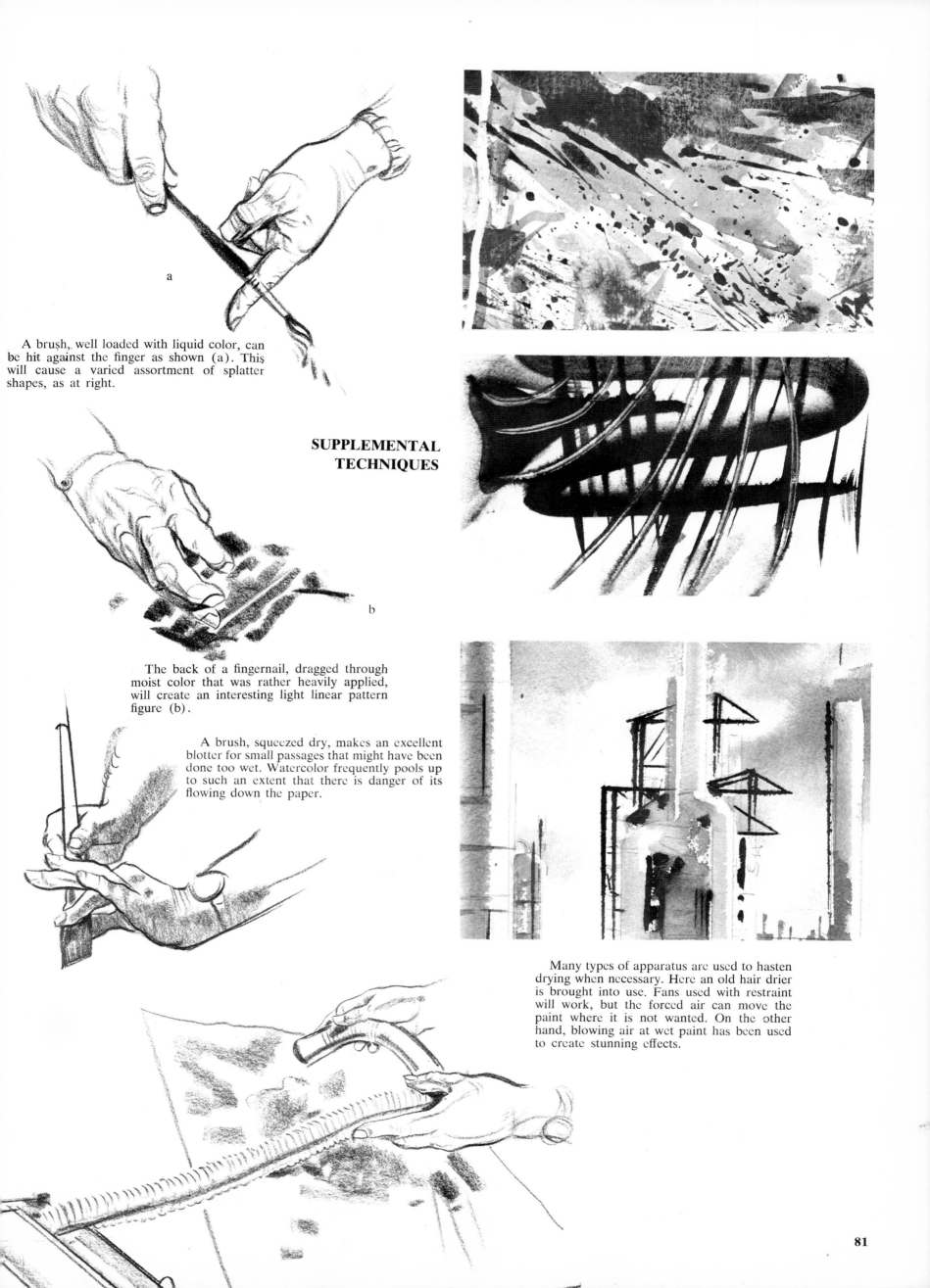

A brush, well loaded with liquid color, can be hit against the finger as shown (a). This will cause a varied assortment of splatter shapes, as at right.

SUPPLEMENTAL TECHNIQUES

The back of a fingernail, dragged through moist color that was rather heavily applied, will create an interesting light linear pattern figure (b).

A brush, squeezed dry, makes an excellent blotter for small passages that might have been done too wet. Watercolor frequently pools up to such an extent that there is danger of its flowing down the paper.

Many types of apparatus are used to hasten drying when necessary. Here an old hair drier is brought into use. Fans used with restraint will work, but the forced air can move the paint where it is not wanted. On the other hand, blowing air at wet paint has been used to create stunning effects.

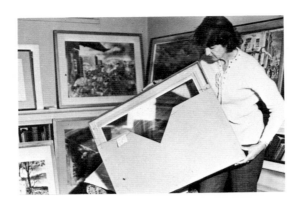

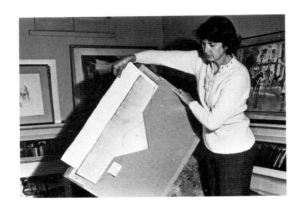

SHOWING PAINTINGS

Sooner or later you will be faced with the problem of showing paintings to sell. A proper frame greatly enhances a painting, but it is financially difficult to frame properly every painting you do. One way is to mat each finished work. This is not completely satisfactory because the cardboard mats become dirty after a few showings. A simpler method is to settle on a few frames strong enough to take a beating during transportation and exhibiting, and to substitute plexiglass for the glass.

Make a simple pocket of corrugated cardboard so that a number of paintings of nearly the same size can be slipped into the back. This makes a fine display with a minimum of weight. With watercolors the artist has the constant problem of weight in getting from one spot to another. With two or three such frames, he can show a variety of sizes and usually have an exhibition of as many as thirty paintings that can be readily carried. An exhibition can then be available in short order.

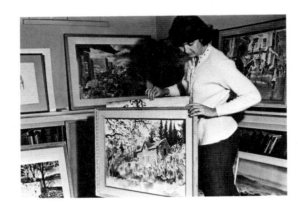

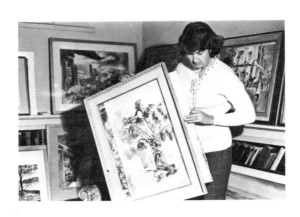

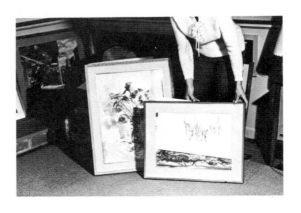

RESTORING WATERCOLORS

Sometimes paintings get damaged and have to be restored. A series of my paintings had been painted in a mixed media of transparent watercolor and acrylic. One was painted completely in watercolor in a simple direct approach. Another was mainly acrylic used as transparent watercolor, and the third was a combination of both.

Six weeks after they were hung, a flood hit the area. Just about all furnishings were a total loss. The paintings were covered with silt and had been under rushing water for quite some time. For those who equate watercolor with delicacy, here is what was done to bring the paintings back to their original state.

The paintings had been mounted on Upsom board because of their size. Library paste was used so that if the need ever arose to remove them from their backing, they could be soaked off. If a watercolor is painted with the best materials, it can be immersed in water without dissolving the paint.

1. These paintings had really gone through hell and high water.

2. A shallow tub made with two-by-fours, the kind available at a lumber dealer's, was lined with pliofilm, and a painting was placed in the tub.

3. A few gallons of water were poured into the tub to cover the painting.

4. A few handy bricks were used to hold the painting under the water.

5. After the painting had soaked a few hours, a soft sponge was carefully used to loosen the silt.

6. After a few more hours of soaking, the painting was removed from the Upsom board and hung up to dry. Once it had dried, the painting was placed under a few mounting boards to flatten it.

7. To remount the paintings, inexpensive paper was cut to the size of the mounting board. This paper was sponged on both sides.

8. Library paste was then spread onto one side of the paper.

9. This was a sticky business.

10. The paper was pasted to one side of the mount board. This was to equalize the strain on the board when the painting was pasted on the opposite side.

11. The pasted paper was smoothed out.

12. Again, after the painting had been carefully sponged on both sides, library paste was spread on the back of the painting.

13. With a windshield squeegee used over a protective piece of paper, all the bubbles were squeezed out.

14. Once it was perfectly flattened, the restored painting was clamped between table tops. After a tiny retouch job on a torn spot, the painting was as good as new.

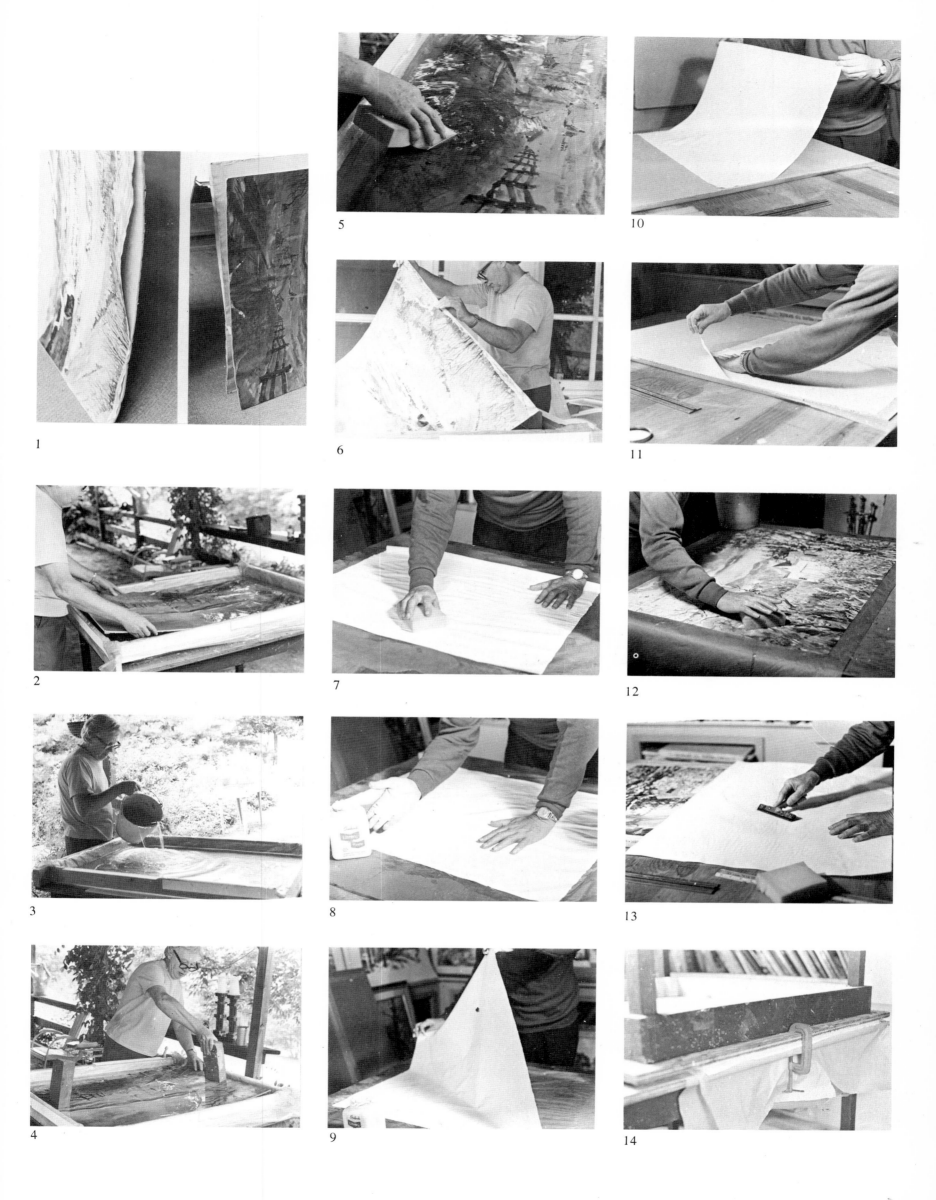

1

2

3

4

5

6

7

8

9

10

11

12

13

14

OIL PAINTING

Whether the brothers Van Eyck were the first to mix their colors with oil or whether they merely perfected an earlier practice employed by boat painters is, for all practical purposes, of little matter. The fact that they opened up the medium to artists is critical. Artists, generally the creative segment of our society, when handed the ball, will run with it.

Using oil as the medium offers a much wider divergence in procedure and end result than did previous methods using wax, egg, mortar, glue, resin, or glycerin. The oil medium adheres to a variety of supports. One superior material is paper. Whether glued to a wood surface or to other support, paper is ideally suited to a spontaneous final painting, with a resultant transparent appearance. First the Flemish, then the French used paper. Paper has been used for the first oil color demonstration that follows.

More popular today is the use of canvas or a solid support such as hardboard, plywood, or composition board. Sometimes a combination of both is used by gluing canvas onto the solid surface. Stretched canvas has two advantages: a resilient surface much favored by some artists, notably portraitists, and the possibility of almost unlimited size.

The best canvases are linen and hemp, both comparatively stable. On the market are combinations of cotton and linen. These are to be avoided. If cost is a factor, it would be wiser to use a canvas of cotton alone rather than any exotic combination. A support that might expand and contract to a greater or lesser degree than the paint may cause the paint to scale off.

Once a support has been selected, it must be covered with some sort of priming. Whereas preprimed canvas is acceptable in the experimental stages of painting, it is better and less expensive for the serious artist to do his own priming. Unless an artist wishes to step back in time to priming methods utilizing size or casein mixed with plaster or carbonate of lime, or a thin coating of white lead over a coating of size, he is much better off using a reliable ready-mixed gesso. Two or three thin coatings applied and sanded after each application work fine. If you insist on using size followed by multiple thin coatings of white lead (unsanded), make certain the white lead is completely dry before each succeeding coat. If this is not done, certain colors (emerald green for one) will begin a cracking process in a week or so. In any priming process a less frightening surface is created if the priming is tinted with a color compatible with the colors the painting will be, perhaps light gray or sepia, generally on the warm side of the palette. This is another reason for priming your own canvas.

It was once believed, with some degree of reason, that earth colors—yellow, ocher, red ocher, and black, along with ultramarine, which was once made from lapis lazuli—were the only desirable colors for an artist's palette. Recently, at least recently in the history of artists' materials, there has been available a much greater variety from which to choose. It is usually impractical for the average artist (if such an artist exists) to research and investigate today's colors. Here is a palette of high quality that will do the job.

List of permanent colors:

Flake white	Cadmium red or vermilion dark
Golden ocher	Madder lake
Stontain yellow	Ultramarine
Deep cadmium yellow	Cobalt
Venetian red	Ivory black
Burnt sienna	Blue black

In addition to the tube colors, which may be used as they are, you may want something with which to dilute them, for some paintings. Aside from drying agents, which should be used sparingly, if at all, use the finest grade of pure, raw linseed oil and rectified turpentine, or a combination of the two.

Brushes

Up until the early 1800s the round sable brush, much like that most generally used for watercolor, was employed almost exclusively. Today the square type, in either hogs' bristle or synthetic fiber, is customary. Add to these a number of special brushes for specific effects, and, of course, the fingers. Courbet is given credit for the first use of the palette knife as a painting tool. This method of painting might well be termed a "clean" application of paint to a surface, because the knife may be wiped clean after each stroke. A brush, after the first stroke, does not carry clear color to the canvas. Entire paintings can be made with a palette knife, but it is used effectively in combination with the brush, the fingers, or a roller.

Paint Application

In oil painting, more than in watercolor, the steps taken in the preparation and completion of the painting are important in assuring the painting's retaining its original appearance. Heavy underpainting in a warm color, with thin overpainting, may eventually lead to the painting's losing its character, or, less likely, improving with age. The old masters are given credit for actually planning on this. It is safer for us, however, to plan for our paintings' permanence.

Some of the greatest paintings in history, when examined, show that the artist has changed his mind about his composition halfway through. An underpainting with a completely different approach has come through. To avoid this, the artist must first scrape off the original paint before changing a painting in the middle of its creation. Whether you are a beginner or more experienced, in order to see what happens to oil paint in the painting, paint a portrait with the limited palette of white, black, yellow ocher, and red ocher. A few of the old masters obtained remarkable results with these, and, yes, with a limited use of an auxiliary color or two. Even a color painted over with the same color of the same value tends to become opaque. Because of this factor almost all quick studies for a final painting appear more brilliant than the final worked-over painting. Direct, spontaneous painting as against painstaking corrections and overpainting will produce a clear and more permanent picture.

We discover, then, that the direct application of paint in the oil medium becomes as important as in the watercolor medium. Few can paint with such assurance. The method, then, to be employed is to sketch the subject on the canvas in thin, very much diluted color. With the mechanics of the subject under control, it is easier to continue into the final painting with greater spontaneity.

Some artists begin a painting by first sketching in the subject in its thinned-out complementary colors and then continuing into the final painting with the colors as seen in life. This is both a difficult and a dangerous approach. Much more satisfactory is doing the sketch in a grisaille made with an undiluted paste of black and white, or brown and white, a method used by El Greco, Titian, and Rubens, among other old masters.

Varnish

It is a simple matter, with a group of oil painters, to bring the discussion around to the use of varnish. A high grade of varnish, applied evenly, has the effect of restoring brilliance to the painting and at the same time preserving the painting from the impurities in the atmosphere. Varnishing, however, also tends to create an overshiny surface. An uneven application can produce a spotty matte and shine effect. Some varnishes tend to darken with time. The impressionists, for the most part, avoided using varnish at all, hoping to retain the full vibrance of the original work. Today the artist has available to him plastic coatings to give either a matte or a gloss finish. In time, they may answer the age-old problems and drawbacks of even the clearest varnish.

Before using any kind of varnish on the finished oil painting, wait at least one year. Always be certain that the surface is free from dust or other particles. At the end of the one-year waiting period, you may find you have progressed so far in your ability as to have become more critical of the old painting.

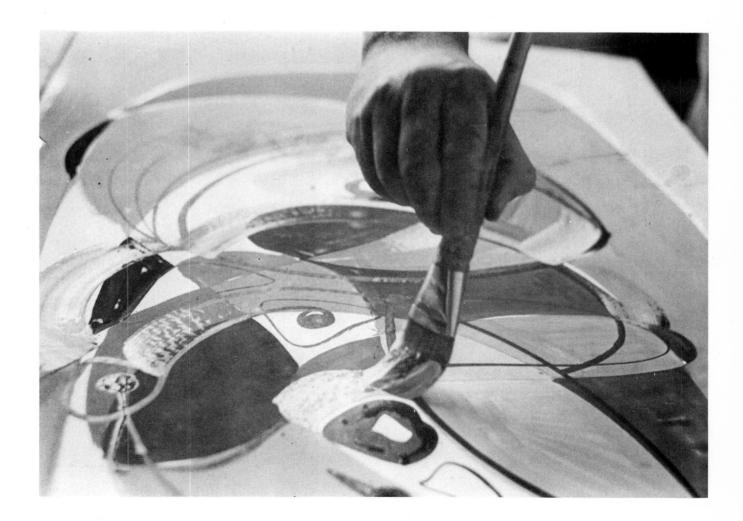

PRACTICE IN OIL TECHNIQUES

Oil paint may be used in a relatively liquid state. For practice in this technique, it is best to mix the paint with turpentine alone. It will dry rapidly, and when used on a scrap-paper surface, it affords an opportunity to become acquainted with the medium.

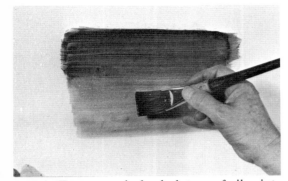

(a) From a pool of a dark tone of oil paint, create a graded area, using back-and-forth strokes with a camel-hair chisel brush.

(b) Using the same pool of paint slightly thinned, paint a fairly even area.

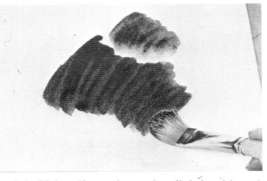
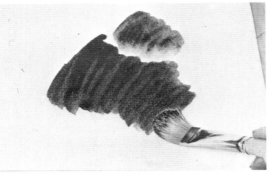

(c) Using the paint only slightly thinned with turpentine, scumble a dark tone with a bristle brush.

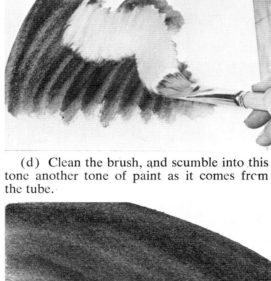

(d) Clean the brush, and scumble into this tone another tone of paint as it comes from the tube.

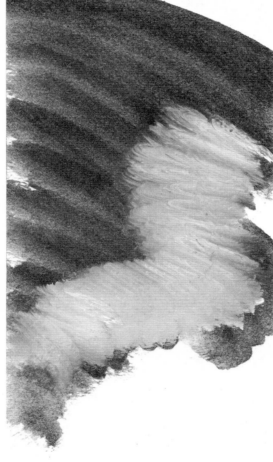

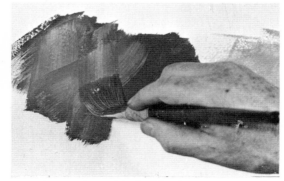

(e) Practice a kind of basket-weave stroke.

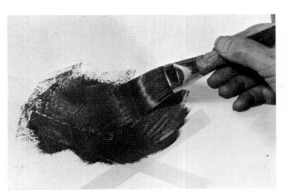

(f) Another practice stroke, as in (e).

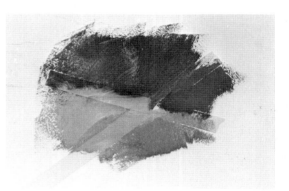

(g) Try the same strokes over a crisscross of tape.

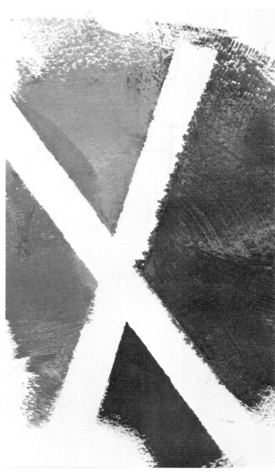

(h) Add a second tone.

(i) The tape was immediately pulled off to illustrate a danger in using oil in "hard edge" techniques. Oil dries slowly, and therefore jagged lines may result unless the paint is allowed to dry before the tape is removed.

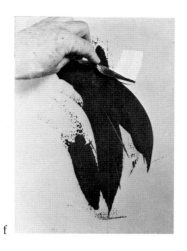

f

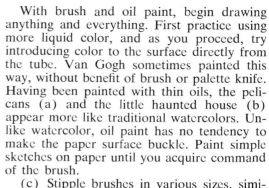

c

With brush and oil paint, begin drawing anything and everything. First practice using more liquid color, and as you proceed, try introducing color to the surface directly from the tube. Van Gogh sometimes painted this way, without benefit of brush or palette knife. Having been painted with thin oils, the pelicans (a) and the little haunted house (b) appear more like traditional watercolors. Unlike watercolor, oil paint has no tendency to make the paper surface buckle. Paint simple sketches on paper until you acquire command of the brush.

(c) Stipple brushes in various sizes, similar to the one shown, are available in art stores. In this case, an old, otherwise ruined brush was selected and the end of it cut off to create a do-it-yourself version.

(d) Stippling, which is merely dipping this blunt brush in a small amount of paint and tapping the ends of the hairs onto a surface, can appear to the casual observer as a kind of idiot busy work, but it is an excellent technique to gain unique effects.

(e) Here, to create a hard edge to show off the kind of graded tone possible with this technique, a bit of Scotch tape was used.

(f) and (g) The other extreme in technique is using a palette knife with great abandon. In immense scale, the technique is very effective.

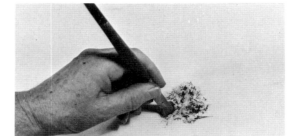

d

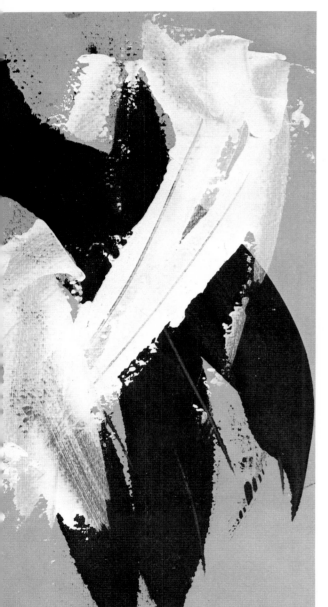

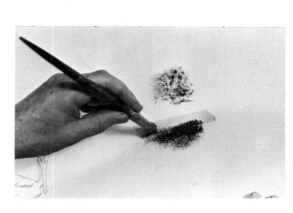

e

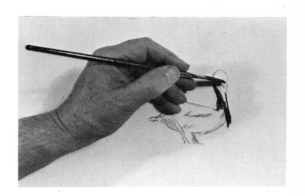

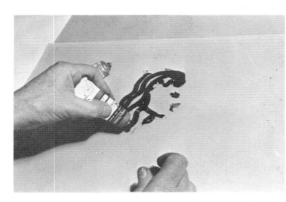

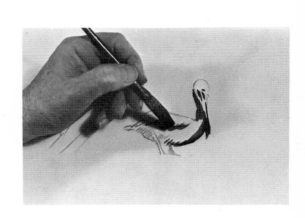

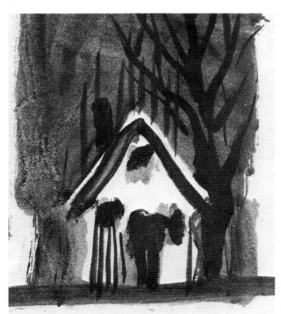

b

d-1

e-1

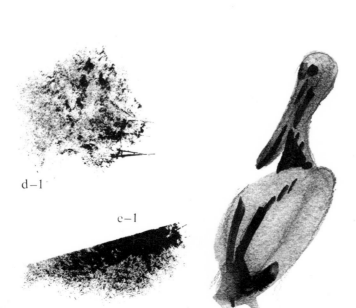

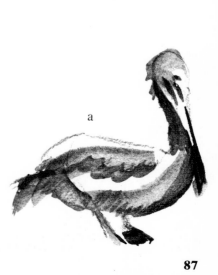

a

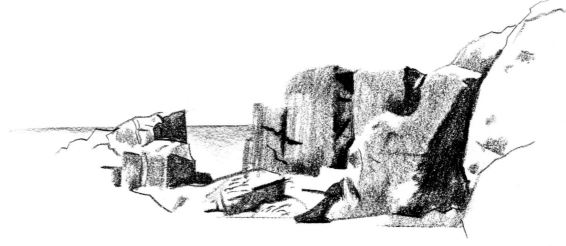

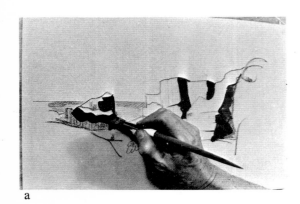

a

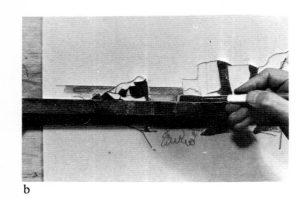

b

(a) Begun from a comprehensive charcoal sketch, the oil painting is drawn in simple lines. The shadow sides of the rocks are laid in.

(b) With a bridge used for a straightedge and to keep the hand off a freshly painted surface, the horizon and water are painted with thin paint.

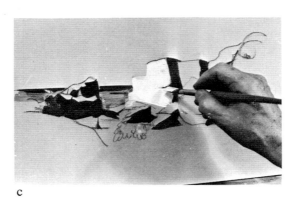

c

(c) The light sides of the rocks are painted with a heavy application of paint. This part can also be done with a palette knife (as seen later).

(d) Again using a bridge to avoid contact with the wet paint, scumble a stormy sky.

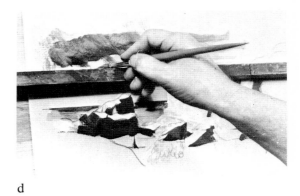

d

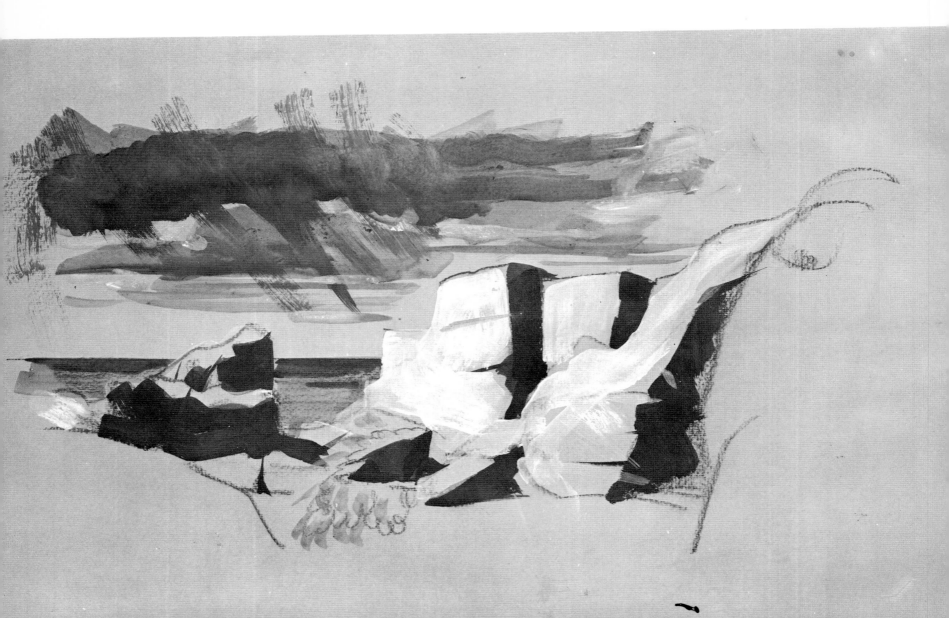

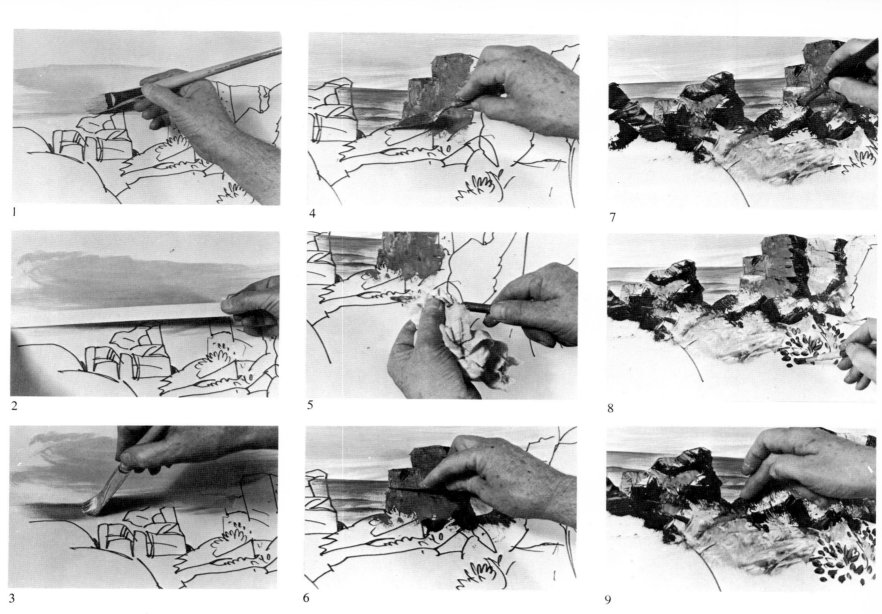

Using the sketch (a) on page 88 as a starting point for this practice study in oil:

(1) Paint a light sky tone.

(2) Once this is dry, place a strip of tape over the area so that the bottom edge of the tape represents the horizon line.

(3) Paint the ocean with broad strokes.

(4) With a palette knife, lay in the light side of the rocks.

(5) Wipe off the palette knife.

(6) Paint the shadow side of the rocks.

(7) Use a stipple brush to indicate spray.

(8) Paint the foreground foliage, seaweed, or whatever.

(9) Use the back of the fingernail for linear effects.

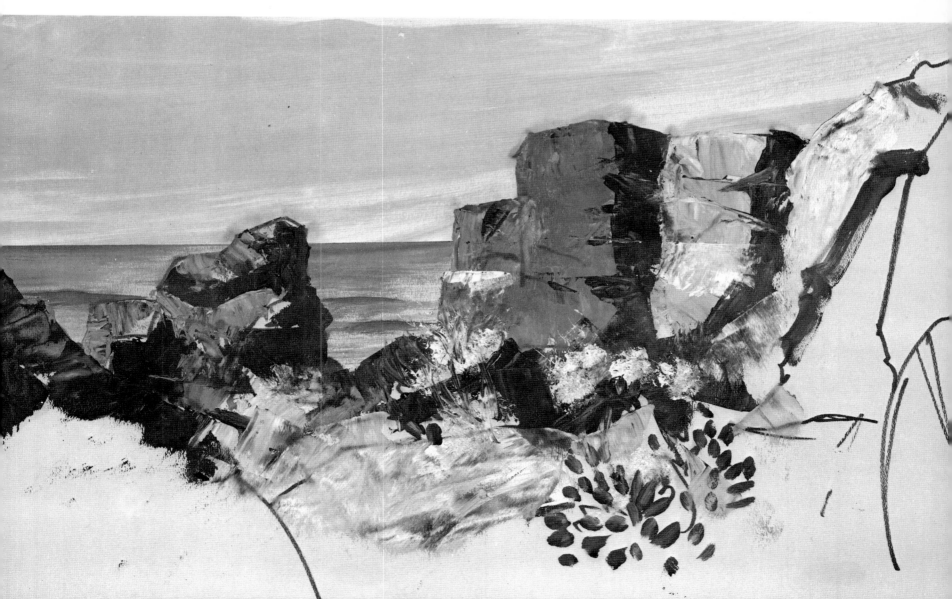

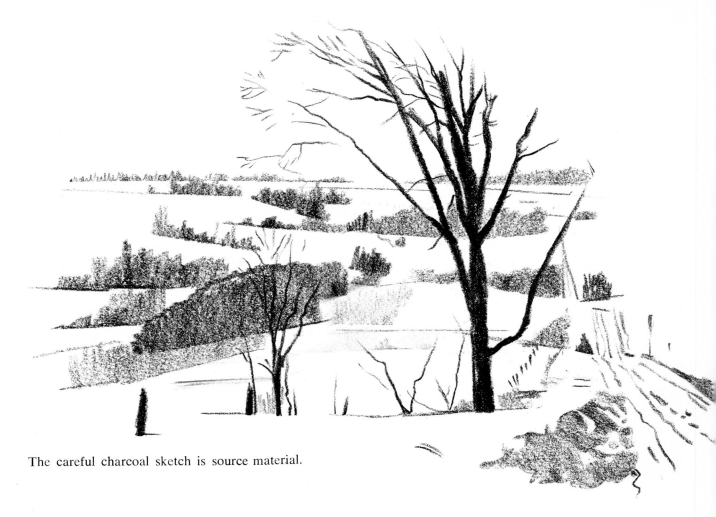

The careful charcoal sketch is source material.

(1) Over a line sketch, the sky area is brushed in with broad strokes of oil paint.

(2) Paint an effect of falling snow by pulling the brush at an angle into the horizon line.

(3) Use broad strokes for the distant areas.

(4) Use scumbling strokes for the middle areas of trees.

(5) Use broad strokes with thinned paint for the foreground shadow areas.

(6) With a palette knife apply paint for brightly lit snow.

(7) Continue with the palette knife.

(8) Now paint the middle-distant deciduous trees and the foreground elm.

(9) A few dabs of paint with a palette knife puts the snow in the crotches of the trees.

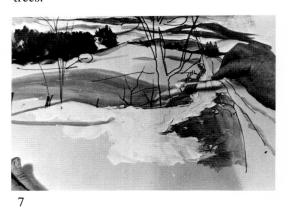

1

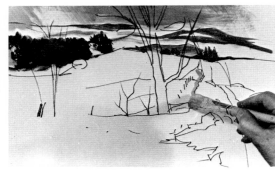

4

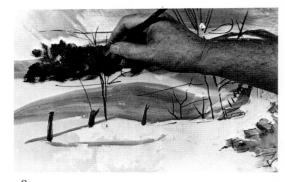

7

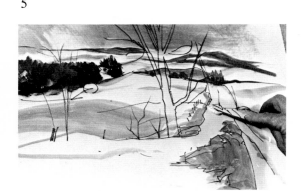

2

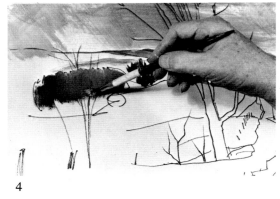

5

8

3

6

9

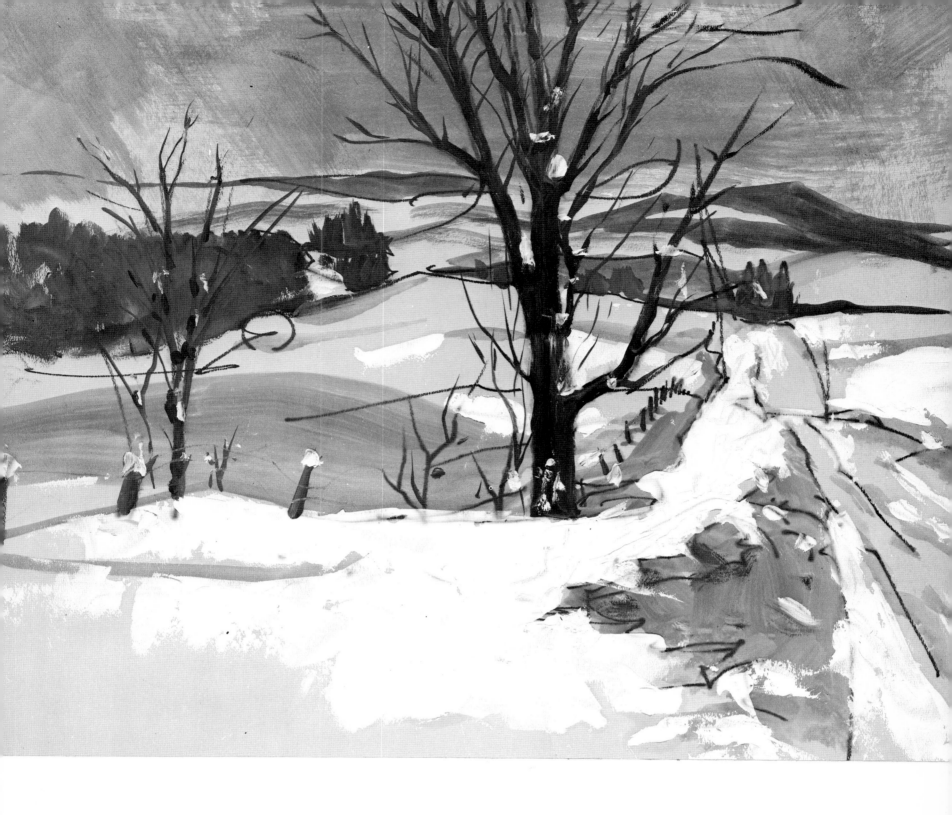

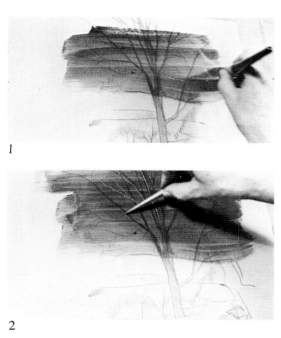

1

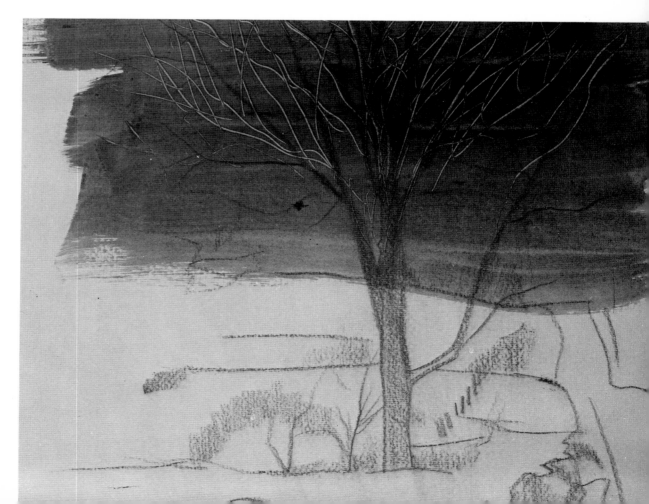

2

An alternate, among dozens of alternate approaches, might be to:

(1) Brush in a heavy-toned sky area, and

(2) Scrape out the branches with the back of a fingernail or the handle of the brush.

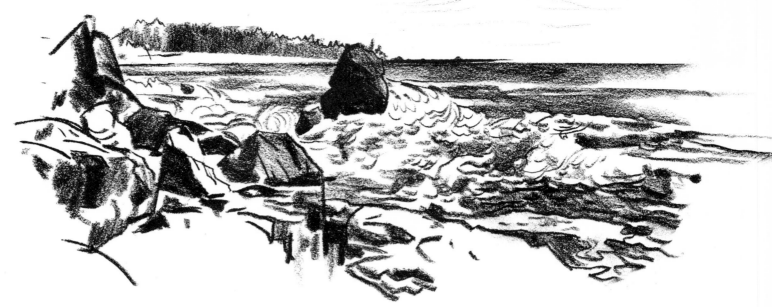

Starting with any sketch, there are unlimited possibilities for interpretation. It could be:

a geometric approach (a),   or a design approach (b),   or a simple abstract with added elements (c).

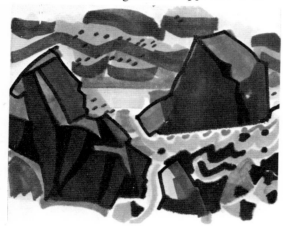
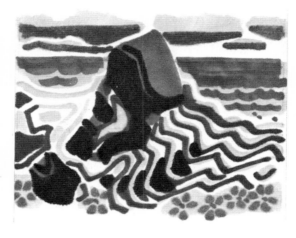
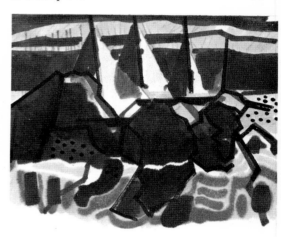

In naturalistic painting, let the strokes of the brush follow the form of the object:

(1) A large chisel brush is used for the rocks.

(2) A smaller, round brush is used for the waves breaking on the rocks.

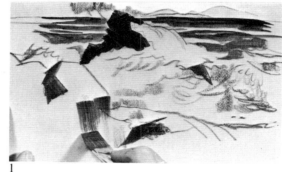
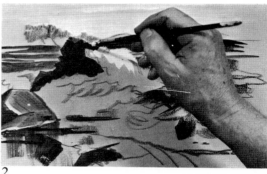

1   2

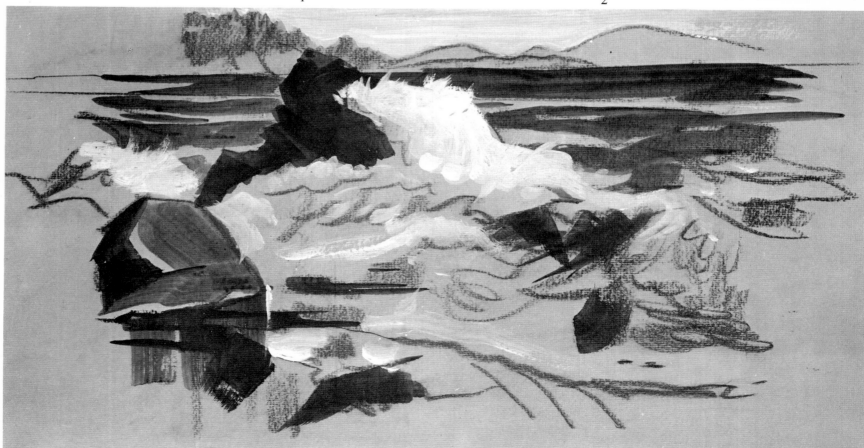

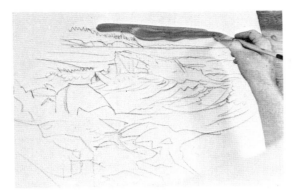 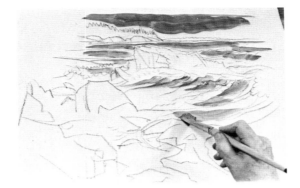 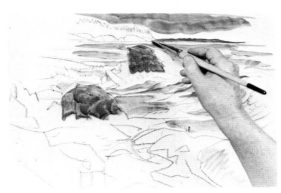

(1) Starting with the sky,

A safe and sure procedure, no better or worse than any other, is to cover the entire sketch with chosen tones of oil paint.

(2) Proceeding to the ocean and surf,

Above all, the artist must constantly think of portraying not only what he sees but what he cannot see. When the artist thinks and feels

(3) And then into the rocks.

that the rocks rest on solid ground, that the waves are breaking, his painting becomes believable.

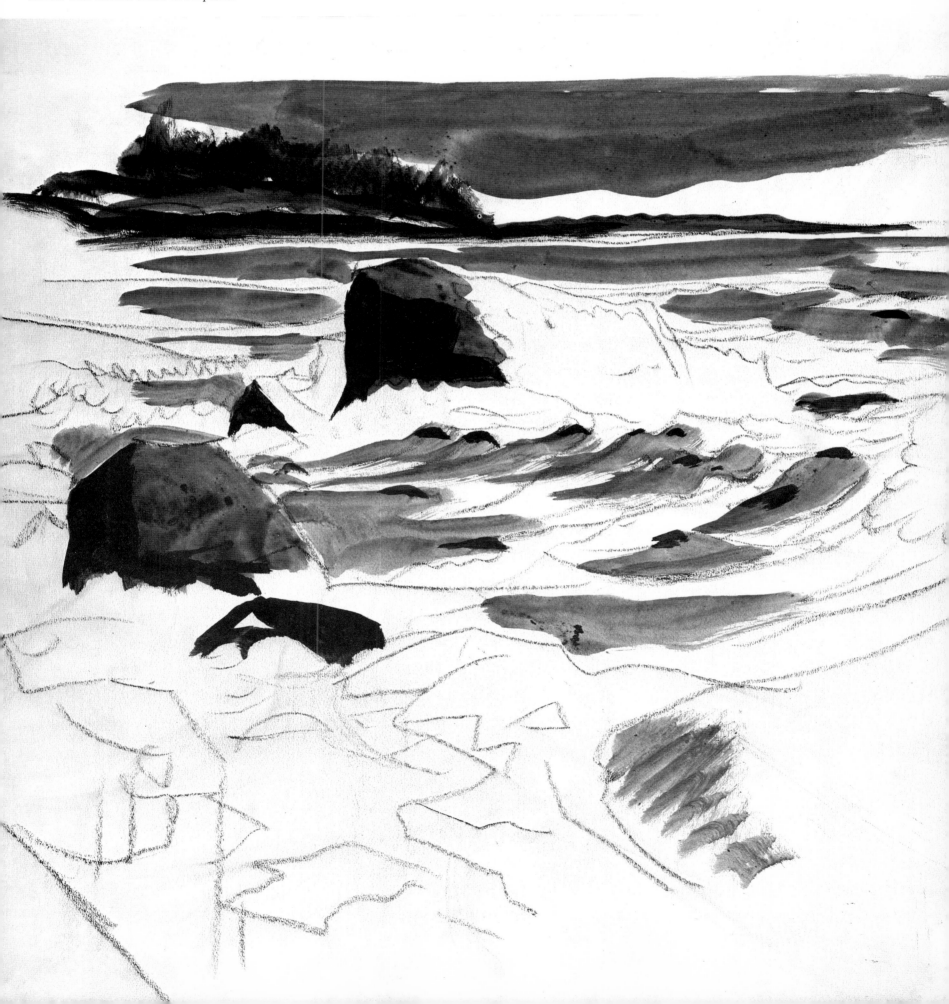

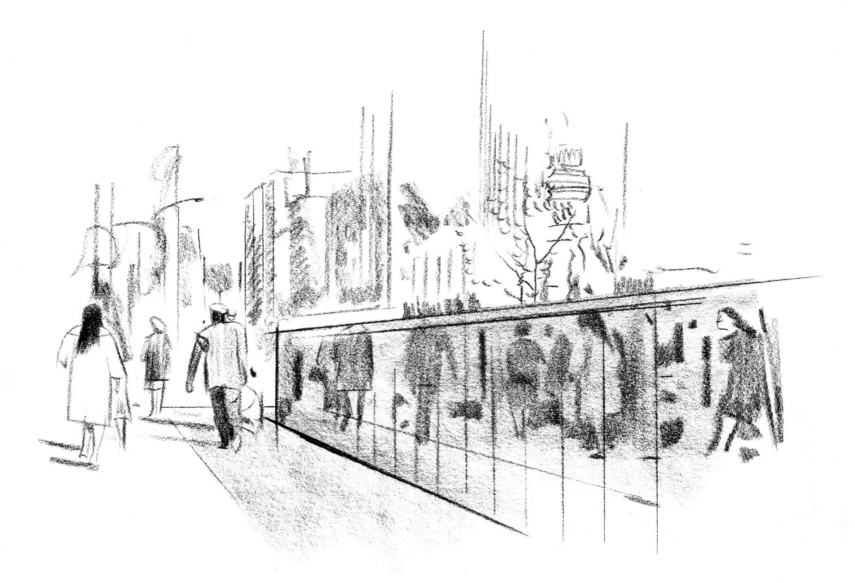

In oil painting a glaze is overpainting with a thinned mixture of one or more colors. Mixed with a combination of oil and turpentine, the glaze is applied water thin. Certain colors are more transparent than others in their full intensity. You can test the relative transparency of various colors by applying small strokes on thin paper and holding the result to the light. The relative opacity will be readily apparent.

This sketch offers an opportunity to show one need and use of glazing. The shiny marble wall reflecting the passers-by is the important storytelling section of the painting.

This is only a simple example. Multiple glazes are often used, each one adding to the depth and transparency of the finished work.

GLAZING

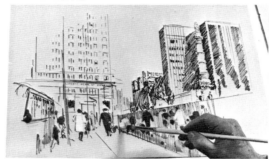

(1) First, the people on the walk and their reflections in the shiny wall were painted.

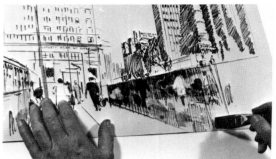

(2) The reflecting marble wall was then carefully painted, over the reflections, with a glaze the color of the marble. Once this was finished, the lines showing the black shapes of the marble were painted in opaque.

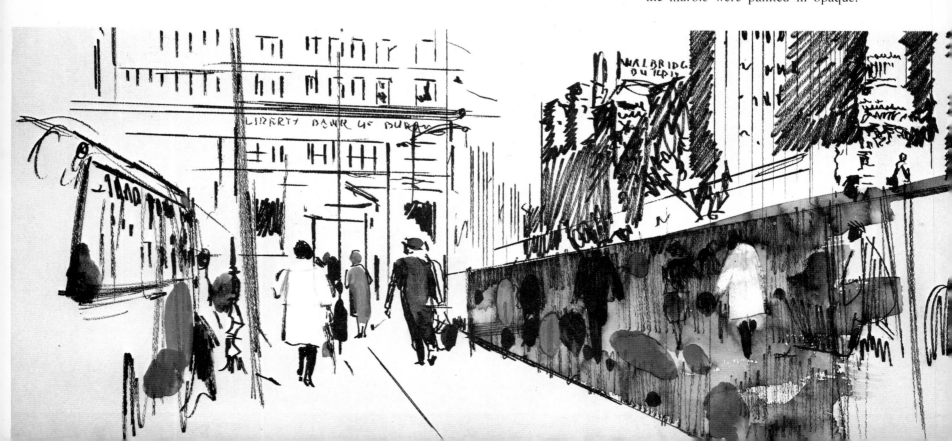

PRACTICE SUBJECTS

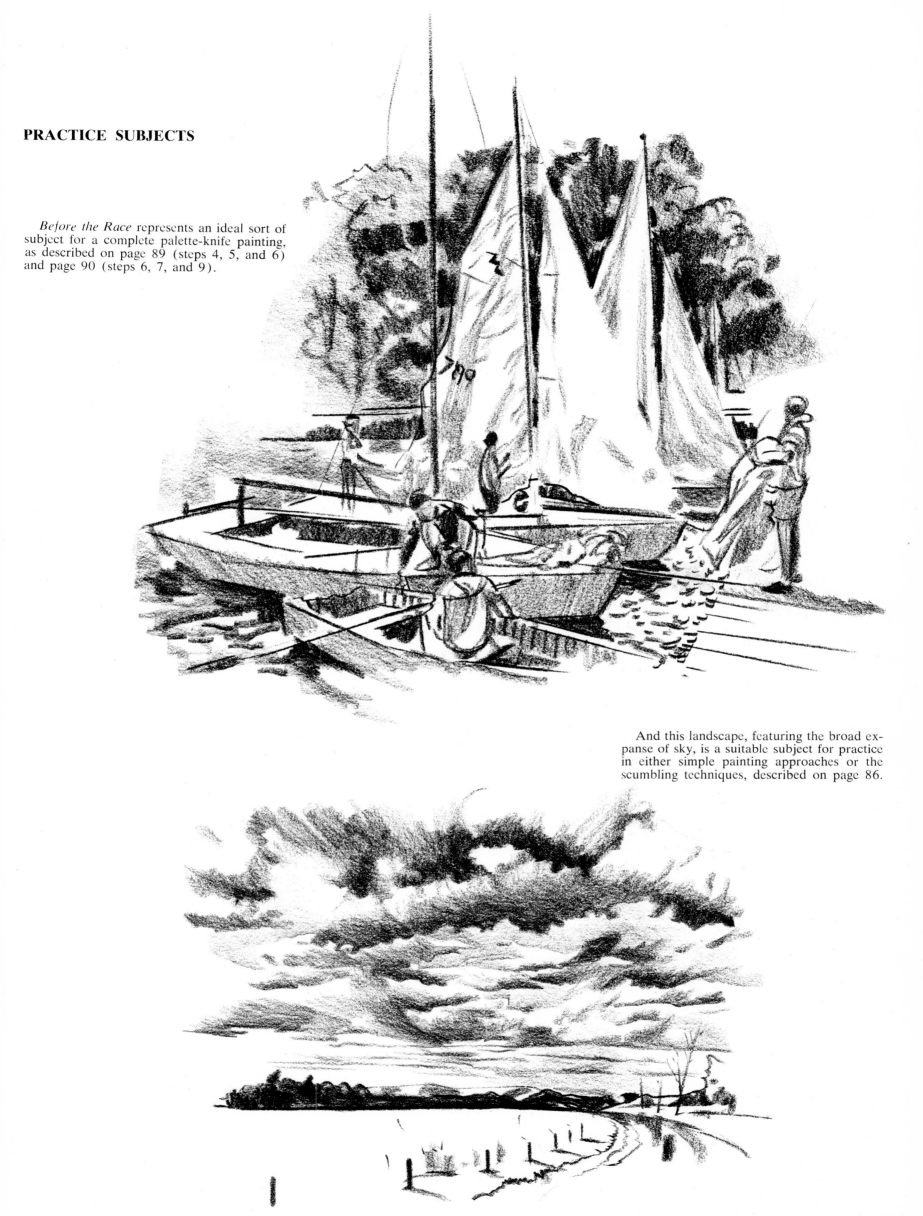

Before the Race represents an ideal sort of subject for a complete palette-knife painting, as described on page 89 (steps 4, 5, and 6) and page 90 (steps 6, 7, and 9).

And this landscape, featuring the broad expanse of sky, is a suitable subject for practice in either simple painting approaches or the scumbling techniques, described on page 86.

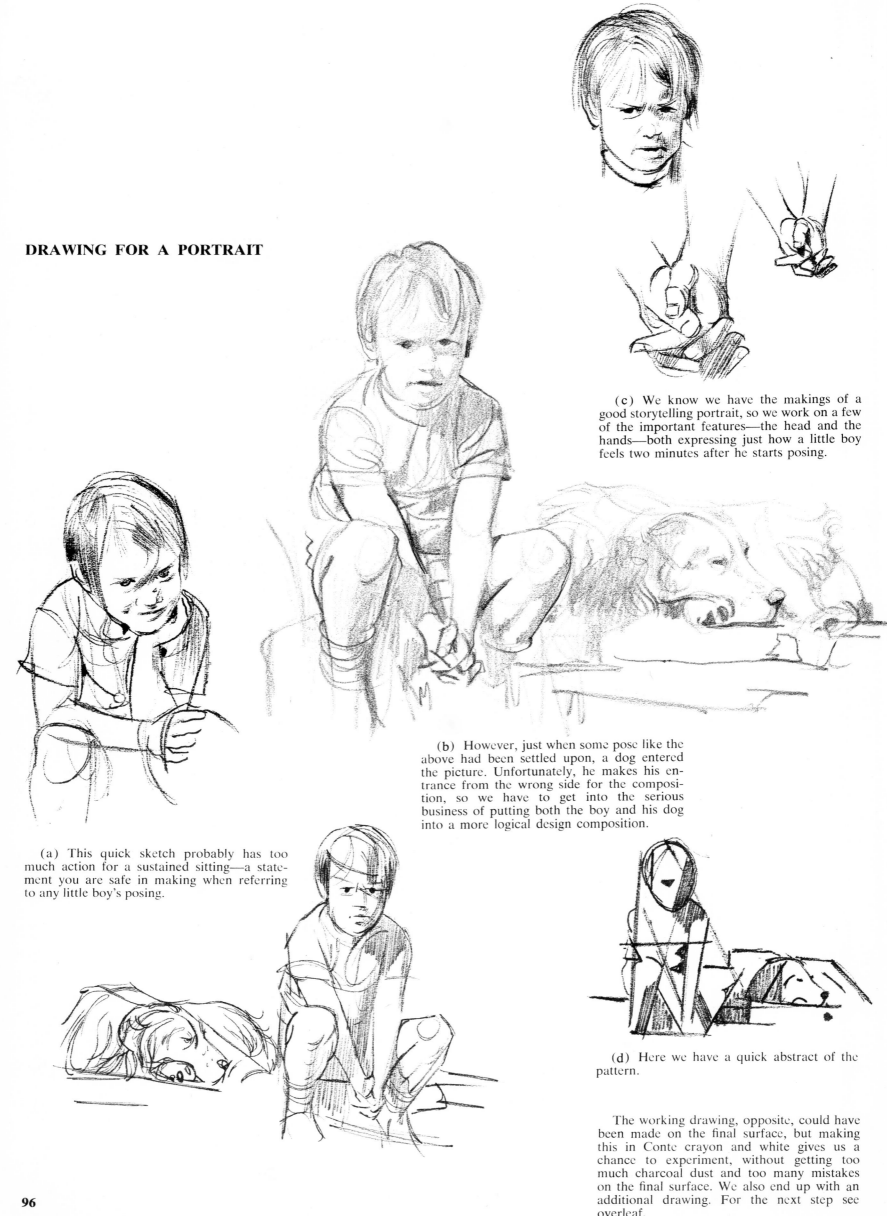

DRAWING FOR A PORTRAIT

(c) We know we have the makings of a good storytelling portrait, so we work on a few of the important features—the head and the hands—both expressing just how a little boy feels two minutes after he starts posing.

(b) However, just when some pose like the above had been settled upon, a dog entered the picture. Unfortunately, he makes his entrance from the wrong side for the composition, so we have to get into the serious business of putting both the boy and his dog into a more logical design composition.

(a) This quick sketch probably has too much action for a sustained sitting—a statement you are safe in making when referring to any little boy's posing.

(d) Here we have a quick abstract of the pattern.

The working drawing, opposite, could have been made on the final surface, but making this in Conte crayon and white gives us a chance to experiment, without getting too much charcoal dust and too many mistakes on the final surface. We also end up with an additional drawing. For the next step see overleaf.

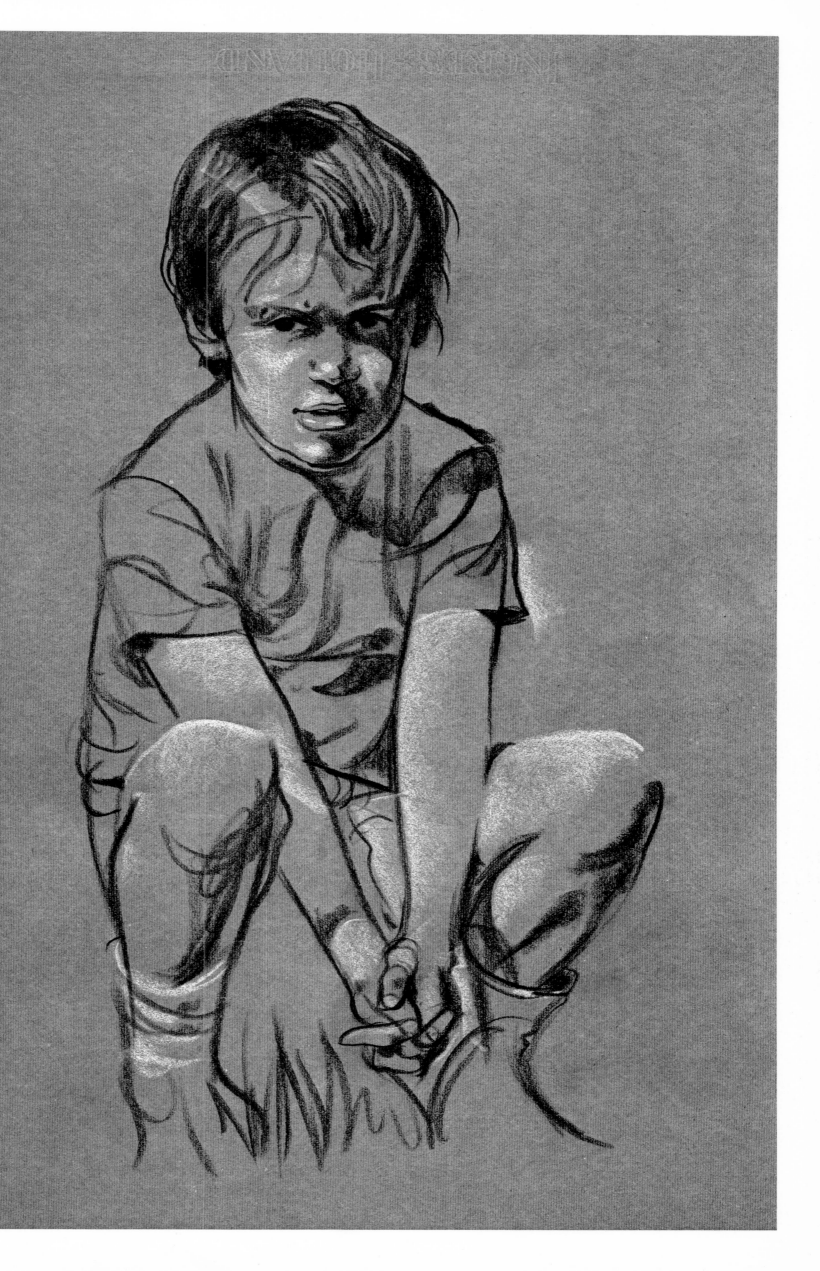

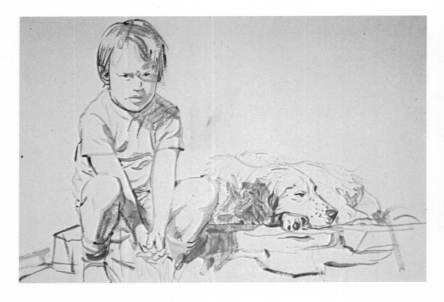

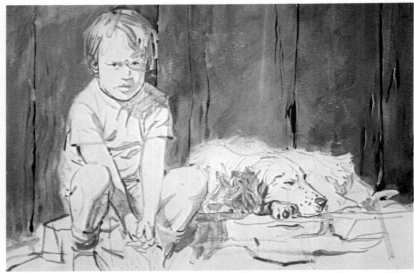

This oil portrait was painted on 300-pound d'Arches rough watercolor paper. Any good rag paper would have worked as well. The oil medium has little tendency to shrink or warp the paper, so it is unnecessary to moisten the surface, as it is in using watercolor. This is not to imply that moistening the paper surface with a mixture of turpentine and linseed oil is not an interesting and rather effective procedure, only that the process was not used in this painting. The brushes and techniques used throughout were the same as in watercolor.

1. First, the drawing was made in sepia and blue paint. Two colors were used as a simple means of isolating different areas of the painting.

2. The barn background was painted in full value. The boy originally was posed against a rather uninteresting background of a clapboard house. The rough boards of a barn seemed more in keeping with the theme of the painting. A few old boards were located and brought into the studio, and then, without benefit of the model, were painted into the composition. Young boys and dogs are singularly impatient models. Any time they can be relieved of the strain of sitting moderately quiet is to the advantage of all concerned.

When practical, it is an interesting experiment to mix what you consider to be the exact color of a specific, such as the barn board background, and then paint a spot on the actual surface. When this method is impractical, it is sometimes wise to paint a dab on a scrap of paper and match it against the subject.

COLOR DEMONSTRATION: OIL ON PAPER

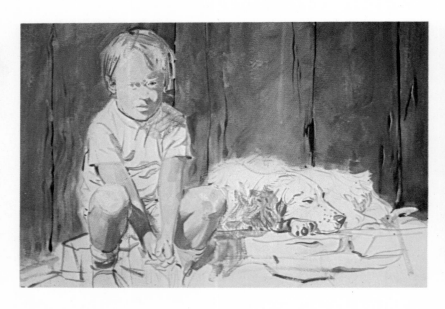

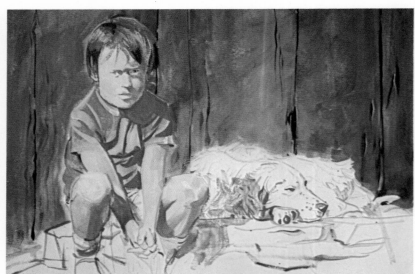

3. With direct strokes, the painting began with the hair and continued into the general tones of the skin. In a more intensive study, not employing an *alla prima* approach, this stage could first have been painted in its complementary colors, greens and blues, as against the predominate reds, oranges, and yellows in this area. In this painting, however, an attempt was made to put down the colors directly as they appeared. The complementary underpainting was used by the old masters. When properly done, with glaze after glaze, it can produce an effect of depth that the *alla prima* method might lack. The direct approach has vibrant qualities sometimes lacking in the less direct approach. It is less likely to look overworked.

4. The over-all color of the clothes and the general colors of the setter were also painted in direct painting. The brush strokes always followed the structure of the material. The strokes that went into making the shirt and its folds always followed the way the shirt hung. The strokes on the socks carried around the ankle, around the anatomy underneath. The strokes that indicated the fur on the setter followed the direction the fur lay. It becomes possible later to emphasize an area by using strokes in opposition to the natural direction. As an example, to paint the area of a highlight on the hair, use strokes in the opposite direction and then, over this, a few lines in the natural direction.

Opposite: The finished painting

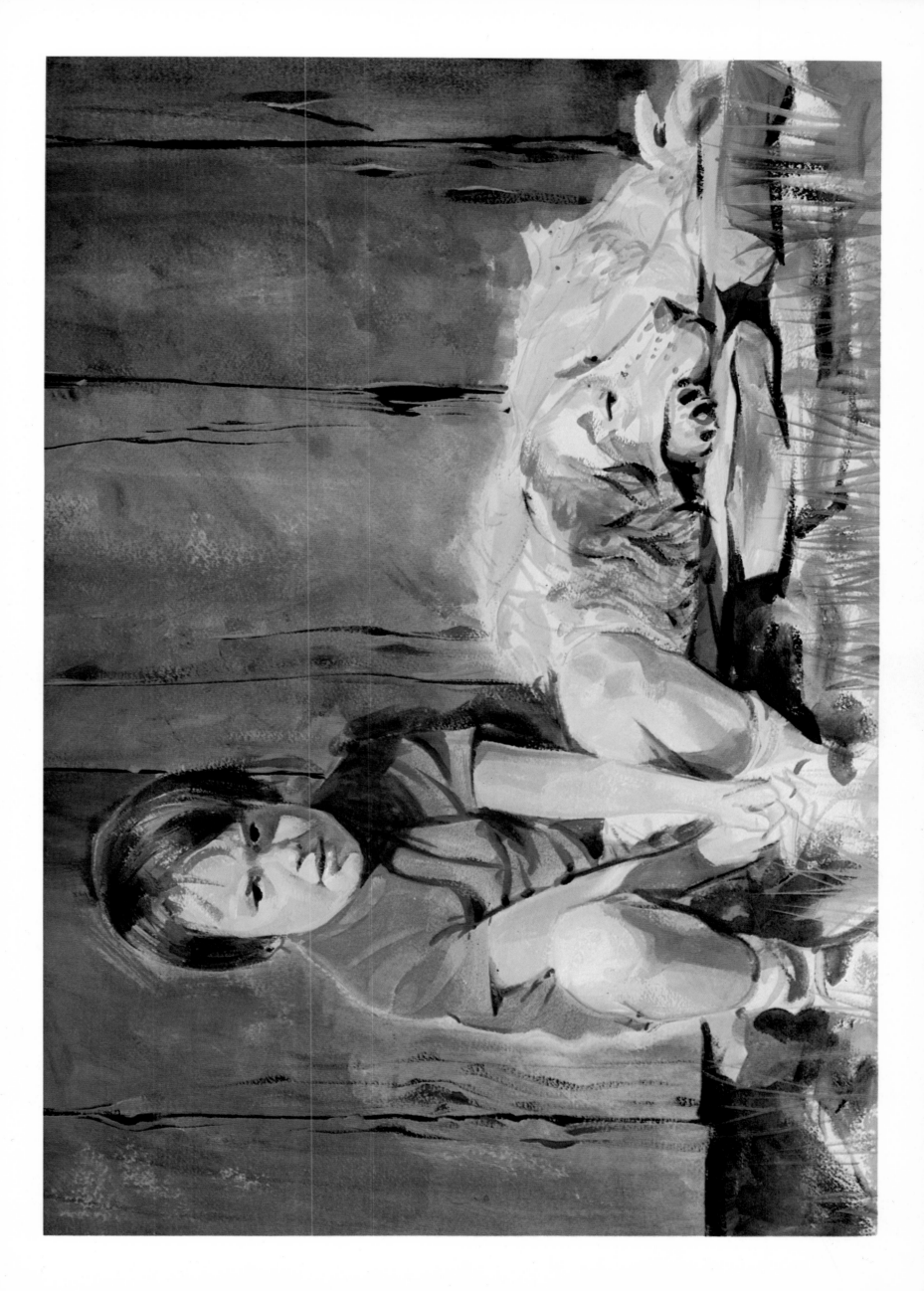

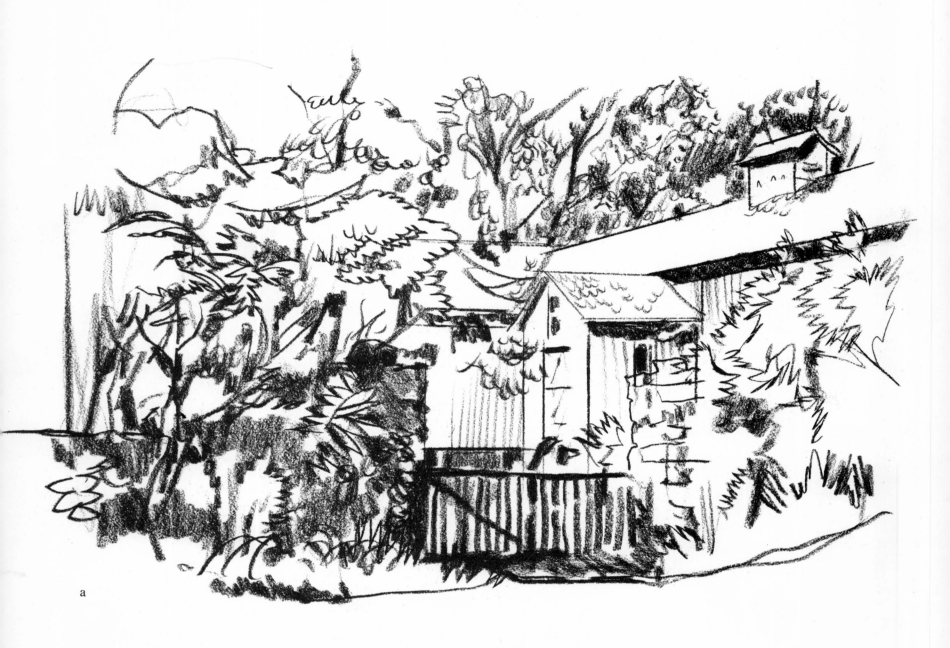

a

PREPARATION FOR A LANDSCAPE

A painter seldom paints exactly what he sees. Even the painter who seems to have reproduced every leaf in its place generally has rearranged the leaves to tell his own story.

My first impression of the barn (a) was of a mass of foliage hiding an unusual structure. Sketching it, I became involved with leaf forms and designs, to the point that the barn began to take second place in the composition.

In (b) I opened the gate to let the viewer walk into the picture more easily. I left no mystery about where the barn ended, and I even included a repeat motif of a little gate in the distance similar to the foreground gate.

Drawing from the same spot, I proceeded to (c). I used the solid stone wall as a foil or frame for the barnyard scene.

It is excellent practice to sketch many compositions from one spot. It is also excellent practice to paint the same spot at many different times of the day.

On pages 102 and 103 is a color demonstration of the barn shown in sketch form here. In it, colors were used as they appear in life, as was best remembered, for the picture was painted in the studio. This is a poor procedure, except in this case of a simple procedural demonstration. It would be far better to experiment with many color combinations. The barn could be any of a number of colors. It could be subdued, with some action going on in the barnyard. It would probably be best as a kind of stage set for a storytelling picture.

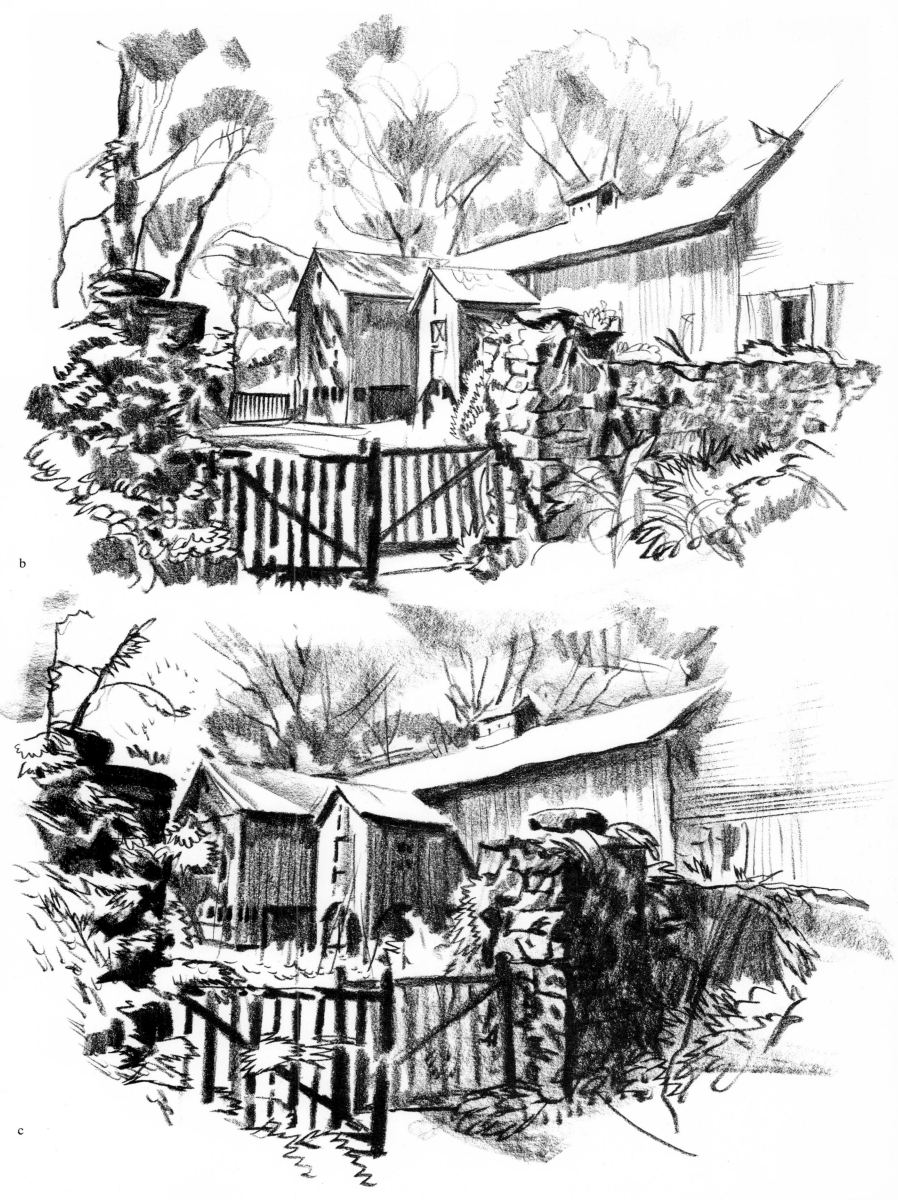

b

c

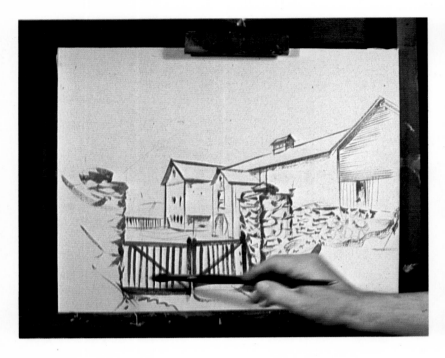

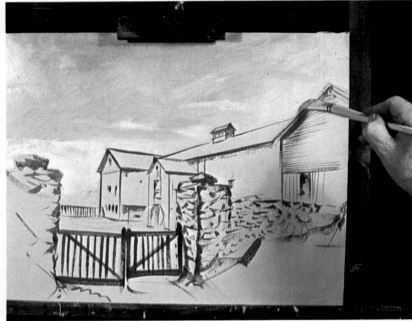

1. This demonstration sketch was painted on stretched canvas. The procedure used, one of many possible approaches, was that of working from distant to foreground planes and objects. First, the anatomy of the painting is drawn in a single color mixed to a thin consistency with turpentine.

2. The sky area is scumbled in, rather thinly, the paint mixed, once again with more turpentine than normally used, to facilitate drying. For a more responsive feel in the application of the paint, use linseed oil mixed with the color. In opaque techniques in oil, about ten times as much white is consumed as any other color. However, a heavy impasto effect at this stage could cause trouble in the next steps.

COLOR DEMONSTRATION: OIL LANDSCAPE

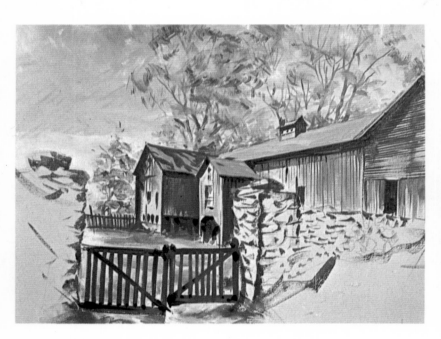

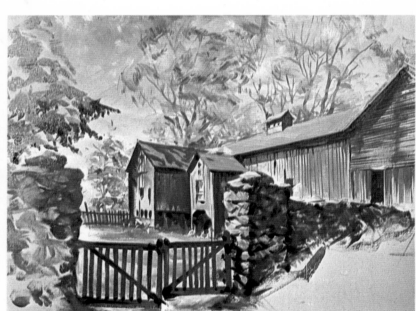

5. The fence is painted over the barnyard foreground. It makes a more inviting picture to have an opened fence.

6. The foreground mass of stone fence and brush is painted in the most contrasting tones so far, in an effort to push the rest of the painting back where it belongs. It becomes obvious that we will need a great deal of weight to accomplish this.

If this were being done in watercolor, now would be a time for a single tone washed over the foreground area. To use a transparent glaze in oil, it would be necessary to wait until the underpaint had dried.

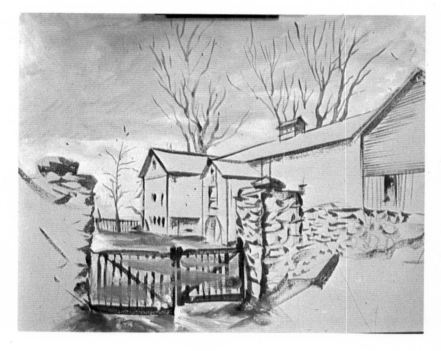

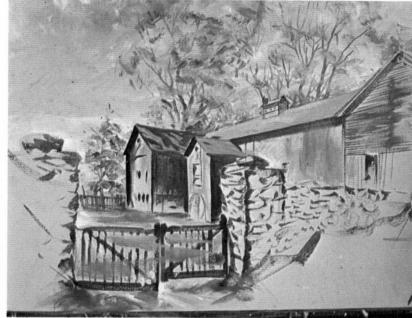

3. The tones and colors of the middle distance, the barnyard and the barns, are indicated. These are not done in a flat, single color mixed with white, but in a multitude of colors, even complements, usually evident in weatherworn surfaces. The branches of the background trees are placed behind the barn roof.

4. The foliage on the background trees is scumbled in. The roof is added. Shadows on the roof begin to give a feeling of form. The major shadows on the barn are painted in warm tones. A few details, barn siding and windows, are underpainted in experimental tones. These colors may be modified as we proceed.

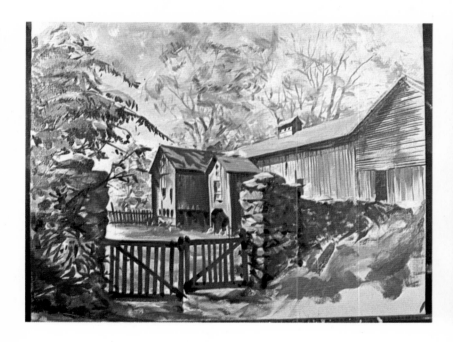

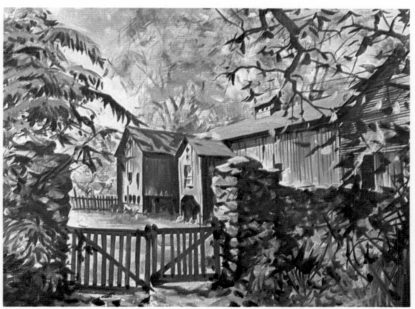

7. Using a direct wet-in-wet technique, it is possible to increase the value of the foreground tones.

8. The final elements in the painting—branches and leaves, painted directly over sky, barn, and stone wall—bring the painting to a finish.

103

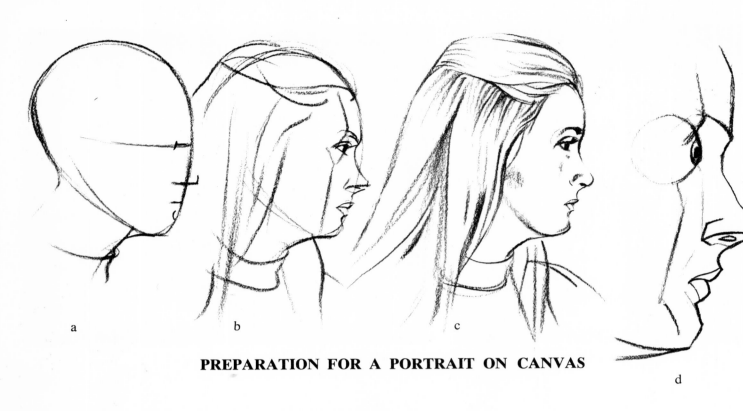

a   b   c

d

e

PREPARATION FOR A PORTRAIT ON CANVAS

In portraiture, the character and the personality of the subject must shine through the more mechanical painting of the features. However, before even a competent portraitist takes on an oil portrait commission, he must have a working knowledge of his subject's features. True, a highly accomplished artist might dash off a portrait with little or no preliminary study. His preliminary work has been in his years of experience.

In the sketches above, the progressive steps in the thinking of the artist are illustrated.

(a) He starts with the simple shape.

(b) He adds the features.

(c) He refines the sketch.

(d) A detail of blocking the features.

(e) A detail of refining the features.

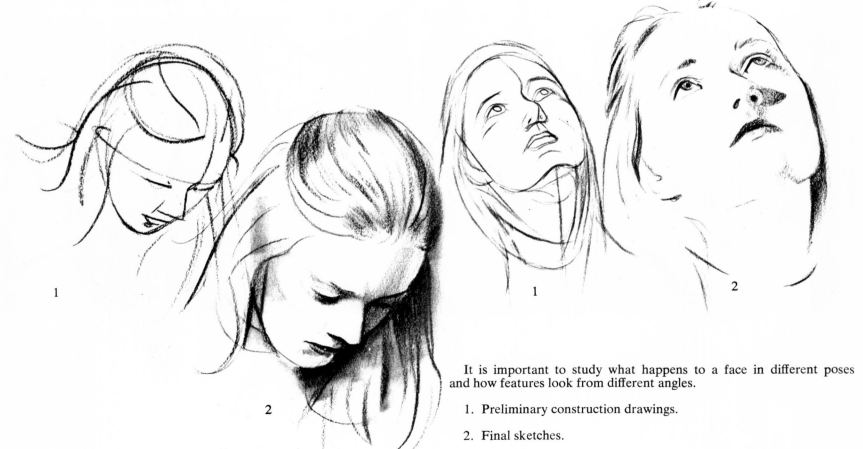

1   2   1   2

It is important to study what happens to a face in different poses and how features look from different angles.

1. Preliminary construction drawings.

2. Final sketches.

Immediately below are stages in a straight, run-of-the-mill pose.

(a) Blocking the head.

(b) Making a tonal pattern.

(c) A study of the structure of the features.

(d) The combination of all.

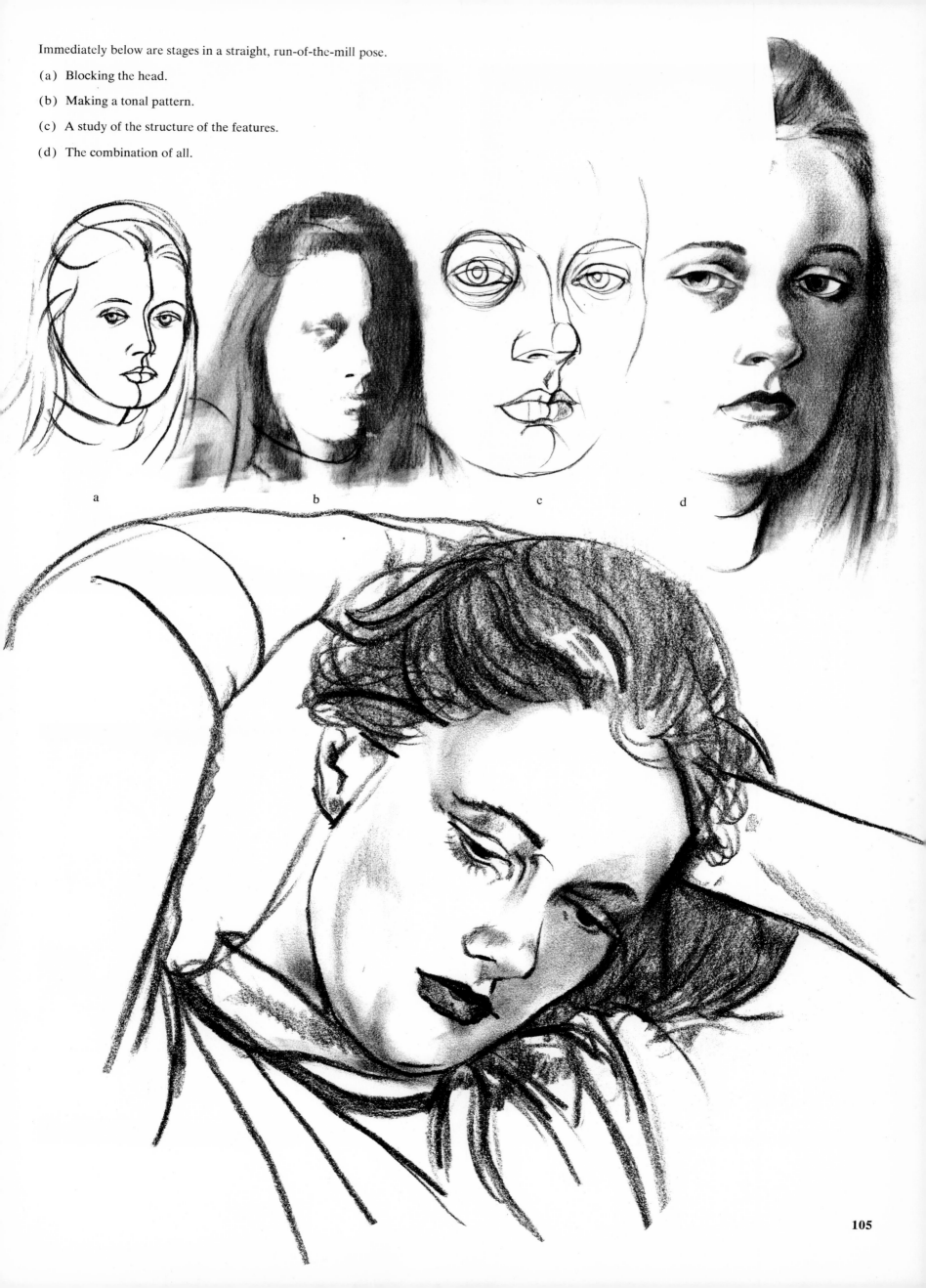

a   b   c   d

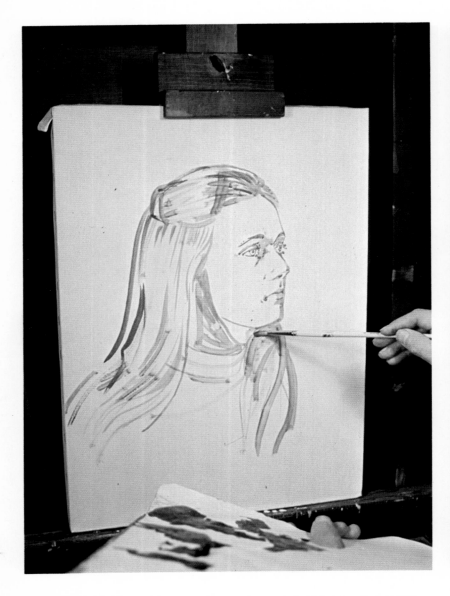

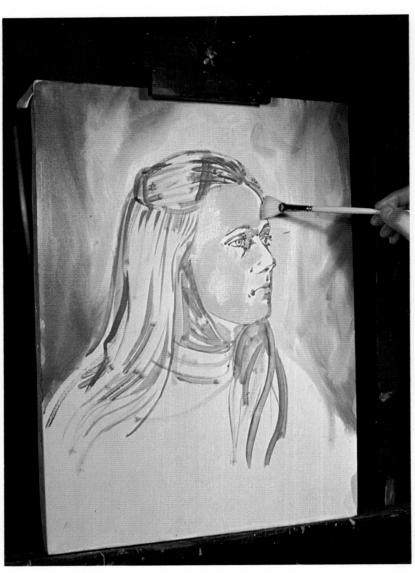

1. For demonstration purposes, I am using the simplest pose. Here, the head is positioned on the canvas. The knowledge gained in sketching the subject begins to pay off.

2. The background is brushed in. The general face color is roughly scumbled in. Here I use a fan-shaped blending brush to soften and blend colors, one into the next.

COLOR DEMONSTRATIONS:

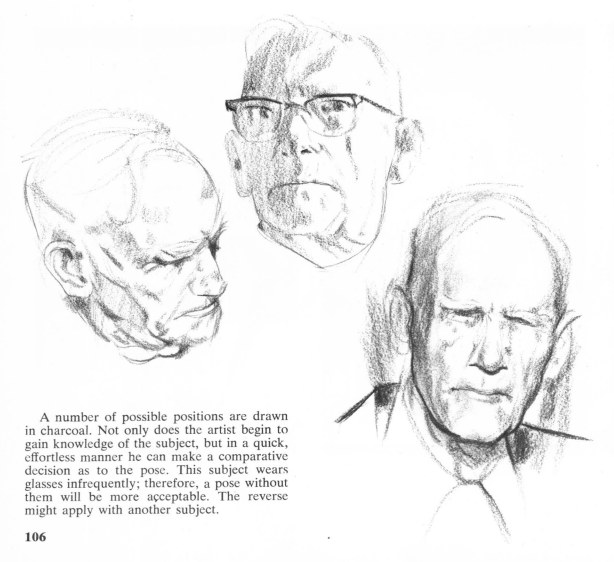

A number of possible positions are drawn in charcoal. Not only does the artist begin to gain knowledge of the subject, but in a quick, effortless manner he can make a comparative decision as to the pose. This subject wears glasses infrequently; therefore, a pose without them will be more acceptable. The reverse might apply with another subject.

1. The quick sketch, using color thinned with turpentine. Hold the brush far from the ferrule to get the action in the pose that comes with a free approach.

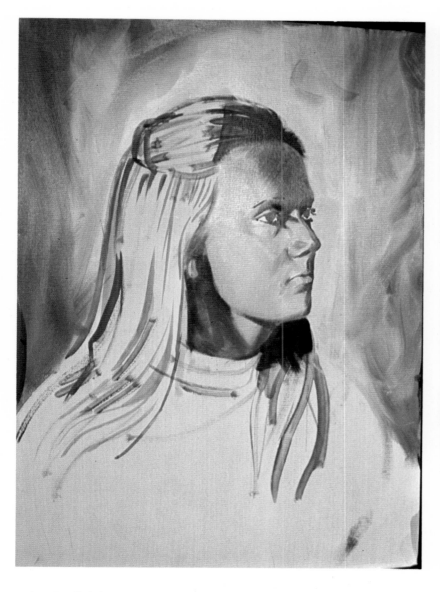
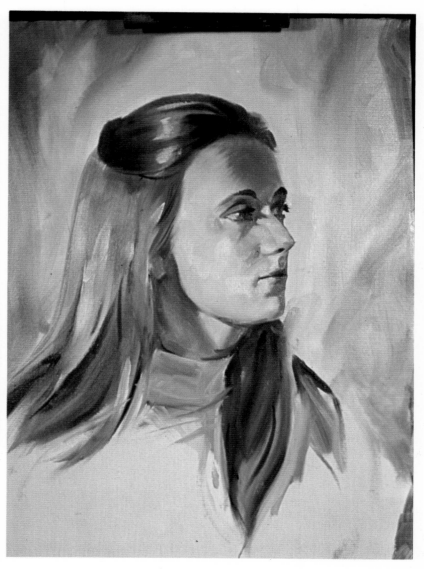

3. The lighting chosen in this instance calls for two major tones, one for the light areas and one for the shadow or darker areas. Having a single source of light makes the painting quite simple.

4. Within the basic tones, introduce the details of the face. If possible, stop before you get so detailed that you destroy the likeness. This can easily happen.

TWO PORTRAITS ON CANVAS

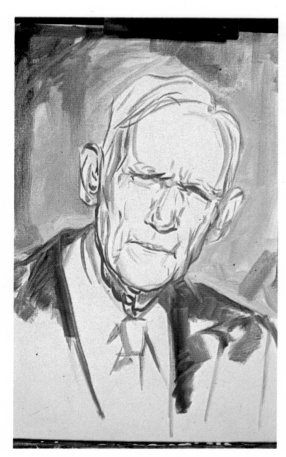
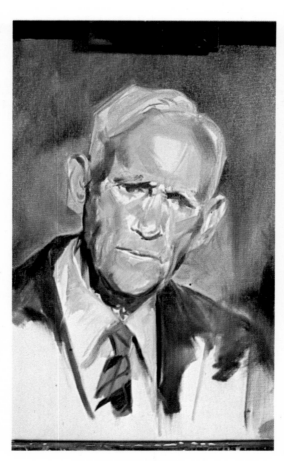
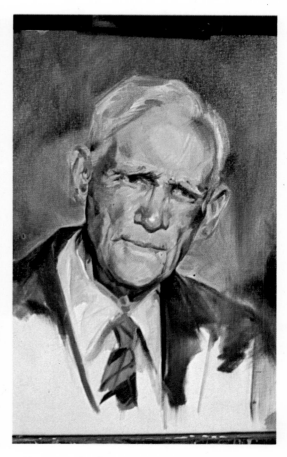

2. The background and the accents of depth. The subject is an elderly man, so there is no concern about lines in his face. The approach, even in the brush strokes, can be considerably more vigorous than in the painting of the girl.

3. The general facial colors are painted in strong strokes with as large a brush as practical. The eyes are indicated by dabbing paint from the tip of the finger.

4. Here the final details, deeper tones in the shadows, the refinements around the mouth and the nose. In a man's portrait, blues may appear where the man has shaved. In a woman's portrait, if blue is indicated, don't use it. It will look as if she had just shaved.

CHARACTER STUDY

The drawing of the old man filing the buzz saw will, in the next few pages, evolve into a display of oil technique. The demonstration is important for a deeper reason. An artist must have knowledge of his subject, must be able to see beneath the surface and understand. He comes to the understanding through past experience, observation, and listening.

The old man was working on a partially disassembled saw. As he filed each tooth, with a sure, definite kind of grace, he talked. His father had built the barn that now stood in ruins, awaiting a present-day salvager of the hand-hewn beams. The beams would be part of a modern house. The scrap wood would become food for the fireplace. He would, with his ancient blade, cut this into proper fireplace lengths.

The old man's single, greatest excursion had been many years ago, to the big town a few miles away. The man's gnarled hands held the blade firmly. The least slip would mean a badly cut set of fingers. His old eyes were intent on the file and the tooth being filed. The artist must catch this feeling. Sometimes a great compliment is paid the artist by a non-art critic who later, seeing the painting, says, "Harry sure can file a saw!"

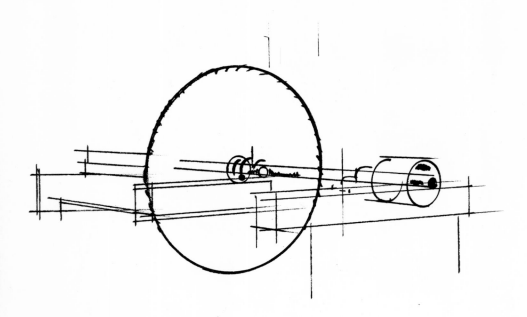

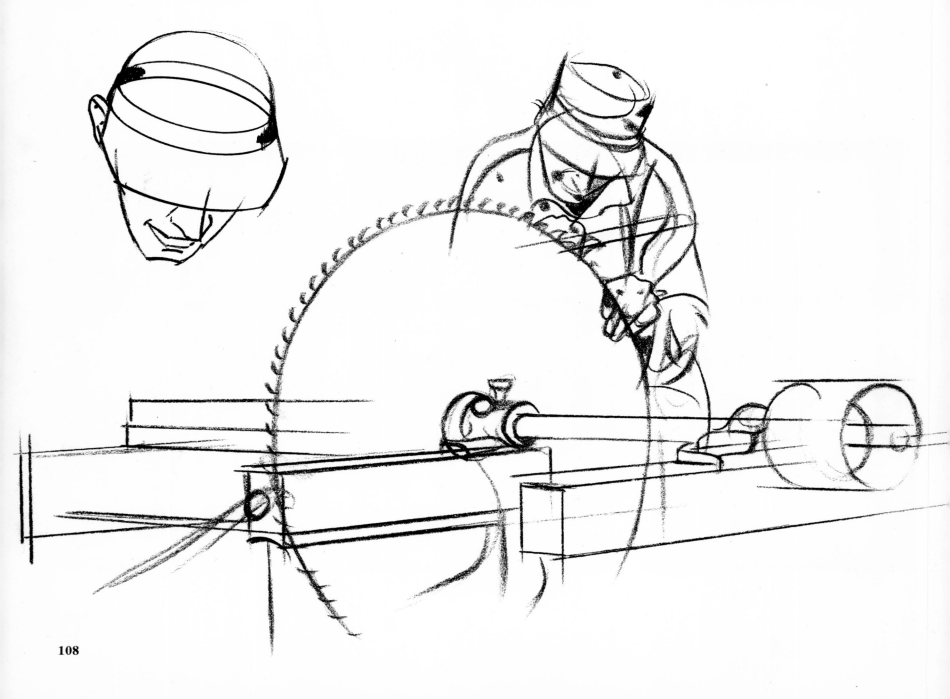

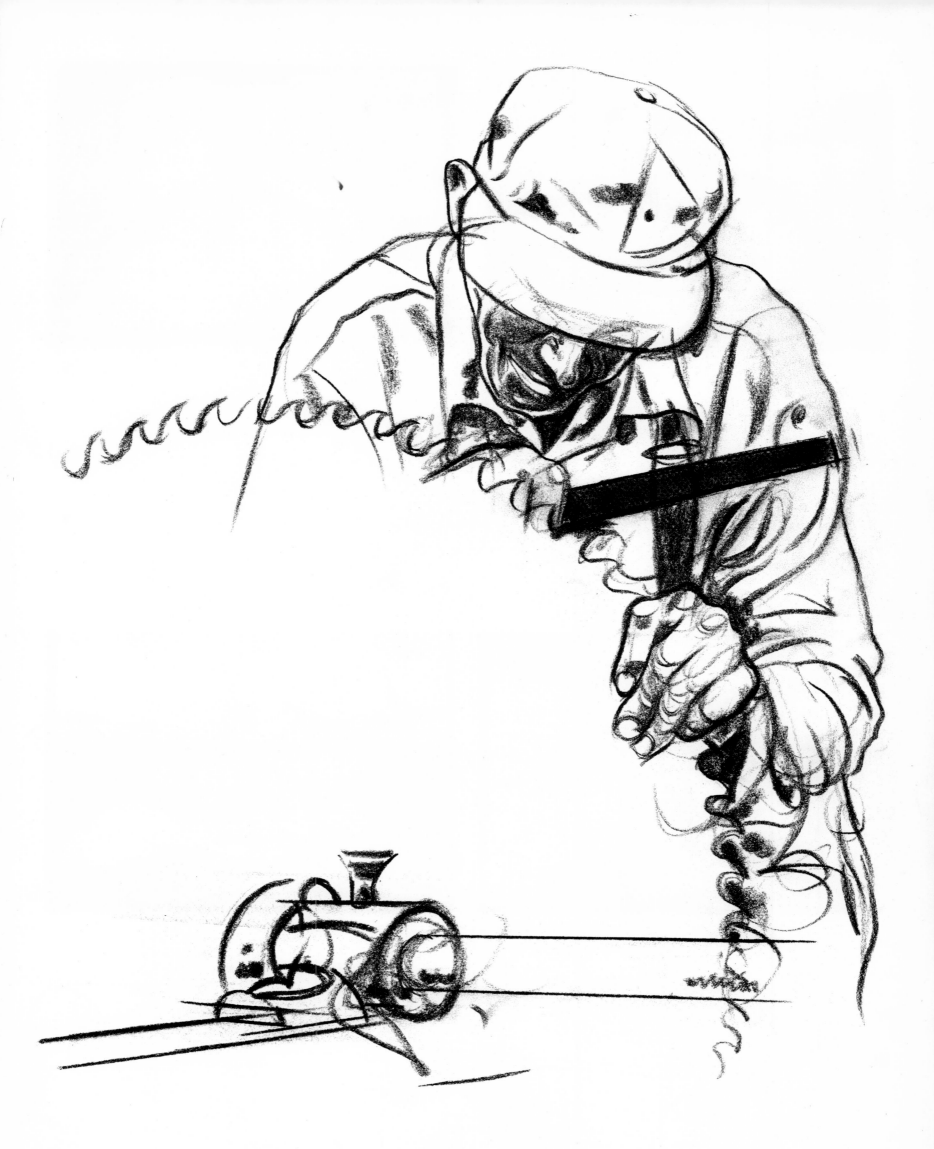

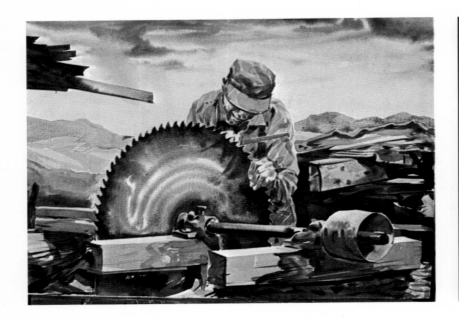

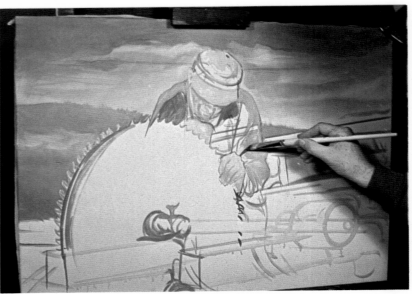

1. Some time prior to this oil demonstration I had painted the subject in watercolor for the Bank of Cattaraugus. It seemed an interesting experiment to finish this oil and then compare the two. The owners of the watercolor gave permission. It is reproduced above.

2. To begin the painting in oil, the sketch was made on the stretched canvas. The broad background of sky was quickly brushed in. It is wise to work with as large a brush as possible to avoid any temptation to do details at this stage.

COLOR DEMONSTRATION: OIL

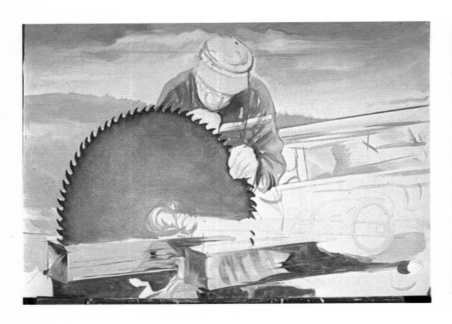

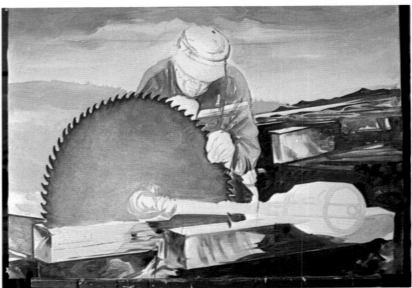

5. The beginning painting on the structure that holds the blades is carefully done. In oil, we may be cautious in our application of paint. The reproduction may seem faded. It is because, for this demonstration, I used mainly turpentine as the medium to facilitate drying.

6. The deep shadows and the forms within the shadows are painted. With the knowledge that oil may be used as an opaque medium, the shadow areas may be painted first. The light areas and the highlights may then be superimposed over the darks.

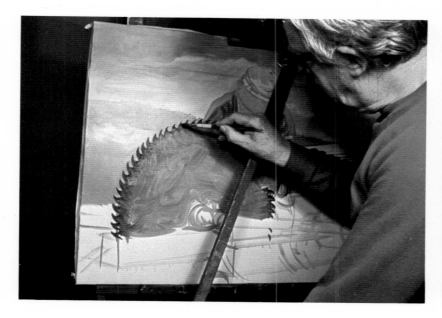

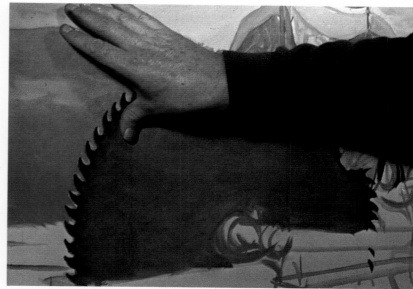

3. The saw blade had been carefully constructed in the drawing. I filled in the area with a combination of colors. When these colors were later blended, they produced a neutral color with greater vibrancy than any premixed color. I am using a maulstick (a stick used as a rest for the arm and hand to avoid touching the wet canvas).

4. Here I am using my thumb to blend the wet oil paint into an interesting all-over tone. Oil paint is singularly adapted to this technique. Used in combination with definite lineal pattern, it can be very effective. Another method is to use a rag instead of the thumb, but the latter is usually more effective.

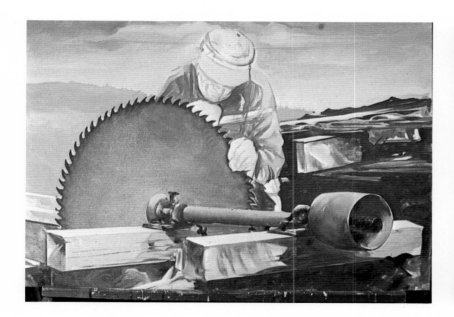

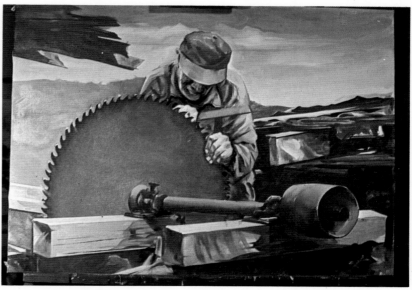

7. The light tones of the wooden structure are painted over the darker tones. The shaft, as well as the remainder of the hardware, was layed in.

8. Finally the figure and other refinements, such as highlights on the just-filed teeth, are painted. At this stage I felt the painting still needed an element in the upper left-hand corner. I put it in.

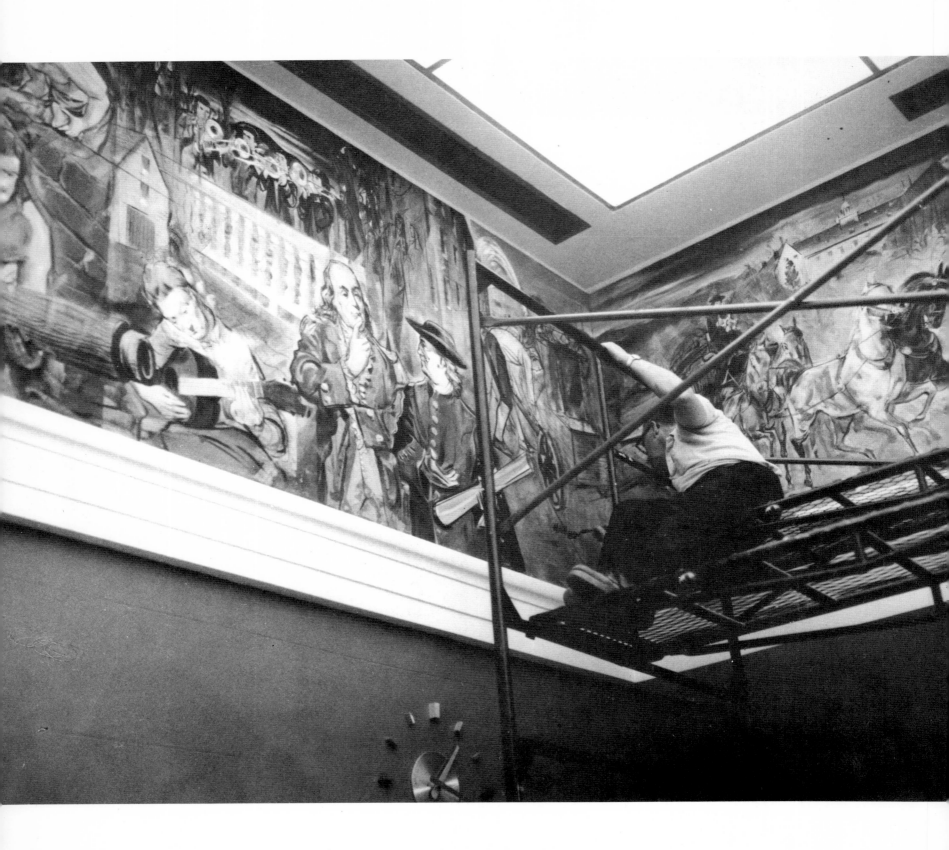

Mural, painted in acrylic for The First National Bank of Bethlehem, Pennsylvania

ACRYLICS

In the art world the advent of plastic paints was revolutionary. From the individual artist's standpoint, the plastic medium is noteworthy because of the versatility in its use. The approach may be that of the transparent watercolorist, the oil painter, or the painter in quick-drying opaques. At first glance, and even upon close examination, the plastic medium seems to overcome all the built-in disadvantages of the more traditional media.

Plastic paints may be mixed effectively with oil, water, or its own medium. This plastic medium is available in either a high gloss or a matte finish. Derived originally from advanced technology in determining permanent color, a complete assortment of colors was developed. They seem to overcome the serious artist's problems in both the water color or oil media. Only experimentation in the traditional media, however, can give the student a true appreciation of the acrylic's possibilities.

Although it is often difficult to distinguish between a watercolor and an acrylic done in a watercolor technique, there is a difference. The student should become familiar with watercolor before attempting acrylics. The artist well grounded in oils will find himself at home in the plastic medium. A problem with normal oil painting is the instability of the vehicle, linseed oil, which, in drying, turns from the liquid to a solid state, eventually forming an entirely different chemical compound. Even when dry, the plastic medium remains exactly what it was in the beginning.

The ability of the plastic medium to simulate the traditional media of watercolor, oil, tempera, or fresco, is of less importance than the plastics' own unique qualities. In heavy impasto applications it does not crack or peel. It is remarkably flexible. A painting may be rolled tightly without danger of cracking. Thin applications may be applied in one glaze over the next. Applications of plastic varnish may be sprayed, brushed, or rolled over completed areas in progress, isolating one from the next. There is not the constant annoyance, as in oil paints, of waiting for long periods of drying. These characteristics allow the artist a spontaneous approach to a degree seldom possible in many oil techniques. It is every bit as direct as transparent watercolor.

The medium itself may be used as clear adhesive in creating a collage. The surfaces to which it will adhere are more numerous than both oil and watercolor combined.

Plastic paints are well suited to resisting the elements. They work well for both indoor and outdoor murals.

Coming into the world of acrylics is best done first through the use of the other media. Only on this road can one quickly appreciate the possibilities and, yes, the limitations.

There are limitations. It is essentially a studio medium, difficult to use out of doors. It dries to a hard substance in the average time taken to complete an outdoor painting. This fault can be minimized by keeping the paint palette covered with a layer of pliofilm, but this is, at best, an annoyance. Because of its tremendous adhesive qualities, it plays havoc with clothes and working surfaces, along with the floor, walls, or ceiling. The greatest disadvantage in the hands of the devil-may-care artist is the high mortality rate of good brushes. When paint is allowed to harden in the brush, that's about the end of the brush. If the ruined brush is left in vinegar, at least partial use of it may be recovered.

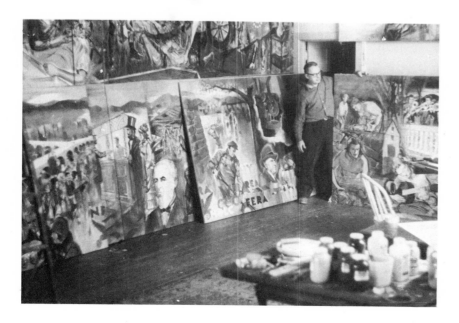

All of the procedures shown in both the watercolor and the oil sections work well with acrylics, the most versatile of the three mediums.

The sketch for painting *Beach at Sanibel* was made on a toned surface. The brilliant bleached driftwood is the first thing to catch the eye. The sunstruck areas of the driftwood were laid in first. It was then possible to continue working into the darker tones. This approach, though possible, is more difficult than working from dark to light.

TECHNIQUES

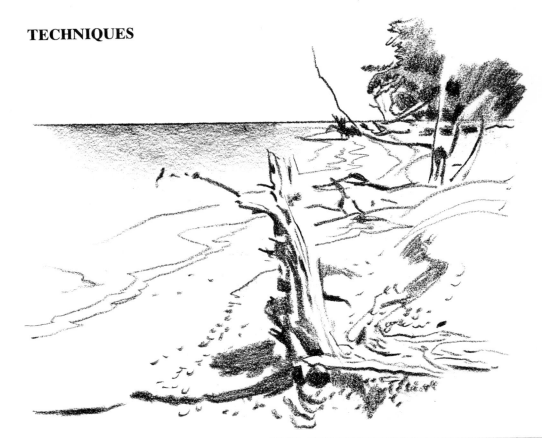

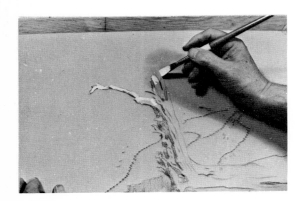

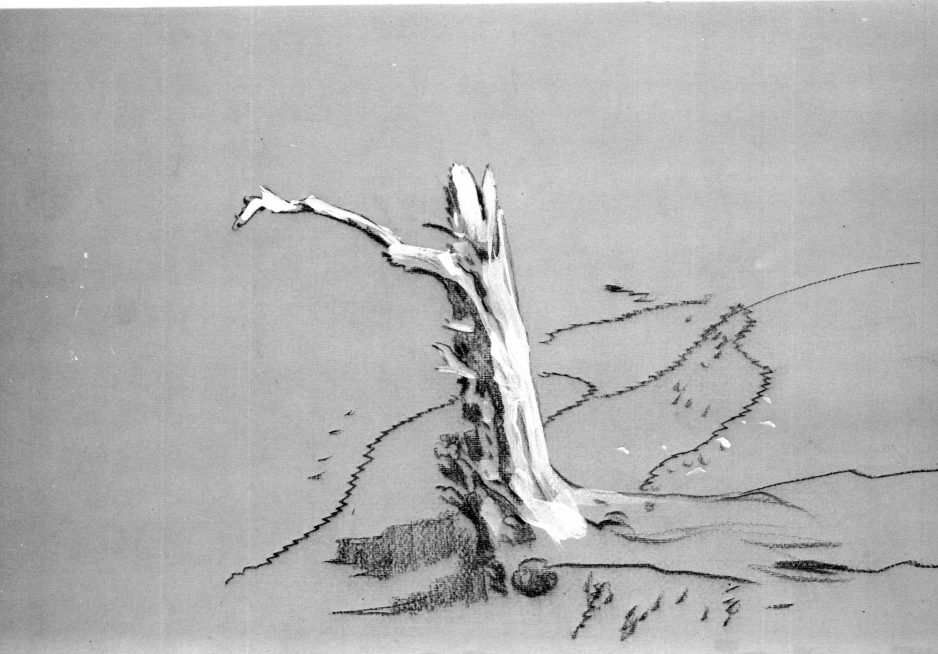

A more orthodox approach to the painting on the preceding page is shown here.

(1) A piece of tape is first placed to frisket the horizon line. If the sky is painted, you must wait until it dries. A brush called a "round" is used here.

(2) An inexpensive ox hair chisel brush adds the sandy shore.

(3) Back to the round brush for detail.

(4) Use a finger to smudge in an area.

(5) Removing the tape reveals the even horizon line.

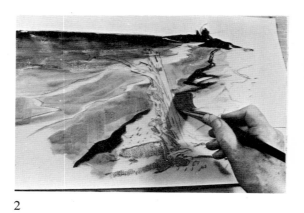

2

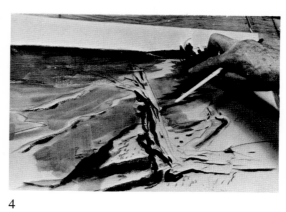

4

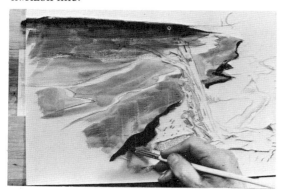

1

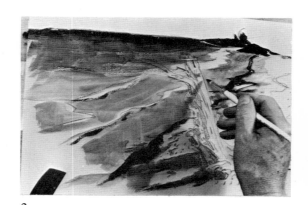

3

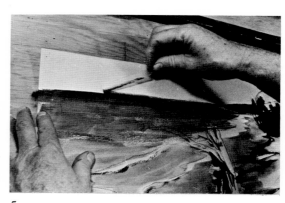

5

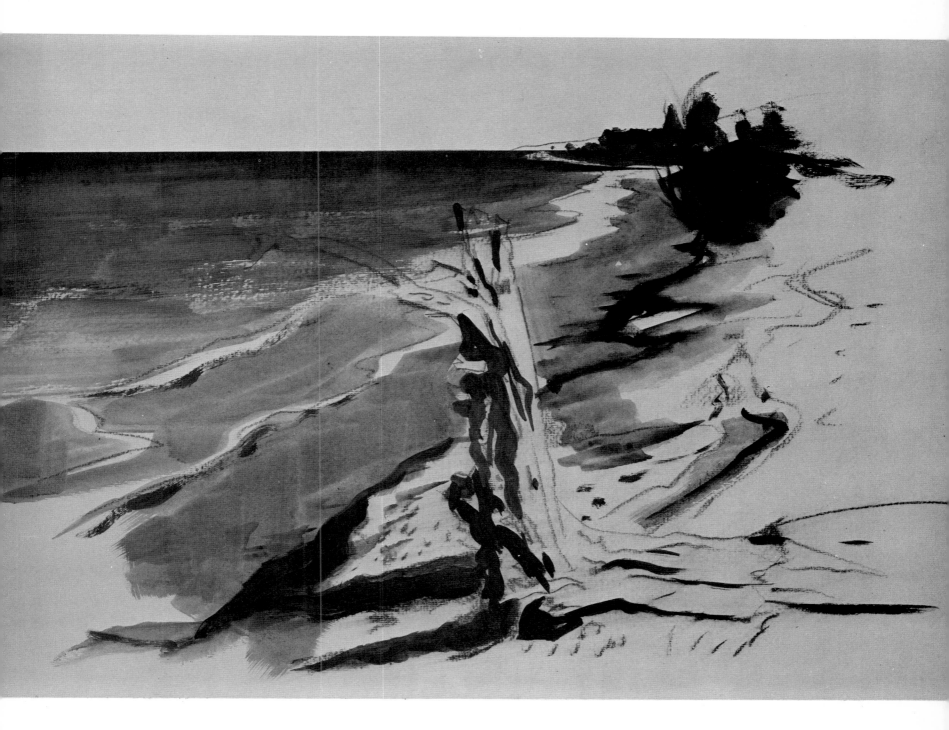

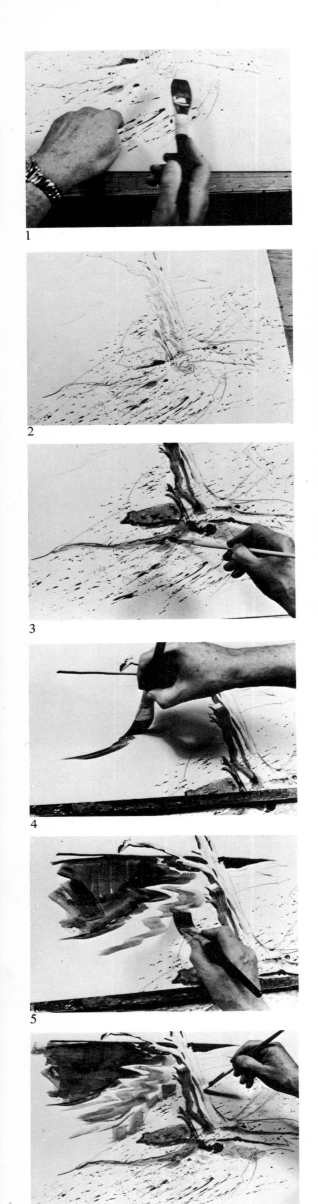

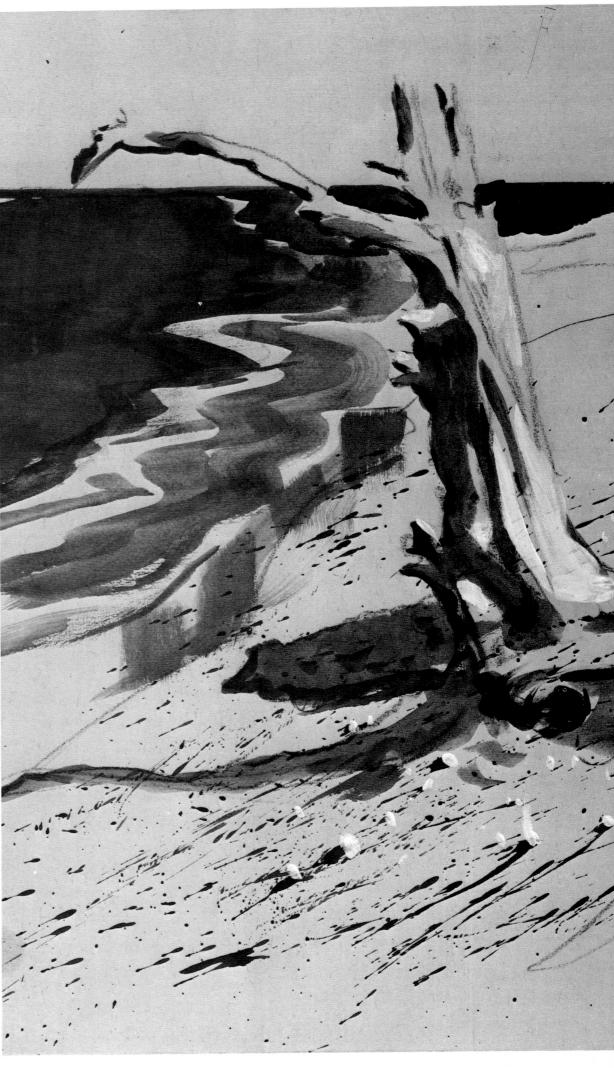

1

2

3

4

5

6

Every so often, tricks can be used effectively. Here, the splatter approach, used by some abstract expressionists, is employed in a realistic acrylic painting of a similar subject to the two previous examples.

(1) Slap a brush filled with liquid paint against the finger to produce the shadows of the beach debris.

(2) It will splatter in many-sized dots in a pattern that will give the effect of directional shadows.

(3), (4), and (5) Paint the major areas much as shown on the preceding page.

(6) Paint in the light sections, including the sun-bleached shells and tidal deposits on the beach.

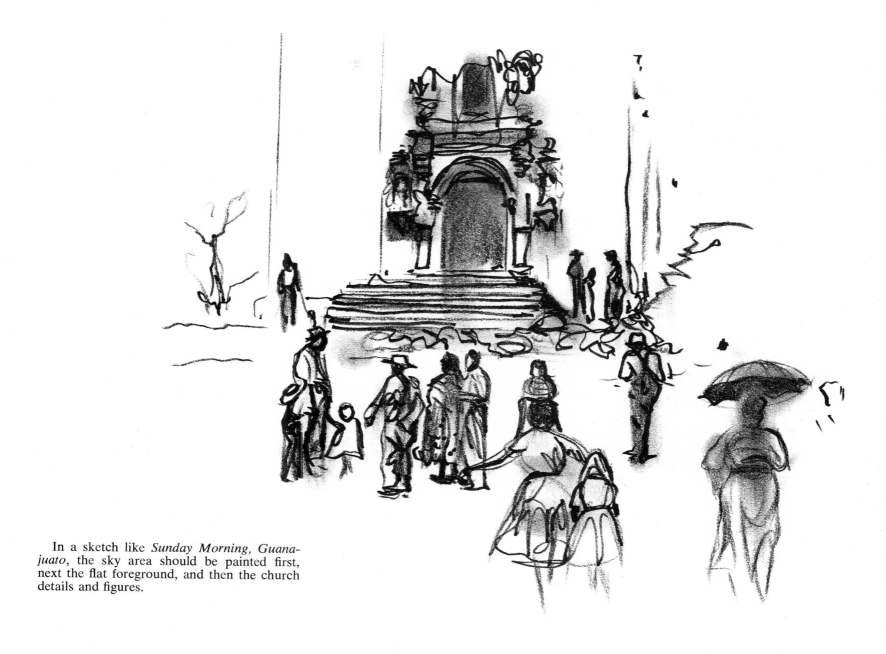

In a sketch like *Sunday Morning, Guana-juato*, the sky area should be painted first, next the flat foreground, and then the church details and figures.

In the sketch *East London*, there are an unlimited number of possible approaches in technique. Try using a subject like this in a variety of finishes.

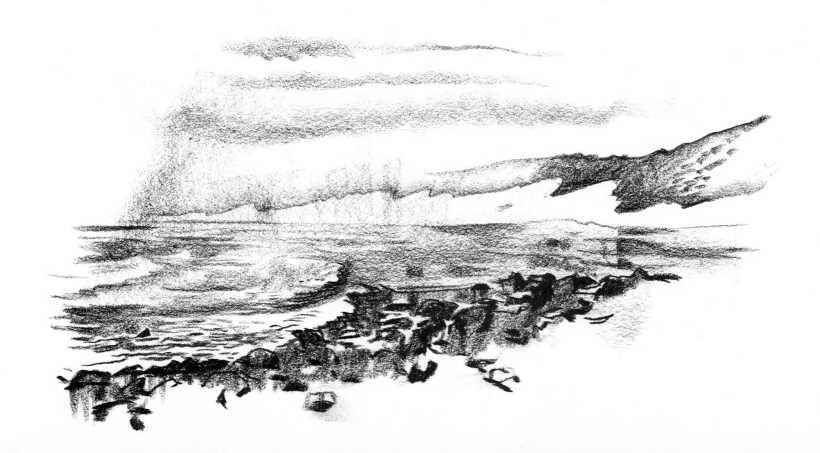

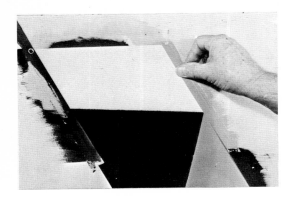

(1) Use a tape to control the edge of any tone you may be using.

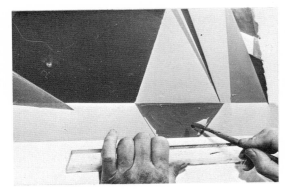

(2) Paint a tone with liquid paint and a brush,

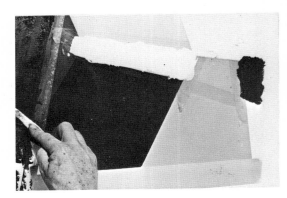

(3) Or apply a tone with heavier paint and a palette knife.

While acrylic paints can make fine flat tones, they are also excellent for achieving a textured surface.

**HARD-EDGE
TECHNIQUES**

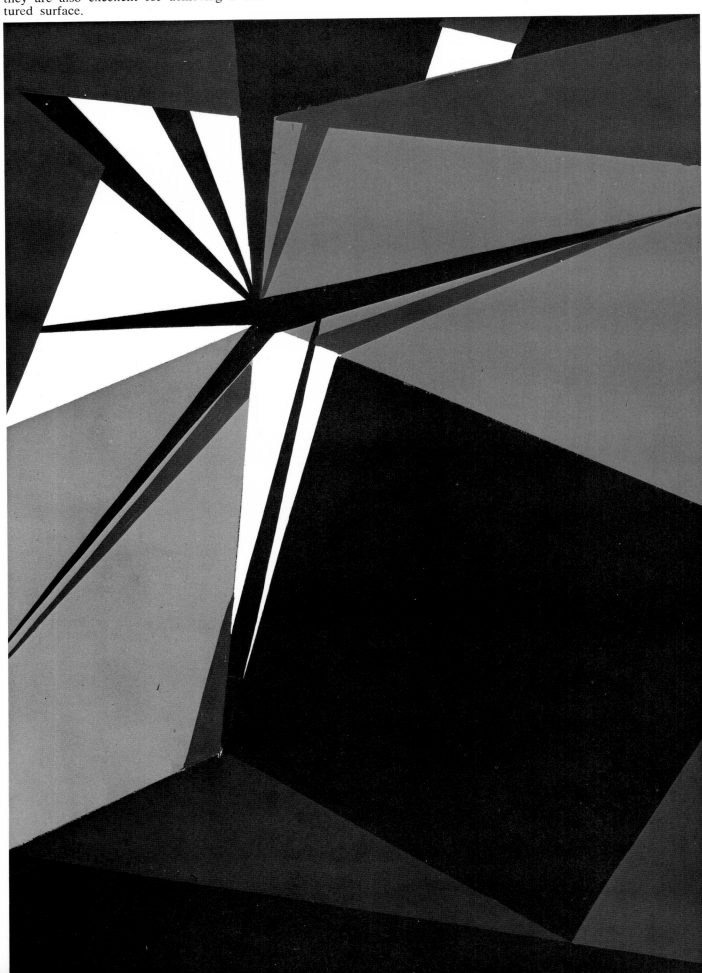

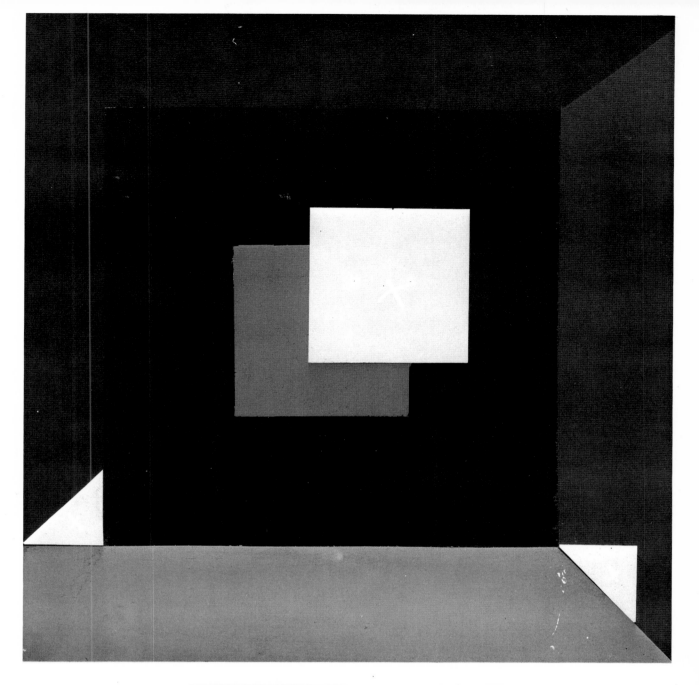

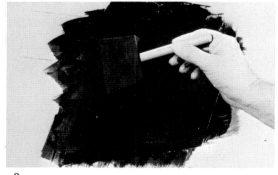

a

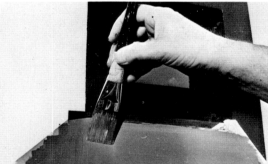

b

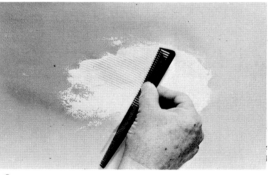

c

To produce granular surfaces, foreign substances such as marble dust or sand can be dropped into the wet acrylic paint (or into oil paint, for that matter, when working with oil). Be sure your additives are fairly inert,

unless you want mold to grow or the sawdust to drop off.

(a) A urethane foam spatula helps to create a flat, even tone.

(b) A wide sable brush used with easy,

even strokes also gives a uniformly flat surface.

(c) When the paint is appled in heavy impasto, textured effects can be added while the paint is wet with most any object at hand, such as a comb or a piece of screening.

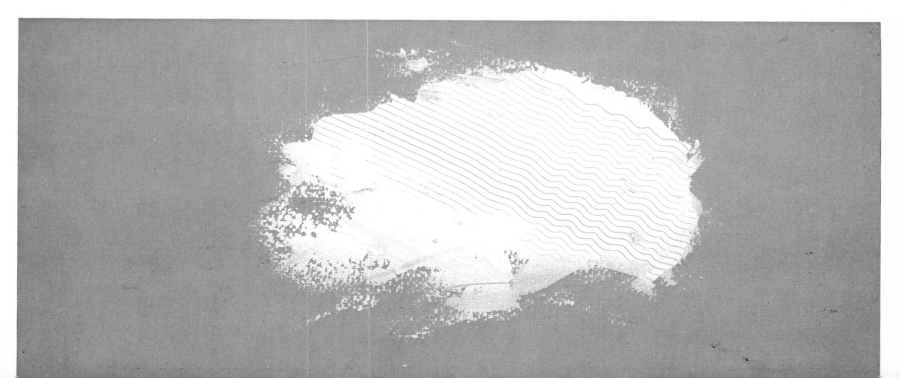

COLLAGES

(1) It is possible to create collages by painting pieces of paper in any number of colors, cutting or tearing them into desired shapes, and then adhering them to a surface with the acrylic medium. One of the qualities of the medium is that it acts as an adhesive as well as a varnish.

(2) The mottled look shows the milky appearance of the medium in a liquid state. Later, when it dries, it becomes completely transparent. Interesting effects can be achieved by using colored tissues in this way. By applying one color over another, liberally brushing the surface with the acrylic medium, the underneath colors can be seen through the transparent tissue.

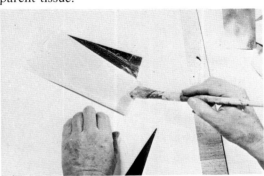

1

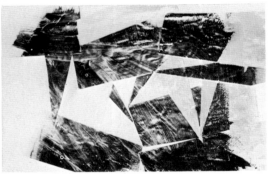

2

Acrylic modeling pastes are available. Added to the paint, they become an extender in fuller-bodied work. They offer an economical method of creating textures in relief or heavy impasto. The relief, once dry, may be painted to any color one likes.

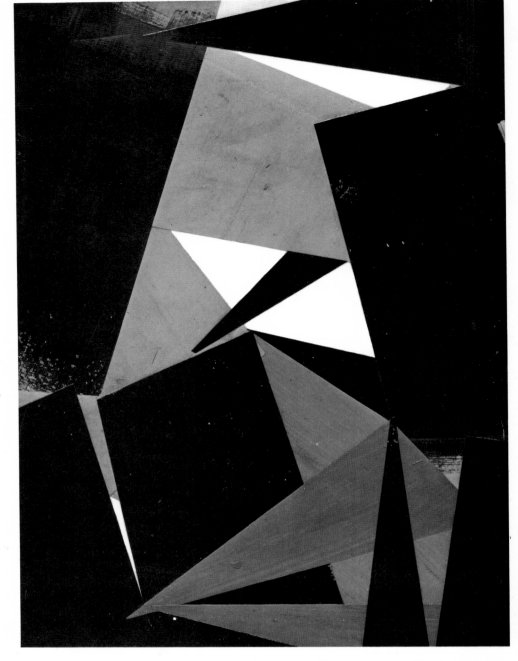

(a) Acrylic can be the basis of designs in bas relief. It is best to limit the thickness to about ⅛ inch to facilitate drying.

(b) Extremely deep reliefs must be built up in layers, with time for drying between applications—otherwise, the difference in drying time will cause cracks. This is important.

(c) The paste may be used much like plaster, but when dry it is considerably more durable and less likely to crack.

(d) Once dry, the paste may be sanded, sawed, carved, or chiseled.

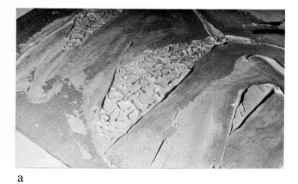

a

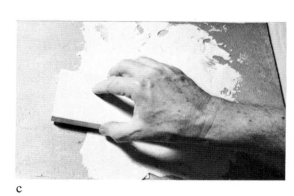

c

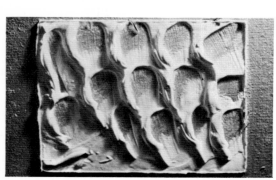

b

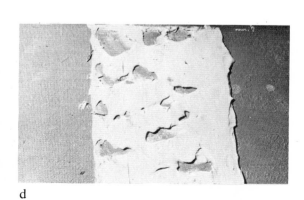

d

Opposite page:

PAINTING ON TRANSPARENT SURFACES

Acrylics may be painted on plastic materials such as acetate, Lucite, or plexiglass. Mixed with water, they do not adhere well, but mixed with the acrylic medium, they do. It is possible to use their transparent characteristics to create works that can be viewed with light coming through in much the same manner as a stained-glass window.

In the half-finished ballet sketch on the opposite page, the colors were separated with strips of black opaque tape. Once the work is finished, it may be sandwiched between sheets of rigid plastic to create an almost unbreakable panel.

120

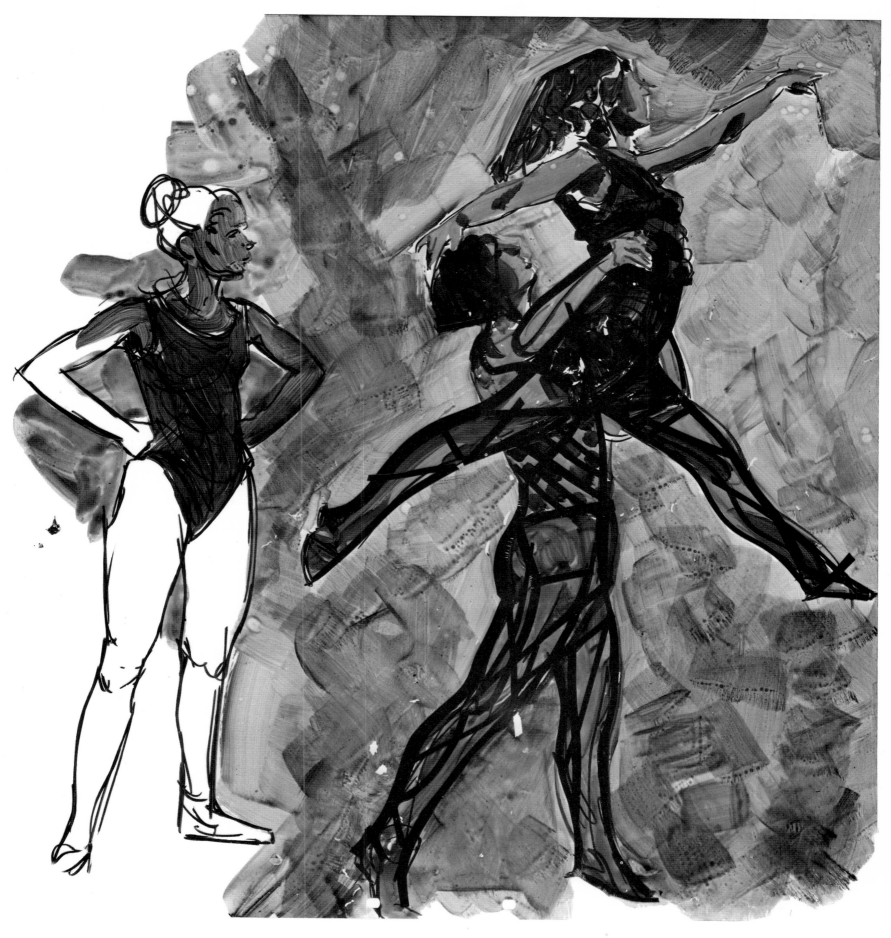

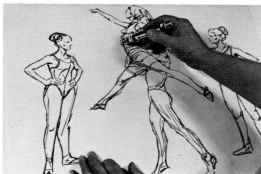

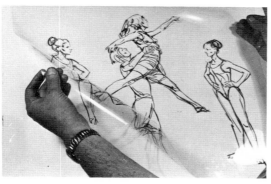

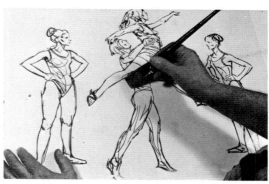

(1) First the sketch is traced or drawn on the back of a sheet of acetate or other transparent surface. A felt pen works well and was used for this demonstration.

(2) Then the drawing is flopped so that a clean surface is ready for the paint. The drawing can be sponged off the back when it has served its purpose as a guide for the painting.

(3) It is possible to paint over a glass surface with light coming through, or to use a light box, to get an even distribution of paint thickness.

MURAL IN ACRYLIC

A mural, by definition, is a painting on, in, or for a wall, and, by extension, for a ceiling as well. A mural is not just a large painting. It must be a part of a building, in one way or another. It need not, of course, be done with acrylic; it may be done with oil or tempera. A muralist has an entirely new set of problems, many of which have little relation to the normal set of vexations peculiar to painting. First, unless he owns the building, he is faced with the problem of pleasing people who have little idea of what they want, but definite ideas of what they do not want.

Second, he is faced with a circumstance usually beyond his control: the surface to be covered, and the practical problem of getting the mural onto the surface to stay, despite all attempts of the elements, vandals, and critics to remove it.

The project, here, was a mural commissioned by the Buffalo Savings Bank to depict the history of Cheektowaga, a community near Buffalo, New York. The historical research took me to the libraries and to the town historian. From this, a number of rough cartoons were sketched. A final selection of subject and style was made. Next came the researching for costume and the specifics that would be incorporated into the mural.

It was decided early in the project that the drawing would be realistic, for simple audience comprehension. It would have been considerably easier to use a more dramatic and abstract interpretation. The first purpose of this mural was to tell a story; the second, to create a work of lasting artistic worth.

(a) Sketches from books that could not leave the library.

(b) Sketches of animals at the zoo.

(c) Sketches of friends who were kind enough to pose in the costume of the period.

(d) Sketches of specific persons of the period.

There were hundreds of these working drawings made prior to the finished cartoon. The cartoon was shown to the client. We ran into the first hassle.

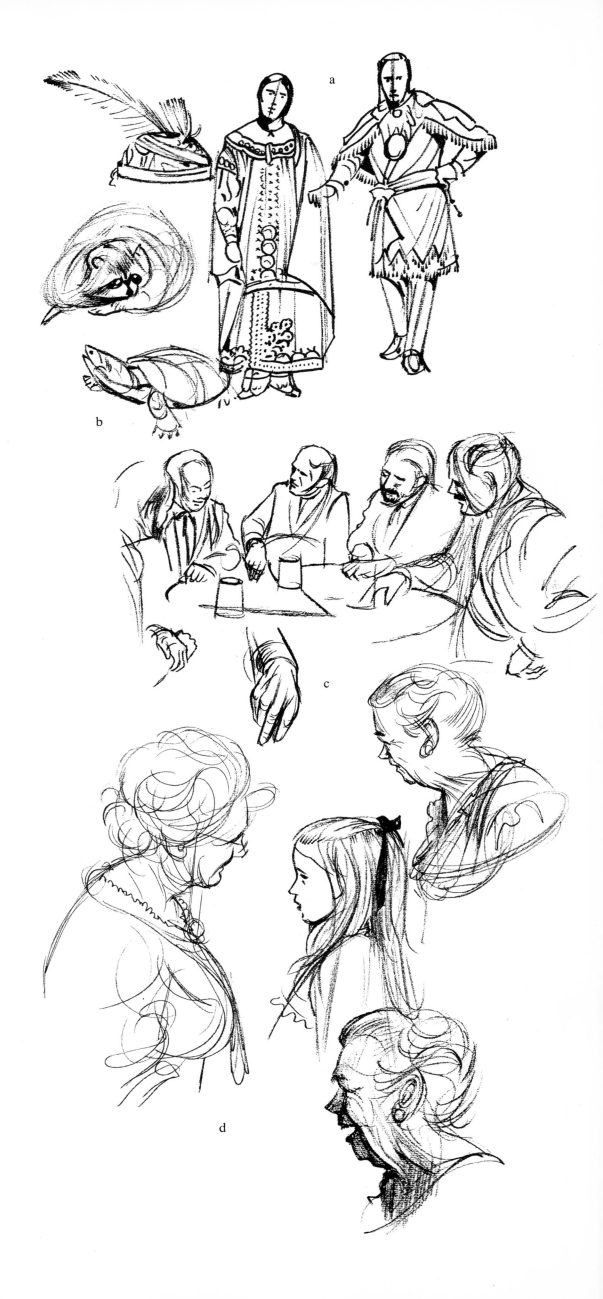

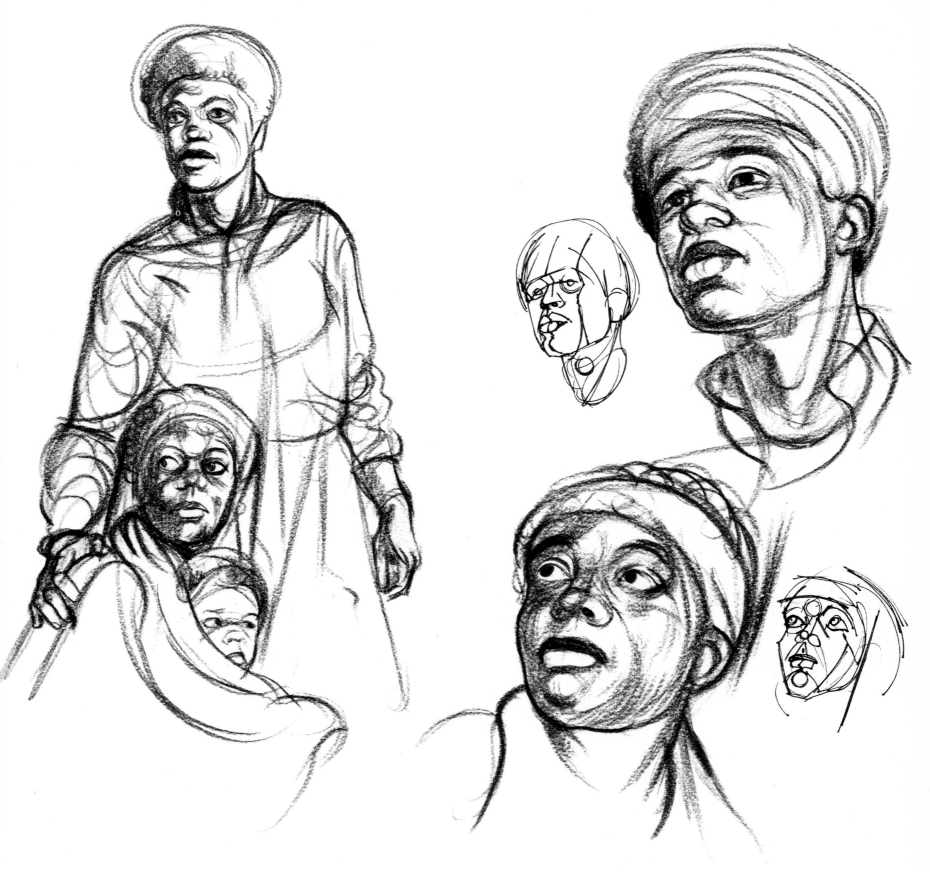

I had found that Cheektowaga was the site of a station on the Underground Railroad. It was a stopping-off hiding place prior to entry into Canada, just across the border. I had a beautiful black family as models, and I put it all together into the finished cartoon. The public relations department of the bank objected. My black friends had no objections, and while the controversy continued, I began the mechanics of getting the cartoon on canvas. To end the bank's concern and simplify the design, which was overcomplicated, I decided to save my interest in the Underground Railroad for another project.

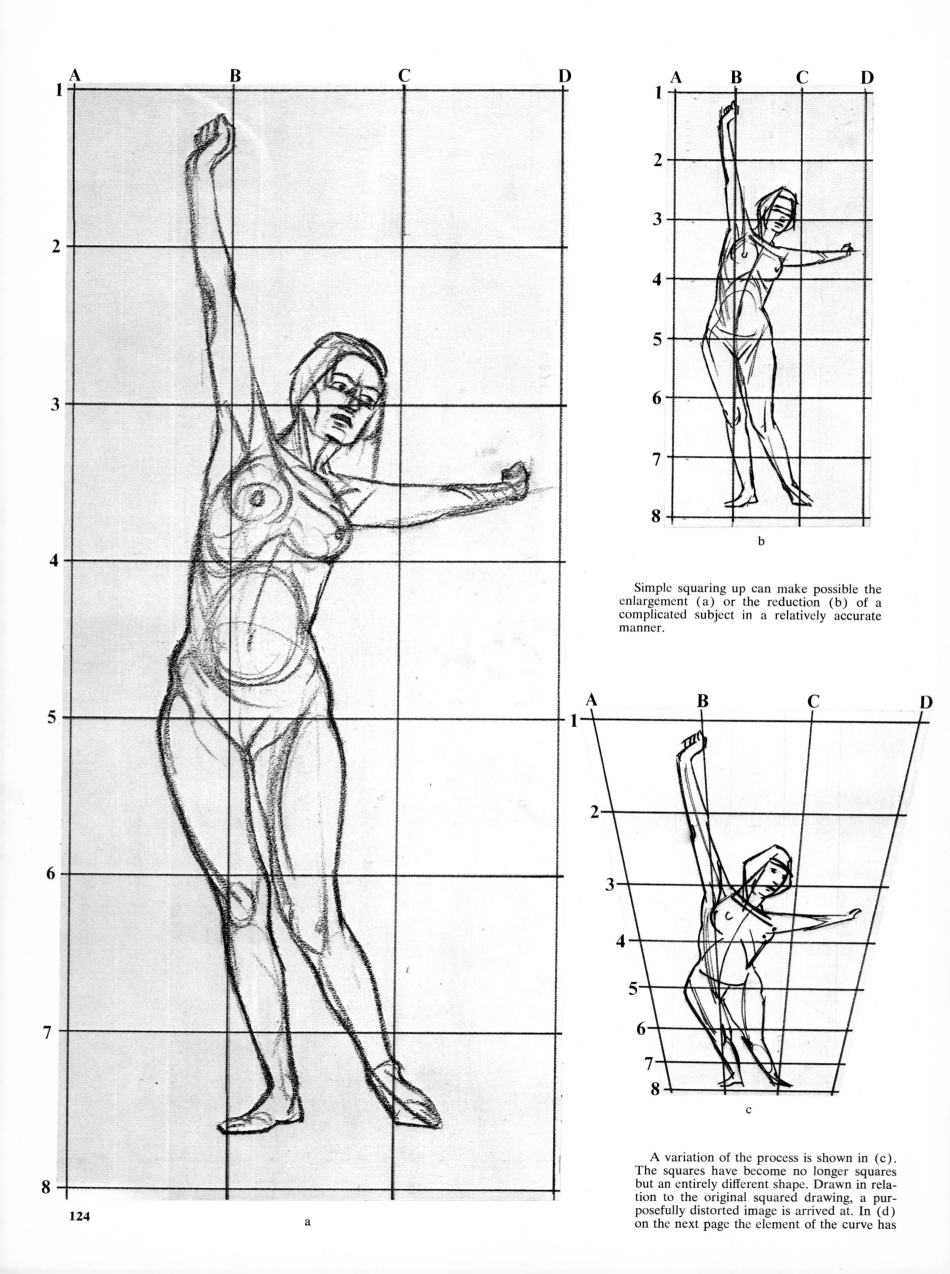

Simple squaring up can make possible the enlargement (a) or the reduction (b) of a complicated subject in a relatively accurate manner.

A variation of the process is shown in (c). The squares have become no longer squares but an entirely different shape. Drawn in relation to the original squared drawing, a purposefully distorted image is arrived at. In (d) on the next page the element of the curve has

a

b

c

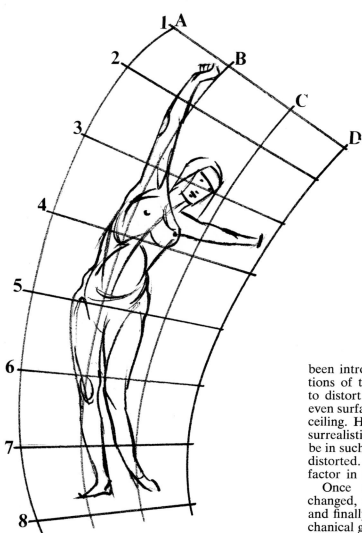

d

been introduced. There are practical applications of this procedure. The artist may wish to distort in order to compensate for an uneven surface, such as a curved wall or a domed ceiling. He may wish to distort as in certain surrealistic works. The painting or mural may be in such a spot that, when viewed, it appears distorted. The artist may compensate for this factor in his projection.

Once a small-scale cartoon is finished, changed, rechanged, discarded, begun again, and finally resolved, the artist begins the mechanical groundwork that will become the mural that the public will see. He squares the cartoon in small scale, and then increases the size of the squares to fit the final size of the mural. Sensible artists follow the agreed-upon cartoon. More individualistic artists enlarge more freely but retain a resemblance between cartoon and final work.

A simple fact that influences the changes, other than just the technique of scaling up to final size, is that scale itself causes a very different final image. Something that in small scale may seem correct, in large scale may appear wrong. If the cartoon is dramatic, it becomes even more dramatic. If it is weak, it is seldom saved by enlargement. The professional improves the work as he progresses.

A good way to get a general idea of how the mural will look in place is to make a slide photograph of the finished cartoon and project it onto the site.

A mural painted or fastened to any wall is at the mercy of the wall surface, which may be less permanent. When the wall surface has a high-risk deterioration quotient, there are ways to minimize the risk.

A new surface can be built and attached to the existing wall. This is expensive but frequently advisable.

The mural can be painted on a stretcher, or a series of stretchers can be constructed to fit the area.

The mural can be executed on a series of hardboard panels.

Another solution is to paint the mural off the site on canvas and adhere the finished canvas to a well-prepared wall with a polyester adhesive. An older method was to set it in a thick coat of white lead. Ineptly handled, however, this method can lead to a comedy scene usually found featuring the Keystone Cops.

A matte acrylic medium acts as a protective finish.

(a) If you wish to use stretchers, there are factory-made re-enforced stretchers in a variety of sizes, usually measured in the metric system.

(b) Shown here is the re-enforcement with hardboard triangles necessary in constructing large-size custom-made stretchers. Making such stretchers is usually a job for the cabinet division of a local lumber mill.

(c) A cross section of the stretcher shows the shape needed to avoid the canvas's contacting the stretcher edge.

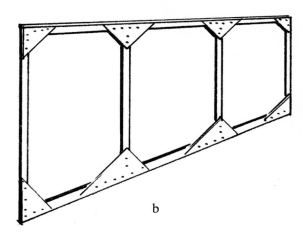

a

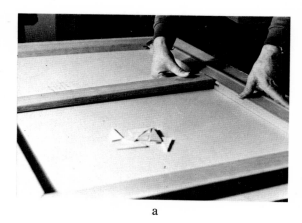

b

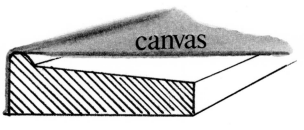

canvas

c

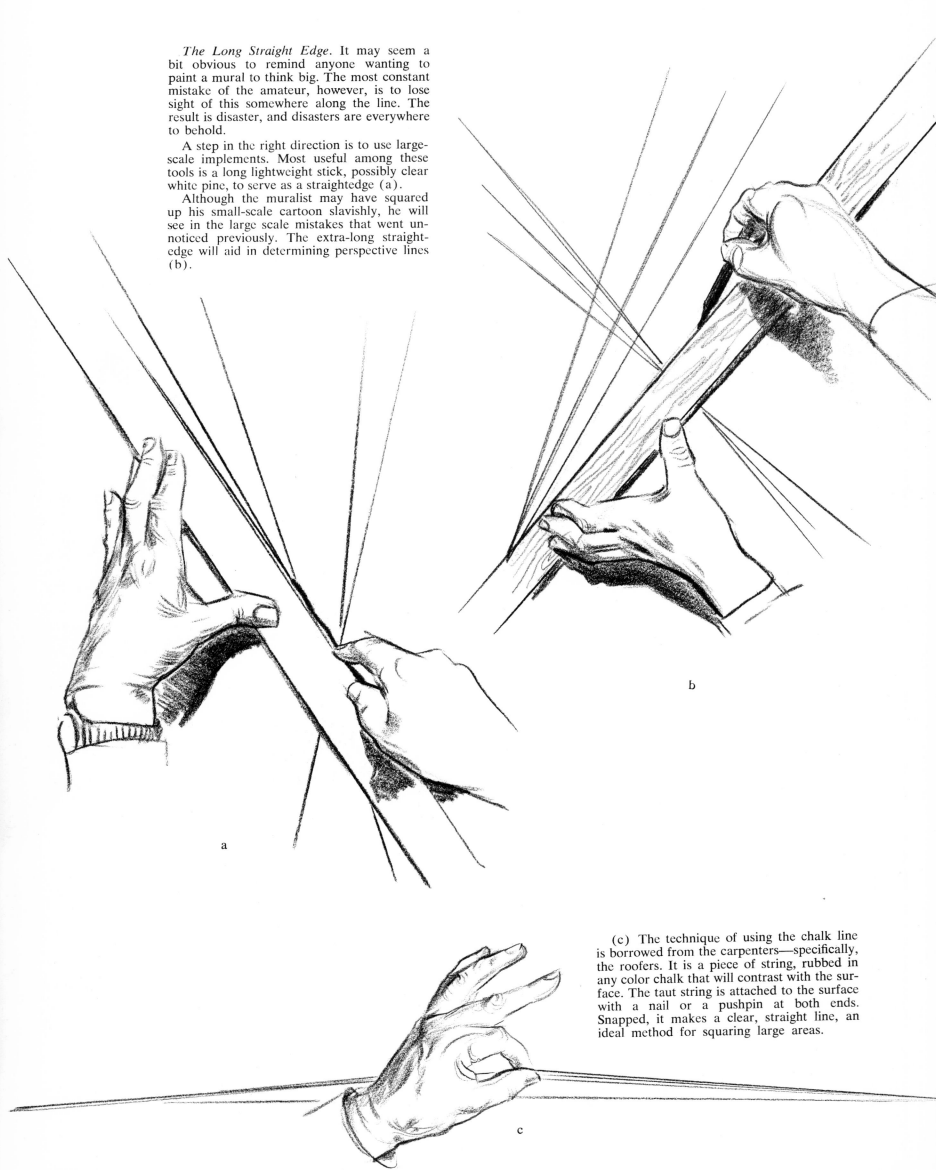

The Long Straight Edge. It may seem a bit obvious to remind anyone wanting to paint a mural to think big. The most constant mistake of the amateur, however, is to lose sight of this somewhere along the line. The result is disaster, and disasters are everywhere to behold.

A step in the right direction is to use large-scale implements. Most useful among these tools is a long lightweight stick, possibly clear white pine, to serve as a straightedge (a).

Although the muralist may have squared up his small-scale cartoon slavishly, he will see in the large scale mistakes that went unnoticed previously. The extra-long straightedge will aid in determining perspective lines (b).

a

b

(c) The technique of using the chalk line is borrowed from the carpenters—specifically, the roofers. It is a piece of string, rubbed in any color chalk that will contrast with the surface. The taut string is attached to the surface with a nail or a pushpin at both ends. Snapped, it makes a clear, straight line, an ideal method for squaring large areas.

c

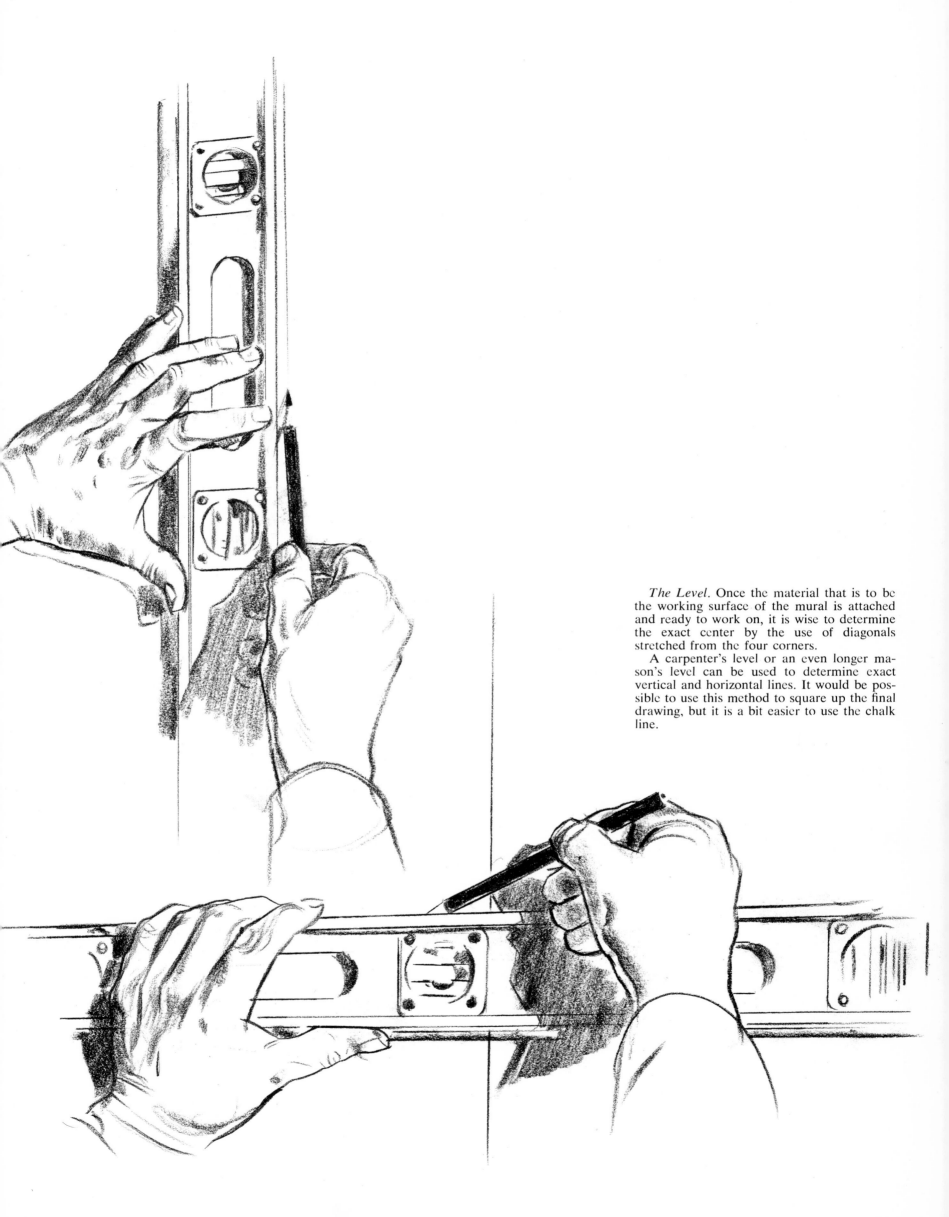

The Level. Once the material that is to be the working surface of the mural is attached and ready to work on, it is wise to determine the exact center by the use of diagonals stretched from the four corners.

A carpenter's level or an even longer mason's level can be used to determine exact vertical and horizontal lines. It would be possible to use this method to square up the final drawing, but it is a bit easier to use the chalk line.

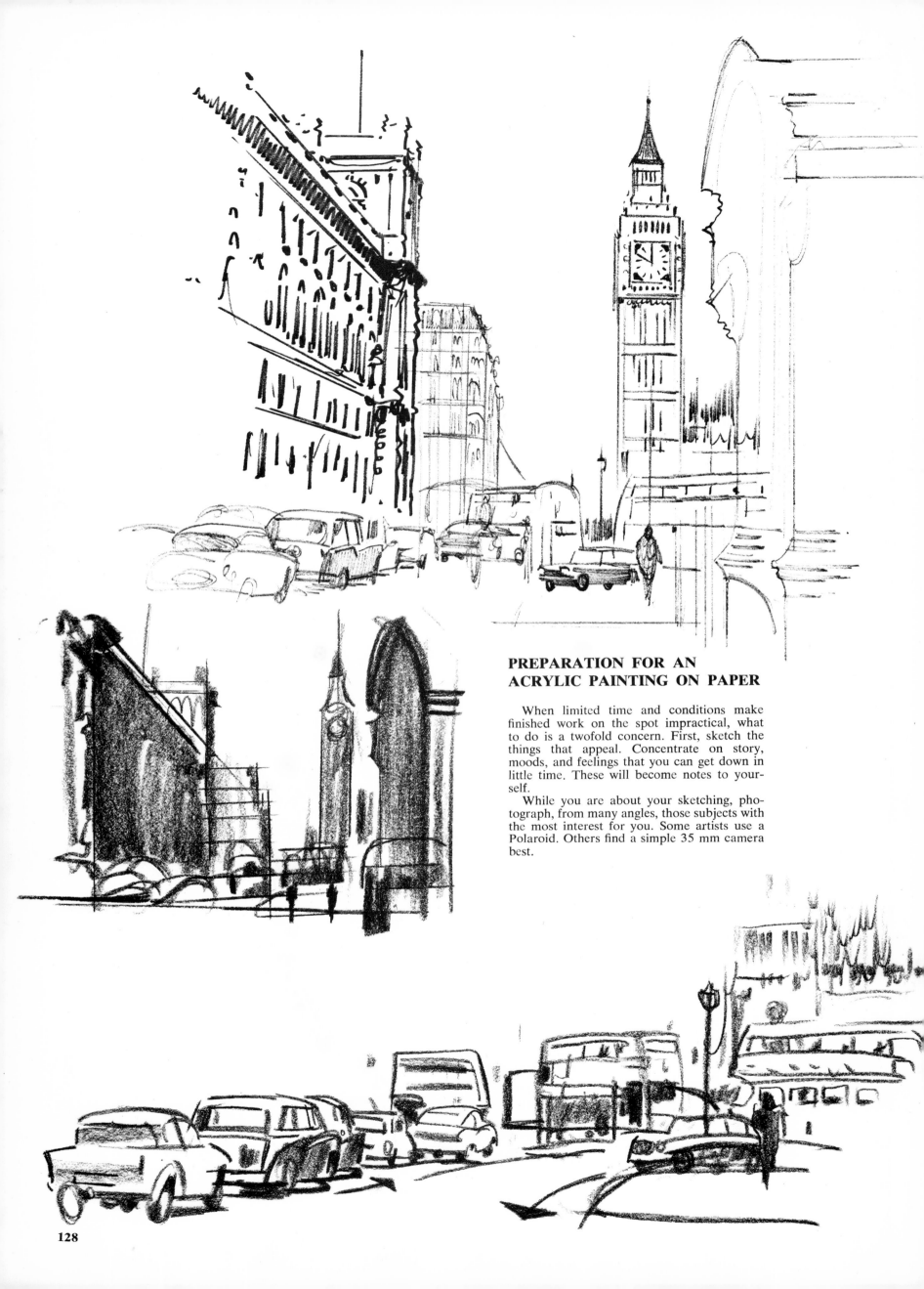

PREPARATION FOR AN
ACRYLIC PAINTING ON PAPER

When limited time and conditions make finished work on the spot impractical, what to do is a twofold concern. First, sketch the things that appeal. Concentrate on story, moods, and feelings that you can get down in little time. These will become notes to yourself.

While you are about your sketching, photograph, from many angles, those subjects with the most interest for you. Some artists use a Polaroid. Others find a simple 35 mm camera best.

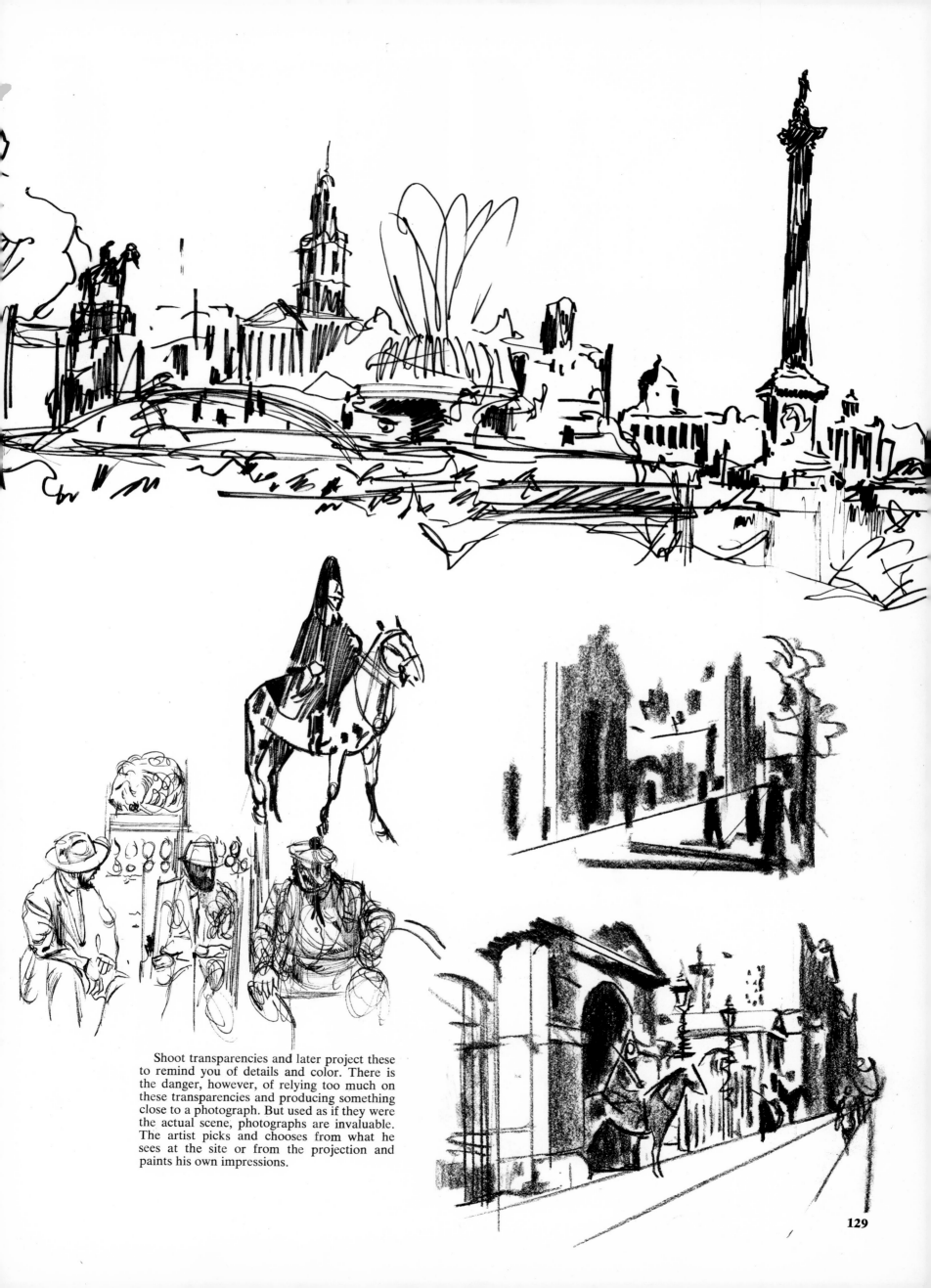

Shoot transparencies and later project these to remind you of details and color. There is the danger, however, of relying too much on these transparencies and producing something close to a photograph. But used as if they were the actual scene, photographs are invaluable. The artist picks and chooses from what he sees at the site or from the projection and paints his own impressions.

129

Big Ben

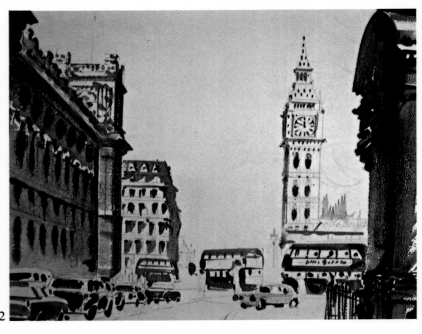

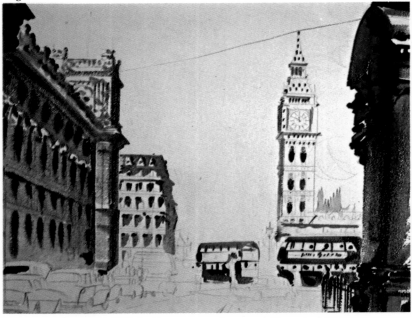

1

2

Big Ben (1) and *The Queen's Guard* (1a) are both painted in typical wet watercolor style. The acrylic medium is more controllable than the transparent watercolor medium, but, until mastered, it is somewhat less brilliant. Shown in the sketch of hands is the use of the large chisel-edge brush, charged on one corner with Indian red and on the other side with ultramarine blue. Applied directly to the surface, the colors blend as they hit the paper, giving an assured appearance.

In *The Queen's Guard* (1a), general definition of the subject was started in the distance and worked toward the foreground. In *Big Ben* (2), the buses and the incidental street activities were dabbed into the painting in brilliant color. In *The Queen's Guard* (2a), the painting is carried farther into the foreground, leaving white sections that will be other than the over-all warm brick color. This could all have been

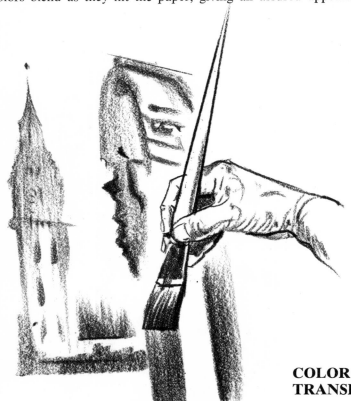

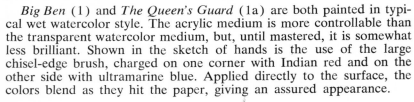

**COLOR DEMONSTRATION:
TRANSPARENT TECHNIQUES**

The Queen's Guard

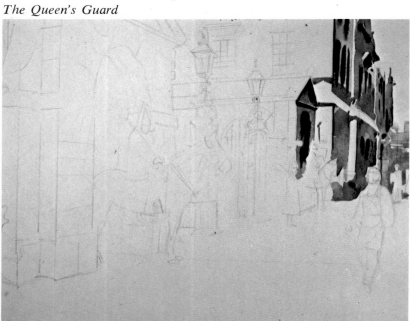

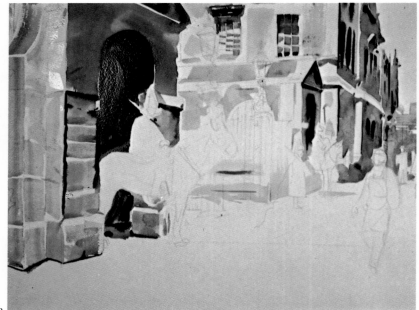

1a

2a

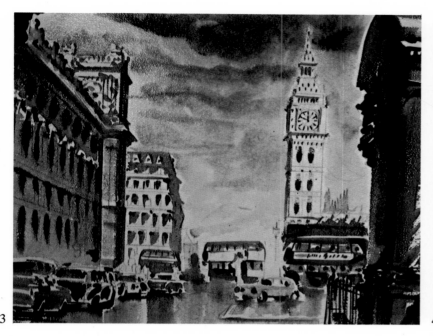

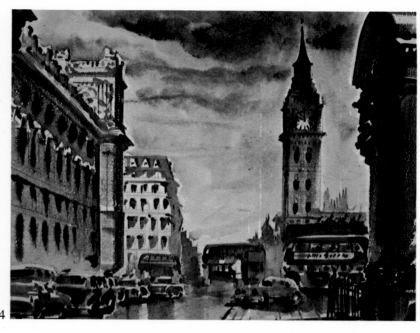

3

4

painted in the brick color and the details added in opaque later, but it seemed best to retain the drawing at this stage. A straightedge was used up to this point for details and windows and such, and now (in 3), it was used in painting the over-all tone of the clock tower. The brisk feeling in tone rather than line is the object. By this time parts of the painted surface are dry enough to accept the filigree fence lines without blossoming (3a).

In *Big Ben* (4), a damp brush was dragged over the almost dry buses, cars, and other street activity. With a certain degree of luck, it put rain on the streets.

In (4a), the guard and the pedestrians were painted in direct strokes. With clear water the sidewalk area was dampened and into this surface the reflections were brushed.

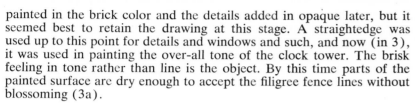

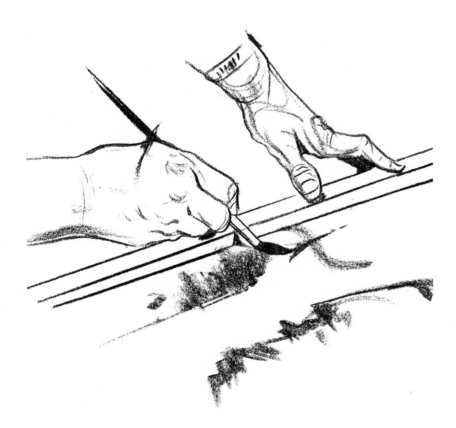

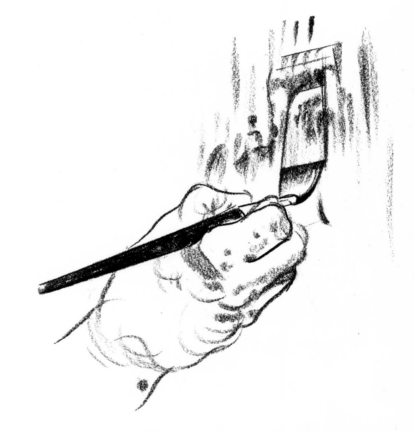

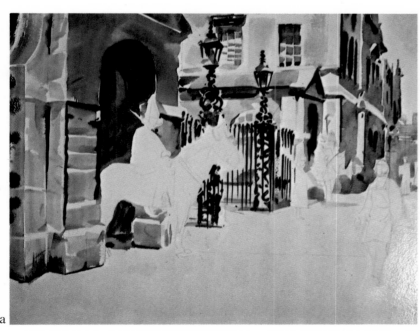

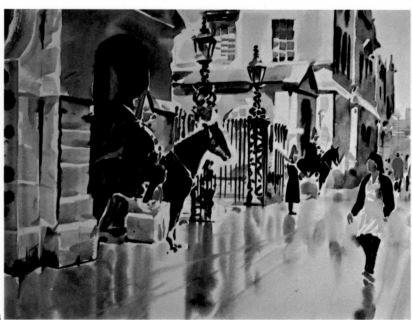

3a

4a

CHOOSING SITES TO PAINT

The artist differs from the casual sight-seer in a singular respect. The artist, while enjoying the scene, observes with the thought of recording what he sees or feels. The drama of a turbulent sky over mountains, for instance, is something to be transferred onto a two-dimensional surface.

Seldom is the subject or composition ready-made. Never, regardless of the statements of the non-artist, can the artist record what he sees in complete fidelity and arrive at any worth-while result. This is so, despite the fact that the casual observer is inclined to relate the ability of an artist to the degree of his absolute fidelity in interpretation. This does not imply that the more incomprehensible the interpretation the better, as critics at the other extreme might suggest.

It is the artist's honest interpretation of what he sees and feels and his ability to transmit this to a surface that counts. And here's the rub. By nature, the artist looks deeply into what he sees. He reacts and in his reacting spreads out on some surface his thoughts and feelings for all to examine. He may have developed, through experience, an ability to see what others pass over lightly. He may be, by nature, more aware than the next individual of what's happening around him. He may, like a child, see directly, unhindered by experience and the direction of others. He is a person alone and set apart, living in a world in which he has the ability to see what those around him are unable to see, until he, in his way, points the subject out to them.

So what happens to the amateur artist as well as the professional when he is traveling through a region of awe-inspiring beauty? He doesn't know what on earth to paint. He is faced with the biggest single problem of all creative people: where to start. If he picks this spot, will he miss a better spot around the bend?

The practical answer is simple. Start. An artist is said to be impractical, but for that split second, when he must begin to put something down on a surface, he must break the pattern and paint. Only someone who has scurried frantically from one spot to another —only an artist—will understand the magnitude of the problem.

To overcome the dilemma of which is *the* one subject to choose, the artist may have to resort to a number of almost ridiculous disciplines. Decide that the first safe, comfortable spot found will be the spot from which the painting will be made. Decide that he will start painting, come hell or high water, at a given mile on the speedometer and have someone drop him off with no hope of return until that someone picks him up later.

Should the composition be basically a dramatic pattern of extreme light against dark? Should it be a vertical composition?

Would the composition be more telling with a foreground of roofs acting as a foil for the illusion of distance? Should the distant objects accentuate the interest in the foreground?

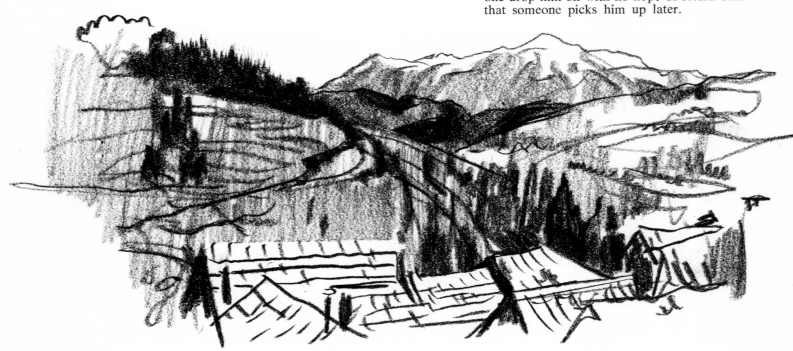

Even within the four walls of a studio, this mental block exists. The way to overcome it is to start, not painting aimlessly, but to start. On a drive through the mountains with the intention of painting an acrylic, the first step in the right direction is to sketch the first vista that catches the eye. A sketch in pencil is no great commitment.

The most consistently recurring question an artist must answer is, "Where do you get your ideas and inspiration?" Since each artist is an individual expressing his personal thoughts in a personal manner, even a clever answer is usually a useless bit of information to the questioner. Every artist will have his own answer to the question. The moment his answer becomes routine, his work becomes sterile. Like a lively puppy, he may finally catch his own tail, only to find he has lost the game.

You gain an ability to draw by drawing. You learn to come up with ideas by getting ideas. People who must come up with ideas every day for a living use many systems. One used is snowballing. A cartoonist's snowballing could go like this: thought, animal . . . animal . . . monkey . . . three monkeys . . . hear no evil, see no evil, speak no evil . . . three monkeys . . . one monkey . . . lighting a cigarette . . . monkey says, "Let's be evil!" *

It makes small difference what the message of the artist is, as long as there is a message. There is a school of thought that claims that the artist must NOT communicate. This is rubbish. A wall painted one single color communicates. It can communicate many different thoughts to many different people.

* From the cartoon strip "Middle Class Animals."

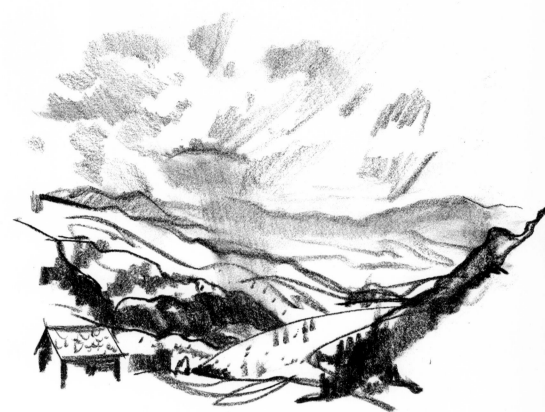

Should it be a direct view looking down the valley?

Perhaps it should be a dramatic one-point perspective into the distance.

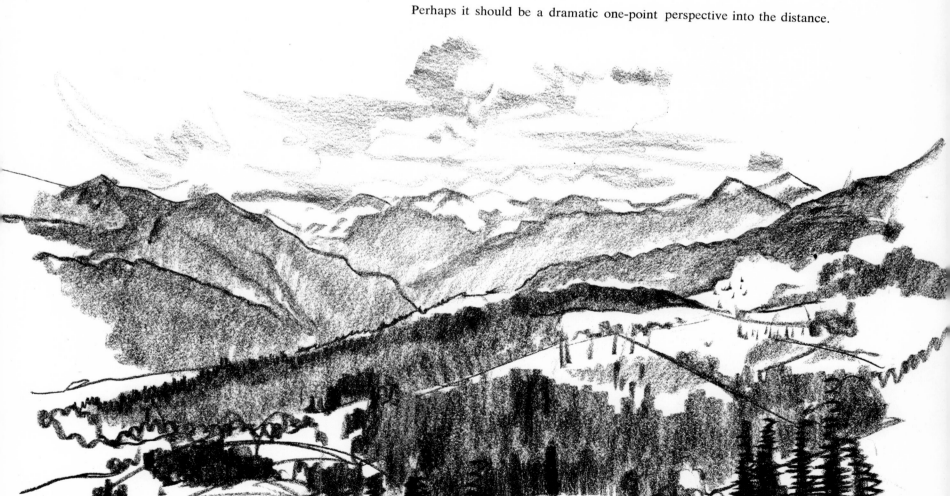

133

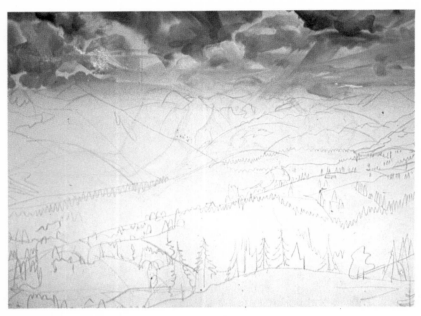

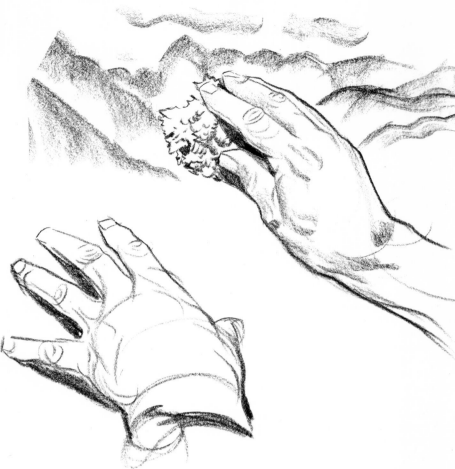

This painting could have been drawn in line on any of the supports suitable for acrylic. It was drawn strongly in detail, not delicately, in charcoal. The acrylic as it is used here, in an *alla prima* technique, is opaque enough to cover the original drawing. In a transparent watercolor, pencil lines can be erased once the painting is complete. With the heavy application of paint as in this painting, this was not possible. Should a drawing in charcoal be liable to smudge when the paint is applied, it would be wise to coat the drawing with either a spray of acrylic varnish or to slap it with a cloth until the loose particles were no longer subject to smudging.

1. The sky was begun first. In this case it is a turbulent, cloudy affair, dramatic, but relatively simple to execute. It should be remembered that the clouds appear smaller the farther they are in the distance, and flatter on the bottom.

2. In the hand sketch the lower section of the sky and clouds was softened by a light rubbing with a sponge.

COLOR DEMONSTRATION: SWISS ALPS

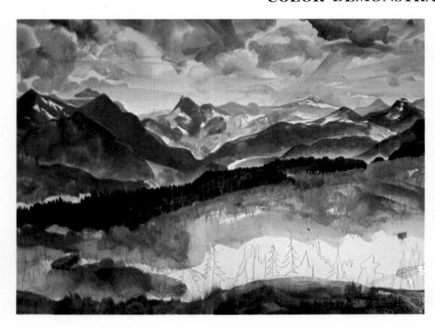

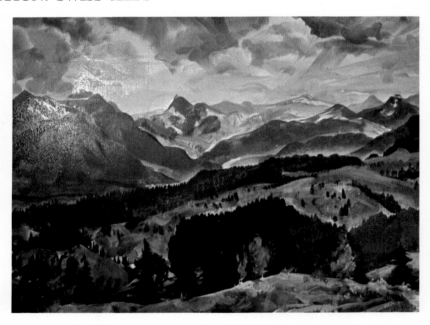

5. By employing high-intensity colors in the immediate foreground, painting the darkest darks next to the lightest lights, and painting in the details, it was possible to push the background back. It would still be possible (because this was an opaque acrylic) to overpaint even stronger elements, such as foreground branches, complete with leaves. Photographers frequently employ just such a gimmick. Before a beautiful panorama, they shoot through a framework of a branch of a tree held a few feet in front of the camera. Imagine, if you will, a winding fence going from immediate foreground into the first clump of trees, a roadway with people, or cows grazing.

6. The dark foreground mass of trees is laid in over the area. The immediate foreground of trees, grass, and flowers is applied over the aforementioned dark mass.

The painting above was reproduced from a transparency and, because of this additional reproduction step, is less true in color than the painting on the right reproduced from the original painting. For artists whose work is to be reproduced this is an example of the advantage of using the original for reproduction purposes.

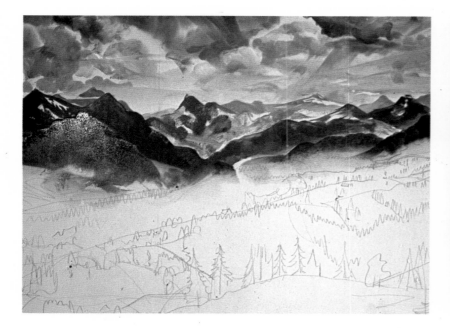

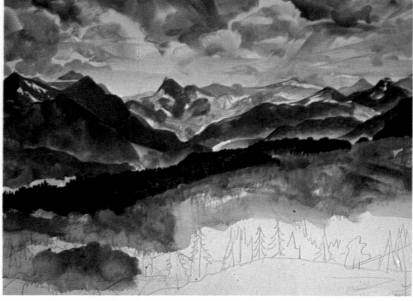

3. The distant mountains then were indicated in faded tones of blue. The snow was applied to these mountains. At this stage the sponge was again used to lighten the base of these mountains before the next nearest range was begun. Complicated as this might seem, it is a simple procedure to paint in the most distant mountains in the right color strength, then with the sponge, in a circular motion first, followed by a horizontal stroke, indicate the low-hanging clouds between the mountains. The danger lies in painting these distant and middle-distant mountains in too strong a value so that as you reach the foreground, you have nothing on your palette strong enough to outvalue the middle ground and background. Two things, aside from the drawing itself, must be borne in mind. The mountains will stay in the distance in direct relation to how light they are in hue and to the degree of intensity of the colors used.

4. Although the faraway and middle-distant hills must certainly have had deep green meadows and dark blue-green fir trees, it is not until the foreground is painted that color of such strong intensity is applied. The middle of the picture area of evergreens still is not in true color, but is rather muted. At the same time, they are strong enough to stand in front of the color in the middle-ground mountains. By sponging between applications of ranges of mountains, the principle of the forced edge was used to lighten subtly the tone as it approached the next dark-edged tone or area. At this stage in the painting it seemed to be falling apart in the foreground. To get an objective look, I held my hand over the immediate foreground. I could see the painting composing itself. This indicated that the immediate foreground had to be in a value or intensity of color to make the rest of the picture recede into the distance.

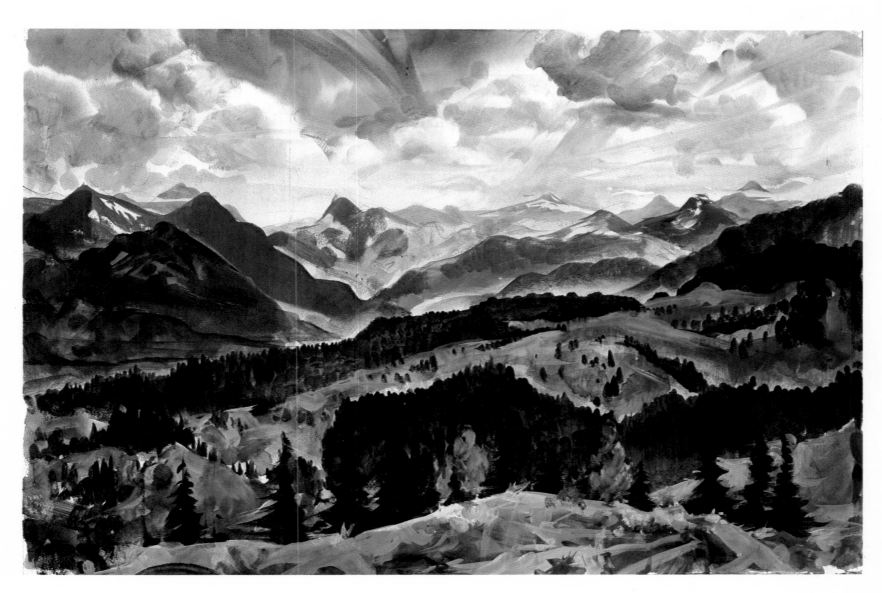

PREPARATION FOR FIGURE PAINTING

In figure work especially, many sketches are usually made prior to starting a painting. A model cannot be expected to hold any pose indefinitely; however, poses should be chosen that can be held for at least fifteen minutes.

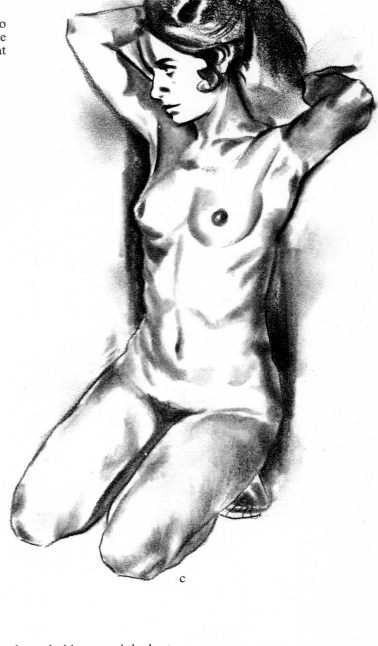

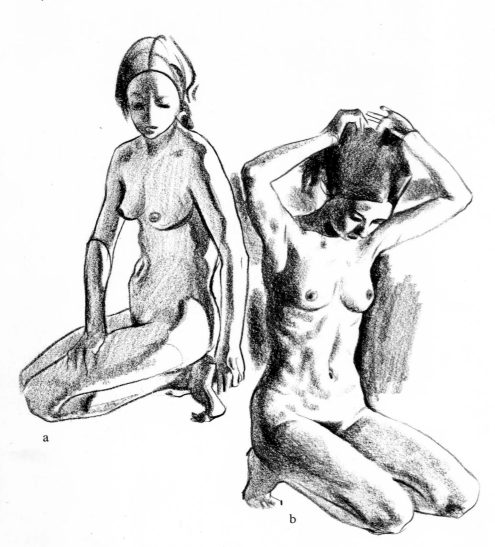

a

b

c

(a) This pose seemed a possible choice, but lacked action and had little design value.

(b) This one seemed better. A model holding arms upstretched, holding her hair, is almost traditional.

(c) In the end, this seemed the best.

On the opposite page is a more complete sketch of (c) done on Ingres paper, using charcoal and white. This was traced for the color demonstration on the next two pages. As the lower torso didn't seem to add to the picture, only the upper section was used in the painting.

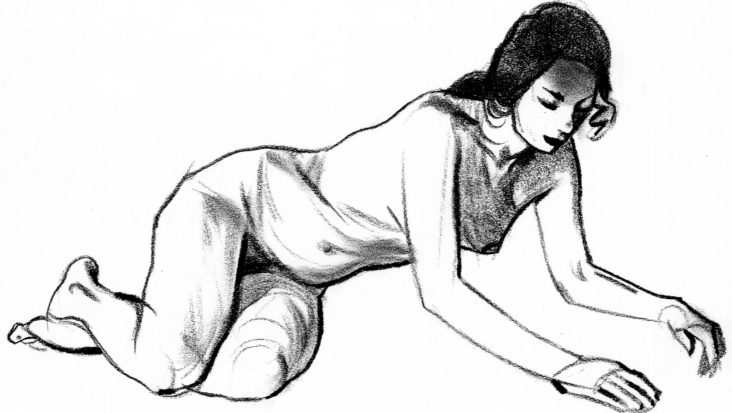

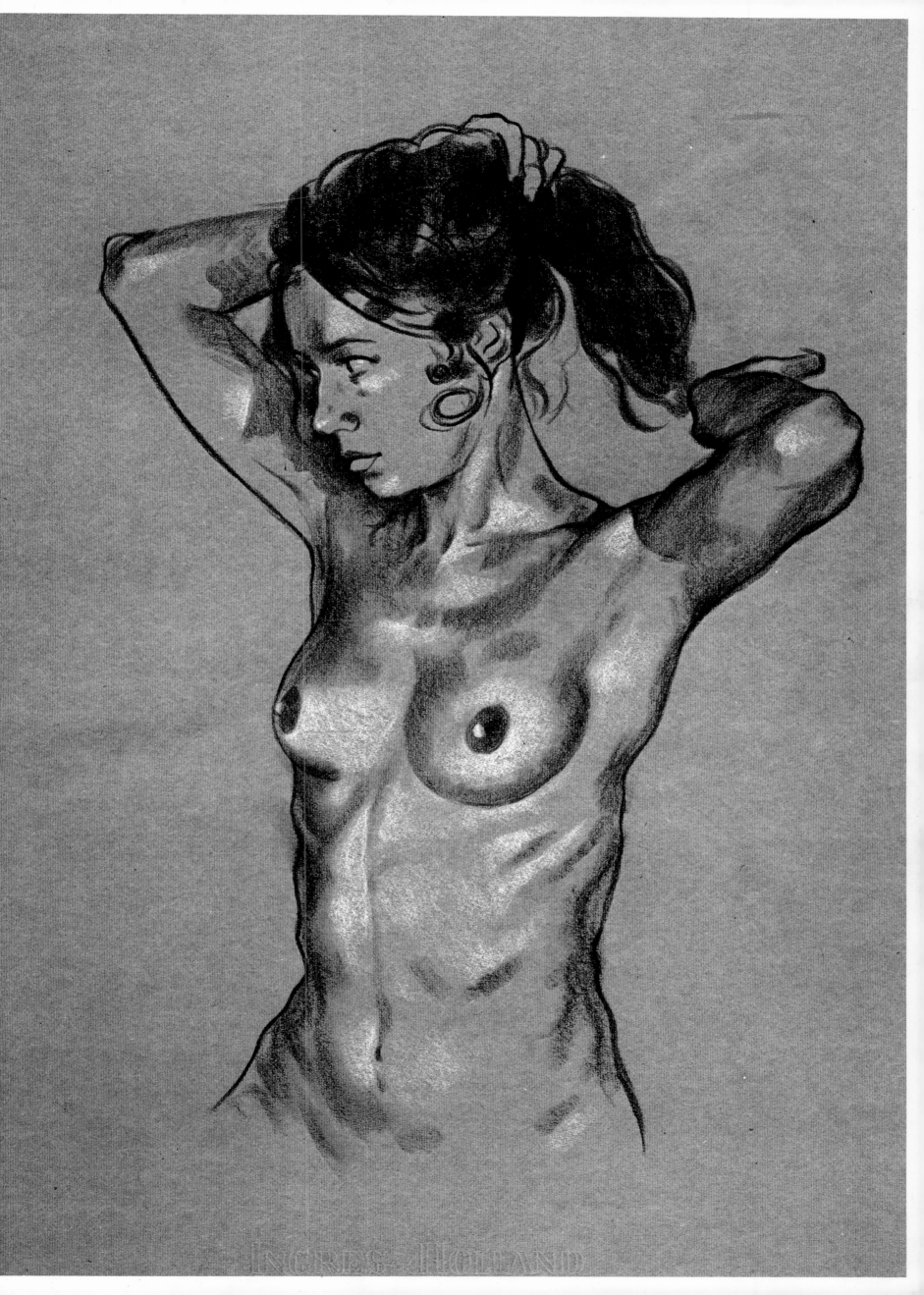

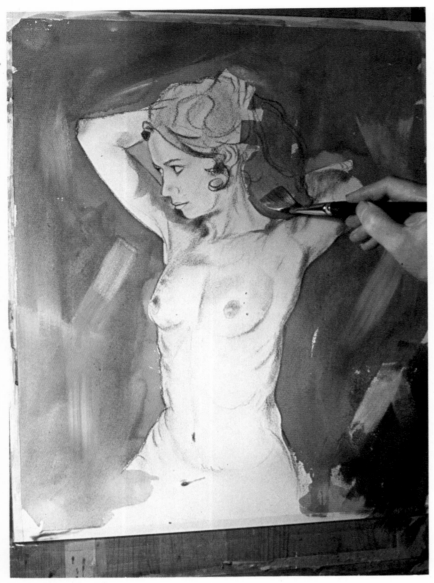

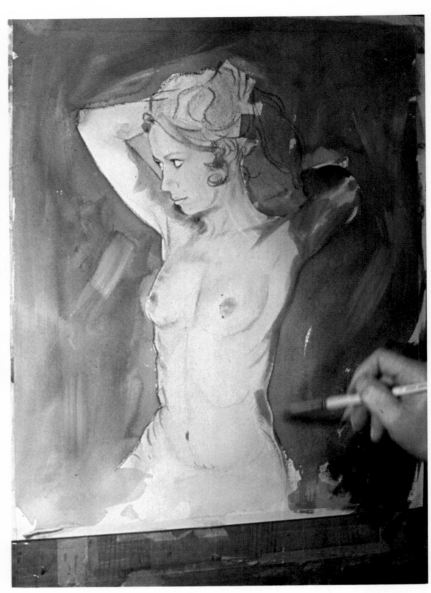

1. The basic sketch was made in charcoal on a board. To remove excess dust, the board was flicked with a soft rag, then the sketch was sprayed with a coating of fixative to prevent the charcoal from picking up into the acrylic paint. A large chisel-edge sable brush was used for painting the background. A heavy impasto can be applied as acrylic dries quickly. The direction of the strokes may either act as a counterpoint to the figure or follow the general rhythm of the design.

2. An over-all transparent flesh tone is applied like a watercolor, thinly to preserve the drawing underneath. Next, secondary shadows were painted in warm tones.

COLOR DEMONSTRATION: FIGURES

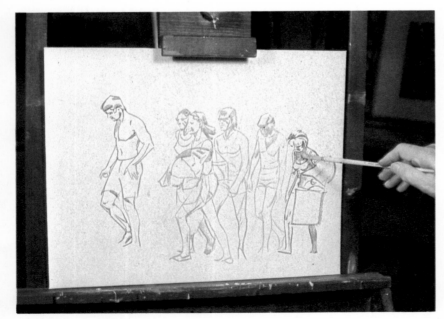

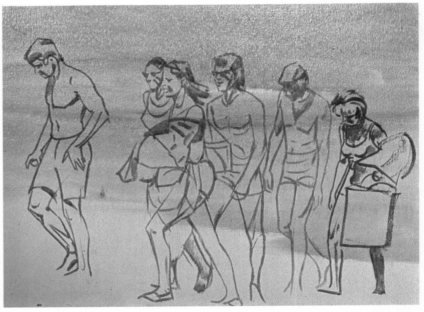

1. An approach to a complicated subject is shown above. A canvas painting panel is the support. This is less expensive than a stretched canvas and slightly more expensive than good paper or heavy illustration board. (Illustration board was used for the painting at the top of the page.) The line painting of the figures is made with the brush held high on the handle.

2. When the line figures are dry, broad over-all strokes are painted over the whole drawing with transparent color, using a combination of the acrylic medium and water.

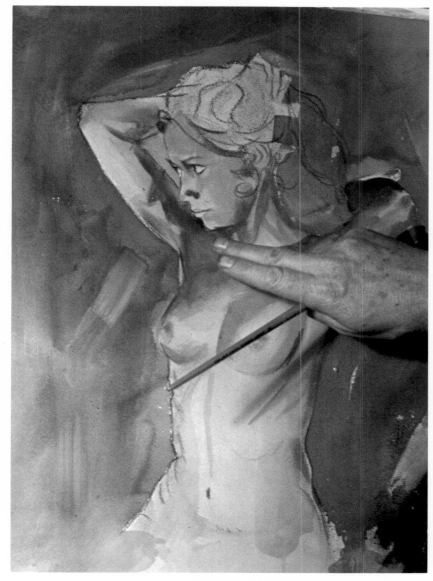

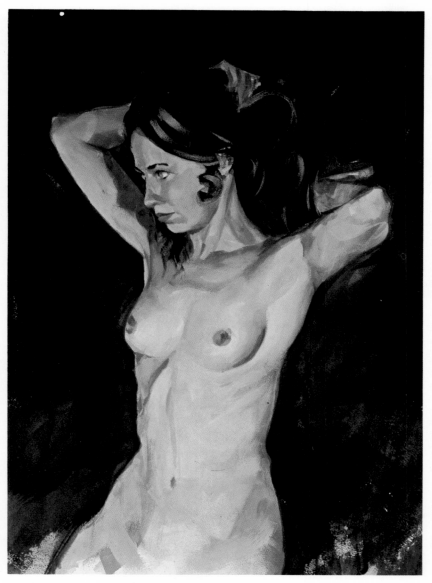

3. Use the fingers to blend the colors softly. To keep the areas fairly moist, use a good amount of the acrylic polymer medium rather than plain water. If you want a shiny finish, use the gloss medium. For a dull finish, use the matte medium. Don't overdo it, but judicious blending of the background is more pleasing than using definite outlines.

4. Only when you have established all the major tones and colors is it time to paint the surface details.

Try painting the identical figure in just cool colors, then warm colors, or paint a completely monochromatic piece. You may want to experiment in using the pointillist technique shown on page 39.

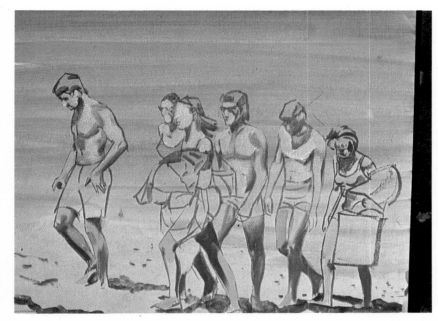

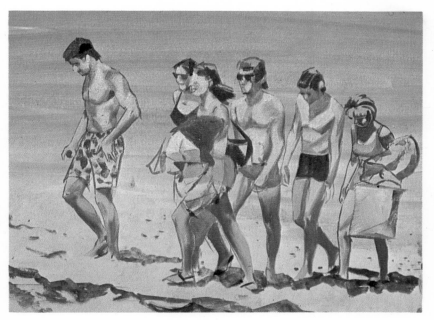

3. The light tones of the figures are then painted with opaque flesh color. This you will arrive at through a liberal use of white mixed with the skin tones. In many cases, the color background of step 2 will become areas of shadow in the final painting. Paint the shadowed sections of the figures.

4. Now is the time for the details, the swim suits and paraphernalia that, strangely enough, only the girls seemed to be carrying.

This painting, like many of the other demonstrations, could be carried considerably further into a more finished piece, but, basically, the procedures would be only an extension of those shown.

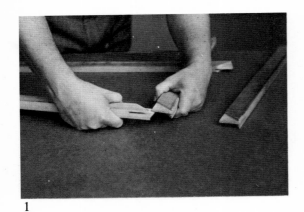

1

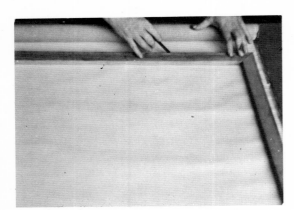

2

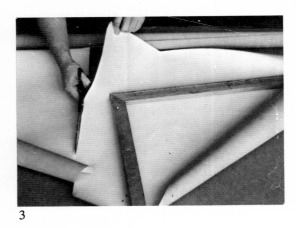

3

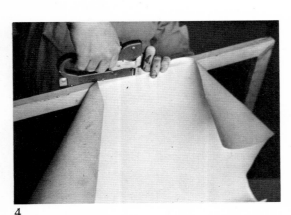

4

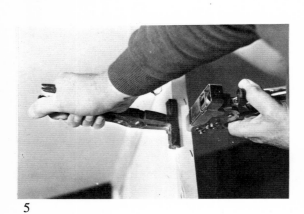

5

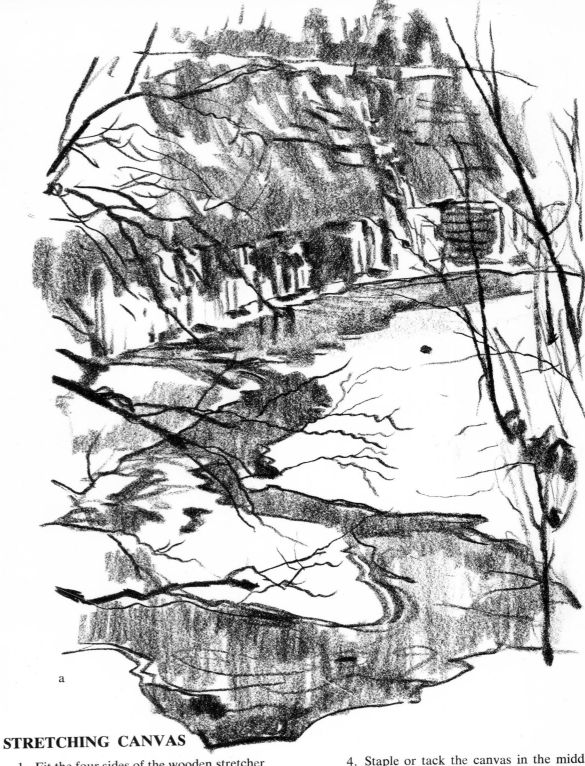

a

STRETCHING CANVAS

1. Fit the four sides of the wooden stretcher together.

2. Use the stretcher to determine the size of canvas needed.

3. Cut the canvas large enough to allow for tacking around the sides. It is sometimes wise to leave more than enough canvas, in case later developments in the composition call for an extension in a given direction.

4. Staple or tack the canvas in the middle of all four sides. Continue the process, stapling toward the corners. If the sides were labeled N S E W, you would staple north, then south, east, then west, etc.

5. A stretching tool is helpful as you staple the final spots. At this stage, hammer into place, in the inside corners, the eight triangular wedges that came with the stretcher strips. This will tighten the canvas.

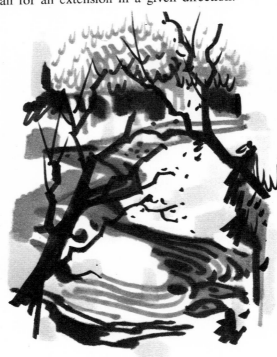

b

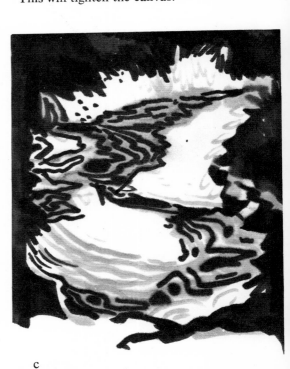

c

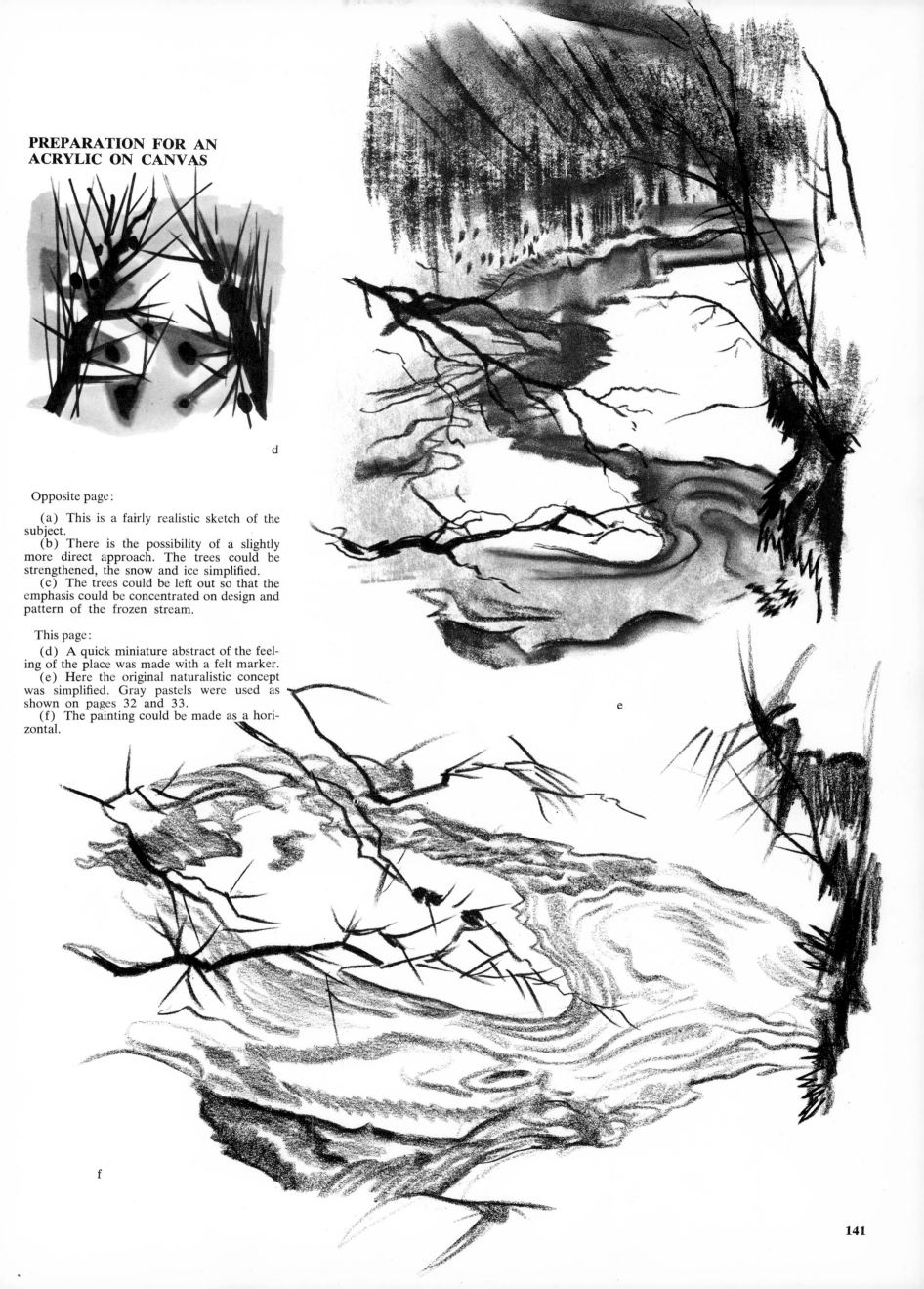

PREPARATION FOR AN ACRYLIC ON CANVAS

d

Opposite page:

(a) This is a fairly realistic sketch of the subject.

(b) There is the possibility of a slightly more direct approach. The trees could be strengthened, the snow and ice simplified.

(c) The trees could be left out so that the emphasis could be concentrated on design and pattern of the frozen stream.

This page:

(d) A quick miniature abstract of the feeling of the place was made with a felt marker.

(e) Here the original naturalistic concept was simplified. Gray pastels were used as shown on pages 32 and 33.

(f) The painting could be made as a horizontal.

e

f

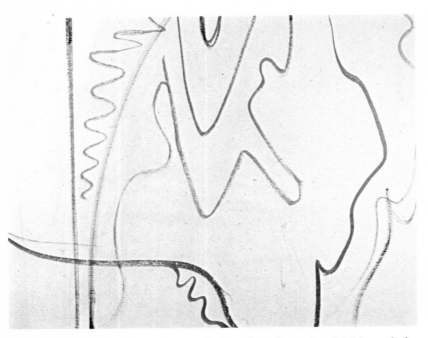

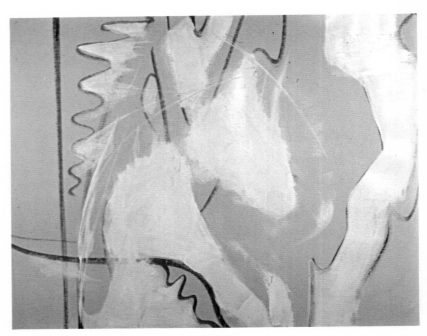

1. An abstract approach to painting, based on the thinking of the preceding two pages. To avoid being too influenced by realism, a horizontal-shaped canvas was chosen, although most of the preliminary sketches were vertical.

2. The stark white in the composition was thought out first and a pattern of white applied.

COLOR DEMONSTRATION: ABSTRACT

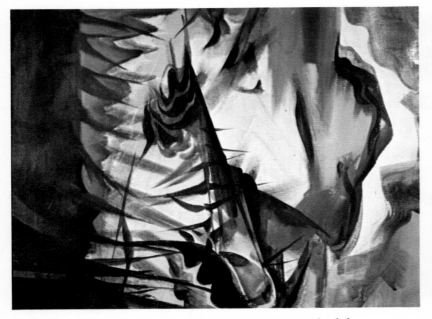

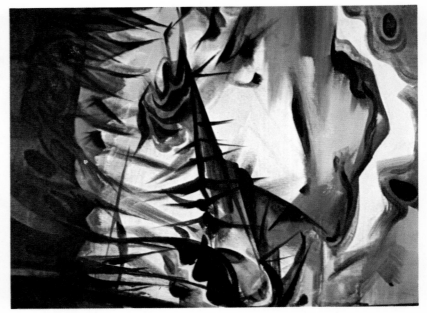

5. The design seems to call for more weight on the left, so a mass is painted in this area. The shape, an important one in the over-all pattern, seems to borrow from natural forms.

6. The details and refinements, including minor changes, are added. This is the stage in nearly all painting where the artist either makes or breaks the work. Add or make changes with great discretion.

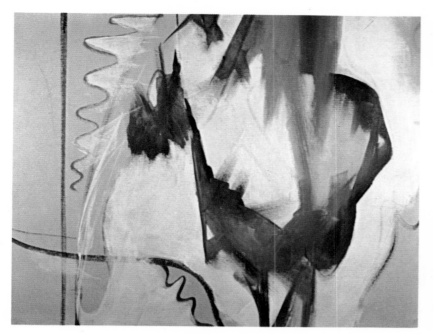
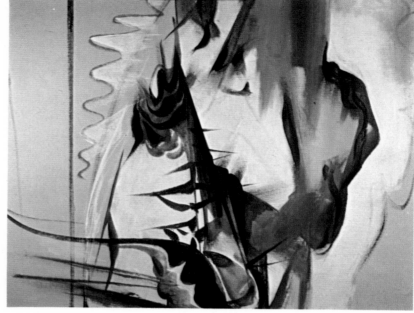

3 and 4. The dark plan of the composition is painted and repainted. In this approach the painting itself suggests the steps.

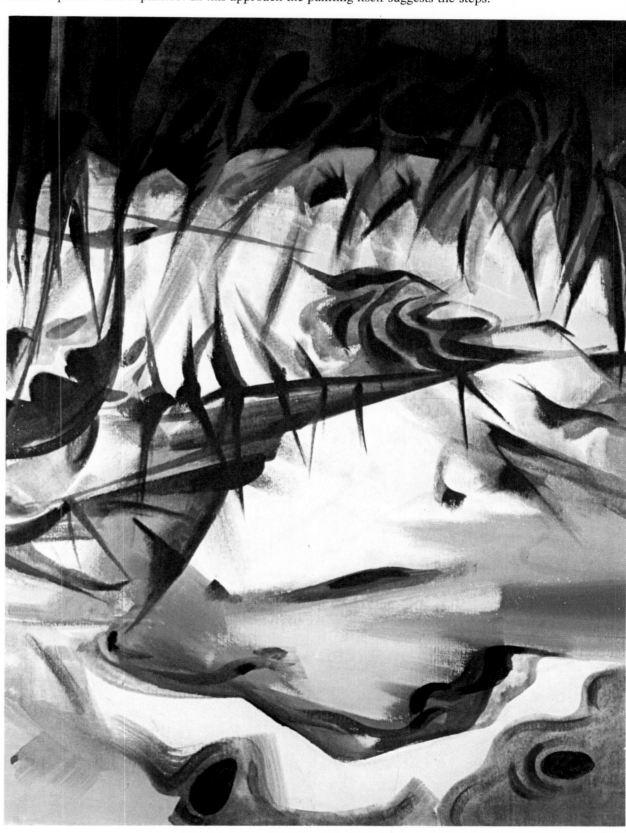

The painting, made as a horizontal, is here viewed as a vertical painting. Not too strangely, it becomes reminiscent of the original subject matter.

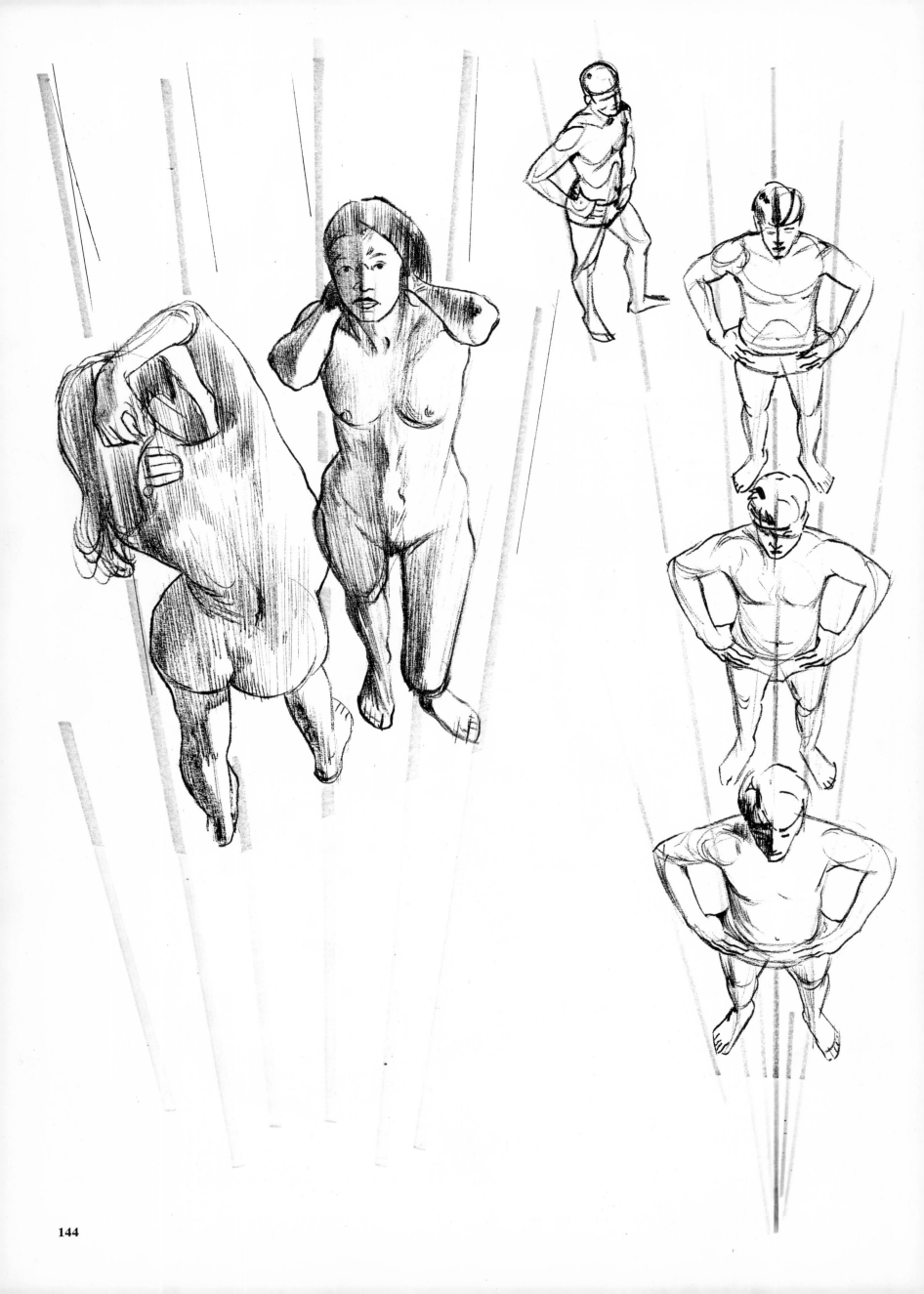

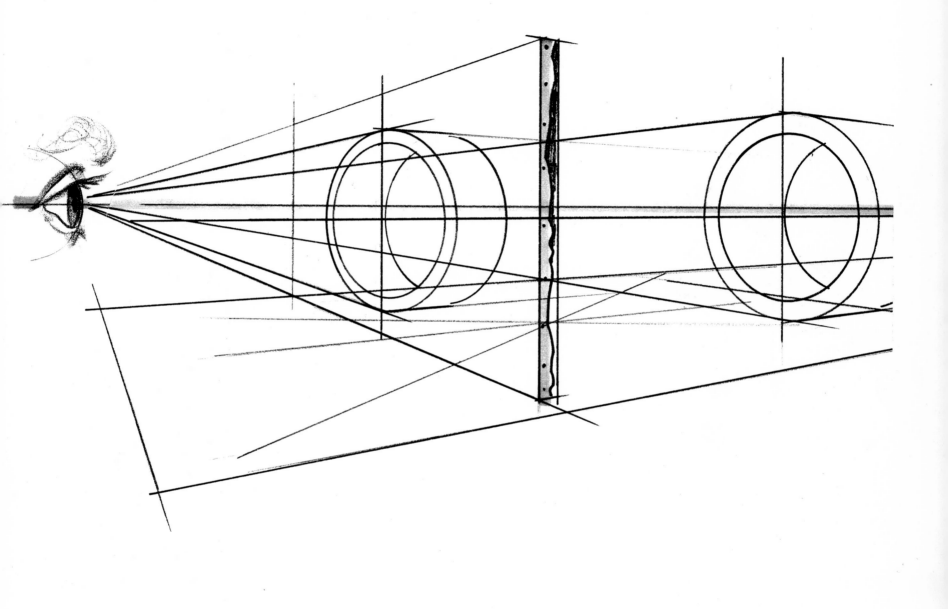

PERSPECTIVE

Perspective is the system of representing objects on a two-dimensional surface to create an impression of three dimensions. Paolo Uccello (Italy, 1397–1475) and Albrecht Dürer (Germany, 1471–1528) were among the first Western artists to study perspective seriously. Tomes have been written on the subject. It is not necessary to go into this in depth, but at least a working knowledge of the science is necessary if we are to create realistic illusions or to distort with intelligence.

In the interests of simplicity and clarity, artists have settled on a few general terms in working with perspective:

Station Point. The point from which the object is drawn, the eye of the artist.

Horizon Line. A line, usually not immediately apparent, that represents the horizon.

Vanishing Point. The point or points where parallel lines appear to converge.

The artist must at all times be aware of the facts of perspective, for if he is not, the first child or casual observer will advise him of his error. This is especially true if the artist deliberately distorts to create a special thought in his drawing. From the first tiny thumbnail sketches, through the finished work, the artist must be constantly aware of perspective, but if this preoccupation becomes apparent to the viewer, all is lost. Like a knowledge of anatomy of the figure, the knowledge of perspective is used only to the point where it enhances the final result.

It is as important for the artist to be aware of the space between objects as it is for him to be aware of the solidity of the objects he is drawing. Certainly the solid objects have solid form, but the air spaces should be considered, if nothing else, as a check on the drawing of the solid forms. For example, when an artist is drawing a street scene, he not only notes the shape of the buildings on each side of the street but the shape of the space between.

For some reason, the term "foreshortening" is usually used by artists in referring to perspective in figure drawing, especially extreme perspective. More accurately, foreshortening should be used when lines of any object are drawn shorter than they actually are to give an illusion of proper relative size.

HORIZON LINE AND ONE-, TWO- AND THREE-POINT PERSPECTIVE

In the rough sketches on the center of this spread, many station points have been used. The sketches have been so placed on the page that they share a common horizon line.

The sketches (a), (b), and (c) of architectural scenes are all drawn from street level. Sketch (d), of the New York Metropolitan Museum of Art, is from a fifth-floor apartment across Fifth Avenue. The sketch of Trinity Church, in the Wall Street area (e), is from street level, and it becomes obvious that there is a slight grade up from the foreground bank to the church. The sketch of Avenue of the Americas and the RCA Building (f) is from a vantage point high above the street.

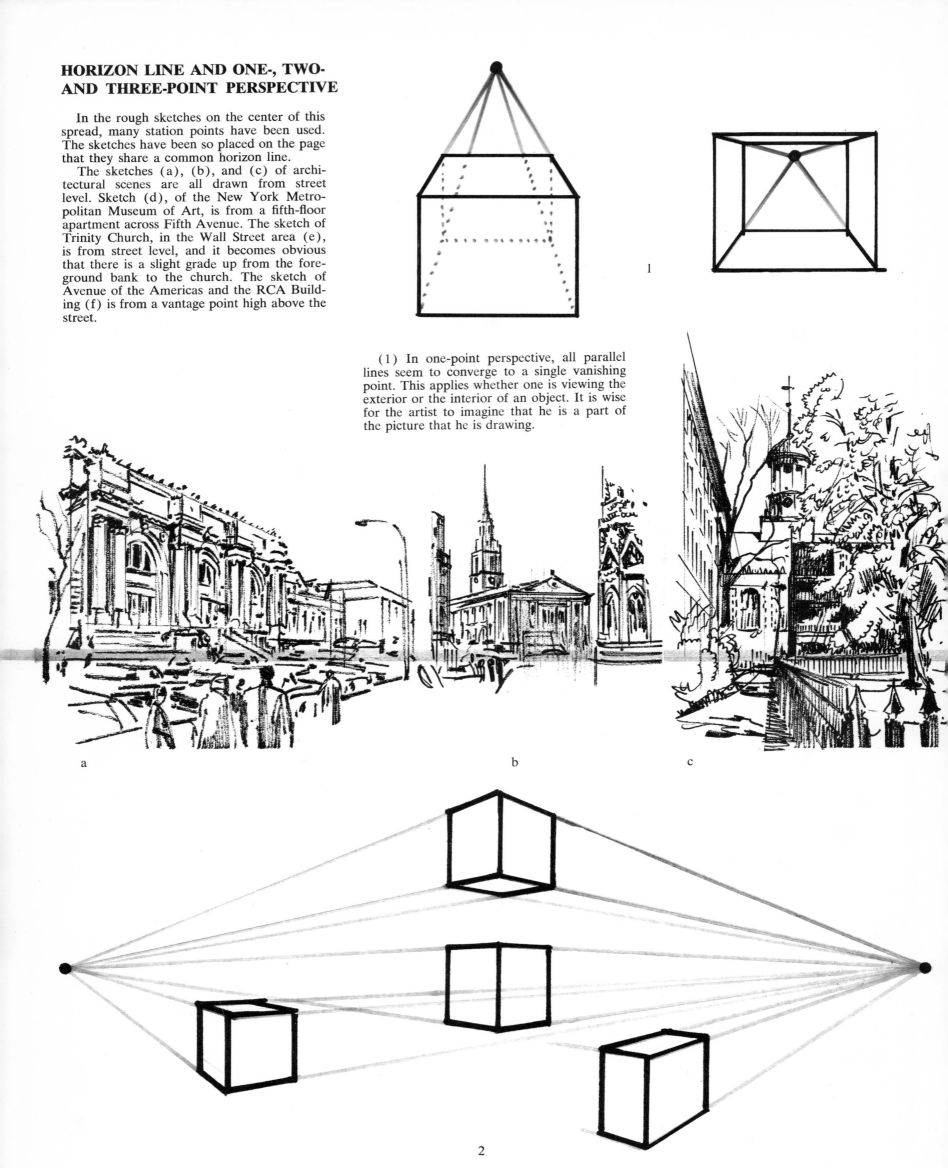

(1) In one-point perspective, all parallel lines seem to converge to a single vanishing point. This applies whether one is viewing the exterior or the interior of an object. It is wise for the artist to imagine that he is a part of the picture that he is drawing.

a

b

c

(2) In two-point perspective, parallel lines seem to converge on two vanishing points on the horizon.

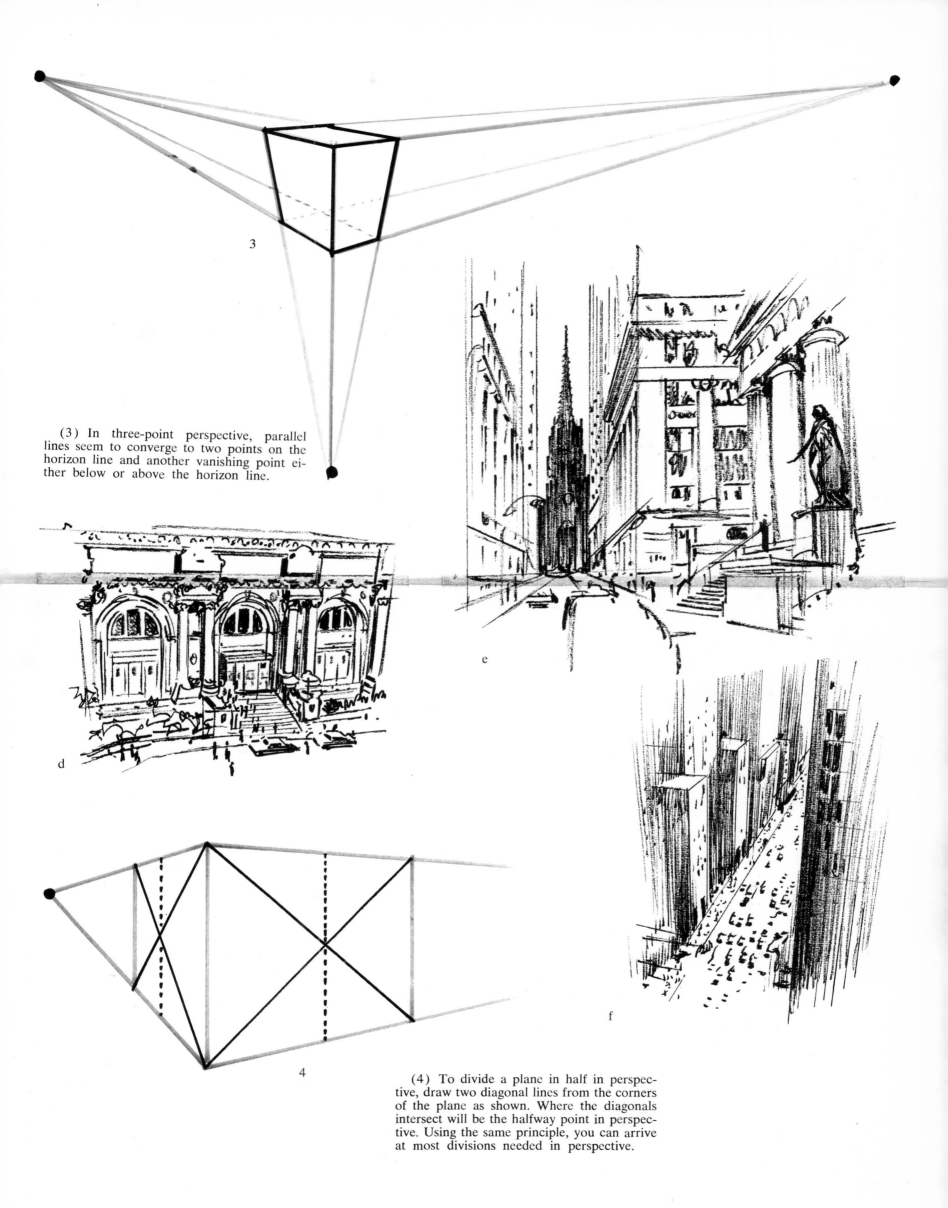

(3) In three-point perspective, parallel lines seem to converge to two points on the horizon line and another vanishing point either below or above the horizon line.

3

d

e

f

4

(4) To divide a plane in half in perspective, draw two diagonal lines from the corners of the plane as shown. Where the diagonals intersect will be the halfway point in perspective. Using the same principle, you can arrive at most divisions needed in perspective.

PICTURE PLANE AND SCALE

(a) As objects recede, they appear smaller. An artist seen holding a pencil at arm's length is usually determining the proportionate size an object will be in his work. He may, of course, be comparing relative sizes.

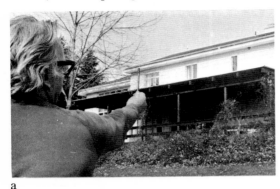

a

(b) If the artist is using a couple of straightedges, he may be determining the angle of a part of the picture in relation to the horizon line.

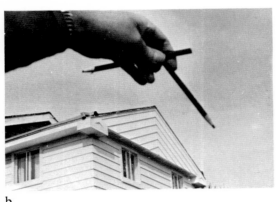

b

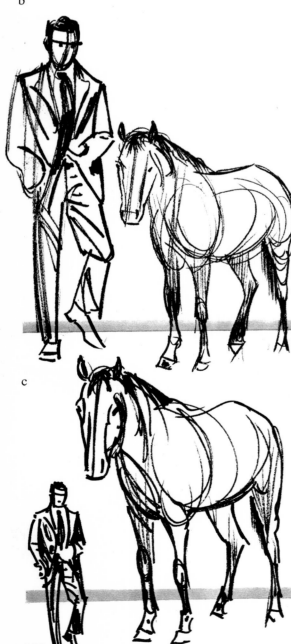

c

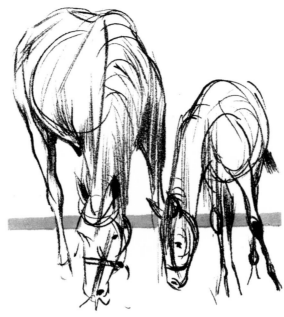

(c) In the two horse and man sketches, the men and horses have been deliberately drawn far out of scale to impress the fact that not only the relationship one to the other is important, but also important is the position in the perspective of the picture, as in the convincing sketch of the mare and colt.

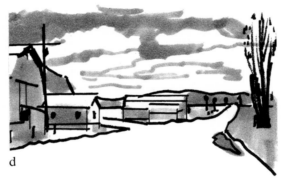

d

(d) This is a scene as it would appear to the camera, with a normal lens—a fairly accurate interpretation.

The artist is not as limited as a camera, however. He can create the message or illusion he wishes. He has taken the first step by simply deciding to attempt the task of creating this illusion of three dimensions on a surface limited to two dimensions.

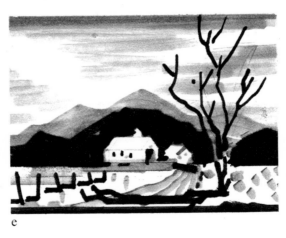

e

(e) In this thumbnail sketch interest is brought to the mountains by increasing their size and importance. The artist has taken the facts as they appear and changed them to conform to his own interpretation of the subject. It is quite possible, then, for an artist to use the same source material, viewed from a single station point, to create endless paintings.

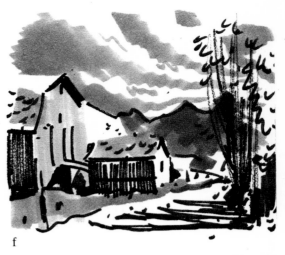

f

(f) In this sketch the buildings are brought into the foreground, and less emphasis is given to the distant mountains.

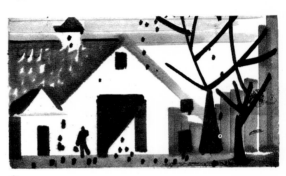

g

(g) In this more abstract approach, concentration is on pattern exclusively. With perspective forgotten, symbols are used to represent trees and parts of houses.

(h) Invariably the artist will be attracted to the dramatic or unusual. Hopefully, if he is impressed by what he sees, he will find it easier to impress the viewer with his feelings. This is no condemnation of the everyday, garden variety of subject matter. It is merely the stock excuse an artist gives to go off on an exciting trip.

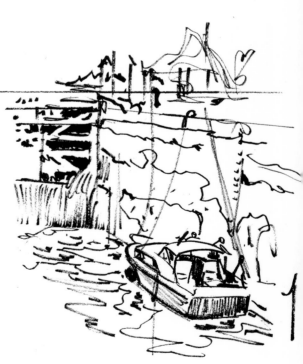

h

Before an artist begins the final work, he should go through many of these possibilities in little sketches. He need not be tied to just what he sees. He may bring a tree that isn't there into his composition. He may transform a dirt road into a winding stream.

148

The diagrammatic lamp, the circle in a square, and the cone were all drawn using ellipses, templates, the wine bottles, jar, and glass on the mirror, drawn (at right) freehand.

The use of the template is valuable as a check against your drawing of ellipses. The template is not truly correct in perspective, but it is close enough to be an aid in drawing.

(a) The difference in the perspective between two ellipses in a small-scale object is slight.

(b) When something is to suggest tremendous scale, the ellipses vary a great deal.

It follows, then, that when a large object is to be suggested in a drawing, the perspective will be much more violent than in the small objects, even though the size of the drawing is the same. It also follows that an artist working from models might find this fact gives away his source material, if he did not bear it in mind when drawing. It is also possible to shoot photographs with a wide-angle lens and accomplish this illusion mechanically.

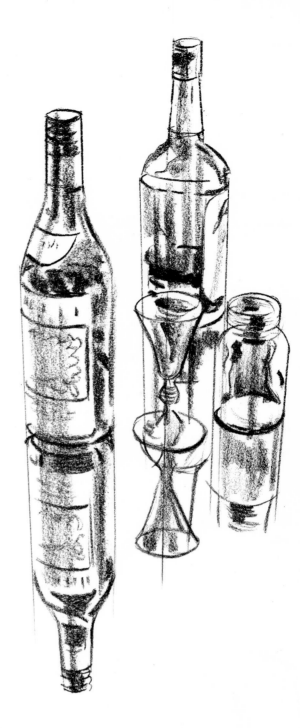

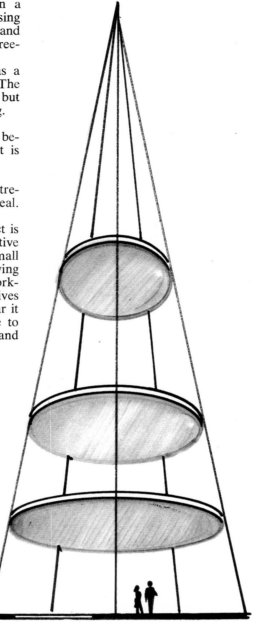

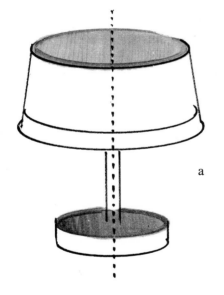

a

b

The bottles, glass, and jar have been drawn as they appear to the eye. A more interesting approach is to draw the individual forms in multiple perspective, much as the cubists did.

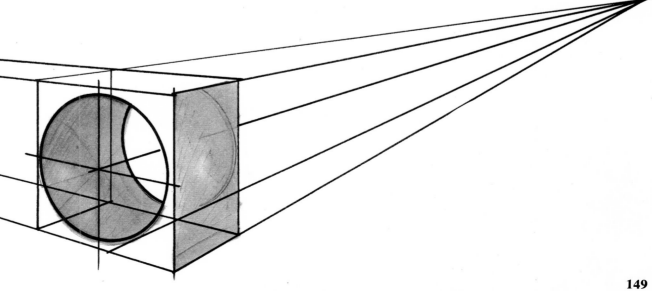

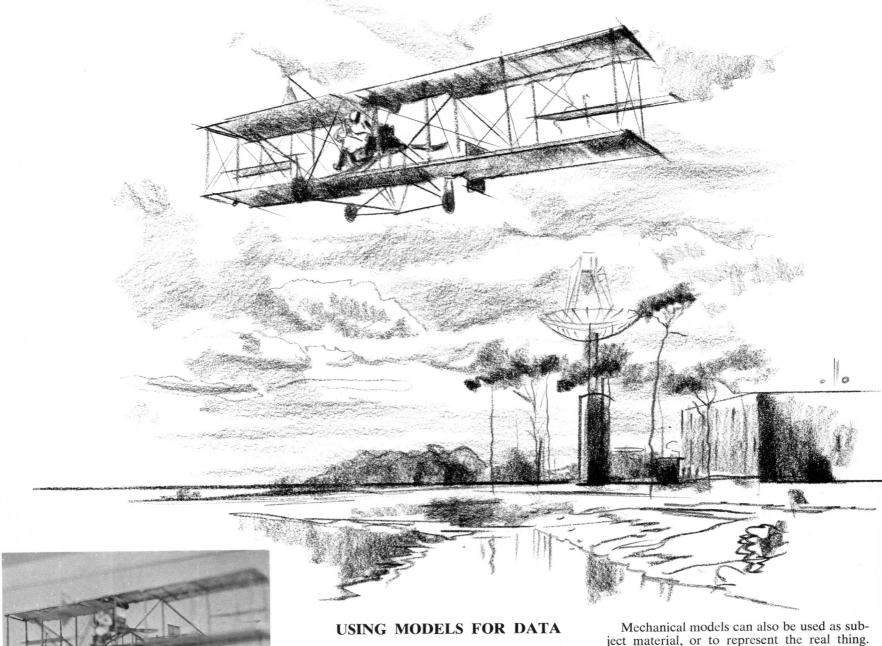

USING MODELS FOR DATA

Mechanical models can also be used as subject material, or to represent the real thing. The model of the early Curtiss-Wright plane (a) was used for the sketch above in which the landscape was added.

(b–d) One of the best methods of projecting drawings from plans (b) is to use blocks (c). In this way you can see where shadows lie and quickly try many angles of view (d). Some artists actually make a diorama of complicated projects before proceeding with the finished painting.

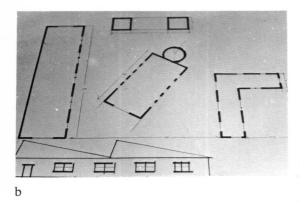

a

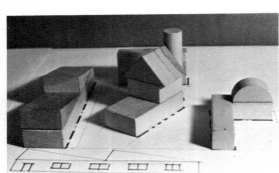

b

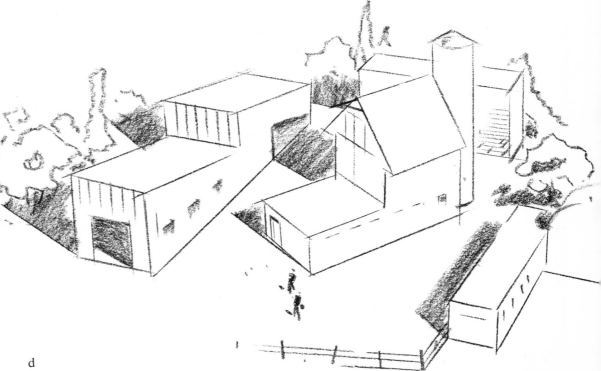

c

d

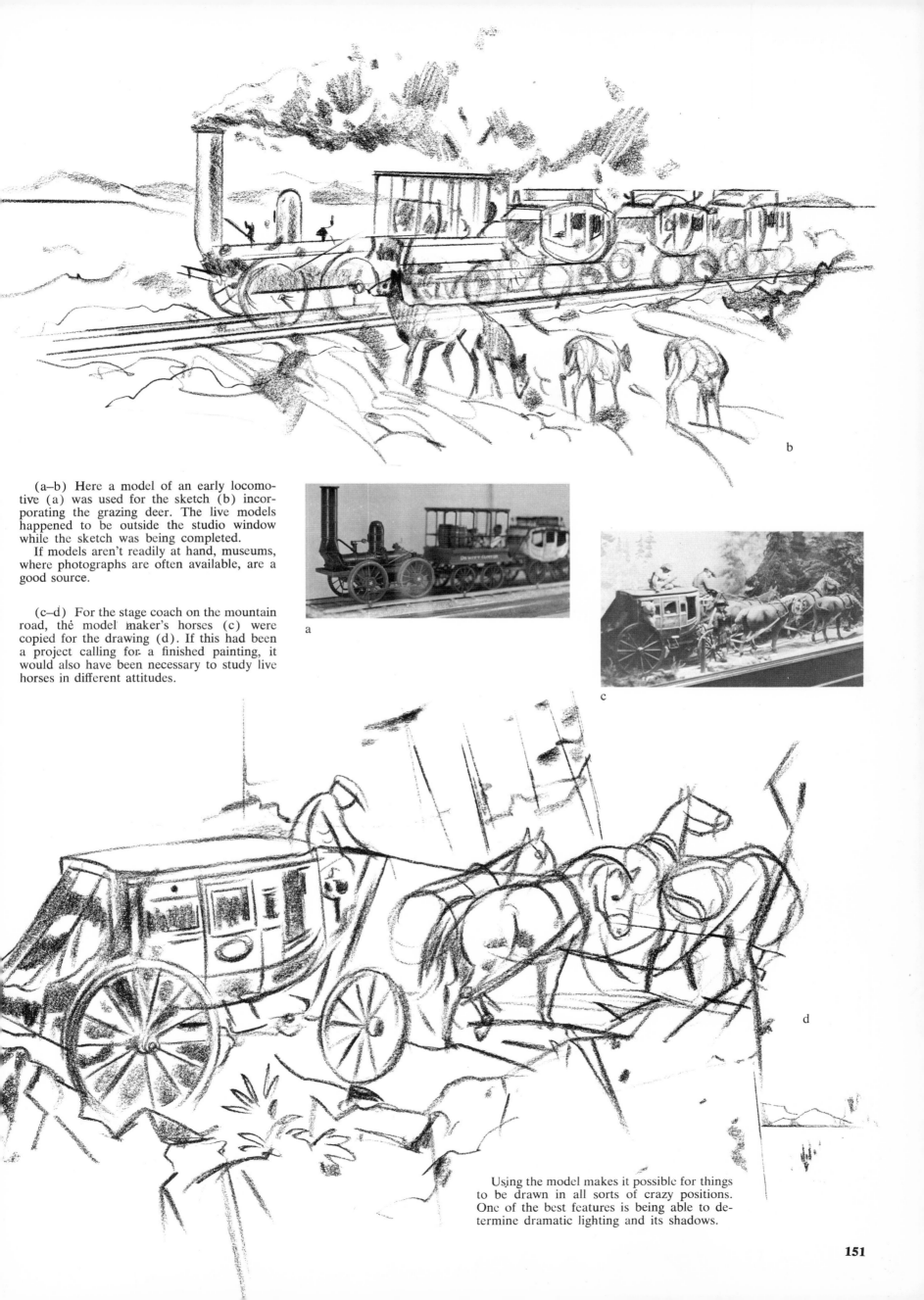

(a–b) Here a model of an early locomotive (a) was used for the sketch (b) incorporating the grazing deer. The live models happened to be outside the studio window while the sketch was being completed.

If models aren't readily at hand, museums, where photographs are often available, are a good source.

(c–d) For the stage coach on the mountain road, the model maker's horses (c) were copied for the drawing (d). If this had been a project calling for a finished painting, it would also have been necessary to study live horses in different attitudes.

Using the model makes it possible for things to be drawn in all sorts of crazy positions. One of the best features is being able to determine dramatic lighting and its shadows.

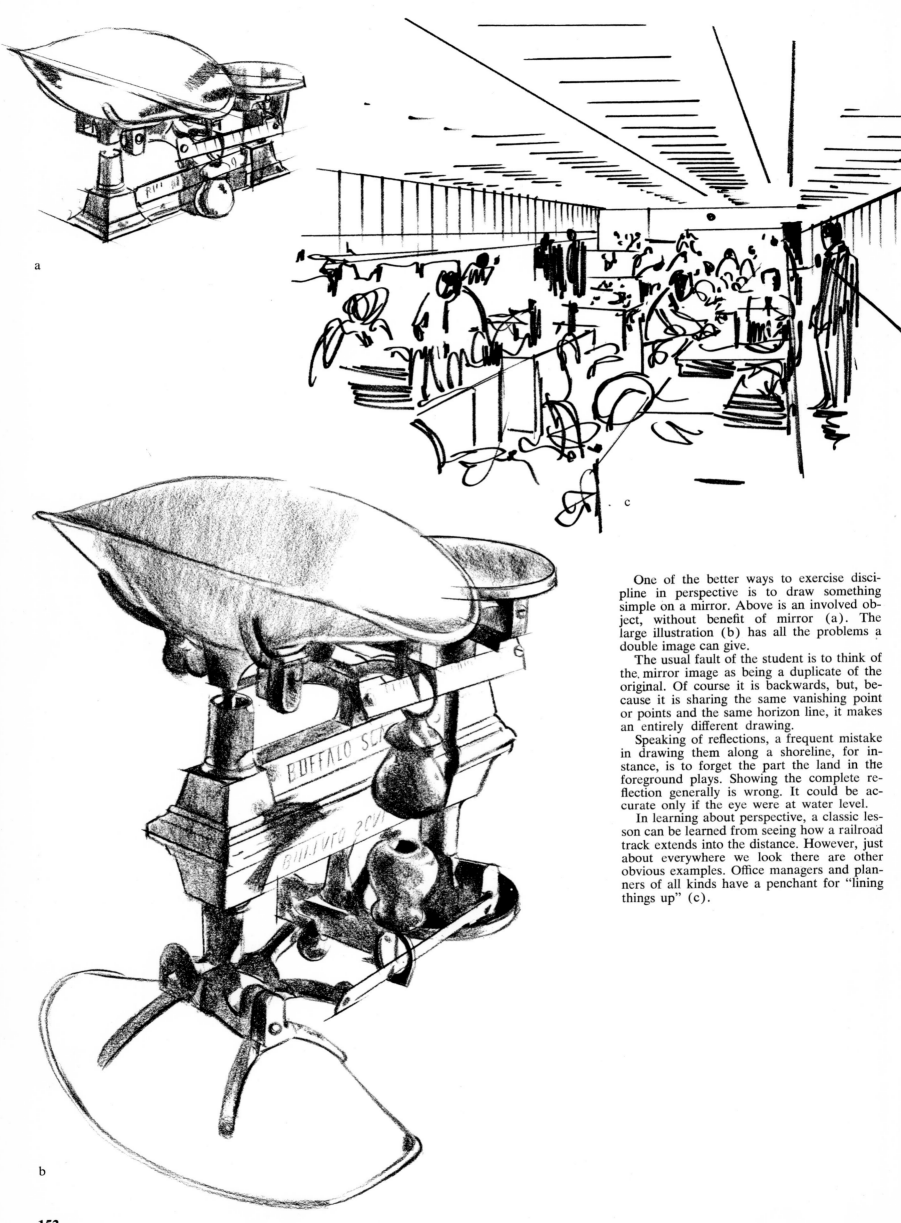

a

One of the better ways to exercise discipline in perspective is to draw something simple on a mirror. Above is an involved object, without benefit of mirror (a). The large illustration (b) has all the problems a double image can give.

The usual fault of the student is to think of the mirror image as being a duplicate of the original. Of course it is backwards, but, because it is sharing the same vanishing point or points and the same horizon line, it makes an entirely different drawing.

Speaking of reflections, a frequent mistake in drawing them along a shoreline, for instance, is to forget the part the land in the foreground plays. Showing the complete reflection generally is wrong. It could be accurate only if the eye were at water level.

In learning about perspective, a classic lesson can be learned from seeing how a railroad track extends into the distance. However, just about everywhere we look there are other obvious examples. Office managers and planners of all kinds have a penchant for "lining things up" (c).

c

b

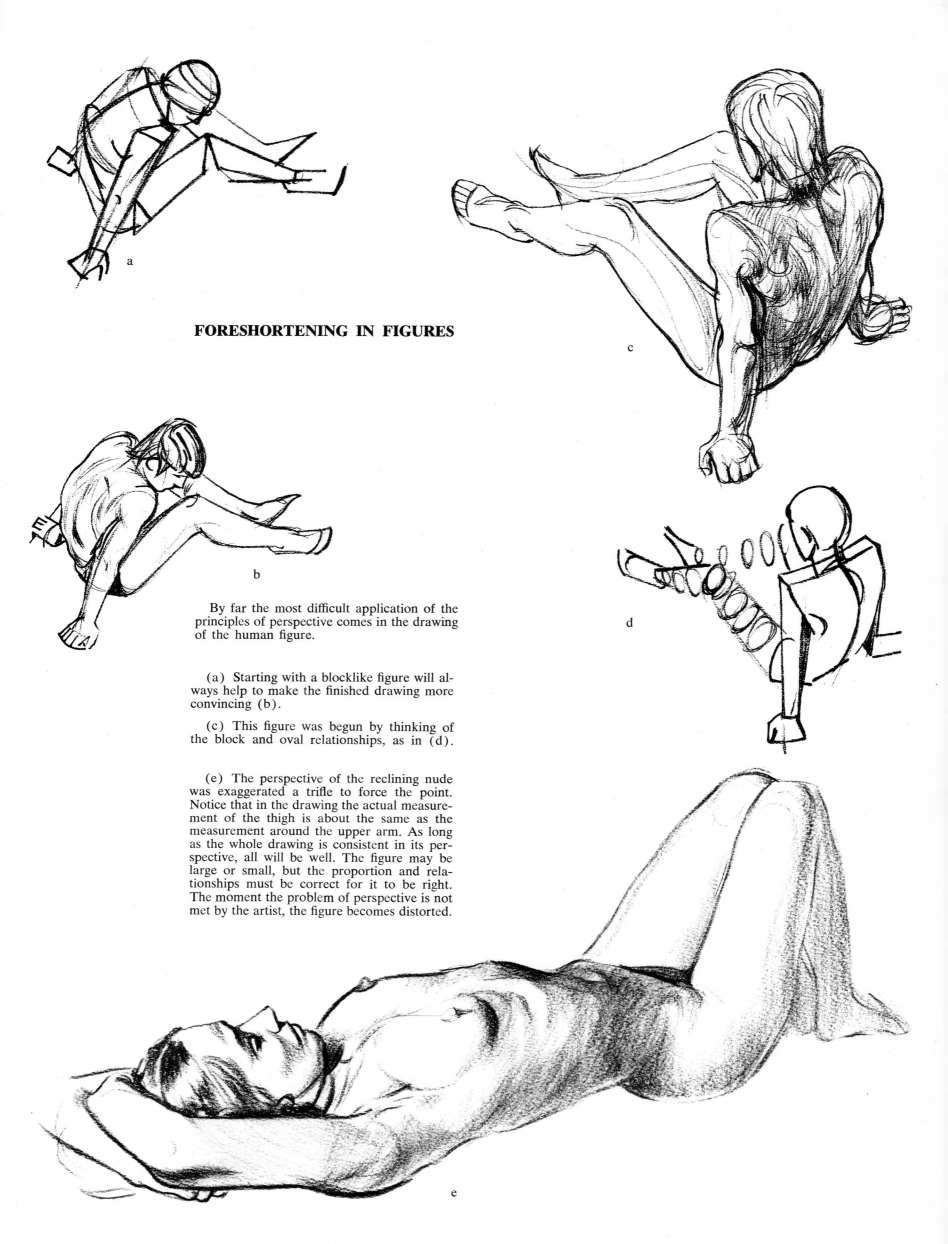

FORESHORTENING IN FIGURES

By far the most difficult application of the principles of perspective comes in the drawing of the human figure.

(a) Starting with a blocklike figure will always help to make the finished drawing more convincing (b).

(c) This figure was begun by thinking of the block and oval relationships, as in (d).

(e) The perspective of the reclining nude was exaggerated a trifle to force the point. Notice that in the drawing the actual measurement of the thigh is about the same as the measurement around the upper arm. As long as the whole drawing is consistent in its perspective, all will be well. The figure may be large or small, but the proportion and relationships must be correct for it to be right. The moment the problem of perspective is not met by the artist, the figure becomes distorted.

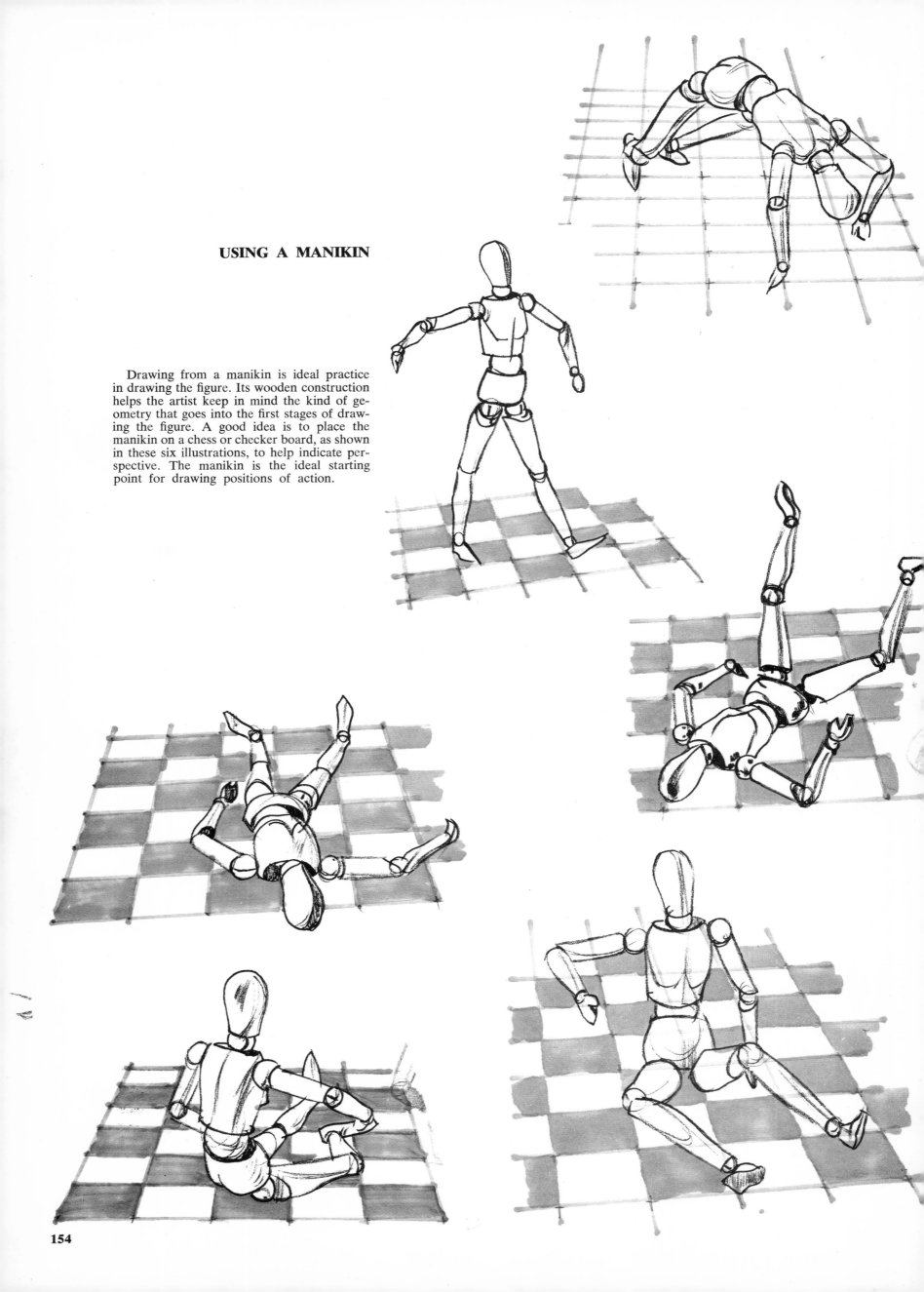

USING A MANIKIN

Drawing from a manikin is ideal practice in drawing the figure. Its wooden construction helps the artist keep in mind the kind of geometry that goes into the first stages of drawing the figure. A good idea is to place the manikin on a chess or checker board, as shown in these six illustrations, to help indicate perspective. The manikin is the ideal starting point for drawing positions of action.

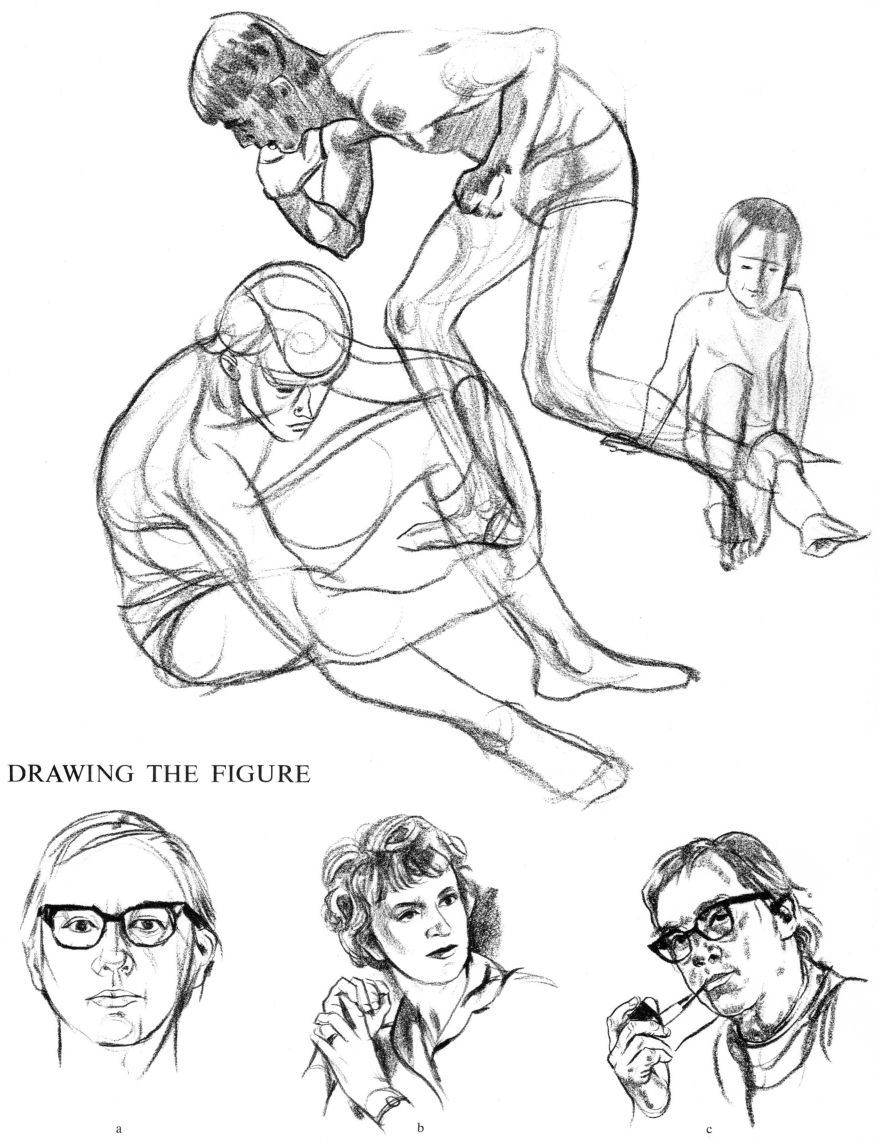

DRAWING THE FIGURE

a
b
c

The first and continuing problem in figure drawing is obtaining a model, unless, of course, you wish to restrict your drawing to head and hands, or to use a manikin, as shown on the previous page. Most people have a vain streak and will pose for their portrait. Remember that poses with hands (b), preferably hands doing something (c), make for a more interesting pose. If the person is wearing glasses (a and c), try to wait until you have completed the head before putting the glasses into the drawing.

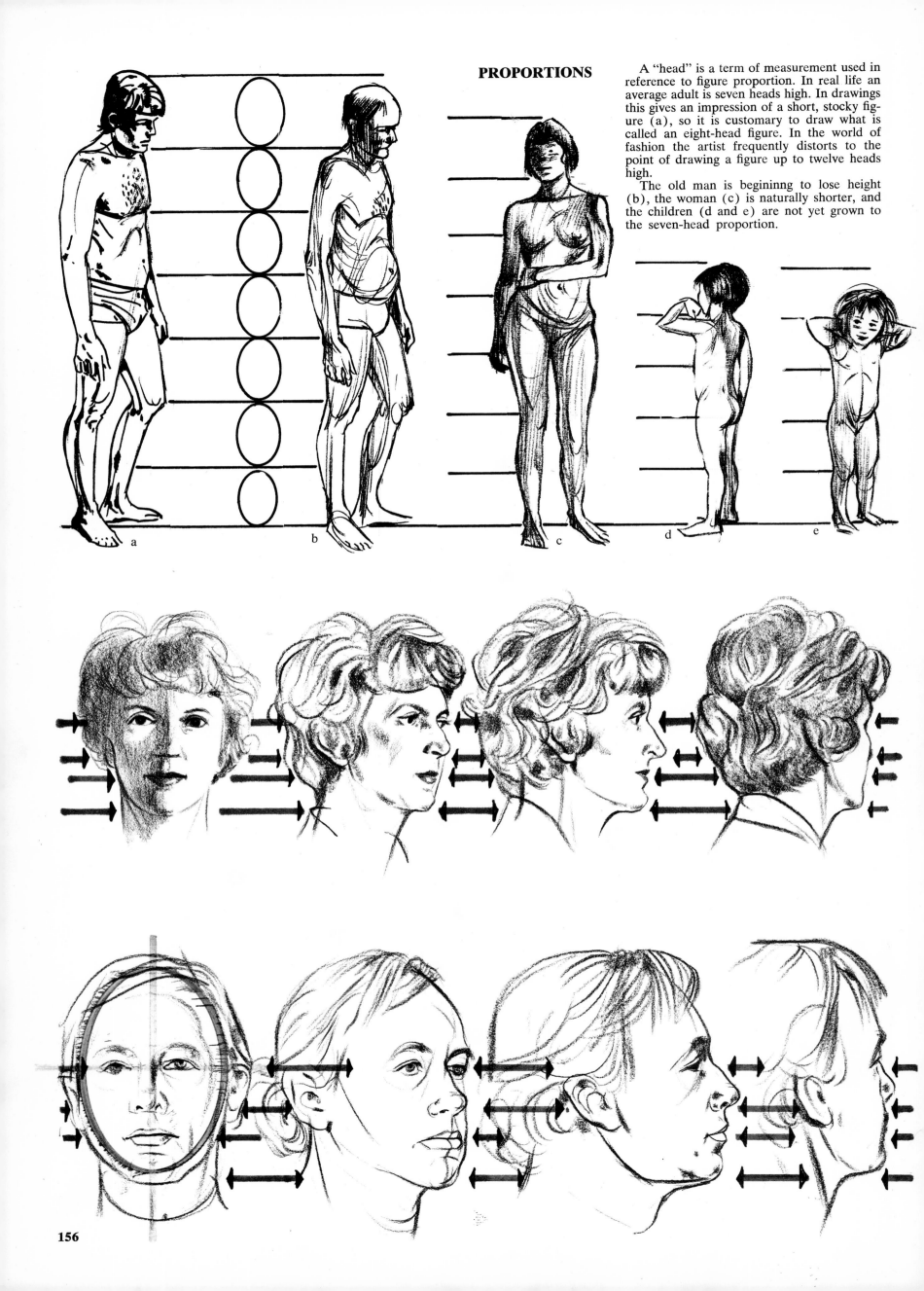

PROPORTIONS

A "head" is a term of measurement used in reference to figure proportion. In real life an average adult is seven heads high. In drawings this gives an impression of a short, stocky figure (a), so it is customary to draw what is called an eight-head figure. In the world of fashion the artist frequently distorts to the point of drawing a figure up to twelve heads high.

The old man is begininng to lose height (b), the woman (c) is naturally shorter, and the children (d and e) are not yet grown to the seven-head proportion.

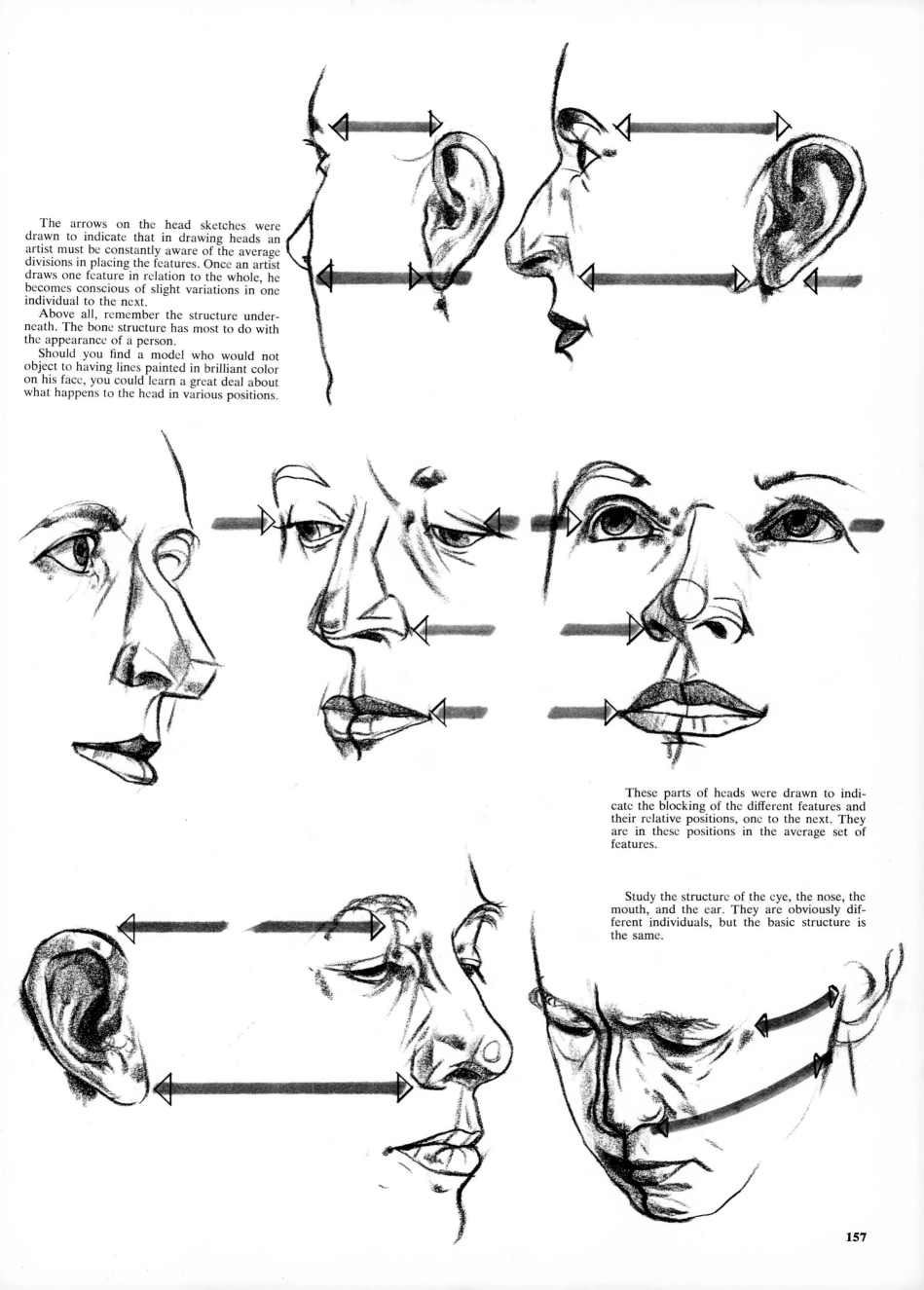

The arrows on the head sketches were drawn to indicate that in drawing heads an artist must be constantly aware of the average divisions in placing the features. Once an artist draws one feature in relation to the whole, he becomes conscious of slight variations in one individual to the next.

Above all, remember the structure underneath. The bone structure has most to do with the appearance of a person.

Should you find a model who would not object to having lines painted in brilliant color on his face, you could learn a great deal about what happens to the head in various positions.

These parts of heads were drawn to indicate the blocking of the different features and their relative positions, one to the next. They are in these positions in the average set of features.

Study the structure of the eye, the nose, the mouth, and the ear. They are obviously different individuals, but the basic structure is the same.

157

STICK FIGURES AND SKETCHING

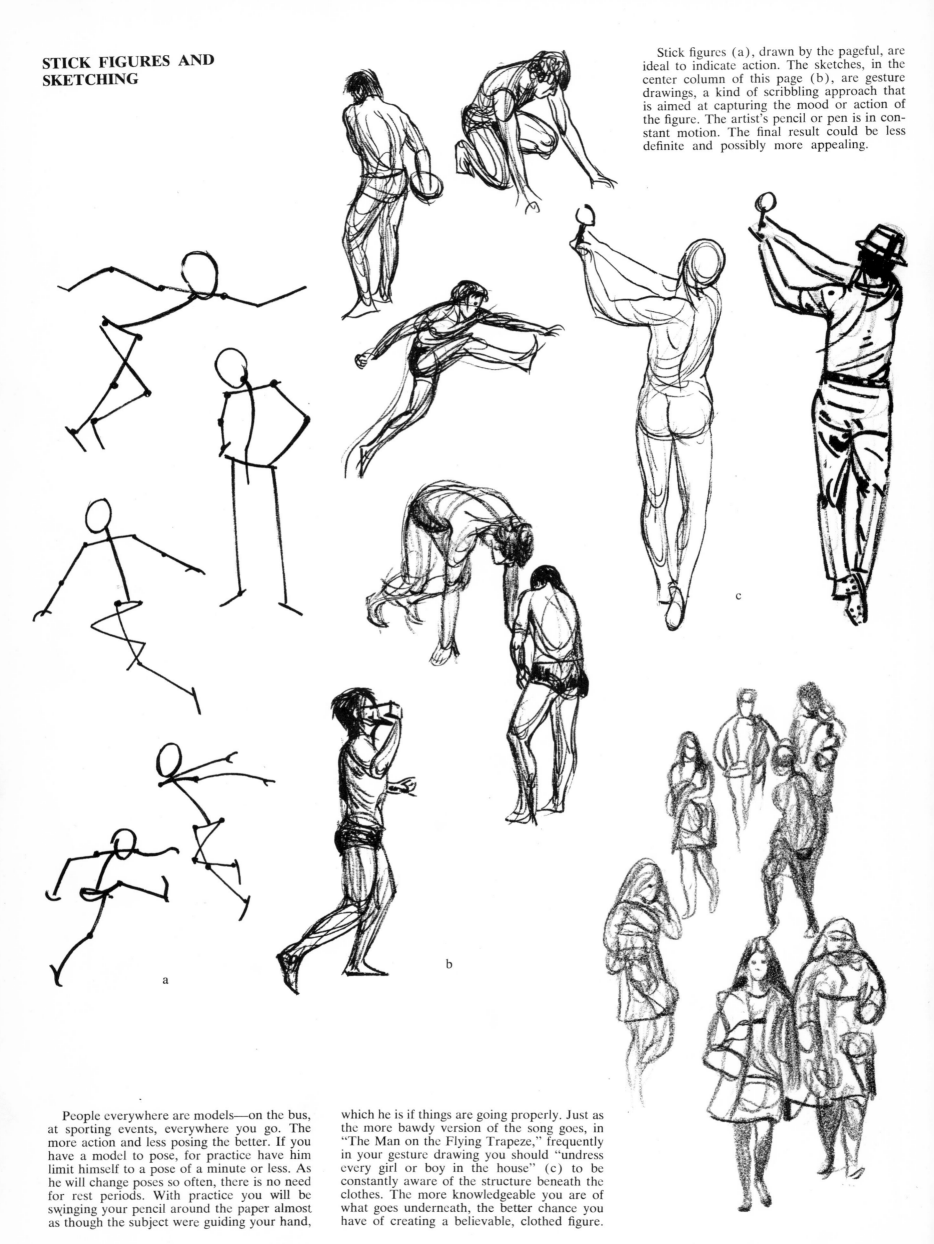

Stick figures (a), drawn by the pageful, are ideal to indicate action. The sketches, in the center column of this page (b), are gesture drawings, a kind of scribbling approach that is aimed at capturing the mood or action of the figure. The artist's pencil or pen is in constant motion. The final result could be less definite and possibly more appealing.

a

b

c

People everywhere are models—on the bus, at sporting events, everywhere you go. The more action and less posing the better. If you have a model to pose, for practice have him limit himself to a pose of a minute or less. As he will change poses so often, there is no need for rest periods. With practice you will be swinging your pencil around the paper almost as though the subject were guiding your hand,

which he is if things are going properly. Just as the more bawdy version of the song goes, in "The Man on the Flying Trapeze," frequently in your gesture drawing you should "undress every girl or boy in the house" (c) to be constantly aware of the structure beneath the clothes. The more knowledgeable you are of what goes underneath, the better chance you have of creating a believable, clothed figure.

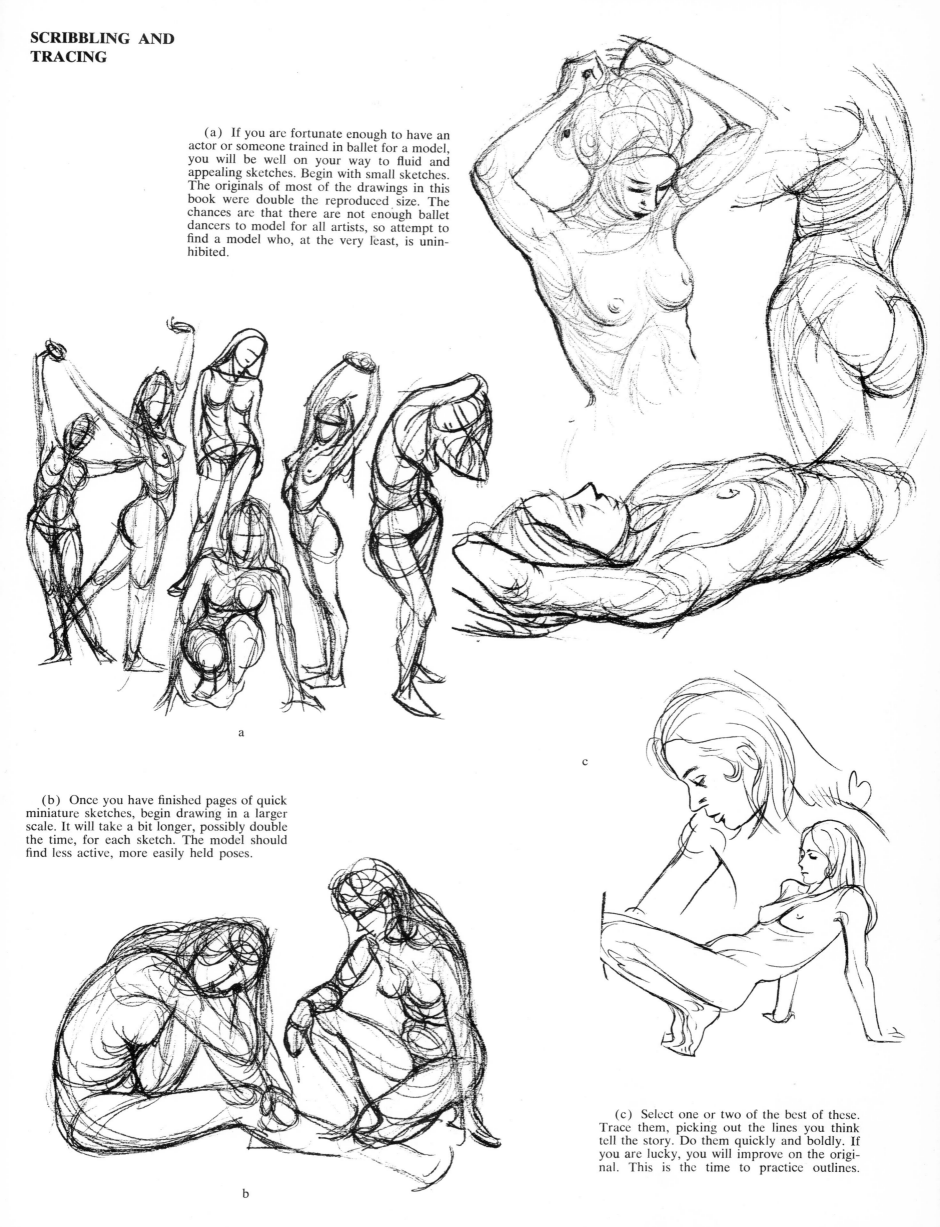

SCRIBBLING AND TRACING

(a) If you are fortunate enough to have an actor or someone trained in ballet for a model, you will be well on your way to fluid and appealing sketches. Begin with small sketches. The originals of most of the drawings in this book were double the reproduced size. The chances are that there are not enough ballet dancers to model for all artists, so attempt to find a model who, at the very least, is uninhibited.

(b) Once you have finished pages of quick miniature sketches, begin drawing in a larger scale. It will take a bit longer, possibly double the time, for each sketch. The model should find less active, more easily held poses.

(c) Select one or two of the best of these. Trace them, picking out the lines you think tell the story. Do them quickly and boldly. If you are lucky, you will improve on the original. This is the time to practice outlines.

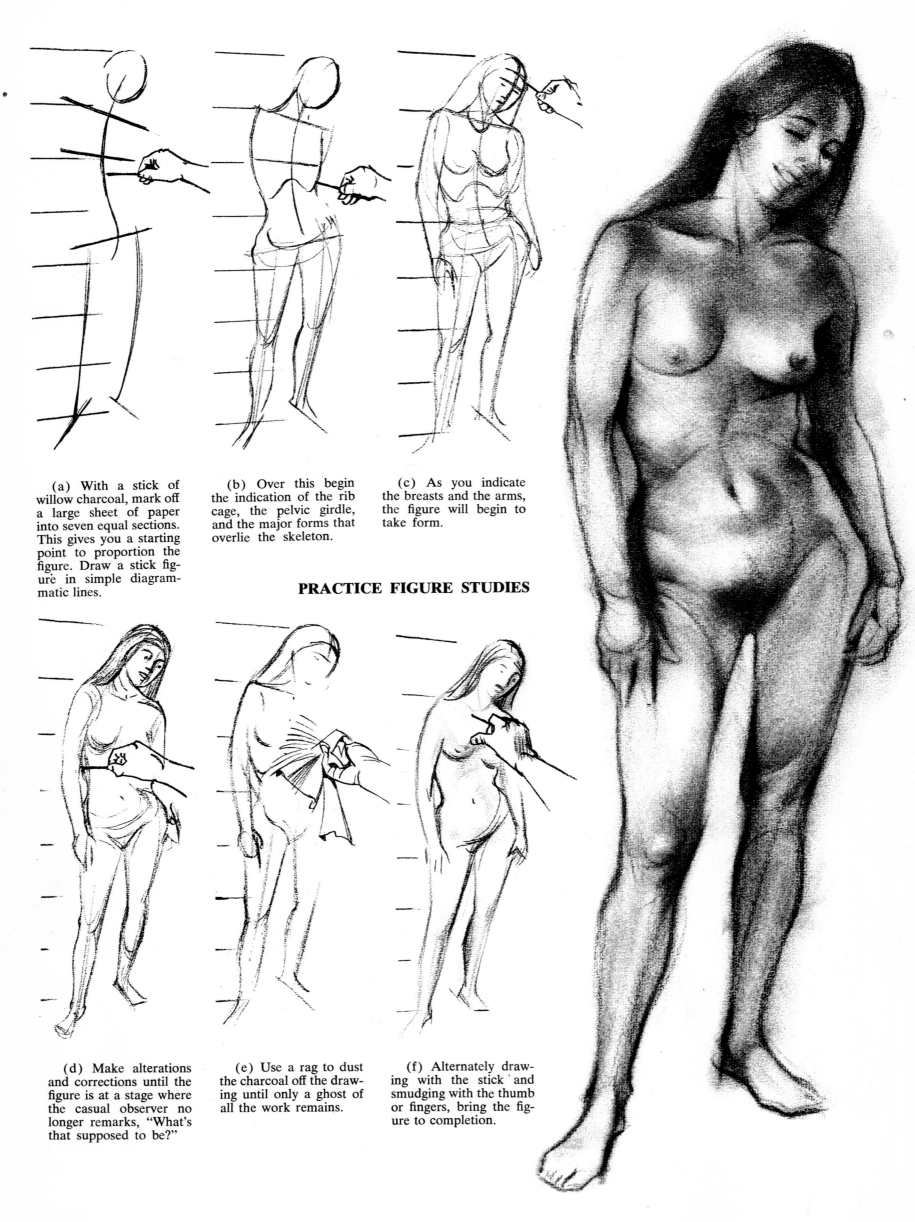

(a) With a stick of willow charcoal, mark off a large sheet of paper into seven equal sections. This gives you a starting point to proportion the figure. Draw a stick figure in simple diagrammatic lines.

(b) Over this begin the indication of the rib cage, the pelvic girdle, and the major forms that overlie the skeleton.

(c) As you indicate the breasts and the arms, the figure will begin to take form.

PRACTICE FIGURE STUDIES

(d) Make alterations and corrections until the figure is at a stage where the casual observer no longer remarks, "What's that supposed to be?"

(e) Use a rag to dust the charcoal off the drawing until only a ghost of all the work remains.

(f) Alternately drawing with the stick and smudging with the thumb or fingers, bring the figure to completion.

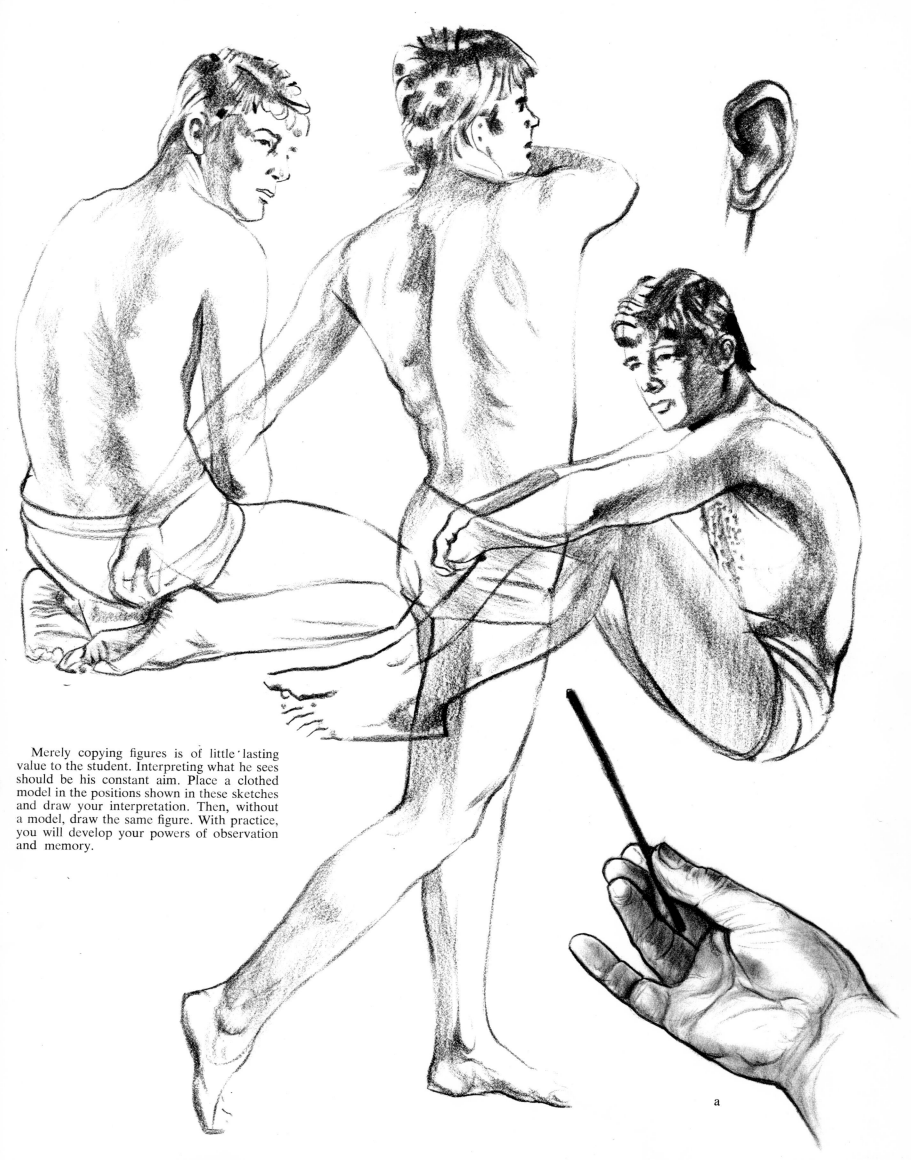

Merely copying figures is of little lasting value to the student. Interpreting what he sees should be his constant aim. Place a clothed model in the positions shown in these sketches and draw your interpretation. Then, without a model, draw the same figure. With practice, you will develop your powers of observation and memory.

a

Art teachers of the past theorized that only through long and intense study of the figure could the student become sufficiently familiar with the subject. Whether or not they carried the theory too far has been the subject of continued argument between the older and the younger artist. Most students, talented or not, are usually turned off. The final drawing is in most cases, of little value, but the practice is invaluable in future, free work. For a free, light touch, the charcoal strokes are made with the hand in position (a).

161

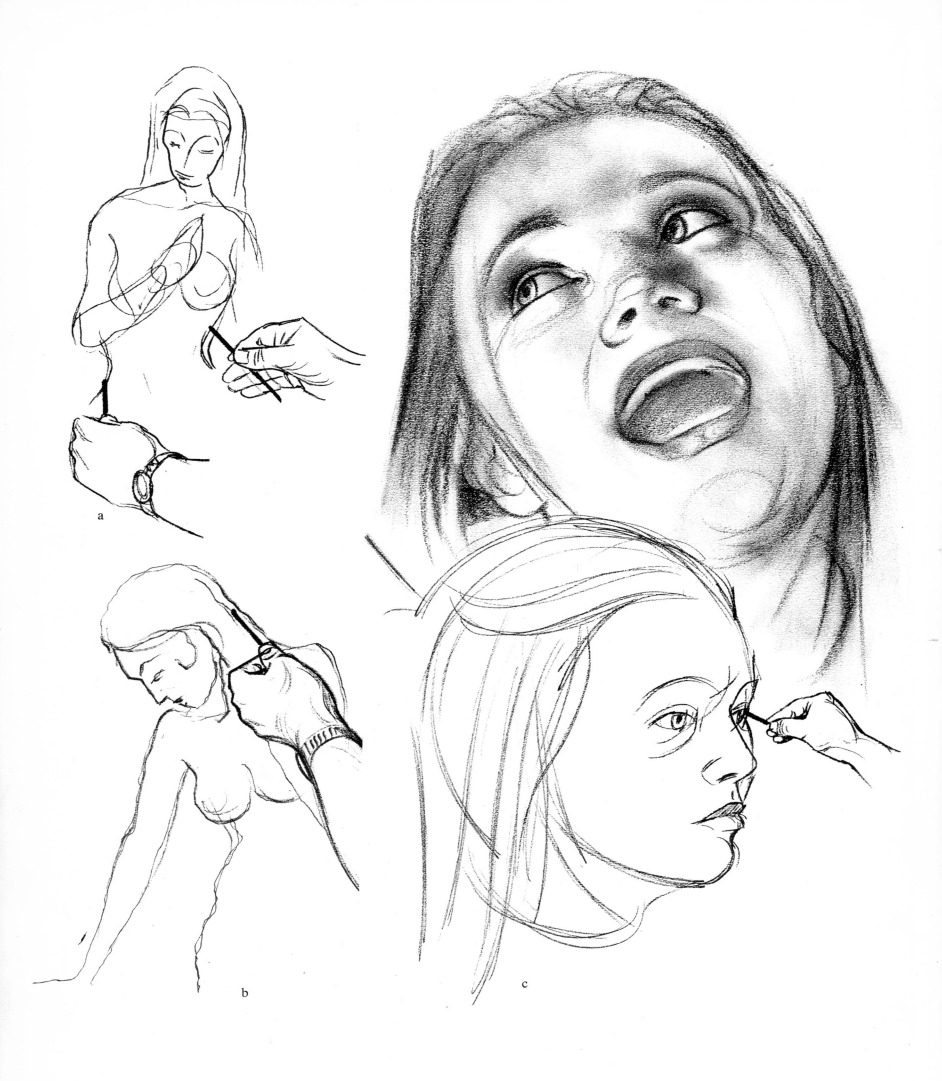

One danger in becoming too knowledgeable of anatomy and all that goes with it is in finally becoming so clever that the finished drawings are sterile and wooden in appearance. Hopefully, the student will avoid this pitfall by alternating between free gesture drawings and finished studies.

(a) One way to free oneself is to use two sticks of charcoal, one in each hand. Attempt to complete an outline drawing of both sides of the figure at the same time.

(b) Another approach is for the right-handed artist to draw with his left hand, or the left-handed artist to draw with his right hand. This makes the mind tell the hand what to do.

(c) There is nothing that quite takes the place of the oversize drawing, made at arm's length, to free an otherwise timid artist.

The hungry, working artist, working in large scale, will devour a tremendous amount of paper. Use old newspapers, such as this market report page in an over-all gray tone, along with felt markers. And the finished result can be interesting enough to frame.

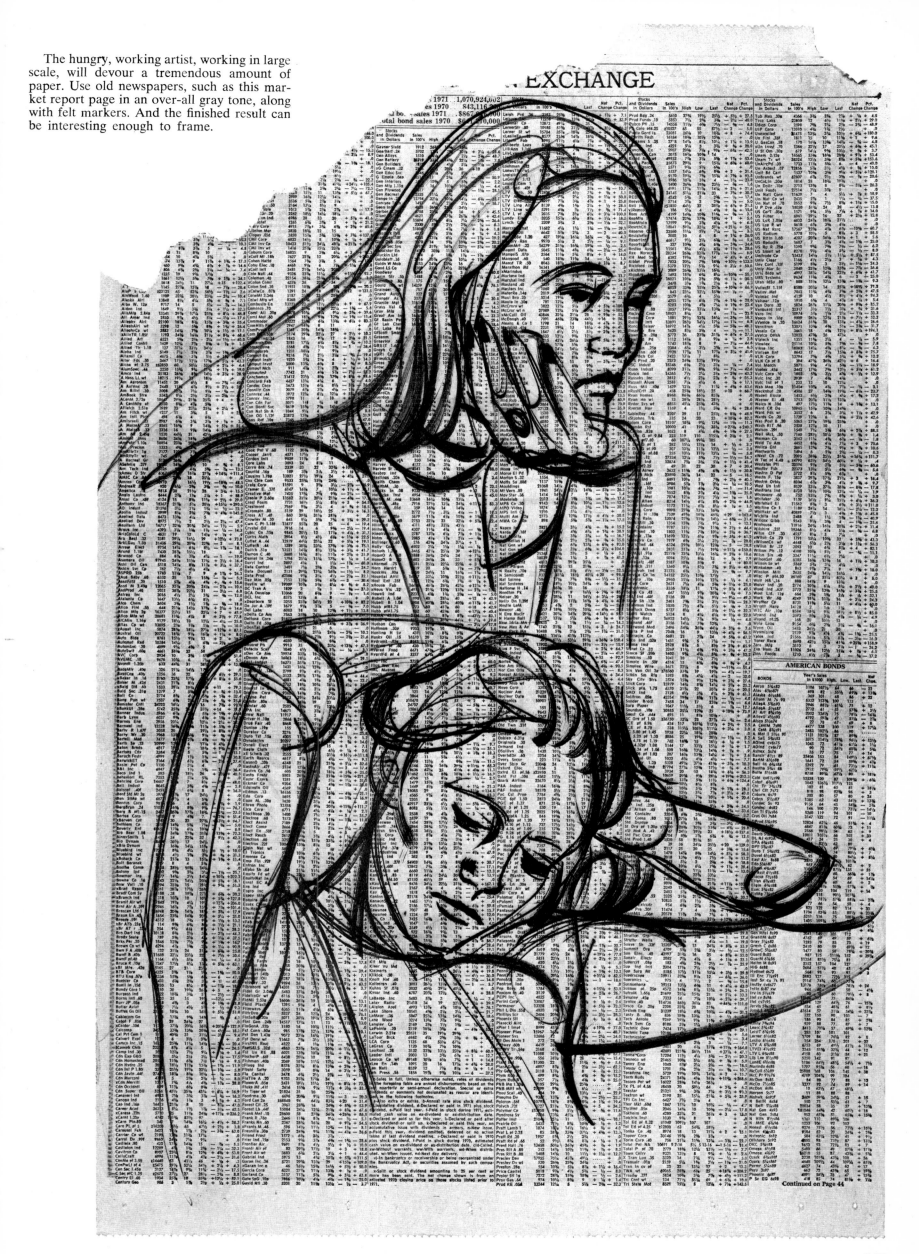

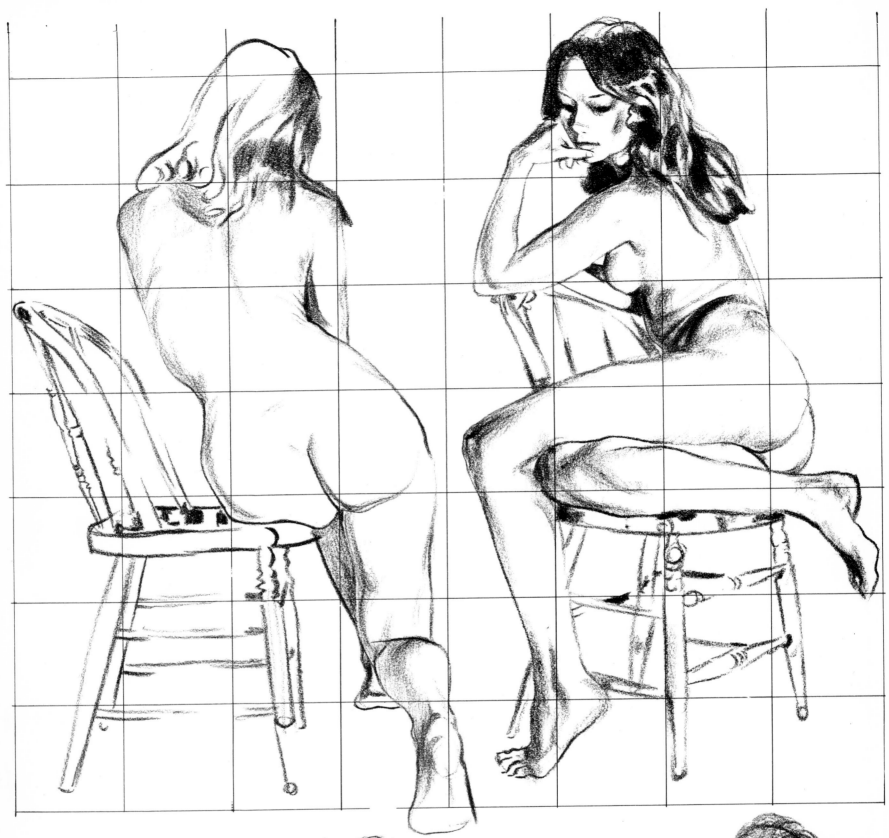

These figures have been squared up, much as the mural painter does with his cartoon prior to drawing it in final size. The squares give points of reference for enlarging the drawing to a larger squared surface.

Make squares of any size on tracing paper. Three-inch squares will match the original size of these sketches. Copy a drawing, scaled up. Once this working drawing is complete, trace it off onto other papers a few times. Practice finishing the figure in a variety of styles as shown on the bottom of the next page. After this practice do a freehand drawing in your own personal style. To what extent can you distort the facts? How best to tell what is in your mind? What would happen if a male figure assumed these poses? Or a child? The object: to make one think about what he is putting down on the paper. The artist becomes acquainted with the facts and then proceeds to give them his own interpretation.

SCALING UP A DRAWING BY SQUARES

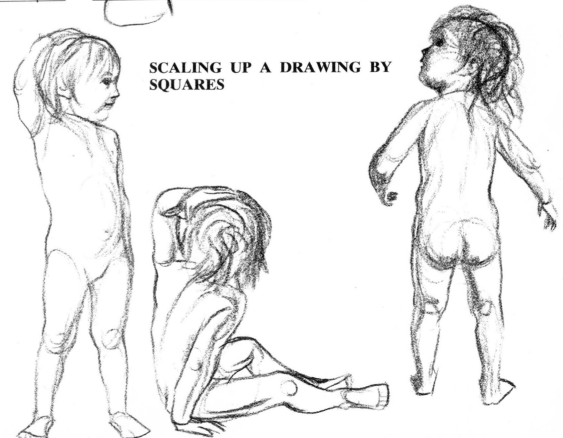

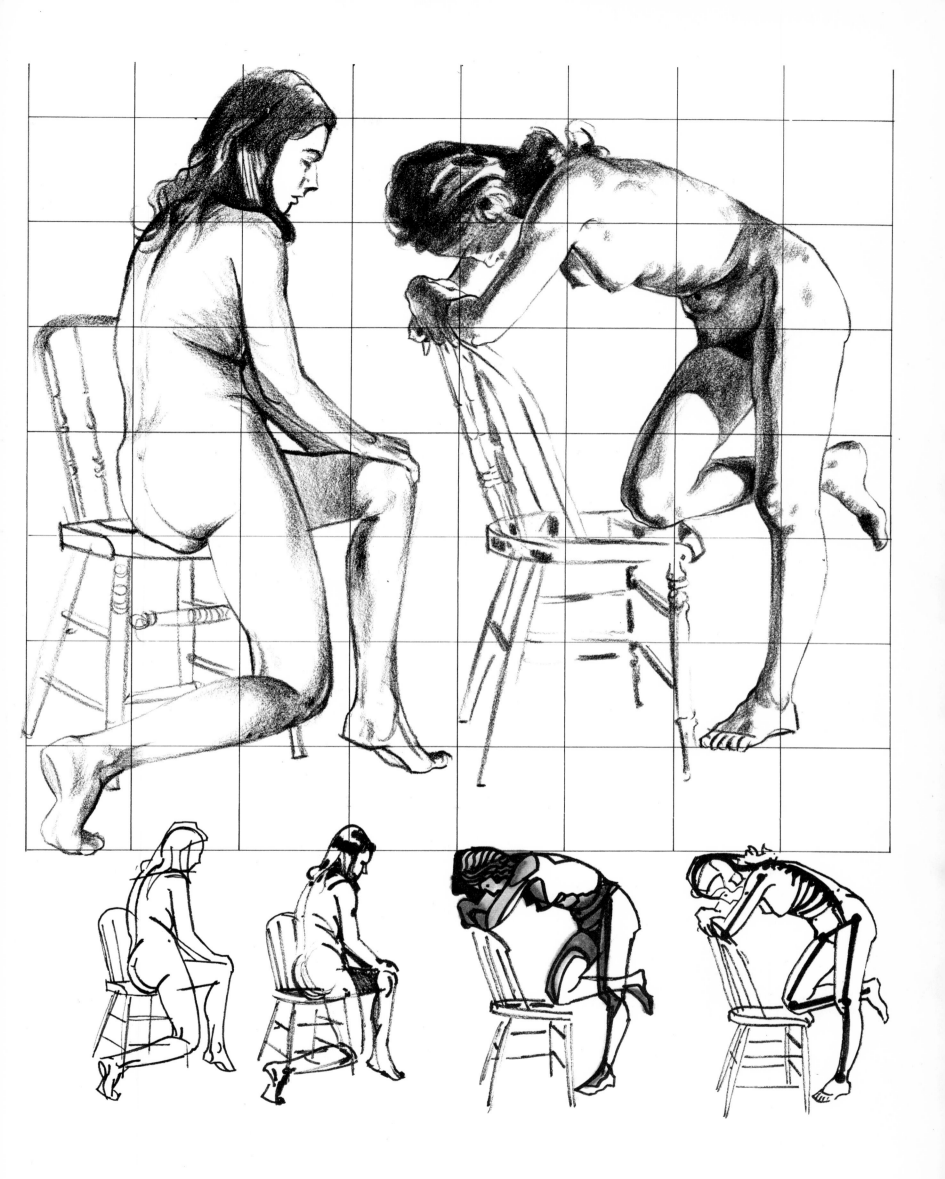

165

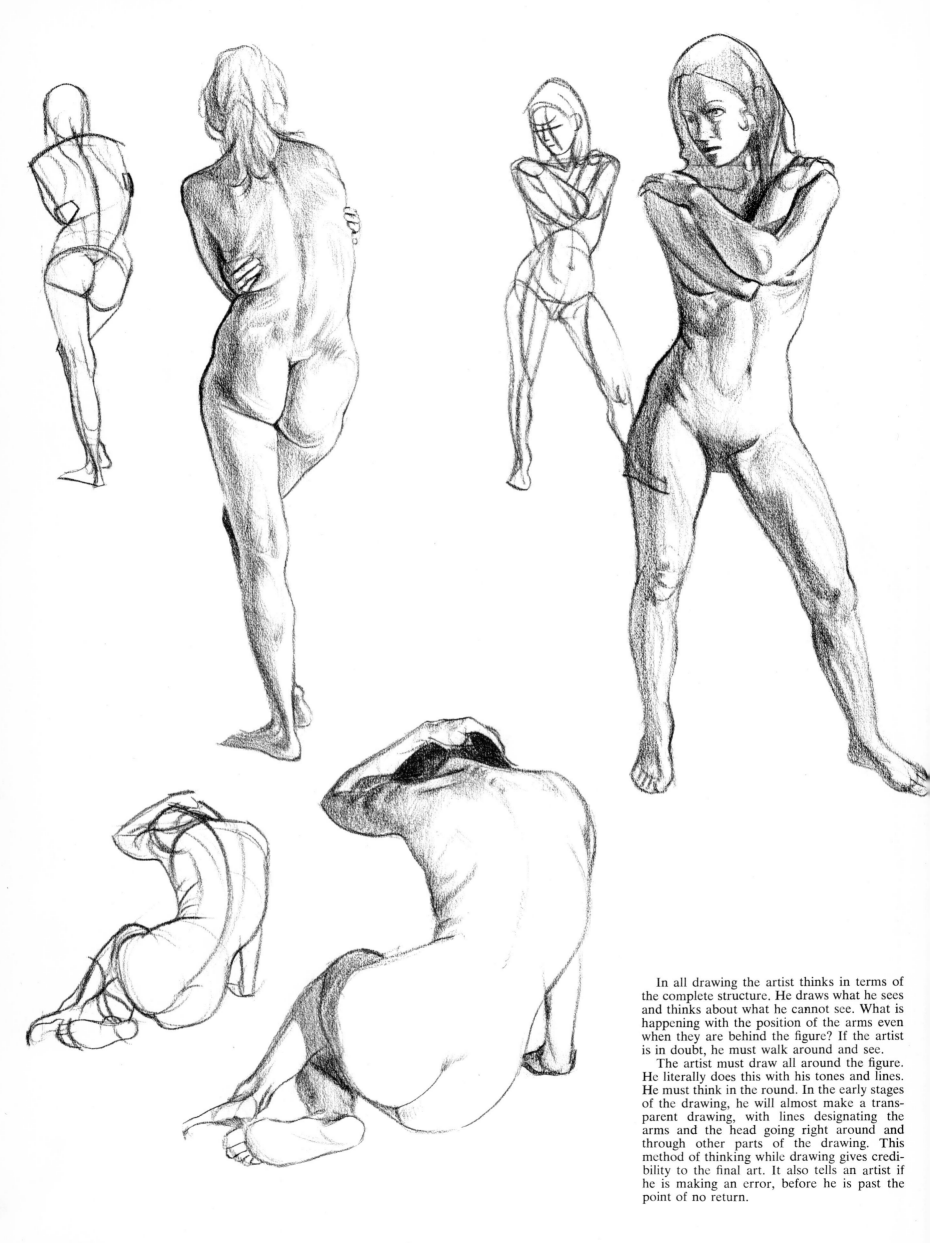

In all drawing the artist thinks in terms of the complete structure. He draws what he sees and thinks about what he cannot see. What is happening with the position of the arms even when they are behind the figure? If the artist is in doubt, he must walk around and see.

The artist must draw all around the figure. He literally does this with his tones and lines. He must think in the round. In the early stages of the drawing, he will almost make a transparent drawing, with lines designating the arms and the head going right around and through other parts of the drawing. This method of thinking while drawing gives credibility to the final art. It also tells an artist if he is making an error, before he is past the point of no return.

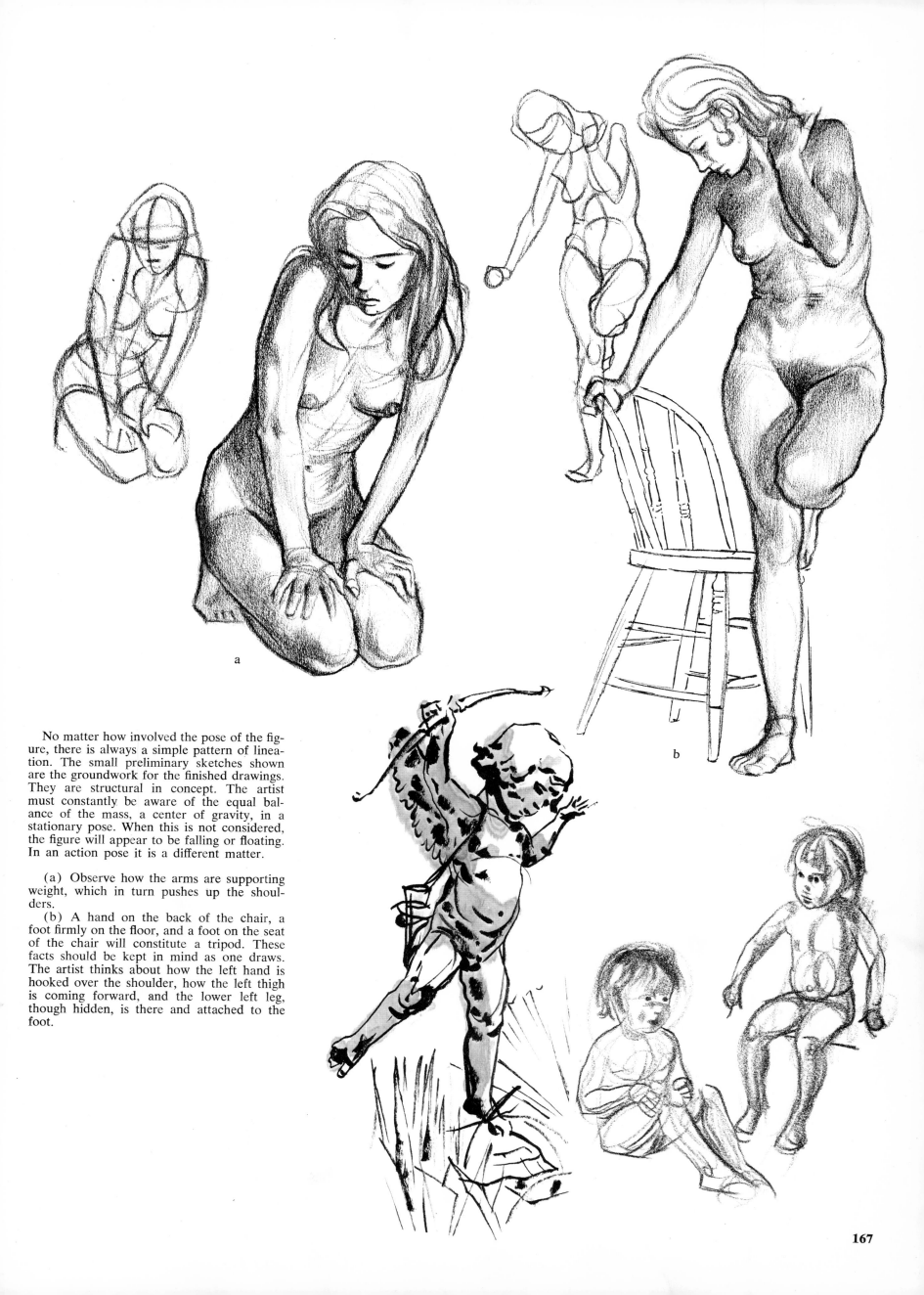

No matter how involved the pose of the figure, there is always a simple pattern of lineation. The small preliminary sketches shown are the groundwork for the finished drawings. They are structural in concept. The artist must constantly be aware of the equal balance of the mass, a center of gravity, in a stationary pose. When this is not considered, the figure will appear to be falling or floating. In an action pose it is a different matter.

(a) Observe how the arms are supporting weight, which in turn pushes up the shoulders.

(b) A hand on the back of the chair, a foot firmly on the floor, and a foot on the seat of the chair will constitute a tripod. These facts should be kept in mind as one draws. The artist thinks about how the left hand is hooked over the shoulder, how the left thigh is coming forward, and the lower left leg, though hidden, is there and attached to the foot.

a

b

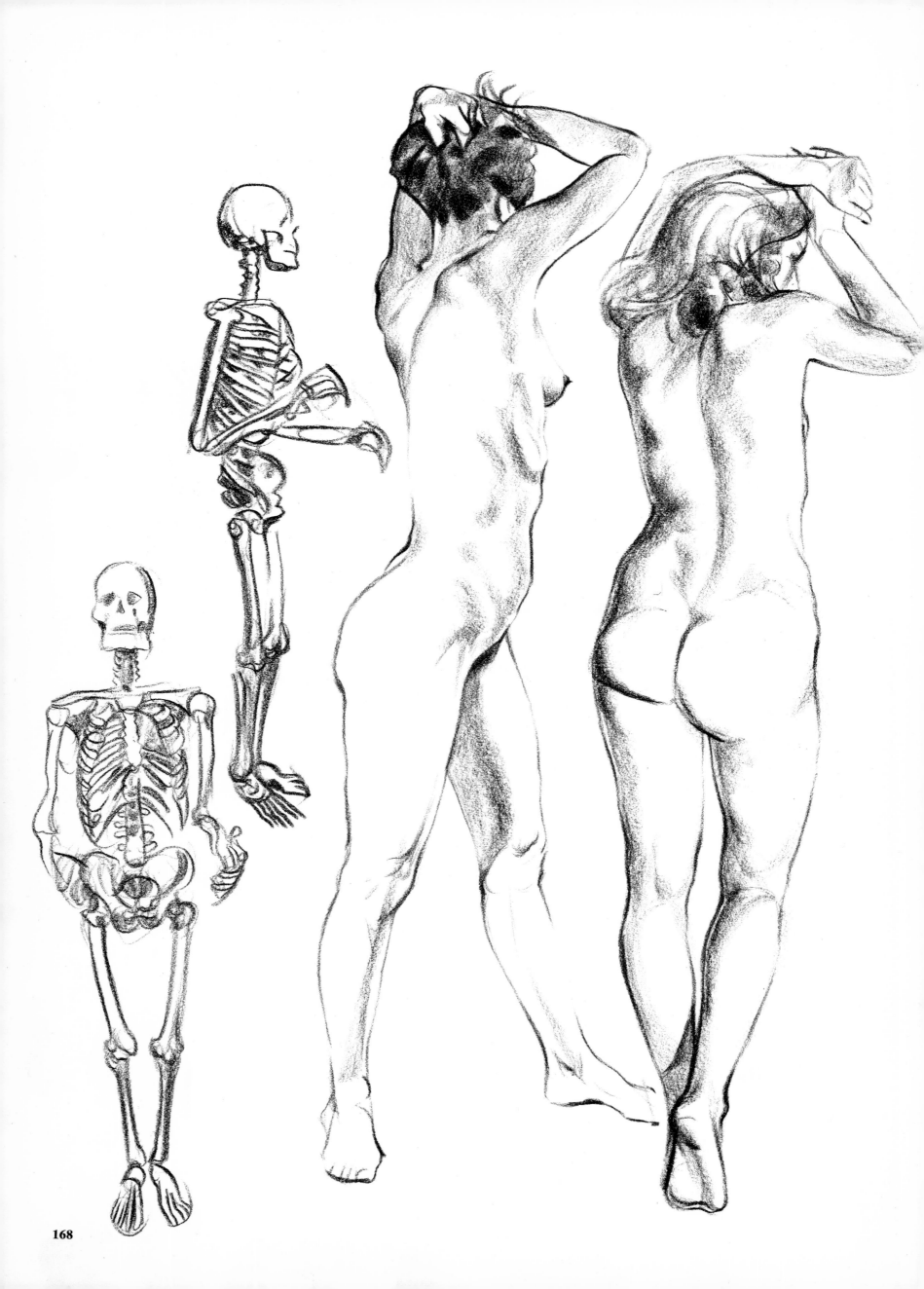

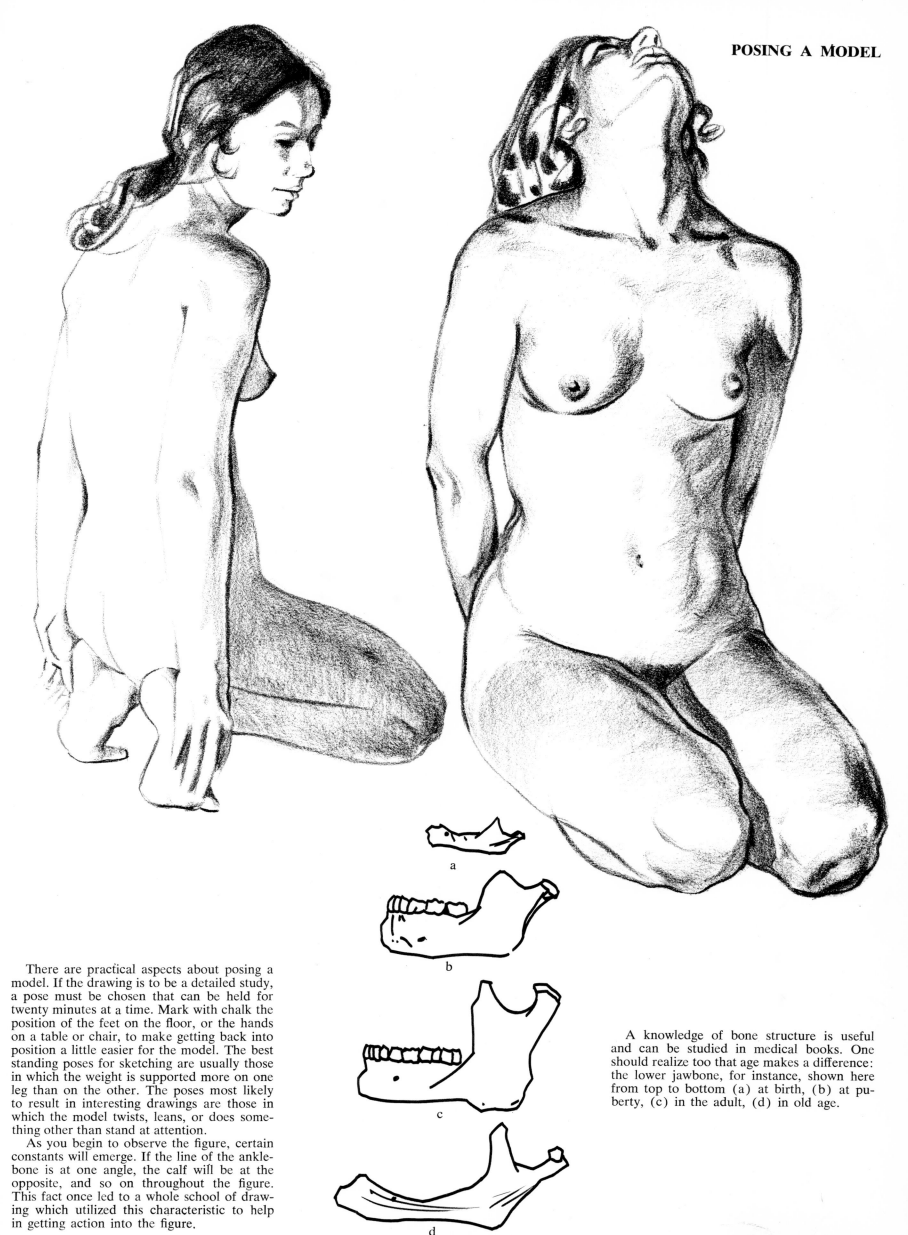

There are practical aspects about posing a model. If the drawing is to be a detailed study, a pose must be chosen that can be held for twenty minutes at a time. Mark with chalk the position of the feet on the floor, or the hands on a table or chair, to make getting back into position a little easier for the model. The best standing poses for sketching are usually those in which the weight is supported more on one leg than on the other. The poses most likely to result in interesting drawings are those in which the model twists, leans, or does something other than stand at attention.

As you begin to observe the figure, certain constants will emerge. If the line of the ankle-bone is at one angle, the calf will be at the opposite, and so on throughout the figure. This fact once led to a whole school of drawing which utilized this characteristic to help in getting action into the figure.

a

b

c

d

A knowledge of bone structure is useful and can be studied in medical books. One should realize too that age makes a difference: the lower jawbone, for instance, shown here from top to bottom (a) at birth, (b) at puberty, (c) in the adult, (d) in old age.

169

ANIMAL DRAWING

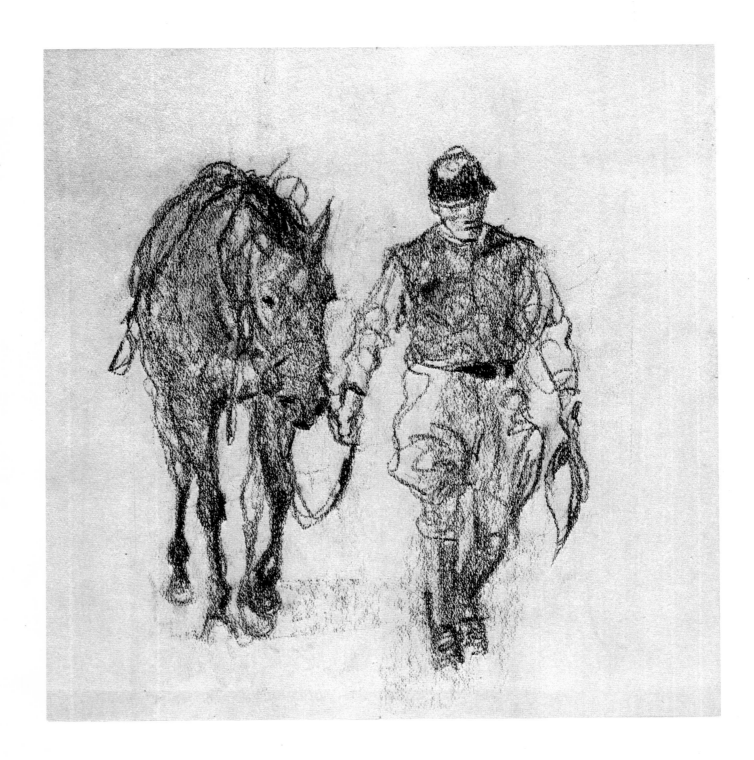

As with the human figure, drawing animals involves a knowledge of the animal, his unique qualities and purposes in life. It helps the artist to know how the animal's form has adapted to fit his life style. For instance, a thoroughbred horse is easily distinguished from the draft horse. The slinky action of the cat is far removed from the jerky motions of the squirrel. It is its role in the system that the artist must think about while drawing an animal. Through understanding, the artist draws the animal in such a way as to make his audience get the message.

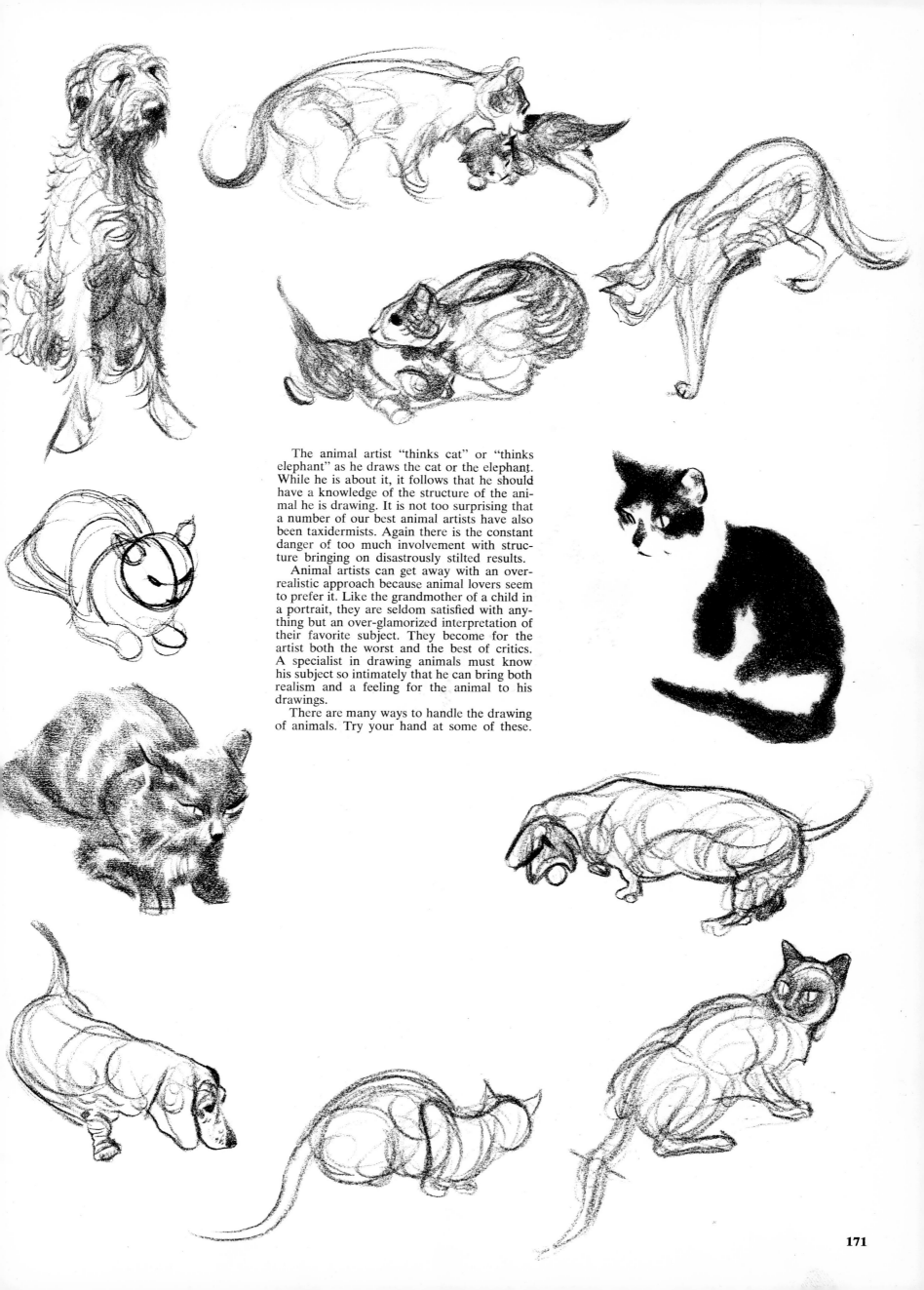

The animal artist "thinks cat" or "thinks elephant" as he draws the cat or the elephant. While he is about it, it follows that he should have a knowledge of the structure of the animal he is drawing. It is not too surprising that a number of our best animal artists have also been taxidermists. Again there is the constant danger of too much involvement with structure bringing on disastrously stilted results.

Animal artists can get away with an over-realistic approach because animal lovers seem to prefer it. Like the grandmother of a child in a portrait, they are seldom satisfied with anything but an over-glamorized interpretation of their favorite subject. They become for the artist both the worst and the best of critics. A specialist in drawing animals must know his subject so intimately that he can bring both realism and a feeling for the animal to his drawings.

There are many ways to handle the drawing of animals. Try your hand at some of these.

DRAWING FROM LIVE AND STUFFED ANIMALS

The sketches below were made from stuffed animals in a museum. Drawing from suc models is the simplest way to get a working knowledge of any species.

The drawing (a) was done in simplified mass, (b) with a line approach.

The heads of the raccoon and the fox, (c) and (d), make use of the sweeping action line. The more swing you can get into the drawing, the more alive the animal will seem.

At the bottom of the column are two sketches of an otter drawn from slightly different angles. Drawing from the stuffed model allows one to study identical action from various angles.

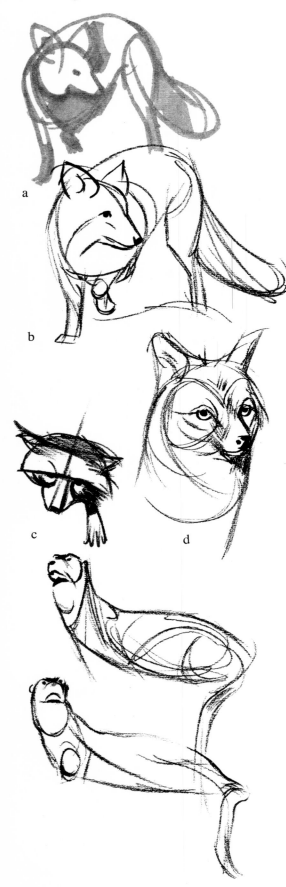

a

b

c   d

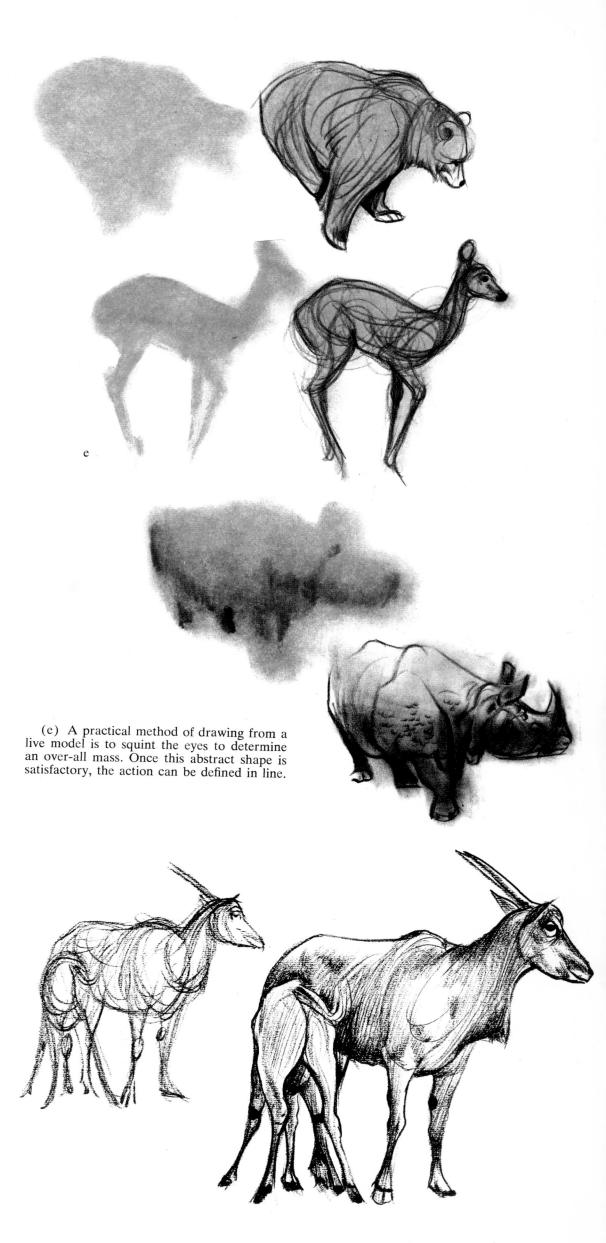

e

(e) A practical method of drawing from a live model is to squint the eyes to determine an over-all mass. Once this abstract shape is satisfactory, the action can be defined in line.

There is always the doodling, gesture sketch from which you can continue into the more finished drawing. Once many sketches from the model and from life have been completed, take photographs of the animals. With a variety of pictures on your drawing board in the studio to study and sketch, a finished drawing with real feeling is more possible than with a single photograph as a basis for your work.

A practical way to start drawing some animals (such as the hippo illustrated here) is by making a variety of oval shapes. Get the action and positioning on the page first and add the details later.

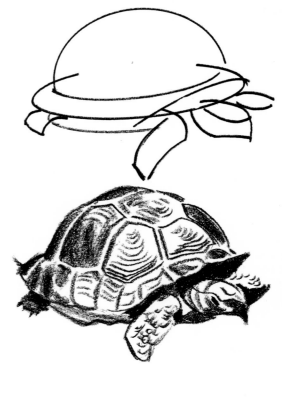

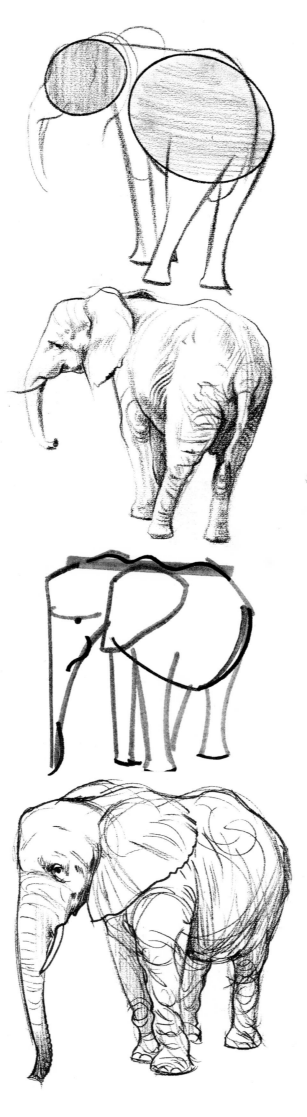

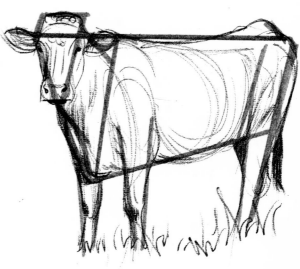

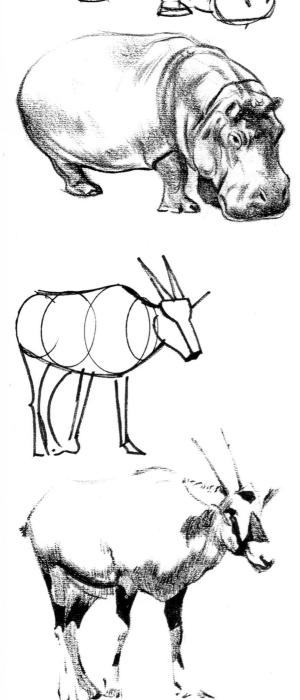

Any geometric shape that coincides with your impression of the animal's form will serve. For instance, one of the cows on this page was first drawn as a rectangular block, the other as a triangular block.

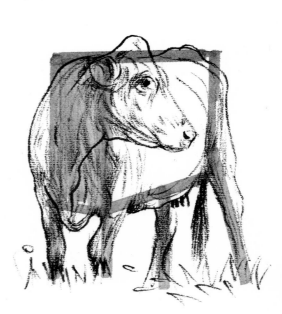

Whether they are lazy, overfed, or egotistical, some animals are inclined to pose for longer periods than others. Camels have a few unlovely habits, but strong action while the artist is drawing is not one of them. In a zoo camels move in slow motion.

Sometimes preliminary sketches have greater artistic value than the final drawing. This is due to the artist's excitement in the early moments of observation and to his immediate, unconscious, strong impressions. The initial impact causes the artist to draw quickly and directly in the beginning. Later, when one becomes involved in the details, there is the danger of losing sight of the picture as a whole.

Once an outline drawing of a strongly patterned animal is completed in pencil, an interesting finish is achieved by putting in only the stripes or spots with a felt pen. Erase the pencil lines. The pattern remaining will tell the story of the animal.

In the beginning of your zoo sketching, choose the placid animals. Draw the entire animal, not just parts. Once you have become familiar with an animal's actions in sketch form, you can concentrate on the details. Stay in one spot. Fill pages of your sketchbook before you move to another animal or another location. Read about the animal prior to sketching. It will help you to know what to look for. Most zoos have a sign telling something about each species. Knowing an animal's characteristics helps in drawing it.

Begin with a single line to get the action.

Try another line.

And another.

The action first, then deeper and deeper into the sketch.

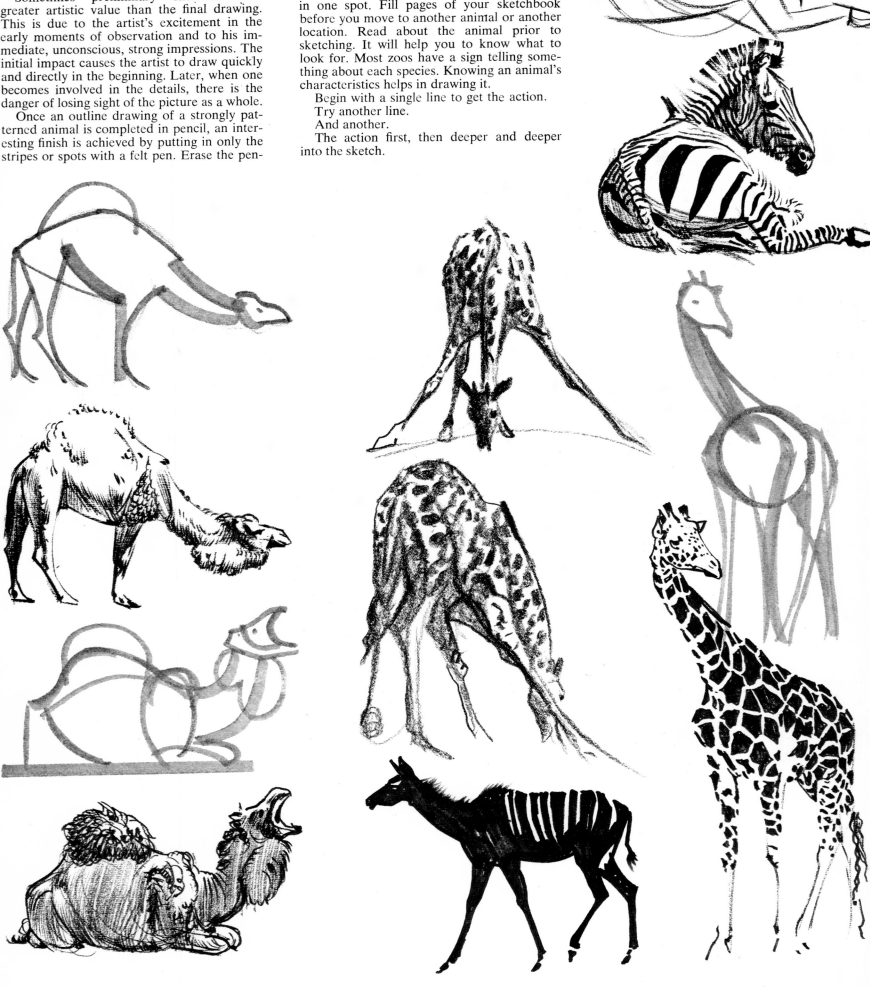

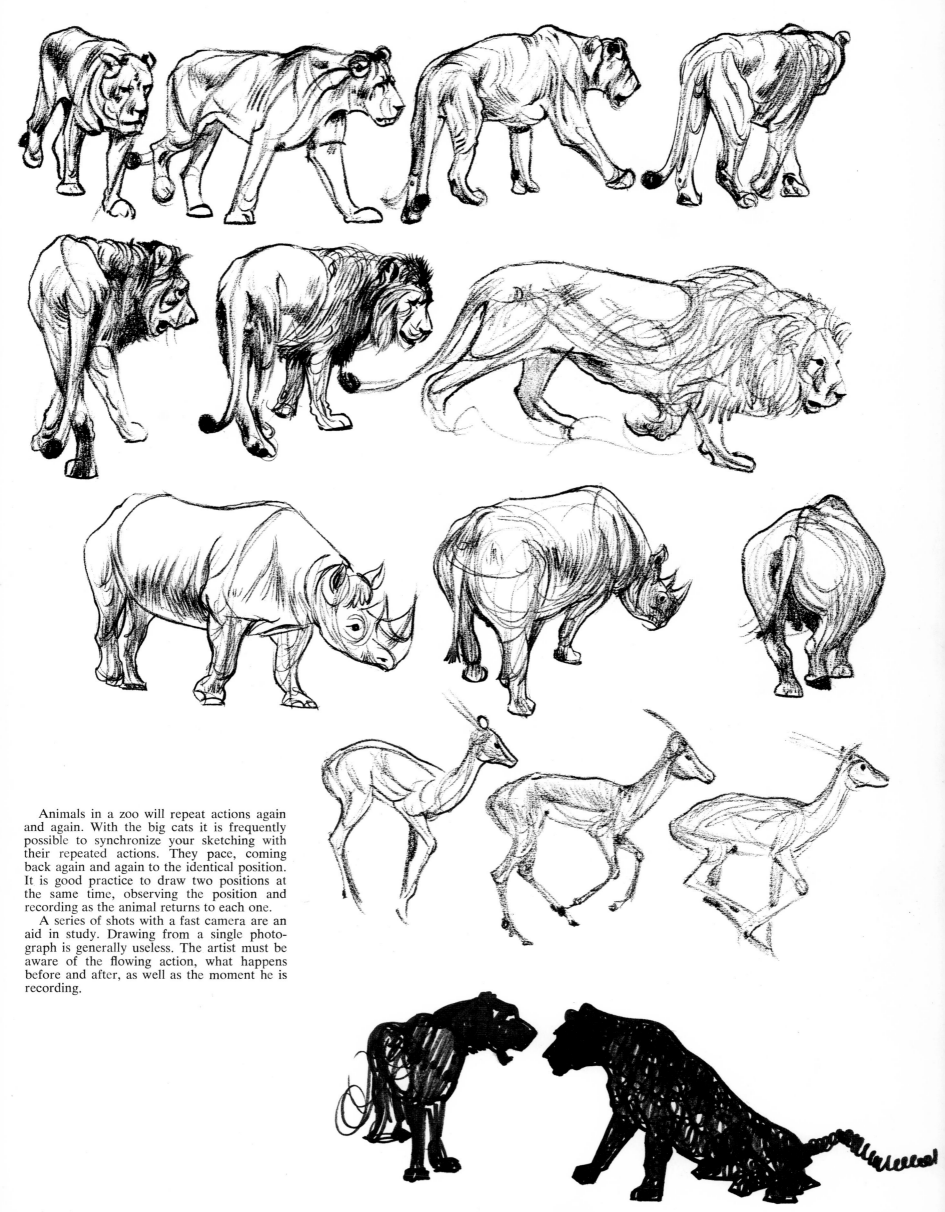

Animals in a zoo will repeat actions again and again. With the big cats it is frequently possible to synchronize your sketching with their repeated actions. They pace, coming back again and again to the identical position. It is good practice to draw two positions at the same time, observing the position and recording as the animal returns to each one.

A series of shots with a fast camera are an aid in study. Drawing from a single photograph is generally useless. The artist must be aware of the flowing action, what happens before and after, as well as the moment he is recording.

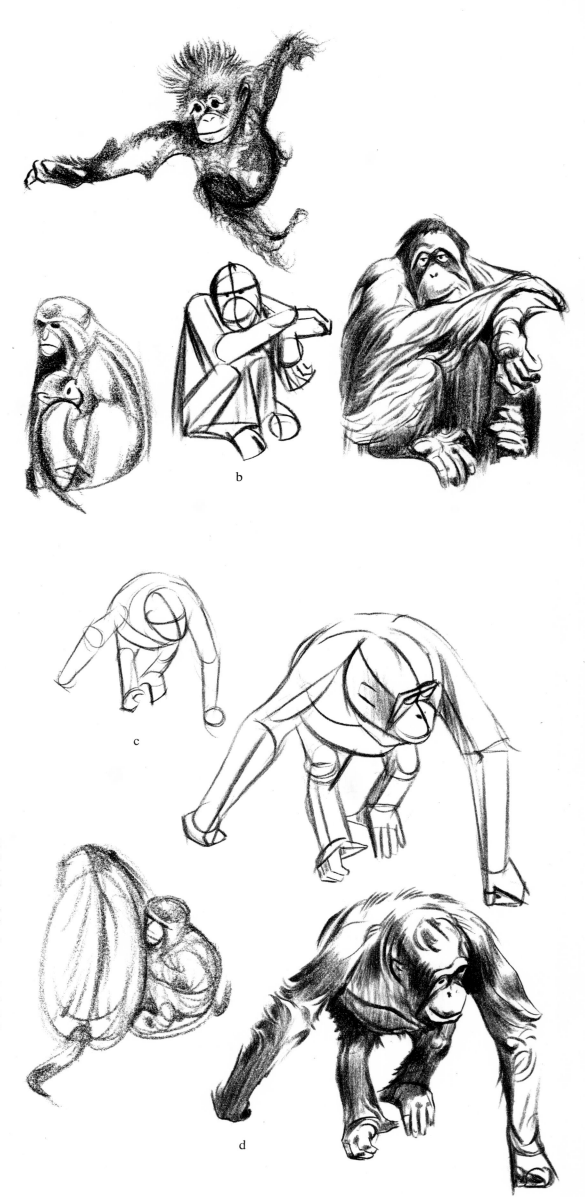

Primates vary in characteristics and physical make-up one from the other to a startling extent. To the uninitiated, they are just big or little monkeys. If the student is ever to become adept at drawing primates, he must become aware of the differences.

(a) The two sketches indicate adolescent orangutans. Their action and proportion say they can be nothing else. Although the casual viewer may remark, "I like your monkeys," you will not be successful until someone like the zookeeper says, "You really caught young Rusty there."

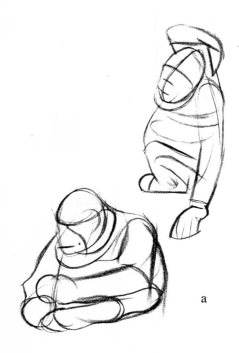

a

(b) Unless the underlying drawing is correct, the final sketch of the mature orangutan will not make logic, despite the furry mass that meets the eye.

(c) The motion of the orangutan has been roughly blocked in.

(d) Details, such as fur and fingers and eyes, are worked in next. The action of the prehensile thumb, the stance—these peculiarities of the orangutan help to identify him as this special primate.
The direction of the lines in the sketch follow the direction of the limbs and the lay of the hair. As the specifics change direction, so does the line of the drawing.

All these sketches were drawn on a bond paper pad with a 4B pencil. However, they could have been drawn with medium Conte or Wolf pencil. If a more lineal effect had been desired, pen or brush and ink would have worked.

b

c

d

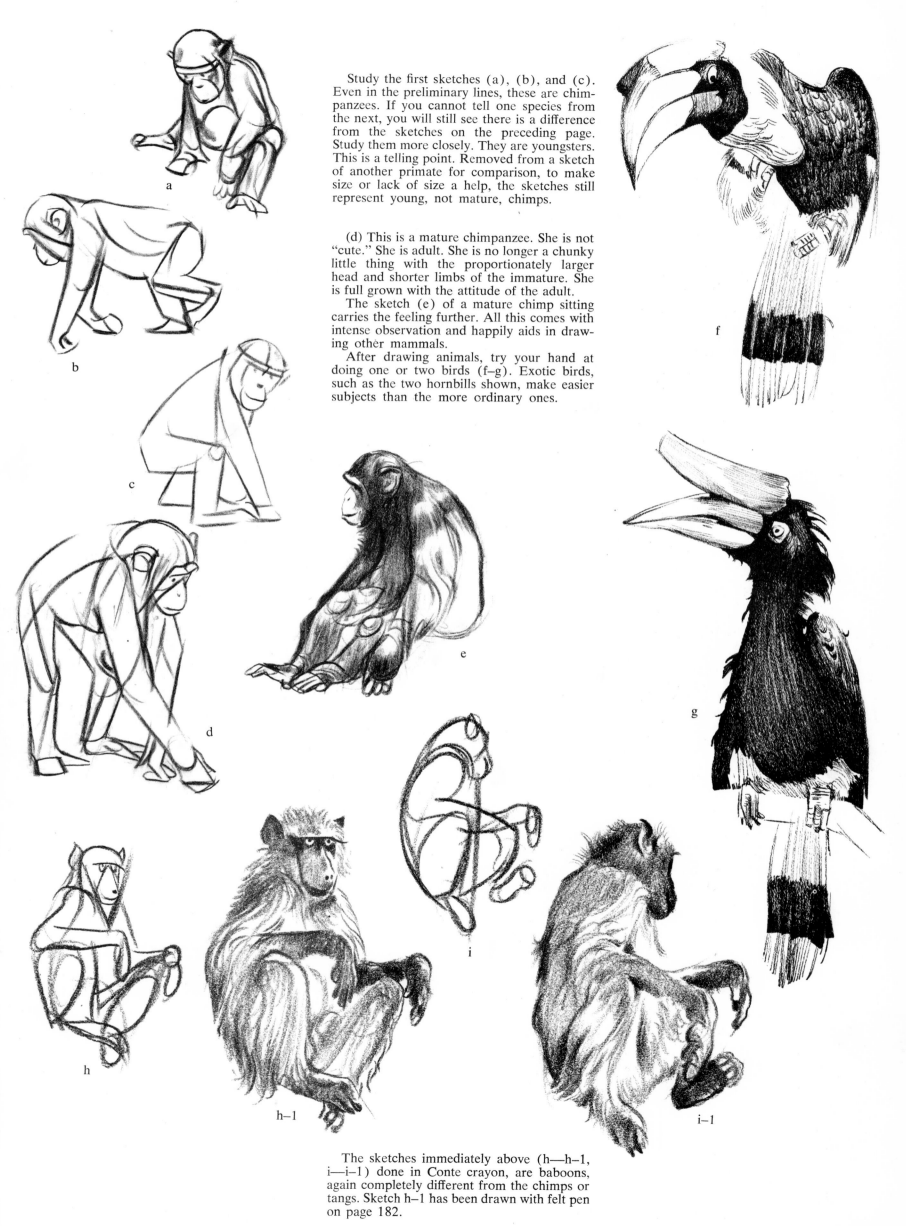

Study the first sketches (a), (b), and (c). Even in the preliminary lines, these are chimpanzees. If you cannot tell one species from the next, you will still see there is a difference from the sketches on the preceding page. Study them more closely. They are youngsters. This is a telling point. Removed from a sketch of another primate for comparison, to make size or lack of size a help, the sketches still represent young, not mature, chimps.

(d) This is a mature chimpanzee. She is not "cute." She is adult. She is no longer a chunky little thing with the proportionately larger head and shorter limbs of the immature. She is full grown with the attitude of the adult.

The sketch (e) of a mature chimp sitting carries the feeling further. All this comes with intense observation and happily aids in drawing other mammals.

After drawing animals, try your hand at doing one or two birds (f–g). Exotic birds, such as the two hornbills shown, make easier subjects than the more ordinary ones.

The sketches immediately above (h—h-1, i—i-1) done in Conte crayon, are baboons, again completely different from the chimps or tangs. Sketch h-1 has been drawn with felt pen on page 182.

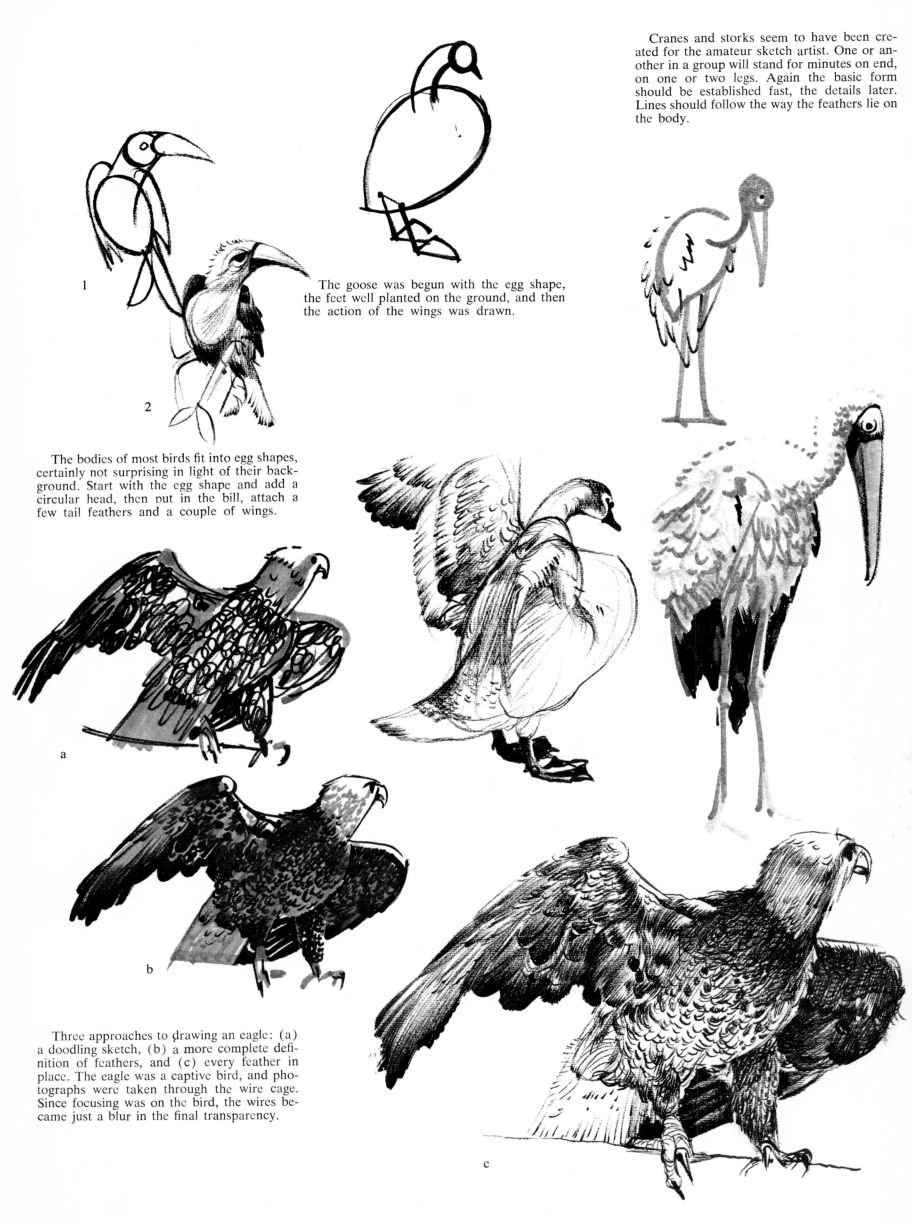

Cranes and storks seem to have been created for the amateur sketch artist. One or another in a group will stand for minutes on end, on one or two legs. Again the basic form should be established fast, the details later. Lines should follow the way the feathers lie on the body.

1

2

The goose was begun with the egg shape, the feet well planted on the ground, and then the action of the wings was drawn.

The bodies of most birds fit into egg shapes, certainly not surprising in light of their background. Start with the egg shape and add a circular head, then put in the bill, attach a few tail feathers and a couple of wings.

a

b

Three approaches to drawing an eagle: (a) a doodling sketch, (b) a more complete definition of feathers, and (c) every feather in place. The eagle was a captive bird, and photographs were taken through the wire cage. Since focusing was on the bird, the wires became just a blur in the final transparency.

c

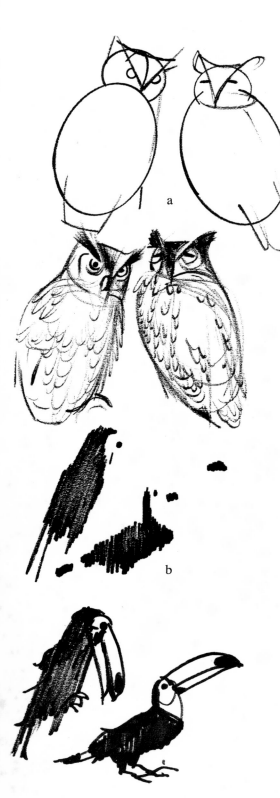

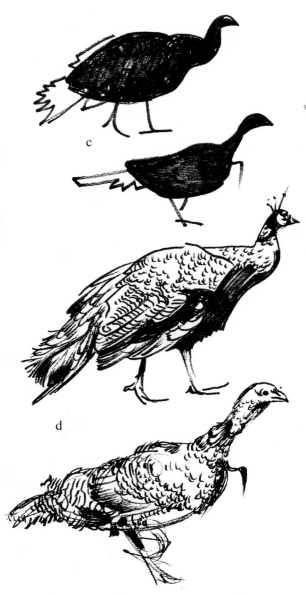

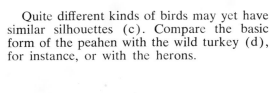

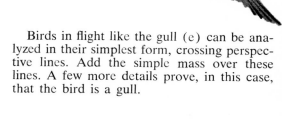

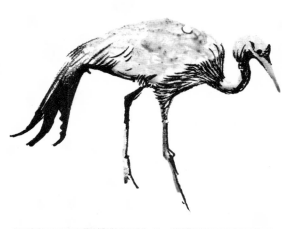

Birds in flight like the gull (e) can be analyzed in their simplest form, crossing perspective lines. Add the simple mass over these lines. A few more details prove, in this case, that the bird is a gull.

Quite different kinds of birds may yet have similar silhouettes (c). Compare the basic form of the peahen with the wild turkey (d), for instance, or with the herons.

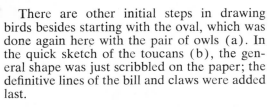

There are other initial steps in drawing birds besides starting with the oval, which was done again here with the pair of owls (a). In the quick sketch of the toucans (b), the general shape was just scribbled on the paper; the definitive lines of the bill and claws were added last.

The two demonstrations to the right (heron and gulls) show a use of liquid frisket. The gull was first sketched, then mystik applied. The background was then painted over this, and later, when dry, the liquid frisket was removed. In the demonstration with the gulls the original drawing was made directly with liquid frisket.

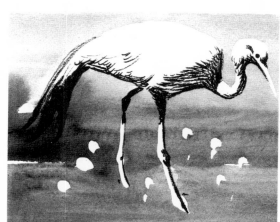

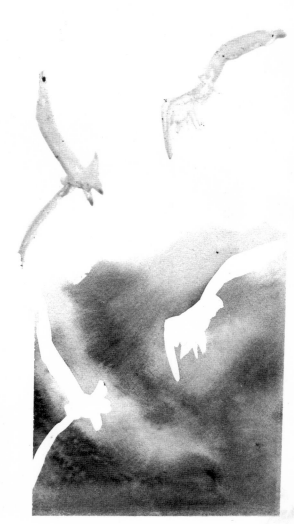

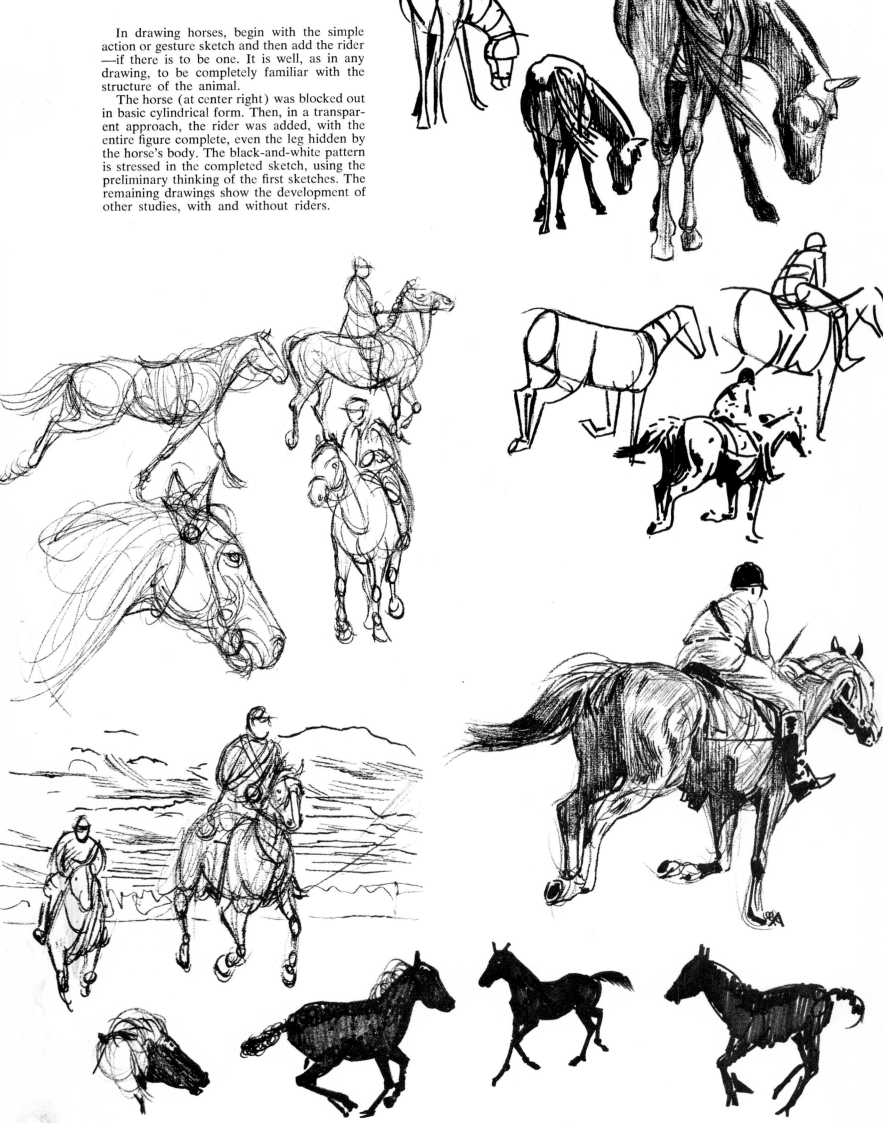

In drawing horses, begin with the simple action or gesture sketch and then add the rider —if there is to be one. It is well, as in any drawing, to be completely familiar with the structure of the animal.

The horse (at center right) was blocked out in basic cylindrical form. Then, in a transparent approach, the rider was added, with the entire figure complete, even the leg hidden by the horse's body. The black-and-white pattern is stressed in the completed sketch, using the preliminary thinking of the first sketches. The remaining drawings show the development of other studies, with and without riders.

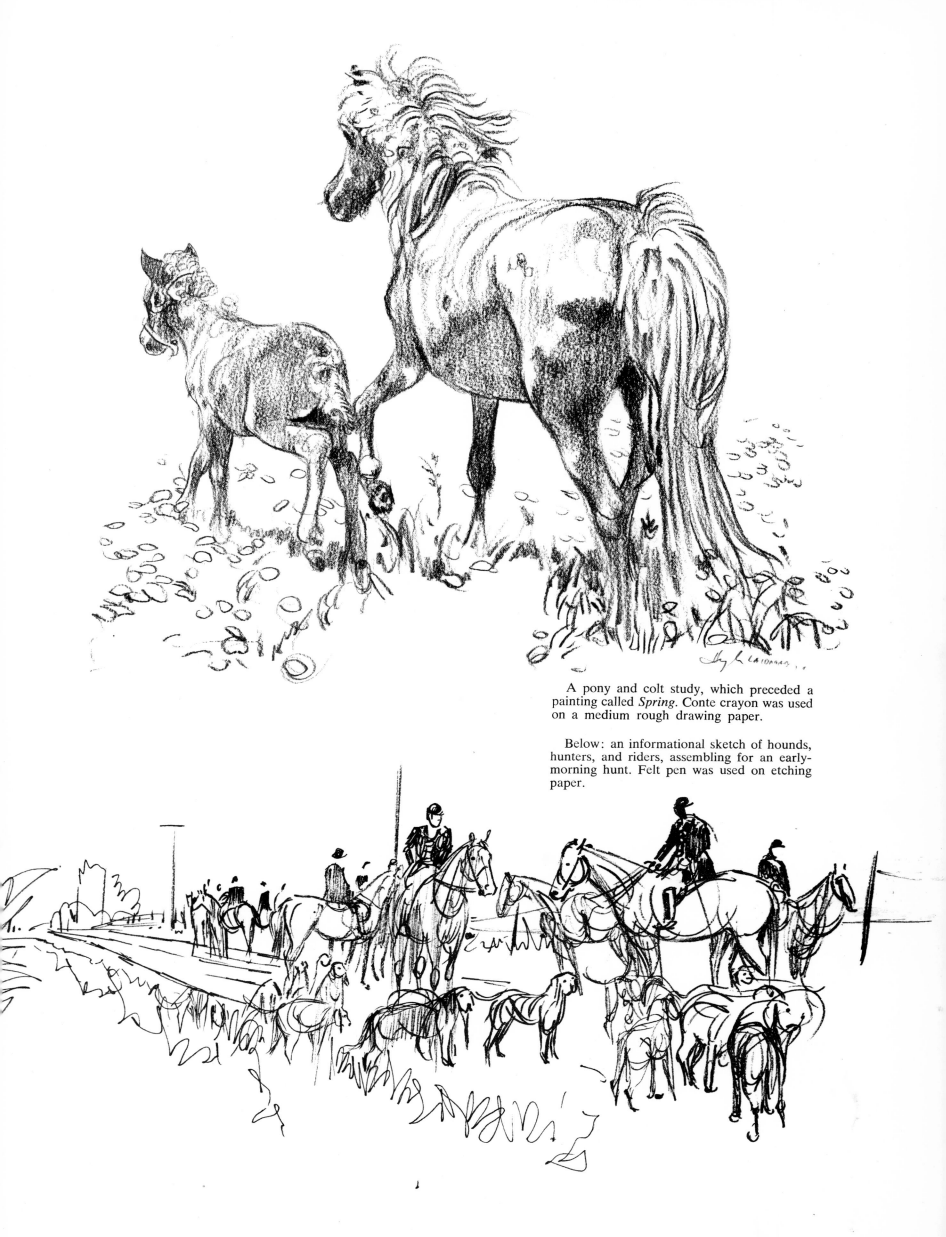

A pony and colt study, which preceded a painting called *Spring*. Conte crayon was used on a medium rough drawing paper.

Below: an informational sketch of hounds, hunters, and riders, assembling for an early-morning hunt. Felt pen was used on etching paper.

The sketches which preceded the drawing at right were made at different times and in very different areas. The foreground wildebeest was sketched at the zoo, while the one in the background was done from photographs made in the African bush. Brought together in this study, they make a believable illustration.

It is interesting to note that the foreground wildebeest, when studied, is a considerably more disreputable-looking specimen than the blue gnu photographed in the wild state. The baboon (below, left) is sometimes referred to as a dog-faced monkey. From the standpoint of the student, these and all of the other animals he draws offer a chance to increase his power of intelligent observation.

Drawing animals is both a frustrating and a rewarding experience. The artist, by keenly observing the shape of an animal, the way it moves, and its character, will discover that most people who claim great knowledge of the creature really don't know as much as he has learned through drawing it.

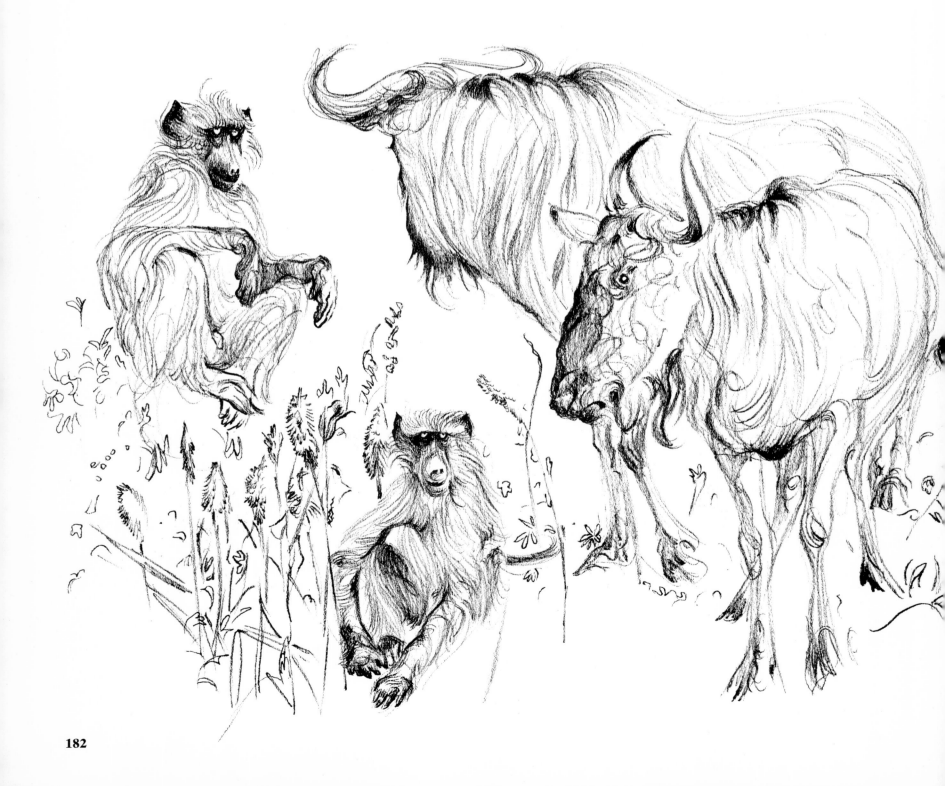

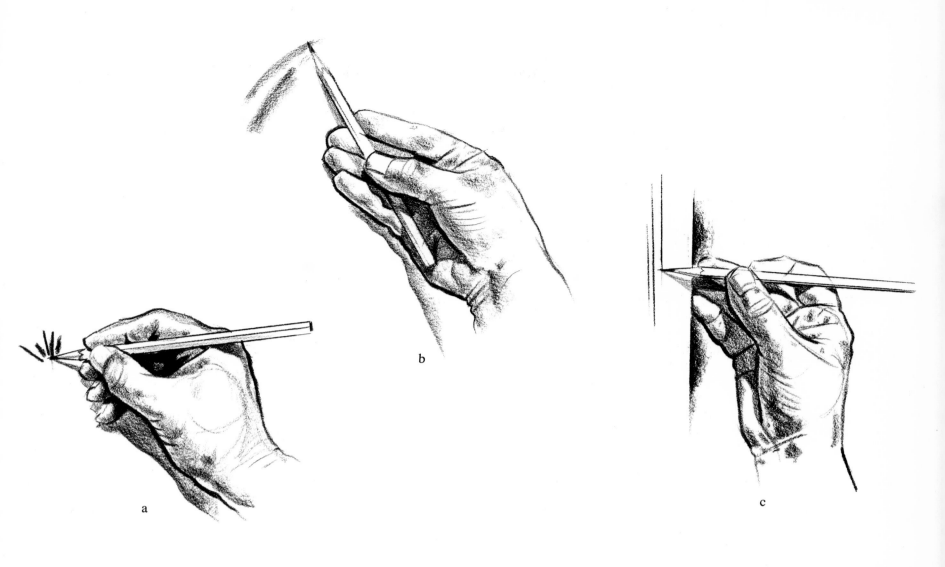

Typical hand positions used in sketching: (a) tight and close to the point, (b) loose for free sweeping lines, and (c) using the side of the pad as a guide to create straight lines.

SKETCHING

Prime considerations in selecting materials for work outdoors are ease of carrying and adaptability to use in the wind. The materials must lend themselves to getting the message down quickly.

There are a number of types of practical pads—the spiral-bound pads and sewed and bound books. The spiral type is generally available in sizes from 4 by 6 inches to 18 by 24 inches; the bound from 4 by 6 inches to 11 by 14 inches. For the most part, the smaller sizes are more practical for outdoor use.

The spiral pad is a bit easier to handle, but has fewer pages than the other types. The bound pad lends itself to flatter storage for viewing at a later date and has more pages, most often of thinner bond paper. It is claimed that the spiral pads are equally responsive to the use of pencil, pen and ink, watercolor, and crayon, but most professional artists find this not to be so.

Felt pens work beautifully because they produce immediate, definite effects.

Pencils are inclined to smudge, but may be used effectively as shown in many demonstrations earlier in this book.

The entire business of sketching both in and out of doors is important enough to the artist to suggest that he carry the necessary equipment with him at all times. It is a good idea to carry a small pad in your pocket or purse so you are always ready to set your thoughts down quickly and effectively when interesting impressions occur.

A clipboard is a practical device that allows the sketcher to use a variety of paper surfaces. Don't work on both sides of the paper. Felt pens frequently bleed through thin paper, and pencils will smudge. There is also the possibility of your wishing at some future date to take out a page or two for exhibition.

Write notes on the sketches to help you in using the work later . . . colors, moods of the day, interesting things that happened. Never scribble aimlessly. Say something in your doodles so you can decipher it later.

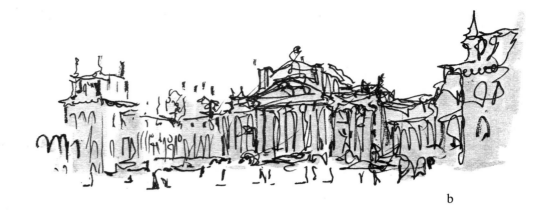

(a) Because of the involved mass of detail in the Rheims cathedral, a gray tone, showing the shadow pattern, was first put down. With the over-all pattern somewhat established, the next step was to draw the major structural elements and, finally, the incidentals.

(b) The sketch of the English mansion followed the opposite procedure. First the façade was drawn in line, then the shadow pattern was drawn in gray magic marker over the lines. This is a more difficult technique but possible in cases where the objective is to strengthen a line sketch that has already been made.

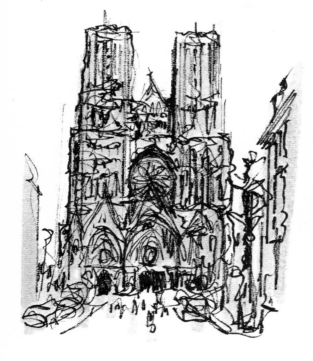

a

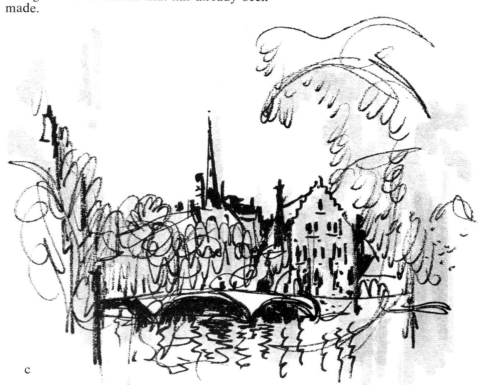

c

(c) The impression of a scene in a Belgian town developed out of a doodle. The intent was to get the feeling of the subject without bothering about mechanics.

(d) For this sketch of New York's East River a straightedge was used in conjunction with finger smudging technique.

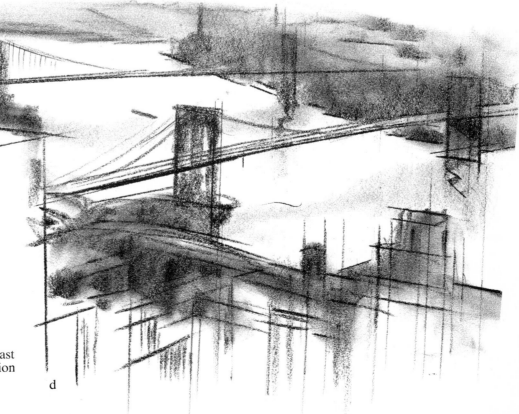

d

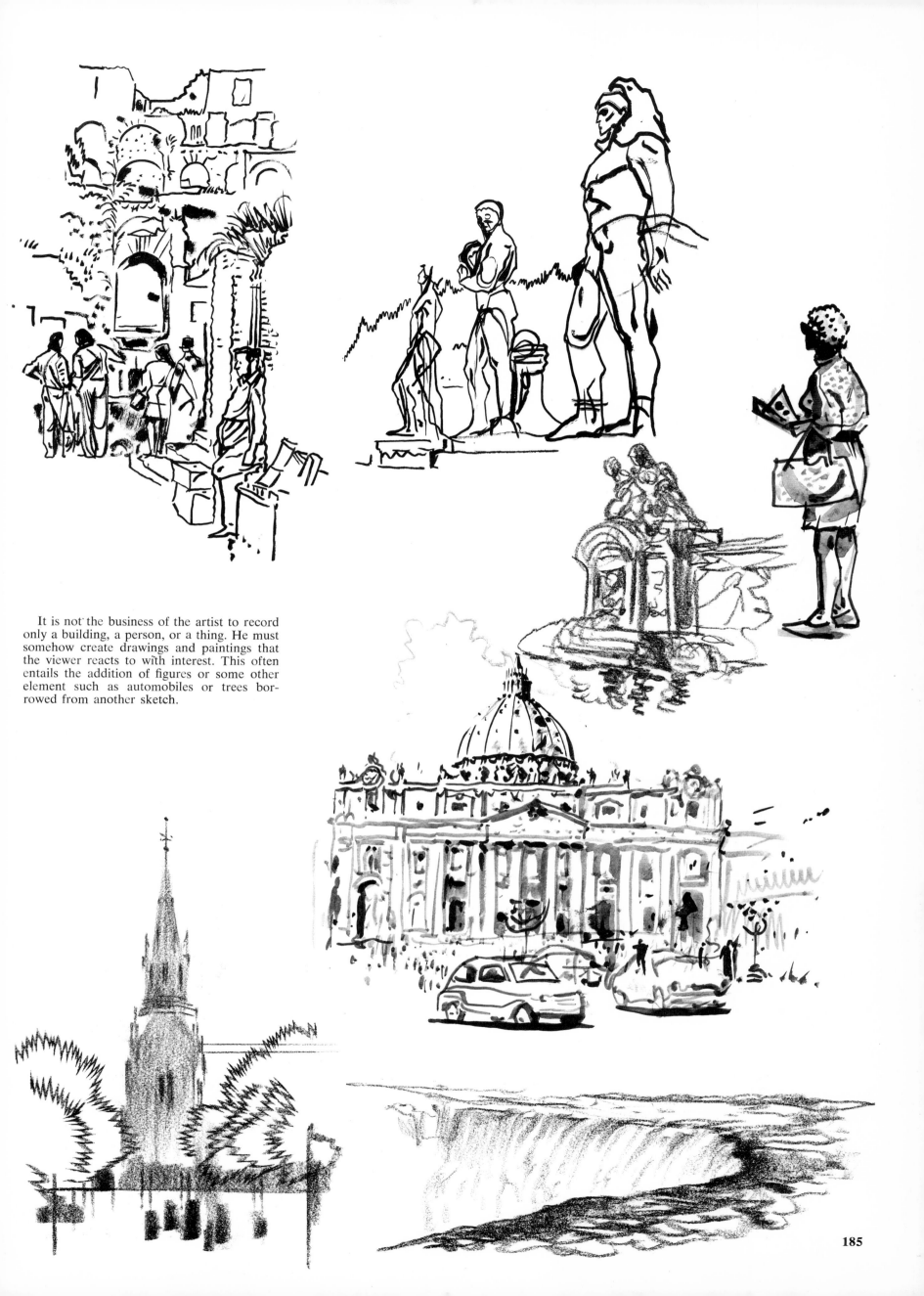

It is not the business of the artist to record only a building, a person, or a thing. He must somehow create drawings and paintings that the viewer reacts to with interest. This often entails the addition of figures or some other element such as automobiles or trees borrowed from another sketch.

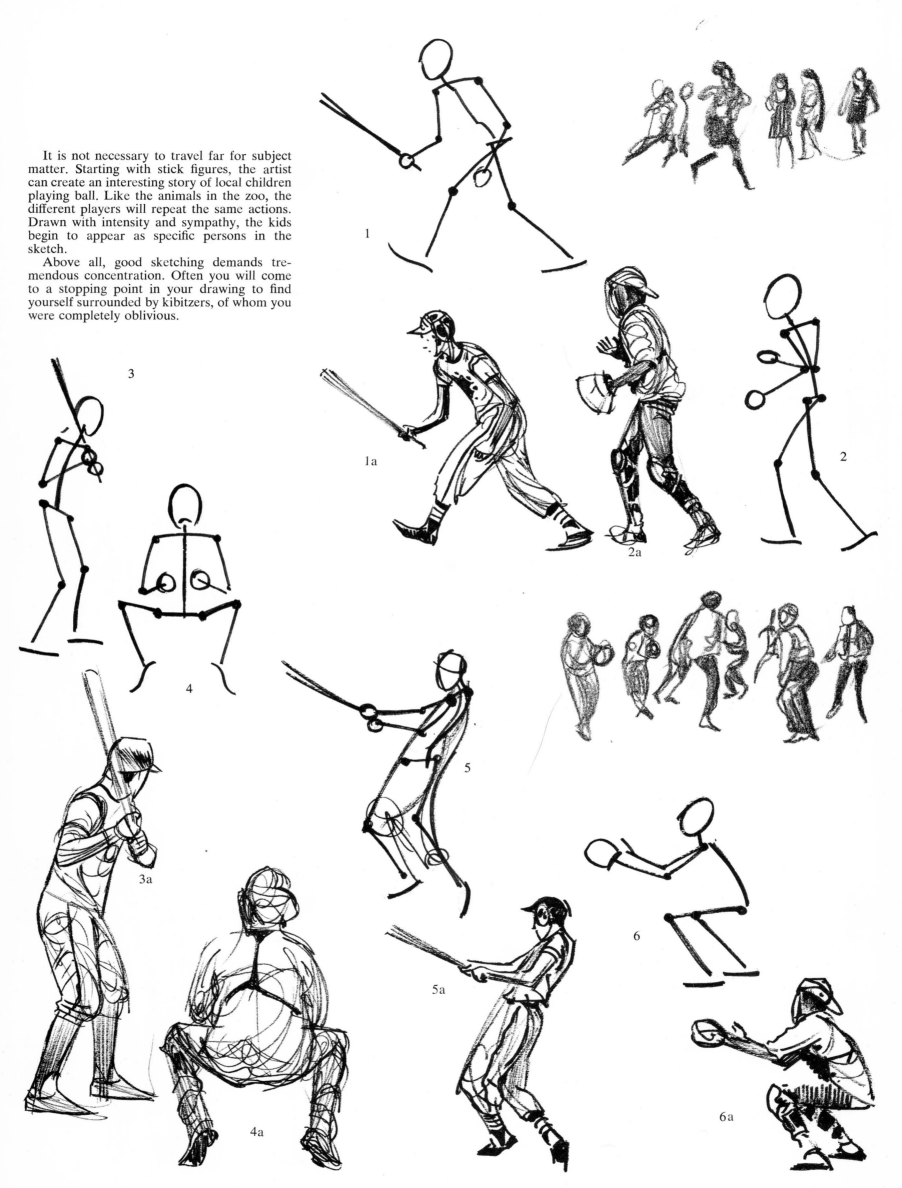

It is not necessary to travel far for subject matter. Starting with stick figures, the artist can create an interesting story of local children playing ball. Like the animals in the zoo, the different players will repeat the same actions. Drawn with intensity and sympathy, the kids begin to appear as specific persons in the sketch.

Above all, good sketching demands tremendous concentration. Often you will come to a stopping point in your drawing to find yourself surrounded by kibitzers, of whom you were completely oblivious.

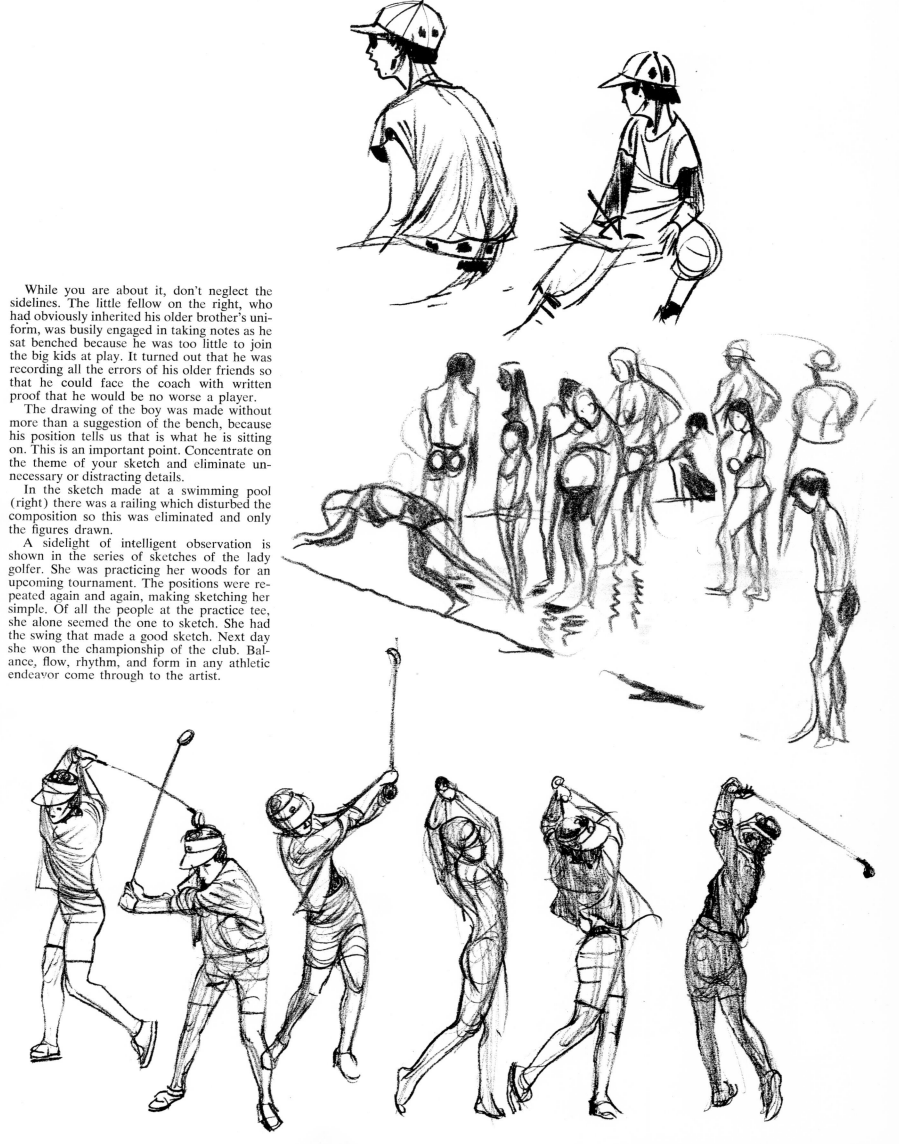

While you are about it, don't neglect the sidelines. The little fellow on the right, who had obviously inherited his older brother's uniform, was busily engaged in taking notes as he sat benched because he was too little to join the big kids at play. It turned out that he was recording all the errors of his older friends so that he could face the coach with written proof that he would be no worse a player.

The drawing of the boy was made without more than a suggestion of the bench, because his position tells us that is what he is sitting on. This is an important point. Concentrate on the theme of your sketch and eliminate unnecessary or distracting details.

In the sketch made at a swimming pool (right) there was a railing which disturbed the composition so this was eliminated and only the figures drawn.

A sidelight of intelligent observation is shown in the series of sketches of the lady golfer. She was practicing her woods for an upcoming tournament. The positions were repeated again and again, making sketching her simple. Of all the people at the practice tee, she alone seemed the one to sketch. She had the swing that made a good sketch. Next day she won the championship of the club. Balance, flow, rhythm, and form in any athletic endeavor come through to the artist.

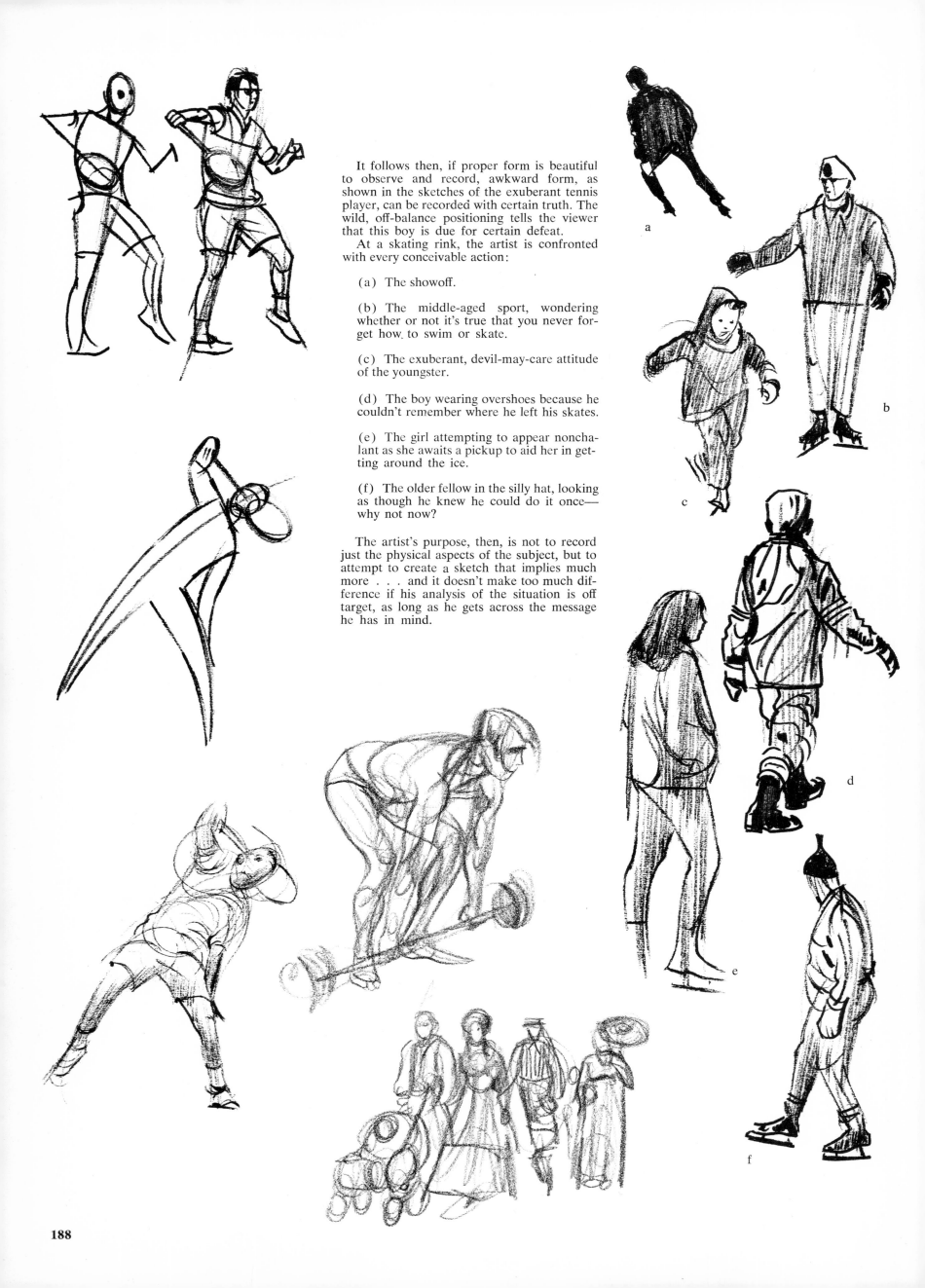

It follows then, if proper form is beautiful to observe and record, awkward form, as shown in the sketches of the exuberant tennis player, can be recorded with certain truth. The wild, off-balance positioning tells the viewer that this boy is due for certain defeat.

At a skating rink, the artist is confronted with every conceivable action:

(a) The showoff.

(b) The middle-aged sport, wondering whether or not it's true that you never forget how to swim or skate.

(c) The exuberant, devil-may-care attitude of the youngster.

(d) The boy wearing overshoes because he couldn't remember where he left his skates.

(e) The girl attempting to appear nonchalant as she awaits a pickup to aid her in getting around the ice.

(f) The older fellow in the silly hat, looking as though he knew he could do it once—why not now?

The artist's purpose, then, is not to record just the physical aspects of the subject, but to attempt to create a sketch that implies much more . . . and it doesn't make too much difference if his analysis of the situation is off target, as long as he gets across the message he has in mind.

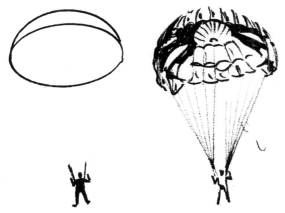

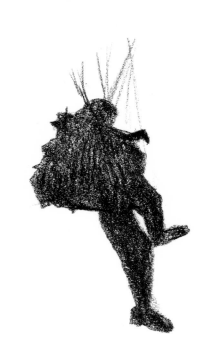

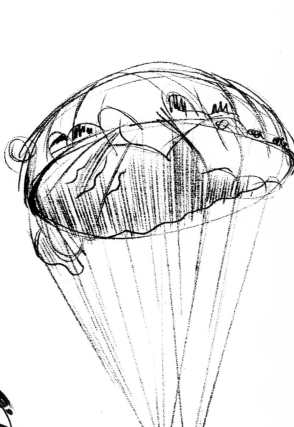

In drawing any subject, the first step is to learn all you can about it before you begin making sketches. With the skydivers, it was easy to have a knowledgeable participant explain in detail every motion of the divers, the reasons and the results, as we observed through binoculars. It seemed inconceivable that anyone could so control his descent as to hit the target in the field. This almost resulted in a minor disaster. From a vantage point right in the middle of the crossed canvas pieces, I observed a diver descending—but for a last-minute scramble on my part—right on me.

The basic shape of the chute and the strings became a cone with a rounded top, a half cone, as the diver spilled the air once upon the ground. Even in as far-out a sport as skydiving, the basic forms can be simplified, the actions understood, until they become a matter of logic. Once the artist has full knowledge of the subject, he can exaggerate and distort intelligently.

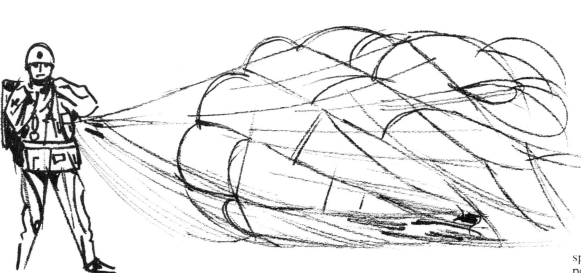

It would be helpful to participate in the sport in order to feel more fully what is happening, but with skydiving just standing on the edge of the field was sufficient, thank you. Again the camera becomes a tool to record, but only as a future aid to the notes the artist takes in his observations.

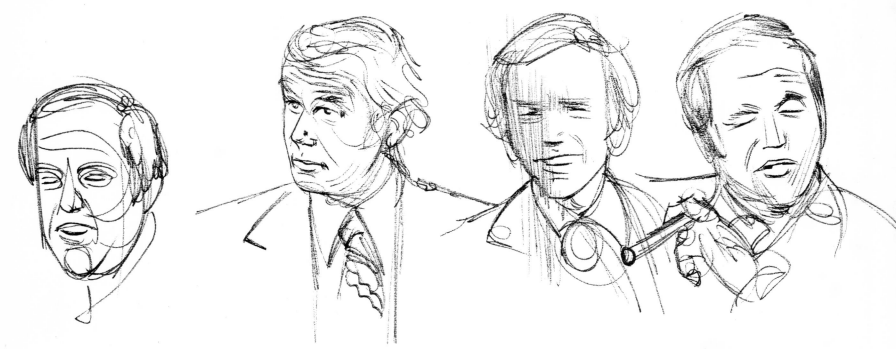

Strictly for practice in sketching, drawing from the television tube is a good pastime. Except in the panel show, where action is limited and repeated again and again, there is generally too little time to do more than make the roughest of sketches. You do have a wealth of models, costumes, and situations, however. If it is necessary to pick up subject matter from television, set up a camera, snap away, and later draw from slides.

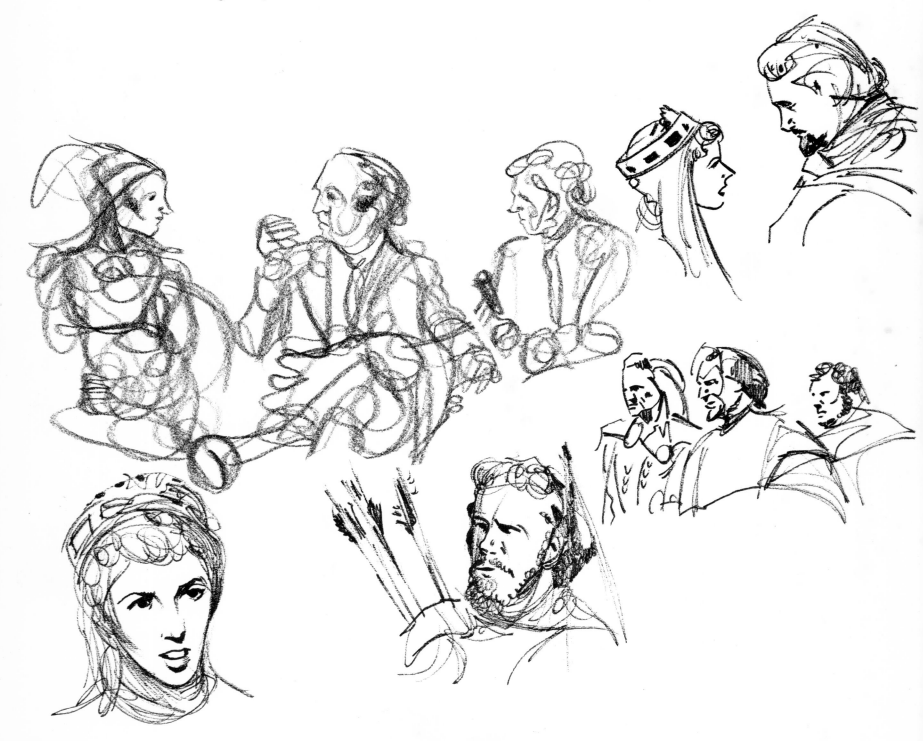

In whatever black-and-white technique seems best for you, fill sketchbook after sketchbook with drawings and notes to yourself. Only through practice, observation, and intelligent comprehension of what interests you can you hope to relay your message in any media. The camera will aid, much as a dictionary helps a writer, but it must not become more than an aid.

These sketches selected from many sketchbooks were made with a felt pen. This tool allows for extremely rapid work, with the added advantage of drying immediately so that it is smudgeproof, and allows one to flip pages with no worry about smudging.

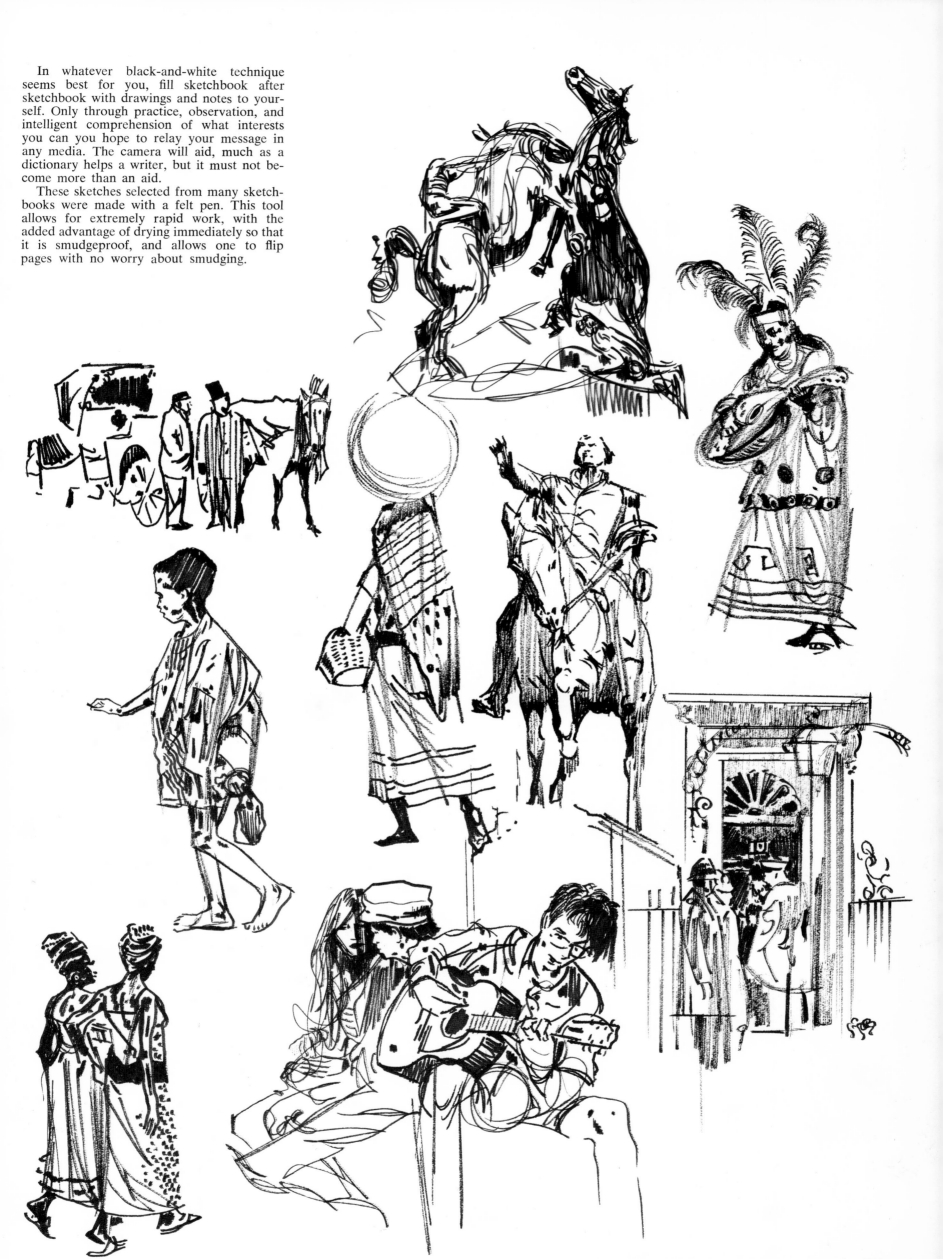

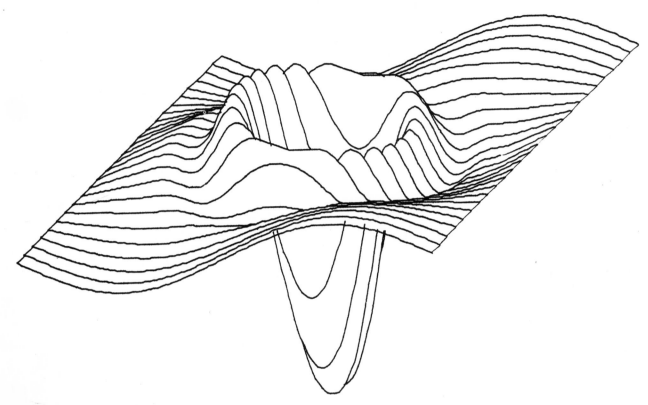

A sketch made by a computer. To an artist, the intriguing aspect of the sketch is the way the graphic technique of the computer has influenced today's art. Acres of artwork in the commercial field are produced in the simple line of the computer. Many more acres of art in the fine art field are adaptations of computer production.

As always, the contemporary artist is influenced by the world around him.